Benjamin Constant and the Making of Modern Liberalism

Benjamin Constant and the Making of Modern Liberalism

STEPHEN HOLMES

YALE UNIVERSITY PRESS
NEW HAVEN AND LONDON

Published with assistance from
the Louis Stern Memorial Fund

Designed by James J. Johnson
and set in Sabon Roman type.
Printed in the United States of America by
Vail-Ballou Press, Binghamton, New York.

Library of Congress Cataloging in Publication Data

Holmes, Stephen, 1948–
    Benjamin Constant and the making of modern liberalism.

    Bibliography: p.
    Includes index.
    1. Constant, Benjamin, 1767–1830—Political science.
2. Liberalism.   I. Title.
JC229.C8H64   1984   320.5′12′0924   84–5118
ISBN 0–300–03083–5

*The paper in this book meets the guidelines for
permanence and durability of the Committee on
Production Guidelines for Book Longevity of
the Council on Library Resources.*

10 9 8 7 6 5 4 3 2 1

Contents

Acknowledgments

It was at the Institute for Advanced Study during the academic year 1978–79 that I began to compile the material for this book. To Albert Hirschman, who invited me to Princeton and whose thoughtful affection for Constant was a model and a spur, I wish to express my gratitude. Acknowledgment also goes to the National Endowment for the Humanities for a prior research grant to Paris in the summer of 1978.

More recently, I have been blessed with a large number of friends and colleagues who took precious time to pore over an earlier version of this study. Sam Beer, Ed Brunner, Pierre Deguise, Don Herzog, Patrice Higonnet, Helge Høibraaten, Charles Larmore, Niklas Luhmann, Nancy Maull, Leo Raditsa, John Rawls, Judith Shklar, Marion Smiley, Paul Starr, Cheryl Welch, Bob Wolff, and Bernie Yack—each read the entire manuscript, raised penetrating questions, and gave heart. I am grateful to them all.

Finally, for their gentle supervision at Yale University Press, I need to thank Maureen MacGrogan, Barbara Folsom, and Marian Ash.

Introduction

N idealized image of the Greek *polis* has haunted political theory since the time of Rousseau.[1] Robespierre extolled Spartan self-sacrifice, denouncing modern commercialism and the miserable principle of self-interest. Schiller, Hegel, Marx, and Nietzsche, in differing ways, all viewed the ancient citizen as a rebuke to the modern bourgeois.[2] In this century, too, philosophical critics of liberal society commonly invoke Greek politics or political thought in condemning the social order of the industrial democracies.[3]

The theorist who most incisively challenged the sanity of this appeal to antiquity was Benjamin Constant. His basic insight was this: the old res publica conception of politics, renewed in modern times, serves only to overlegitimate a bureaucratic agency with police powers. The Aristotelian belief that man is essentially a political animal makes it difficult to understand why citizens might wish to set boundaries to the political.

The importance of this idea was what originally drew me to the study of Benjamin Constant. My aim has been to dissect Constant's central argument and to explore its implications when integrated into his political theory viewed as a whole. Such a project has been worth undertaking because of the subtlety and sheer intelligence of Constant's thinking about modern society and the kind of freedom it makes possible.

Numerous overviews have been published of Constant's political career and writings.[4] I have attempted a more philosophical book. Without neglecting psychological background or social context, I have reconstructed Constant's theoretical position with an eye to examining his fundamental claim that the antiliberal longing for ancient citizenship is both inappropriate and dangerous in the modern world. Taken seriously, Constant's insights

1

suggest a major reassessment of the categories that still dominate the debate about liberalism.

For example, one of the shibboleths of twentieth-century theory is the fundamental "opposition" between liberalism and democracy. The liberal tradition is said to have focused one-sidedly on private rights while discouraging popular participation. In line with this interpretation and because of his intense concern with drawing boundaries to the political, Constant is conventionally but mistakenly read as an antidemocratic liberal. Yet his distinction between ancient and modern liberty did not at all imply that the public should give way to the private. This interpretation, although common, is erroneous. In fact, an attentive reading of Constant throws doubt on the myth of an intractable conflict between liberalism and democracy.

Eighteenth-century attacks on mercantilism, religious orthodoxy, and the remnants of *féodalité* were important sources of inspiration for Constant. Yet he rethought the older liberal tradition in response to his own generation's experience of the Revolution, the Empire, and the Restoration. From the Revolution, for example, Constant learned that communitarian cant may serve the purposes of bureaucratic murder. A handful of individuals had invoked the name of the community in order to perpetrate sickening crimes for the sake of concealed self-interest, spite, or whim. The deceitful rhetoric of the Jacobins spurred Constant's lifelong concern with political pretexts and hypocrisy.

Liberal distrust of community also reflected another common experience of the Revolutionary age: the need to escape police surveillance and local spies. Fear of being denounced by one's neighbor, not simply the stirrings of entrepreneurial capitalism, accelerated the disintegration of communal bonds in France after 1793. Antisocial strategies of disengagement and deception served the interests of all parties. Masks, disguises, and escape routes became integral components of "modern freedom" in the midst of a fratricidal civil war.

According to Constant, Napoleon drew his considerable support not merely from a nationalistic longing for glory, but also from civic privatism. He was able to seize power because the French public was disgusted with pseudorepublican politics and eager to retreat to the safety of private affairs.[5] Napoleon became dictator while citizens were recoiling from politics in relief and disbelief. Constant was attracted to this idea because it was paradoxical. The postrevolutionary urge to avoid politics, to draw sharp boundaries around the political sphere, led to the emergence of an all-invading form of Caesarist dictatorship. The atrophy of political life, far from encouraging the state to wither away, dismantled the last barriers to governmental intervention. Antipolitical, if not anarchist, instincts lay close to the surface of Constant's mind. It is therefore useful to record the lesson he drew from the Bonapartist experience: private rights are endangered by excessive privatization; individual independence cannot survive without some form of citizen involvement.

The portrait of liberalism painted by its recent critics is distressingly flat and unconvincing. Liberal theorists are typically indicted for their naive psychology, insensitivity to the problem of false consciousness, and individualistic repudiation of community. Liberals are said to have conceived political power exclusively as a threat to freedom and never as a means to its realization.[6] They are blamed not merely for their one-sided focus on private rights, but also for their ahistorical abstractness, blindness to social context, definition of man as an economic animal, inability to learn from the past, and, of course, their optimistic belief in progress.[7] There are, however, liberalisms and liberalisms. Some versions may be dismissed with such sweeping charges. Constant's may not. While his political thinking can be criticized in a number of ways,[8] it is largely untouched by allegations such as these. He was a representative liberal whose position eludes many of the standard assaults on liberal thought.

Equally striking is Constant's addiction to paradox and ambiguity. His writings, while never obscure, are slippery and difficult to summarize because they are responsive to sharply opposed aspects of the problems of his concern. Half-truths make telling impressions. They are easy to formulate and simple to recall. No matter how many times contractualist libertarianism and romantic communitarianism are theoretically demolished, they will reappear on the scene. Theories like Constant's suffer a different fate. Even when brilliantly defended, they tend to slip out of sight. We must ceaselessly struggle to hold their complexities in mind. This may explain why a leading voice of nineteenth-century liberalism, while frequently cited,[9] has attracted relatively scant attention from political theorists.

Constant's aversion to half-truths[10] might be interpreted as a timorous refusal to take bold stands. But it also reflects a theoretical strength. His discussions of modern liberty, *publicité,* journalism, Rousseau, Napoleon, historicism, hypocrisy, commerce, federalism, individualism, progress, representation, secularization, and romanticism are all marked by a studied ambivalence. To rescue the significance and cogency of Constant's ambiguities is another central purpose of this book.

THE SHAPE OF CONSTANT'S CAREER

While it is simple to chart the phases of Constant's career, it is difficult to say anything precise about the development of his thought. In a convincing analysis of the private correspondence, Pierre Deguise has demonstrated that Constant routinely warped what he had to say, accentuated one aspect over another, in order to make the most powerful impression on his addressee of the moment.[11] What was true of the letters also held good in public life, in his speeches and brochures. Constant's audience under the Directory was quite unlike his audience under the Restoration (and the latter evolved radically between 1816 and 1830). France's problems also changed. Constant incessantly reworked his arguments in order to make them effective in new and unprecedented situations. But his basic theoretical position did not evolve in a radical way. He had established the fundamental outline of his political views quite early. From the beginning of his career as a publicist until his death, he adhered steadily to the principles of 1789. He never wavered in his advocacy of the disestablishment of privilege, jury trials, the career open to talents, popular sovereignty expressed through representative institutions (including the right of opposition), absolute freedom of speech and the press, unconditional religious toleration, and the laicization of politics and education. Consequently, a developmental approach to his political thought, while interesting biographically, is of little theoretical importance.[12] To be sure, some significant variations are observable; but they usually reflect nothing more than strategic adjustments to political problems of the moment. Two broader shifts of emphasis, however, require special attention.

Under the Directory, faced with a helpless government and an ungovernable country, Constant toyed with various *psychological* mechanisms that he hoped might stabilize the Republic. These mechanisms all failed to bring about the desired result, and by 1800 Constant began to express his commitment to the impersonality of the liberal state: constitutionalism must achieve stability without excessive reliance on the psychological traits of individuals.

The second untypical period of Constant's career occurred between 1814 and 1815 and was indeed much more anomalous than the first.[13] Having been politically inactive for more than a decade, Constant was suddenly asked to respond publicly to Napoleon's imminent fall. Hastily expressing his belief that another Bonapartist tyranny could be thwarted only by effective counterweights, he uncharacteristically endorsed the central principle of aristocratic liberalism: freedom can survive only in symbiosis with hereditary privilege. The tenets of aristocratic liberalism were defended by Mme. de Staël and can be traced back to Montesquieu. But they clashed jarringly with Constant's earlier and later egalitarian writings. By 1816, he had disengaged himself from the de Staël[14] circle and publicly recanted his suggestion of 1814–15 that heredity was a legitimate principle of social organization. He reverted to the Sieyèsian position he had advocated in the 1790s: nobility is excess baggage and an insult to the nation. There was no place for hereditary privilege in the liberal state.

Because Constant's position from 1795 to 1806 is broadly consistent with the views he advanced after 1817, I have felt justified in focusing on the underlying pattern of his thought. In a secondary way, I have attended to strategic concessions and amendations. I have tried to explain in detail his shift away from political psychology as well as to analyze the aberrant royalism and defense of hereditary institutions in 1814–15. I have also examined the apparent change in his view of the suffrage. In my interpretations of "Ancient and Modern Liberty" and *Conquête et usurpation*, I have placed substantial emphasis on date of composition. But I have found no evidence of deep philosophical realignments, only strategic redirectionings that occurred in response to new crises and new audiences. To explain even such minor swerves convincingly, it is indispensable to begin with a brief sketch of Constant's political and intellectual career.

The essential facts to remember about Constant's earliest years are these. He was born in Switzerland in 1767 to a family of marginal nobility, Protestants who believed their ancestors had been expelled from France by religious bigotry and persecution. His family was affluent, so, although he frequently lived in straitened circumstances, he was never compelled to earn a steady income. Excluded as he was from the Catholic schools of France, he suffered an erratic education at the hands of various incompetent tutors until, still a very young man, he was enrolled at the University of Erlangen in Germany (1782–83) and subsequently at the University of Edinburgh (1783–85), then an intellectual center of the Scottish Enlightenment. The upshot of these nomadic early years needs little emphasis: by birth and background, Constant was an outsider, a European vagrant, a *déraciné* without a country. Even after he acquired French citizenship in 1798, he was annoyingly but accurately perceived by most of his contemporaries as *un français du dehors*. He was very anxious to stake out a place for himself in French political life. Yet his origins and itinerant childhood ensured a certain ineliminable civic detachment.[15] Raised as a truant, he never imagined that individual lives could or should be totally enmeshed in the destiny of a single nation-state. On the other hand, while he was later to identify "modern freedom" at least partly with political absenteeism and estrangement, he never forgot the emotional distress of his extraneous early life.

It was probably at Edinburgh that Constant first learned to appreciate the skeptical, reformist liberalism of Adam Smith and to admire the constitutional machinery of British government. The liberalism of the Enlightenment had been preoccupied with abuses characteristic of the old Europe such as primogeniture, entail, and the myopic interventions of mercantilist regimes. Between that earlier tradition and its nineteenth-century heirs a sequence of cataclysmic events had intervened in France: the Revolution, civil war, the paralysis of the Directory, the disastrous cycle of Napoleonic wars, and, finally, the vengeful return of the ultras of which the White Terror was only the goriest episode. To the dismay of European liberals, new and largely unprecedented threats to freedom, security, and civility had burst upon the political scene. Even without absolute monarchs and hereditary inequalities, postrevolutionary regimes had succeeded in imposing ruinous oppression and suffering. Constant's main intellectual problem arose from these circumstances. New political realities forced him to rethink eighteenth-century liberalism in a fundamental way. Only a radical revamping could make it into an adequate response to the shattering events that followed quickly upon 1789. And, indeed, what was a theorist steeped in the writings of Voltaire, Montesquieu, and Adam Smith to think *after* the Revolution? This was the problem that provoked Constant's efforts to elaborate a new philosophical perspective on political authority and social freedom.

In 1789, Constant was only twenty-two years old. The previous year, at the court of the duke of Brunswick, he had assumed the position of chamberlain, a ceremonial post which he occupied off and on, and with varying degrees of disgruntlement, until the spring of 1795. Irked by the émigrés who by 1790 were streaming out of France, Constant managed to make himself unpopular at court. Acerbic remarks were responsible for his bad relations with other courtiers, but also to be blamed were his coy displays of sympathy for the Revolution. In letters dating from this period, he mischievously located himself somewhere to the left of the constitutional monarchists, applauding the leading Girondins. For a brief period during the Terror he experienced a flare-up of enthusiasm for the Jacobins but, as could have been predicted, the flame rapidly guttered out. Otherwise, he regularly referred to Robespierre as a deranged zealot. In a revealing description of the emotional disparity between his own and the Jacobin temperament, the young Constant wrote: "I have very little talent for admiring myself when I feel vivid indignation."[16] Indeed, he always remained leery of crusades for moral purity and postures of heroic martyrdom for the sake of humanity. This distrust of the righteously indignant was not merely an abiding trait in his character; it also had formidable implications for his political thought.

The alienated young courtier's self-consciously defiant stances on the Revolution, by contrast, are of trifling importance for a study of his political theory. After all, Brunswick and Lausanne were remote from the flash point of events. Of utmost significance, on the other hand, was the intellectual encounter mirrored in his fascinating correspondence with Belle de Charrière, the bulk of which was written between 1787 and 1794. Constant was barely twenty when he wrote these letters; so they must be treated with some caution. Nevertheless, we seem to discover here for the first time the all-corrosive skepticism that formed the deepest grounding of his liberal beliefs.[17] Lack of certainty is often depicted as a purely private debility from which Constant escaped by plunging headlong into a career of political reform.[18] While this may be true psychologically, it is false philosophically. The skepticism revealed in his early letters to Mme. de Charrière remained the basis of his mature political thought and action. A permanent deficit of moral authoritativeness was the ultimate reason why he believed the liberal state must remain neutral toward conflicting ideas of the good life.[19]

It is sometimes assumed that disbelief in the objectivity of values, or in the knowability of objective values, disarms liberalism in the face of tyranny. In Constant's case, liberal militancy was born out of the spirit of doubt. Convinced that no group of mortals can be certain about the nature of virtue or the human good, he was ready to oppose any regime that claimed such certainty. Reasonably enough, he perceived the Jacobin attempt to outlaw dissent, legislate public morality, and inculcate civic virtue as a monstrous violation of his moral uncertainty. A true skeptic could not accommodate himself to such a paternalistic regime. No social *telos* could be so unquestionable as to justify legal enforcement. Constant identified freedom not with the state-orchestrated realization of an ideal man but with institutional arrangements that kept open and accessible a wide variety of social and political possibilities. His early and enduring skepticism was an important source of his later willingness to fight for liberal reforms.

In the spring of 1795, Constant returned to Paris in the company of Mme. de Staël (they met the previous autumn). The Convention was in the process of dissolution and the transition to the Directory—a "régime of improvisations"[20] that limped along unconvincingly until toppled by Napoleon in 1799—was under way. In their attempt to patch together a moderate representative government in France, the leading centrists were buffeted by gusts from the Left and the Right. In May 1795, three days before Constant arrived in Paris, the last sans-culotte *journée* had been put down. In September, the right-wing insurrection of Vendémiaire was also crushed, this time with the help of Constant's near contemporary, General Bonaparte.

Government by means of the army had replaced government by means of Parisian mobs. From the outset, Constant identified the fundamental obstacles facing liberalism in France as a state too weak to govern without spasmotic appeals to force and an acrimonious climate of ideological intransigence and *guerre civile*.

Firsthand experience of civil war had a decisive impact on the elemental pattern of Constant's political thought. Scholars bent on unearthing the "social basis" of his approach should examine the fierce polarization of French political life after the Revolution, the irreconcilable conflict of legitimacies, rather than the interests of a supposedly consolidated and self-aware business class. Constant's liberalism was founded on the void at the center of a polarized political scene.

Nineteenth-century European liberals adduced a wide spectrum of ancestors and precursors. In confronting political zealotry and national disintegration, Constant quite naturally returned to a precapitalist source of liberal thought. In the sixteenth century, various *politique* theorists such as Jean Bodin and even Montaigne began to formulate a modern concept of "sovereignty" in response to a civil war, a primarily religious struggle between Catholics and Huguenots. Since reconversion of the Calvinists seemed impossible and the social costs of suppressing all dissent would have been exorbitantly high, the *politiques* proposed a fundamental rethinking of the basis of political legitimacy.[21] No longer able to furnish theoretical resolutions to theological conflicts, the state had to lower its sights and be satisfied with the lesser goal of establishing a modus vivendi between conflicting groups. It had to aim at peace and prosperity, not the salvation of souls. There was no thought of eliminating religious dissonance. The plan instead was to loosen the conditions for social order, to create a political system more laxly tolerant of religious conflict and thus less threatened by it. The state had to lift itself to a higher level of abstraction, no longer pretending to confer moral perfection on its lucky members but becoming instead a legal framework in which moral antagonists could coexist and cooperate. The sovereign state could fulfill this neutral role only if it refused to endorse the aspirations of any single faction. The legitimacy of authority, as a result, could no longer depend on a monarch's moral credentials but only on his secular capacity to keep the peace. The *politiques* saw peace, in turn, as a nonideological goal. Indeed, they did not view it as a *telos* at all. As Constant reformulated their insight: "Peace does not represent any sort of precise goal. It is a condition in which each person forms plans freely, meditates on his means, and sets in motion his individual calculations."[22] Within certain obvious limits, the *politiques* argued, the sovereign state should strive for impartiality. It should help secure the preconditions under which rival groups might realize their various aspirations.

The influence of this *politique* tradition on Constant's thinking was decisive. That the liberal state must remain neutral toward conflicting conceptions of the good life was one of the cardinal tenets of his thought. No ideal was to have an official or privileged status. This principle registered the underlying egalitarianism of Constant's liberalism. The liberal state must focus on securing conditions that allow *all* individuals to pursue their discordant goals. Any ideal compatible with social order and cooperation should command legal recognition. This egalitarian tolerance was pressed upon Constant by his underlying skepticism as well as by his experience of the ideological intransigence of opposed factions within French politics. Doubt about the demonstrably objective status of values was reinforced by independent prudential considerations concerning the best way to exorcise the demons of the past, that is, to put an end to a fratricidal civil war.

The weightiest eighteenth-century heirs to the *politique* tradition were Voltaire and Turgot.[23] They supported the monarchy in its admittedly feeble attempt to secularize society and introduce egalitarian reforms, especially in the area of taxation. They did not view sovereignty as an undesirable intrusion that must be strictly hedged to make room for freedom. They did not believe that a widening and consolidation of sovereign power necessarily entailed the constriction of liberty. Instead, their very liberalism demanded that they conceive of sovereignty as a potential vehicle for freedom. At the very least, they thought that sovereignty and freedom could expand simultaneously. Their enemies, the *parlementaires,* defended the vested interests of the clergy and the nobility. These reactionary opponents of legal and fiscal reform, amazingly enough, portrayed themselves as defenders of "freedom" against a despotic king.[24] According to parlementary ideology, the disestablishment of privilege led inevitably to tyranny. Voltaire and Turgot rejected this view. They attacked the *parlementaires,* affirmed sovereignty, and strove to detach "liberty" from its absurd association with caste and corporations.

The Revolution looked quite different when viewed through parlementary and Voltairist eyes. Considered from the parlementary perspective, the Revolution went wrong when it turned against the aristocracy and sustained the antinobilism of the centralizing and rationalizing monarchs. Robespierre, in the parlementary view, was a gutter Richelieu; and the Revolution was more royalist than the king. This nobilary thesis was still faintly echoed by Jacques Necker in his *De la Révolution française,* and even to some extent by Mme. de Staël in her *Considérations sur les prin-*

cipaux événements de la Révolution française.[25] As she wrote, "in France, liberty is ancient and despotism is modern."[26] From Montesquieu and others she had learned to identify freedom with a pluralism of notables whose power, in France, had been eroded by administrative centralization. Later, Tocqueville brilliantly interpreted the Revolution from a similar ideological perspective.[27]

Constant belonged to a distinct and contrary liberal tradition. He was a *politique* reformer, not a nostalgic *parlementaire*. He emphatically denied that liberty of any sort had flourished in feudal Europe: "the most habitual oppression, that which has weighed the most constantly on the majority of the inhabitants of French territory, has been that of the nobles over the commons."[28] In 1797, he expressed his radical dissent from Necker's interpretation of the Revolution and made a strong plea for the compatibility of freedom and centralized power.[29] In 1818, he sharply criticized Mme. de Staël for her association of "freedom" with the independence of a hereditary class.[30] At the end of his life, he said that Sieyès, who identified the Third Estate with the nation and strongly favored an energetic executive, was one of the truly great political theorists of the age.[31]

Constant was in some ways closer to Voltaire and Turgot than to Montesquieu.[32] His desire to restrict the discretionary authority of the police was not a sign of hostility toward the concept of sovereignty.[33] He did not think that power was the antonym of liberty. He agreed that the public and the private, sovereignty and individual independence, could coexist and even expand simultaneously. The horrors of the Revolution did not make him nostalgic for the old regime.[34] He was unswervingly loyal to the Encyclopedists, "the honorable and useful adversaries of an absurd and hateful regime,"[35] and to the Enlightenment values of legal and fiscal equality, freedom of the press, and the privatization of religion. He also favored popular sovereignty so long as it was organized within the framework of a liberal constitution.

Constant's first major publications were *De la force du gouvernement actuel de la France* (1796)[36] and *Des réactions politiques* (1797).[37] Neither work achieved the lucidity and logical coherence characteristic of his mature writings. They are nevertheless among the most brilliant pamphlets of the revolutionary period. Both were written to buttress the imperiled Directory and to urge it to steer a moderate course between residual Jacobinism and resurgent royalism. *Des réactions politiques* contains some of the earliest examples of the word *liberal* used to signal a position of political moderation.[38] Drawing on the original meaning of the term as broad-minded, generous, and expansive, Constant employed *liberal* to characterize a stance of political nonpartisanship, indiscriminately tolerant toward Left and Right so long as violence and vendetta were kept under control.[39]

Some commentators have assumed that these early works were products of Constant's youthful "republican period," to be contrasted sharply with the constitutional monarchism he espoused during the Restoration.[40] Between 1795 and 1799, it is true, Constant defended the Republic.[41] In many respects, however, the regime created by the Constitution of the Year III was not radically different from the regime in place after 1814. Moreover, the young Constant's arguments for republican government already reflected a desire to sidestep irresolvable conflicts of ideology and moral faith. Among other reasons, a republic was the best form of government for France because it was the closest thing to a nonpartisan regime possible given the circumstances. The restoration of the Bourbons would only fuel the fires of social mistrust, escalating the "vengeances de parti" which had already cost France so dearly.[42] This may have been republicanism, but it was a hesitant and, above all, *conditional* republicanism. The young Constant valued republican institutions for their role in dedramatizing political conflict, preventing a return to sectarian conflict, and guaranteeing a few elemental human freedoms while remaining amenable to gradual reform. The conditional royalism of Constant's later writings represented a concession to reality without signaling a doctrinal conversion.

Constant shared the liberal concern with limiting the power of the state, but during the four years of the Directory he was also forced to confront the contrary problem: a government so feeble, disoriented, and insecure that it was unable to maintain a minimal degree of social order. What France faced was the threat of "anarchy," a term used literally in this period and not as a euphemism for democracy: "anarchy . . . is a condition in which society is subjected to the irregular action of opposed and enemy forces."[43] A power vacuum had exposed French society to a grisly cycle of terror and counterterror. Theorists such as Locke and Montesquieu had been so fixated on the problem of excessive authority that they provided little instruction about how to deal with governmental incoherence or paralysis, with a state unsure of its objectives, unable to act consistently, and helpless to get its decisions enforced. It was the chaos of a sovereignless nation, not merely a personal lapse of principle, that led Constant to support the *coup d'état* of the Directory in Fructidor 1797,[44] and eventually (though not initially) Bonaparte's *coup d'état* of Brumaire 1799.[45] Although there may have been a measure of opportunism involved here, there was no philosophical inconsistency. Before a government's power can be limited, its power must exist, and where it does not exist it must be constructed or reconstructed.[46] Recognition of this fact underlay Constant's reluctant acquiescence in the Directory's extraconstitutional measures and eventually in Bonaparte's seizure of power.

Indeed, the complex story of Constant's tangled relations with Napoleon began at precisely this point. At the end of 1799, the first consul appointed Constant to the Tribunat. By the opening session, Napoleon's spectacular success in consolidating power had become clear and Constant (without any particularly discreditable motives) immediately revived the cause of Locke and Montesquieu. The speeches he delivered between 1800 and 1802 revealed a new self-confidence, simplicity of language, and rigor of thought. Under the Directory he had veered uncomfortably close to associating himself with the regime's intolerance of opposition. The Consulate's inherent strength allowed him to find his voice, to enter the ranks of the opposition without worrying about the atrocities that might follow if the government collapsed. He continued the liberal struggle to limit state authority, until Napoleon's patience became exhausted. Along with several other trouble makers, Constant was purged from the Tribunat in 1802.

Expelled from what promised to be a difficult but effective public career, Constant spent the next dozen years of his life, from the time he was thirty-five to the time he was forty-seven, in a state of compulsory civic privatism: "I have banished from myself all talk of politics. I agree with the authors of the day that it is a subject we should think about as little as possible. It is of no importance, in fact, except to our security, our property, and our lives. What madness to weary ourselves reflecting on bagatelles such as these!"[47] When reflecting upon Constant's complicated attitude toward freedom-from-politics, we should always recall that he experienced the one unpolitical stint in his career as an involuntary expulsion.

After 1802, Constant oscillated between a hermetic or scholarly and a salon-style existence, living much of the time with the exiled Mme. de Staël at Necker's Chateau de Coppet near Lausanne. That is where he settled down to complete his own "great treatise" of political theory, begun around 1800 and originally conceived as a commentary on Godwin. The fruits of this effort were two bulging manuscripts, the *Fragments d'un ouvrage abandonné sur la possibilité d'une constitution républicaine dans un grand Pays*[48] and the original version of the *Principes de politique applicables à tous les gouvernements*.[49] (The former remains in manuscript today, while the latter was published only in 1980.) These two treatises contain the first systematic sketch of what became Constant's mature political theory, and they served as a private stockpile regularly pillaged for many of his later works, especially works dashed off in the heat of political crisis. Here we find most of the themes central to his later writings: the irreversibility of long-term social change, legalism as a cure for the seesaw of anarchy and tyranny, limited government as a precondition for self-government, the subtly qualified critique of Rousseau, concern for strategies of constitutional design, the ancient/modern pattern of analysis, the depiction of modern Europe as a culture tortured by self-doubt, and the abomination of democratic "pretexts" that veil acts of governmental oppression. These themes will occupy us at length below.

If Constant had published these systematic works, he might have eventually come to be known as the most original political theorist in France between Rousseau and Tocqueville. But his failure to publish was no accident. In times of rapid and unpredictable change, a writer struggling to respond directly to events will seldom rest easy with past formulations. As Constant wrote in the *Fragmens:* "In recent times, our institutions have become so ephemeral, change so compliantly, succeed one another so quickly, that in proceeding to analyze them, we can never be sure that they will not be destroyed before our examination is complete."[50] Only the Restoration brought the sort of stability to French politics, not to mention the grudging tolerance for legal opposition, that allowed Constant to publish rewritten sections from his two great tracts, adapted, with some strain, to the framework of a constitutional monarchy.

Another of Constant's most remarkable works was also initiated during the early years of his forced retreat. The amazing set of diaries known collectively as the *Journaux intimes* cover the period between 1803 and 1816.[51] Here we have an anecdotal, aphoristic, insider's view of freedom from politics. These daybooks, alongside Constant's voluminous and equally riveting correspondence (including his letters to Mme. de Charrière), are immensely important for the study of his political theory.[52] They provide invaluable information about Constant's attitude toward contemporary intellectual movements, especially German romanticism. Even more important, they allow us to penetrate deep to the psychological roots of liberal politics. The same can be said for Constant's autobiographical sketches, La Cahier rouge and *Cécile* (both composed around 1811), and of his harrowing novel *Adolphe* (begun in 1806, though not published until 1816).[53] Adolphe is in many ways a prototype of the liberal individual, and his story is a commentary on the human emptiness of negative freedom. He is preoccupied with "independence," obsessed with disengaging himself from a tyrannical Ellénore. But when he finally achieves the freedom he craves, he becomes utterly wretched and irreconcilable with life.

The pessimism so evident in Constant's "private" works is usually sublimated in his political writings. It disappears from the focal point of attention but lurks on the edges of consciousness. The political meaning of *Adolphe,* or part of it, is this: while modern individuals will relentlessly seek freedom, finding it will not necessarily make them happy or fulfilled or "whole." In fact, modern freedom may be indistinguishable from anomie. But though Constant had no illusions about modern freedom, he also saw no alternative to it. He never considered flight into camaraderie as a possible solution to the personally troublesome and unfulfilling nature of modern freedom. Without glorifying private independence or believing it self-sufficient, he clung to it fiercely. Radically communal alternatives seemed less attractive still.

It was during these same years that Constant did much of the research and some of the preliminary writing for his massive study of the history of religions, published at the end of his life as *De la religion* (in five volumes)[54] and *Du polythéisme romain* (in two posthumous volumes).[55] These works are also indispensable for an understanding of the theoretical underpinnings of Constant's liberalism. By 1804, Constant had abandoned the happy atheism he had flaunted as a youth in fashionable imitation of Helvétius and d'Holbach. He remained a skeptic, but his attitude toward religion revealed more genuine uncertainties and waverings than had been visible among his predecessors. Vehement diatribes against the beliefs of others would have been incompatible with his permanent state of doubt. Rejecting the self-satisfied Enlightenment view that all practitioners of religion were either wicked or stupid, he nevertheless advocated the total disestablishment of religious authority and the extension of perfect tolerance to privatized belief.

His analysis of religion, while principally scholarly and historical, was also psychological. A spontaneous "religious sentiment" is implanted in all men. It may be exploited by ecclesiastics but was certainly not created by them. Although the ceremonial and institutional "forms" of a religion may be quite corrupt, its underlying substance—the dimension of pure religious interiority—is worthy of respect.

One of the most remarkable features of *De la religion* is Constant's unhesitating repudiation of the Enlightenment principle of "self-interest well understood." He argues that self-interest is only one possible motivation of human behavior and that a life dominated by self-interest would be humanly intolerable. Indeed, he suggests that the undying hold of religious sentiment on the human mind stems from an innate desire to escape from the blight of egocentric concerns. In politics, Constant resisted Rousseauist and romantic suggestions that men should dissolve their petty individuality into the incandescent life of the nation. But this resistance was provoked by his observation of the group pathologies characteristic of the revolutionary age, not by inherent admiration for the marvels of self-interest. Indirectly, Constant's political thinking reflected the same mistrust of utility and self-interest that is so prominent in his studies of religion.

De la religion and *Du polythéisme romain* represented important departures from the Enlightenment perspective on religious life. Yet it would be a mistake to neglect the continuities between Constant's approach and the views of his eighteenth-century predecessors. Despite his antisensationalism and repudiation of utility and self-interest, he remained a son of the Enlightenment. The "inward religion" he admired had nothing to do with that ancient palace of imposture, *l'infâme*. Both treatises were revised for publication during the 1820s, while liberals were engaged in an intensive anticlerical propaganda campaign. Ultra attempts to renew Catholic exclusivism and control of education gave Constant and his allies a perfect opportunity to detach the nation from the party in power. Thus, the books published during these years were largely concerned with power and its abuse, with subjection, caste, and privileges based on a monopoly of knowledge. Central to the entire study was a distinction between sacerdotal and nonsacerdotal religions.[56] What troubled Constant most was "the despotism of priests." He did nothing to disguise the contemporary relevance of this obsession: "Every time the priesthood has had the aristocracy or the king as an accomplice, it has pronounced anathema against the freedoms and the rights of the people. Consider, even today, the works of those who wish to resuscitate theocracy."[57] In sum, *De la religion* should be read as one of the last major expressions of modern anticlericalism.

Constant's intellectual universe was animated by the belief that the model of the ancient city should never be adduced, in a Rousseauist manner, to condemn the social order of modern Europe. But during the 1820s, when the ultras were dominating the political scene, he systematically and aggressively reinvoked Greece. The Greek city was enormously creative because its religion did not bestow political power on a caste of priests: "In Greece . . . the priesthood was not a *corps,* and it had no political influence."[58] As a loyal disciple of Machiavelli and Montesquieu, Constant praised antiquity in order to attack the Catholic church.[59] By attending to the unyielding anticlericalism of Constant's works on religion, we can reinforce our sense of his permanent debt to the Enlightenment tradition.

Between 1811 and 1813 Constant secluded himself in the university library at Göttingen to pursue his research. He had already spent a good deal of time in Germany. For example, he had accompanied Mme. de Staël in 1803–04 when she descended upon Goethe and Schiller in Weimar. The impact which these various sojourns in Germany had on Constant's political thought is hard to gauge. The principalities he knew most intimately presented a curious amalgam of authoritarian government based on a totally privatized citizen body and quite broad intellectual and literary freedoms.[60] One antirepublican conclusion he could have drawn was the following: at least *some* kinds of liberty are compatible with the complete atrophy of political life. The image of the library at Göttingen (an oasis, a walled garden, an escape from the turmoil of Europe ravaged by war) may have been assimilated into Constant's sense that freedom from politics was a fundamentally ambivalent or merely compensatory good, but a true good nevertheless.[61]

In October 1813, Napoleon was defeated at Leipzig and French troops began to evacuate Germany. Abruptly, Constant debouched from his cloister and, after twelve years of forced abstention from politics, found himself again in the thick of political struggles. He had scant time to acclimatize himself to such a dramatic change of scene. In November he met privately in Hanover with Jean Bernadotte, former marshal of the Empire and now crown prince of Sweden as well as an aspiring candidate to the French throne. With Bernadotte's encouragement, Constant uncrated the sheaf of political papers he had composed between 1800 and 1806 and in great haste spliced together one of his most famous works, *De l'esprit de conquête et de l'usurpation*.[62] No one can deny that this is an explosive book, written brilliantly and with emotional intensity. In some ways, *Conquête et usurpation* is vintage Constant. Yet virtually every commentator since Laboulaye has made the mistake of viewing it as a theoretically representative work. In several important respects, it is an eccentric pamphlet, a product of the anomalous years of 1813–15 when Constant had not yet fully regained his political bearings. I have already mentioned that *Conquête et usurpation* contained the antiliberal argument that "heredity is legitimate."[63] It also echoed the émigré diagnosis of the Empire: Napoleon was destined to tyranny because he had not been born to the throne.[64] It was therefore inconsistent, essentially so, with Constant's writings of the 1790s as well as with the works he published after 1816.[65] When Constant collected his pamphlets on representative government in 1818, he omitted *Conquête et usurpation* not (I believe) principally because of embarrassment over his subsequent relations with Napoleon, but rather because of a theoretical dissatisfaction with the disconcertingly Legitimist flavor of the work.

Louis XVIII acceded to the throne in the spring of 1814 and Constant returned to Paris to resume his interrupted career as a journalist. In response to the government's new censorship laws, he published two important pamphlets defending freedom of the press, a subject that was to become one of his parliamentary avocations as well as a pivotal issue of Restoration politics. Already in May, several days before the promulgation of the Charte,[66] he had published his *Réflexions sur les constitutions,*[67] which contained the sketch of a constitution for a constitutional monarchy based on a nationally elected representative assembly and the rule of law. It was in this period, moreover, that he had his first public encounter with Catholic France, previously in hiding. The extreme reactionary party, the ultraroyalists, were gathered around the comte d'Artois and were already attacking Louis XVIII for his concessions to constitutionalism. Their principal theoretical spokesmen were Louis de Bonald and Joseph de Maistre. By this time the Jacobins had ceased to exist politically. The ultras were therefore Constant's prime adversaries for the last fifteen years of his career. The political thrust of his mature writings can only be understood in the context of the victorious conservative ideology that dominated France and all Metternich's Europe at this time.

The increasing strength of the ultras during the winter of 1814–15 had prepared public opinion to welcome Napoleon (or at least not to regret the Bourbons) when the emperor escaped from Elba in April 1815: "a universal hatred of the nobility lent Napoleon formidable support."[68] On hearing the calamitous news, a panicky Louis XVIII confessed that the uncompromisingly ultra slant of his government had been an error and added that he was now prepared to offer further concessions to the constitutionalist party. At this juncture, Constant briefly rallied to the Bourbon cause and, in the *Journal des débats,* published his notorious attack on Napoleon as a second Attila, as the new Genghis Khan.[69] His timing was not auspicious. The day after Constant's article appeared, Napoleon had installed himself at the Tuileries and the newly accommodating court had absconded ignominiously to Ghent. Constant first withdrew into hiding, but before long he received an invitation from Napoleon, an offer to become a councillor of state and to collaborate on an *Acte additionnel* meant to liberalize the imperial constitution. Exhilarated by the prospect of being involved in large affairs, Constant accepted. The question will always be asked: how could he have believed Napoleon capable of becoming a constitutional monarch?[70] Even a partial answer is complex. His personal involvement with Juliette de Récamier gave him a nonpolitical motive for remaining in Paris. Insecurity about his citizenship and residual embarrassment over his ties with Bernadotte also made it attractive for Constant to rally to the national cause in the face of a foreign invader. Moreover, as we learn from the apologetic *Mémoires sur les Cent-Jours* (1820–22), the Bourbons did not seem better prepared to accept the "yoke of the Charte" than did Napoleon. This is what Constant had come to understand since he published *Conquête et usurpation*. No one imaginative enough to picture the comte d'Artois as a constitutional king could object too strenuously to Napoleon. There is virtue in consistency. And like Plato before Dion, Constant was pleased to have the ear of one of the world's most powerful men.[71]

Finally, there was a deeper reason for Constant's precipitous about-face, his shift from being Napoleon's bitterest enemy to being a collaborator and ally. While Napoleon was a tyrant who suppressed representative government and failed to institute the rule of law, he was also a living symbol of the demolition of the old regime. Napoleon had created *la couronne ouverte aux talents,* providing a visible expression of the organizing principle of the new society, a society making the transition from status to contractual rights. It was not surprising that after a year of rankling under ultra exclusiveness Constant felt attracted to Napoleon's socially progressive credentials, even while he remained skeptical of the emperor's political intentions.

During the Hundred Days, Constant published more rewritten excerpts from his manuscript reservoir, this time under the title of *Principes de politique* (1815).[72] Conceived as a commentary on the *Acte additionnel,* this pamphlet was more straightforwardly liberal than *Conquête et usurpation,* advocating a representative system that contrasted sharply with Napoleon's previous reign. Constant put special emphasis on government by discussion among freely elected representatives, absolute freedom of opinion and the press, the publicity of parliamentary debates, and the political responsibility of ministers. Taken together, these institutions were expected to "maintain in the nation . . . a constant participation in [public] affairs, in a word, an animated spirit of political life."[73] Dynastic legitimacy and the magic of tradition went unmentioned, though the *Principes de politique* of 1815 did contain a pragmatic argument for a hereditary peerage. Citing Montesquieu and the example of England, Constant wrote: "in a hereditary monarchy [such as Napoleon's], the heredity of a class is indispensable."[74] Moreover, Constant claimed that the right to vote should be restricted to owners of land, industrial wealth being declared an insufficient basis for citizenship. He was to reverse himself on both issues by 1817.[75]

After Waterloo, the initial order for Constant's exile was revoked by a reconciliation-minded Louis XVIII. Nevertheless, Constant repaired to England, where he remained for over a year. In London he published *Adolphe,* written a decade earlier. The minor scandal of his personal indiscretions eclipsed to some extent the major scandal of his collaboration with Napoleon. While he was away, France continued to suffer the carnage of the White Terror, a symptom of crippled sovereignty,[76] as well as the more ceremonial indignities of the *Chambre introuvable*, the ultra-dominated assembly elected through intimidation in a France occupied by foreign armies. The second Restoration turned out to be more conservative than the first, and its reactionary nature accelerated Constant's return to his earlier *quatre-vingt-neuvisme*. He took his distance from the Anglophiles of Mme. de Staël's circle and eventually joined the "Independents" of the Left. In September 1816, Louis XVIII (who realized that he was alienating the nation from his dynasty), dissolved the extremist Chamber. Constant immediately returned, to remain in France for the rest of his life. Although persecuted by the ultras, the liberal opposition could not now be driven from the scene. Constant's first work upon his return was *De la doctrine politique qui peut réunir les partis en France*,[77] a polemic against Chateaubriand, who had shifted toward the ultras at the onset of the second Restoration, and in support of the (relatively) moderate Richelieu ministry. But Constant soon broke with the ministerial party and its Doctrinaire supporters such as Guizot and Royer-Collard.[78] The rupture was triggered by a dispute over the electoral and censorship laws. Constant took a more radically democratic position than the Doctrinaires. He declared conservative English institutions maladapted to postrevolutionary France, and called for a broadening of the franchise. He found himself suddenly on the left fringe of the political spectrum.[79]

Constant's celebrated lecture comparing ancient and modern liberty was delivered in 1819. Its renown stems from the simplicity and intuitive appeal of its basic theme. Instead of apotheosizing liberty, Constant anatomized it: there are two distinct and irreducible types of freedom, popular self-government and private independence; the former was most fully actualized in the ancient *polis*, while the latter was the aspiration of all those inhabiting modern, large-scale commercial societies. Any attempt to revive ancient liberty in modern society can lead only to political brutality and terror. This dramatic contrast and stirring conclusion have attracted a good deal of scholarly attention. Yet they do not exhaust the theoretical implications of Constant's argument.

The crucial sentence in "Ancient and Modern Liberty" is the following: "the danger of modern liberty is that, absorbed in the enjoyment of our private independence and in the pursuit of our particular interests, we will renounce too easily our right to share in political power."[80] Constant had witnessed the atrophy of political life under the Empire and seen how depoliticalization served the cause of tyranny. The advocacy of wider and intensified political participation, characteristic of Constant's works after 1816 (a classical statement can be found in the final pages of "Ancient and Modern Liberty"), not only showed what Constant had learned from the Napoleonic experience; it also reflected his violent struggle with the ultras, who were seeking to restrict the suffrage to an even narrower group than the paltry ninety thousand wealthy citizens who possessed the vote in 1819. Constant's call for a rebirth of public spirit[81] and a *partial* resurrection of ancient liberty, reiterated throughout his Restoration writings, must be understood as a militant return to the principles of 1789, provoked by the aggressive ultra campaign to resuscitate Catholic and corporate France.

It would have been nothing short of astonishing if, in 1819, Constant had embraced the cause of civic privatization with the enthusiasm some commentators have ascribed to him. Here, as elsewhere, Constant's liberalism was skeptical. He was not only an advocate but also a critic of freedom from politics. His devotion to private independence was matched by his commitment to an intensification of political participation in France. To point this out is to refute the claim that Constant's liberalism was essentially antidemocratic.

Modern society is exposed to two diametrically opposed dangers: overpoliticization and overprivatization. Too much and too little civic spirit are equally destructive of both freedom and social order. The power of Constant's analysis of the revolutionary age derives largely from his capacity to combine these two antithetical ideas, ideas that are usually viewed as hostile alternatives. Stated positively, Constant's thesis is that, in modern Europe, political participation and individual rights are interdependent and indeed inseparable. The participation of citizens in public debate and electoral politics, and the participation of their representatives in the control of policy, is one form of freedom. The protection of citizens from police harassment and enforced orthodoxy is another form. Although analytically distinct, these two freedoms are in reality mutually reinforcing. Just as civil liberty presupposes political liberty, so political rights are meaningless without a guarantee of personal independence. Limited government and self-government sustain one another. Constant used the image of ancient participatory democracy as a warning to modern citizens about the dangers of choosing civil liberty alone. Yet he managed to do so without romanticizing the classical city in the manner of Rousseau.

Like the other writings of this period, Constant's lecture comparing modern with ancient liberty revealed his indebtedness to the eighteenth-century liberal tradition; but it also showed the extent to which he had been driven to rearrange its basic categories in response to the events of his own time. First of all, Enlightenment loathing of *l'infâme* was redirected against the intolerant and inquisitorial sectaries of the antichristian campaign. To Constant, antireligious zealotry seemed as brutally unenlightened as religious zealotry. After the secularizing fanaticism of the Revolution, even a disciple of Voltaire might write sympathetically about religion.

The Napoleonic experience may have cracked the frame of eighteenth-century liberalism even more dramatically than the Revolution. In many ways, Napoleon represented the best in the tradition of reforming monarchs. He confirmed the disestablishment of privilege, arrested the civil war, and promulgated the Civil Code. On the other hand, because he monopolized power and banished political opposition, his military adventures, in which almost one million Frenchmen had died, had been unstoppable. After 1816, Constant recognized the need to discover counterweights to governmental power that were both plausible and liberal. He was not willing to invoke medieval corporations and intermediary bodies in the manner of Montesquieu. He turned in the only direction he could; toward the gradual extension of voting rights to more and more citizens.

Significantly, Constant never forgot the dangers of invoking ancient liberty against the remnants of the old regime. A similar appeal had helped legitimate the atrocities of the Terror. Under the First Republic, "politics" had largely been a web of plots and counterplots, propaganda and counterpropaganda. To constrict the scope of this sort of political life had seemed a reasonable goal. Even in 1819, Constant conceded that there were limits to the importance of political participation in a modern society. He recognized the limitations of citizenship, however, because he wished to mobilize citizens in an effective rather than merely a theatrical way.

In this same period, besides the brilliantly sardonic speeches delivered in the Chamber[82] and countless articles,[83] Constant also published a thorough restatement of his political theory. It took the form of a commentary on the voluminous *Science of Legislation* authored in the late eighteenth century by an Italian philosophe, Gaetano Filangieri. At the time, Filangieri was considered a major social theorist, and his great work was even translated into English by Benjamin Franklin. Constant's running commentary on this book, the two-volume *Commentaire sur l'ouvrage de Filangieri,* was published in 1822–24.[84] In this treatise he came to terms with the one aspect of Enlightenment thought he found most disturbing, the pervasive suggestion that states should be responsible for the moral health of their citizens. Filangieri's "principal mistake," he argued was "to contemplate with superstitious respect the doctrines, the institutions, in a word the wisdom of ancient peoples."[85] Constant was especially concerned to discredit the widespread eighteenth-century admiration for the Great Legislators of antiquity. Impressed by Solon and Lycurgus, Filangieri "consider[ed] man a passive creature in the hands of authority."[86] Moral legislation, modeled on ancient examples, was conceived by many philosophes as a cure for the moral disease of Catholicism.[87] For the ignorant and the superstitious, the only hope was reeducation at the hands of secular lawgivers. The intractable problem of centuries-old miseducation explains why the most progressive party in the eighteenth century was not democratic but paternalistic.[88] The brutal Jacobin endeavor to create a new republican man forced liberals to reassess this custodial strand in Enlightenment thought. Indeed, the autocratic itch to modify the behavior of "lessers" was one aspect of the philosophes' legacy which Constant repudiated without hesitation. In the *Commentaire*, he argued emphatically that political officials have no business imposing their eccentric schemes for moral regeneration on fellow citizens.

In the course of his discussion, Constant also presented a compendium of his own theoretical views on every issue from the maltreatment of prisoners to overpopulation, from corruption to espionage, from progressive taxation to public education, from protective tariffs to trial by jury. In all this, Filangieri was less the subject of his analysis than an occasion for it.[89]

In 1819, Constant was elected deputy from the Department of the Sarthe. He lost this seat in 1822, but in 1824 was reelected as a Deputy from Paris. In 1827, although elected once again for Paris, he decided to represent instead the Lower Rhine, where he had been simultaneously chosen as a Deputy. He held this position until his death late in 1830. All in all, he was a member of the Chamber of Deputies for nine of the last eleven years of his life. As a leader of the Left and coorganizer of opposition journals such as *La Minerve française* and *Le Courrier français*, Constant fought for all the typical reform causes. Especially noteworthy was his impassioned crusade to have the slave trade declared punishable as homicide.[90] He also fought against the ultras for absolute freedom of the press and a widening of the franchise. In 1827 and again in 1830, he interpreted the electoral successes of the opposition, which indirectly hastened the Bourbons' fall, as personal triumphs.[91] Arguably, Constant had no enemies to the left. The *Charbonnerie* existed underground and had ties to Lafayette, Constant's closest parliamentary ally. There was also an inchoate "patriotic party" that wished to carry the tricolor to the Rhine. In general, however, there was no responsible or effective political party to his left. The nonenfranchised artisans and small shopkeepers of Paris viewed the liberal constitutionalists in the Chamber as their natural allies and virtual representatives.[92]

The untypical period between 1814 and 1815 revealed Constant at his most conciliatory toward the Right. Thereafter, and in response to ultra intransigence, he became increasingly militant in his struggle for liberal-egalitarian and liberal-democratic causes. The *Commentaire sur l'ouvrage de Filangieri*, and even "Ancient and Modern Liberty," reveal the radicalism of the mature Constant. In the bitter climate of Restoration politics, militant liberalism was the natural outcome of his skeptical and critical approach.

Having consigned the government to Polignac and the extreme ultras in 1829, Charles X was swept from the throne during the July Revolution of 1830. Constant was widely hailed as the spiritual father of the Revolution; and Louis-Philippe even appointed him to the Council of State. But by this time he was a very sick man, and he died shortly thereafter, in December 1830.

Constant always insisted that liberals should adjust flexibly to the regime at hand in order to exploit available opportunities for reform. His practical temperament led him to the belief that "it does not suffice to indicate what is just; it is also necessary to convince those in power that what is just is also useful."[93] During the Restoration, successful reformism required circumspection and even self-censorship. His most militant speeches and articles were interlarded with tactical concessions to entrenched powers.[94] While Constant recognized the need for such accommodation, he found it painful. In one of his last speeches before the Chamber, in September 1830, he made these revealing remarks: "So far as I am concerned, I declare it, it is only during the last two months that I have been able to breathe in liberty. Heretofore, I have always been inhibited. Even when I invoked the principles of liberty and justice before this Chamber, I carried a weight on my heart. Wanting to remain within legal channels, I was obliged to repress half my sentiments."[95] There is no suggestion here of a covert teaching. Constant was simply more radical than the moderate Legitimists he wished to convert to the cause of reform. To be convincing, he had to employ their language and adopt their point of view. Intensely practical, he strove to avoid acts of confrontation that might push potential allies into the right-wing camp. His position was always a compromise between Enlightenment ideals and the possibilities of the moment. Caution, though necessary, was an emotional burden.

Constant's interpreter must know how to disentangle the structure of his underlying arguments from his practical concessions. The common misunderstanding of Constant as an antidemocratic liberal, I believe, has resulted from a failure to negotiate this distinction successfully, to comprehend Constant's decision to suppress temporarily half his ideals for the sake of effective political reform.

In this brief chronicle of Constant's career, I have omitted many well-known facts. No mention has been made of his ridiculous duels, unsettlable court cases, speculations on *biens nationaux*, passionate love affairs, quickly aborted attempts to "find peace" in pietism, recurrent bouts of heavy gambling, or dismaying failures to be elected to the French Academy. While not irrelevant, these petty foibles and vaguely scandalous details are of little significance to a study of the philosophical foundations, sociological implications, and historical background of Constant's political thought.

THE APPARENT AND THE REAL

Much more significant than any personal weakness was Constant's ambivalent attitude toward pretexts and public falseness. There was no outright contradiction, but a sharp tension marked his ideas concerning truth and lying, appearance and reality. On the one hand, he viewed masks and hoaxes as the loathsome tools of political charlatans. On the other hand, he found ample reason to consider public dissimulation and fraud integral components of modern freedom.

Constant was almost obsessively aware of the potential deceptiveness of all forms of political thought. As any reader of *Adolphe* would expect, he was disturbed that his own thoughts, the very ideas he cherished most, might be transformed into gullery and imposture. This fear was at the heart of what I call Constant's skeptical or critical liberalism: not even the best ideas, ideas such as freedom, justice, and equality, are immune to clever misuse by seekers and wielders of power. Such an insight was not Constant's alone. He lived and wrote in what was arguably the first great age of ideology and ideological strife, of horrible acts beautified by fine-sounding words. Although there may have been a few isolated precedents, 1793–94 crystallized a new pattern in European politics. Abusive governments could thenceforth justify their actions by calling themselves democracies. Against the backdrop of the old regime, this populist trumpery stood out as a portentous innovation. Constant's historical importance lies here. His political thought can be understood as an original response to a crisis in the concept and experience of freedom. Reflecting on the Revolution, Constant always stressed that arbitrary imprisonment and judicial butchery had been justified in the name of liberty.[96] Although he stubbornly refused to attenuate his commitment to liberty and democracy, he was forced, as his eighteenth-century predecessors were not, to incorporate into his thinking some reaction to bloody tyranny publicly justified by an appeal to freedom and popular sovereignty. His response took the form of a theory of political pretexts and hypocrisy. Constant applied this theory not only to "the tyranny of governments which claim to be republican"[97] but also to the Empire. Counterfeit liberty and simulations of public consent were pervasive themes throughout his writings.

When John Plamenatz refers to Constant's "antidemocratic liberalism," he is acquiescing in a myth. Neither the Terror nor the populist dictatorship of Bonaparte were genuinely democratic. Indeed, "ever since 1789, the revolution had been marked by a succession of dictatorships exercised by groups which seized power by means of violence."[98] It is therefore unreasonable to assume that the Revolution could have produced "a kind of liberalism hostile to democracy."[99] In truth, Constant's hostility was never directed against democracy itself, but only against *the pretext of democracy*. He did not fear popular government, though (like Rousseau) he took it for granted that direct, *polis*-style self-rule was impossible in large modern states. He did not worry that if democracy were carried too far it would be transmogrified into its opposite. What he dreaded was the perverse exploitation of democratic rhetoric to justify the concentration of all power in a few hands and to conceal acts of oppression. In other words, Constant did not share the apprehensions of Tocqueville and Mill about a potential tyranny of the majority. He could not have been more explicit on this point. In 1829, he wrote: "during the last forty years, every time there has been tyranny in France, minorities have governed."[100] Even more emphatically: "The majority never oppresses. One confiscates its name, using against it the weapons it has furnished."[101] Not the majority but the all-justifying *name* of the majority, confiscated by a few, was his fundamental concern.

By focusing on his theory of pretexts and public falseness, I hope to dispel the myth of Constant the antidemocrat. I aim to demonstrate that his liberalism was more compatible with democracy, more open to democratic and egalitarian reforms, than has hitherto been assumed to be the case.

The general misinterpretation of Constant as an antidemocratic thinker (or at best as a reluctantly democratic one) has skewed the perception of other aspects of his thought as well. Constant's relation to Rousseau is regularly presented as one of unnuanced enmity and opposition. In fact, Constant's attitude toward Rousseau was remarkably complex. His egalitarianism and his uncompromising opposition to the old regime was an issue on which he was closer to Rousseau than to Montesquieu. He denounced Rousseau in harsh terms because he had a practical purpose in mind: he wished to eliminate Rousseau's apparent praise of unlimited popular sovereignty from the rhetorical arsenal of political deceivers. He understood that Rousseau had only invoked the image of Sparta as a rebuke to his contemporaries, not as a blueprint for the future; but he felt that, after the revolutionary cults of antiquity, the Spartan ideal ought to be made unavailable, even as mere rhetoric. Furthermore, the aspect of classical politics glamorized by Rousseau and toward which Constant felt most antagonistic was *not* democratic participation. It was, instead, the ideal of a monoethical state and the affiliated image of a superhuman Legislator who tried to mold the inchoate souls of citizens according to his own uniform conception of virtue and goodness. Constant loathed the Terror, but not because it was excessively democratic (which it was not). The Revolution veered "off course" because a small elite seized power and tried to impose its own stern morality on the laggard and the wayward.

Thus far, I have mentioned only the skeptical side of Constant's thinking about public deceit, his wholesale distrust of political creeds and moralistic professions. He had, however, a more hesitant attitude toward truth and lying than this discussion suggests. His works reveal no trace of a romantic obsession with total sincerity. He did not believe that if men removed their masks they would divulge their pure, uncorrupted souls. Fiction and artifice are not merely illusory facades that might easily be peeled away to reveal the authentic inner man. They are constitutive of human life. That was Constant's considered view, as is made clear in the *Journaux intimes* and in the other autobiographical works, as well as in *Adolphe*. Antiromanticism did not weaken his desire to "unmask" those rulers, such as Robespierre and Napoleon, who decorated cruelty with democratic symbols. But it did complicate and subtilize his overall view of political hypocrisy.

At times, moreover, Constant attributed a creative function to masks, lies, and public feigning. This turn in his thought took two forms. On the one hand, he argued that public deceit can have an educative or reformatory function: men become by habit what they first wish to seem by hypocrisy. One of Constant's main arguments in favor of representative government ran as follows: periodic popular elections will force wealthy elites to *pretend* they are concerned with the well-being of average and poor citizens. By dint of habit, this pretense will eventually become a genuine concern. Men are not psychologically robust enough to be consistent fakers. In social life, appearance has a tendency to become reality. As a result, it is not always advisable for political reformers to pierce through "the apparent" in order to expose "the real." It is sometimes best to cultivate the hypocritical façade until it is transformed into reality.

This is only one of the ways in which Constant lent a positive connotation to the idea of political deceit. He also did so in a more straightforward manner, one that did not depend on extravagant hopes for moral education or reform. This second approach came out most clearly in his exchange with Kant, the first installment of which appeared in the *Réactions politiques* of 1797. Against Kant's deontological admonition that man must always tell the truth, even if the heavens should fall, Constant argued that under revolutionary conditions, in situations of mutual distrust and fear, selective lying is a precondition for the survival of personal intimacy and civilized culture. Lies can serve as shields which protect fragile channels of social communication from being infiltrated by spies and informers. Without the ability to privatize certain relations, to withdraw mutuality from surveillance by grudge-bearing neighbors and the police, even the small enclaves of trust that survive in the midst of civil war will be destroyed. As a strategic response to a climate of fear, feigning can be an effective way to maintain pluralism and foster disinvolvement in the politics of paranoia and revenge. Because Constant was anxious to promote such strategies, his attitude toward pretexts and masks remained ambivalent despite his distrust of the ideologies wretchedly abused during the Revolution.

The Anatomy of Liberty

Qui est-ce qui savait, dans ces temps d'inexpérience et d'orage, ce que c'était que la liberté?

P ROGRESSIVES ritually deplore not only the low level of popular participation in politics but also its characteristic lack of intensity. Conservatives reply that the feverish involvement of ordinarily apathetic citizens can destabilize and even topple a democratic regime. Benjamin Constant attempted to *combine* these two one-sided ideas, ideas that are conventionally kept at an aseptic distance from one another. In modern societies, political tyranny may be closely associated with attempts to reglorify the public realm. But tyranny can also be encouraged and sustained by excessive privatization. Too much and too little civic spirit are equally dangerous. This double claim forms the theoretical core of Constant's 1819 lecture on "Ancient and Modern Liberty."[1]

PRECURSORS

The "quarrel between the ancients and the moderns" which flourished in France toward the end of the seventeenth century was not merely a dispute about poetry. It reflected a cultural cleavage between religious conservatives, who viewed history as a process of degeneration, and their opponents, who exalted the refinements of modern *politesse* over the crudities of the barbaric *polis*.[2] Defenders of "the moderns" hoped that a liberation of literature from unsurpassable classical models would accompany the gradual emancipation of science from the authority of Aristotelianism. Constant's vindication of liberal democracy against the would-be imitators of classical democracy was certainly influenced by these literary and scientific contests.[3] He drew more heavily, however, on a narrower tradition of political theory.[4]

For example, David Hume's "Of the Populousness of Ancient Nations" contained a lurid portrait of the classical *polis*.[5] The Greeks and Romans "were extremely fond of liberty, but seem not to have understood it very well" (p. 406). Hume focused on four basic features of the classical city which, taken together, convinced him that ancient liberty was much less attractive than its modern admirers assumed. This list was to reappear virtually unaltered in Constant's *Principes de politique* of 1802–06 (pp. 421–29). Hume described how the inhumane cruelty of domestic slavery destroyed all sense of compassion among Greek and Roman citizens (pp. 385ff.) and observed that "the ancient republics were almost in perpetual war." This bellicosity was "a natural effect of their martial spirit, their love of liberty, their mutual emulation, and that hatred which generally prevails among nations that live in close neighborhood" (p. 403). Ancient battles, moreover, were "much more bloody" than their modern counterparts; and soldiers were "wrought up to a degree of fury quite unknown to later ages" (p. 404). Hume also emphasized "the disorders which arose from faction throughout all the Grecian commonwealths" (p. 407). Internally, the ancient city was characterized by the "slaughters and massacres" that normally accompany struggles between the propertied and propertyless classes (p. 408). Finally, Hume stressed that "commerce and manufactures were more feeble and languishing" in ancient cities than in modern states.[6]

Stylized contrasts of this sort between primitive militarism and advancing commercialism were quite common in the eighteenth century. But the proximate and primary source for Constant's dichotomy between two kinds of liberty was Montesquieu. Among its other achievements, *De l'esprit des lois* drew universal attention to the astonishing differences between modern England and ancient Sparta.[7] Although he never used the phrase "modern liberty," Montesquieu had a clear enough conception of it. In modern societies, such as England, the essence of liberty was security.[8] In Europe, security was notably threatened when nobles were excessively independent and engaged in anarchic self-help (as in Poland) and also when monarchs (as in Richelieu's France) gathered too much power into their own hands.[9] In either case men feared one another and the calculability of life was drastically reduced. "In order for men to have this [modern] liberty, the government must be such that a citizen cannot fear another citizen."[10]

Constitutionalism, including the separation of powers, could arrest the seesaw of anarchy and despotism, introducing a salutary predictability into civic life. Protection from both baronial reprisals and *lettres de cachet* was the essence of English liberty. Men knew that, if they did not break the law, they would not be harassed by the police or by marauding private armies. Security made it possible to plan one's life and enter into long-term cooperative ventures with one's neighbors. A state based on this modern conception of liberty enabled its citizens to engage in a promiscuous variety of actions and lives. All citizens contributed to a common pattern, but only as "dissonances in music agree in the concord of the whole."[11]

The compatibility of the modern constitutional state with unregimented human diversity was one key to Montesquieu's contrast between modern England and ancient Sparta. He called Sparta free (that is, free from foreign domination), but he quickly added that "the only advantage of its liberty was glory." It was a small "society of athletes and combatants," where money was proscribed, where men were made cruel by harsh discipline and were always ready to immolate their private lives for the sake of their *patrie*.[12] Sparta represented the apogee of politics based on virtue.[13] Motivated exclusively by patriotic virtue, Spartans subordinated themselves unflinchingly to a single overriding purpose: to live and die for the glory of their state.[14] They participated in public life, but only in the sense that they played their parts; they certainly did not "influence" the course of deliberation in personal, idiosyncratic ways. In this "warrior's guild,"[15] collective deliberation was less important than gymnastics.

Montesquieu could compare Sparta to a monastery that, paradoxically, secured the undivided loyalty of its inmates by starving them of all human possibilities except those associated with the official functions of the group. Duties were intensified by self-sacrifice. A modern state cannot expect extraordinary devotion from its citizens precisely because of its munificence: it lavishes so many extrapolitical possibilities on the individual that he feels "he can be happy without his *patrie*." Intense politics based on virtue is thus out of place in the modern state. Personal honor or avarice may motivate modern citizens; but self-abnegating patriotism cannot. That the English revolutionary attempt to resurrect a polity based on virtue in the seventeenth century would collapse in ridiculous hypocrisy was perfectly predictable.[16]

Montesquieu's striking counterposition of England and Sparta had a decisive impact on numerous writers besides Rousseau.[17] Jean-Louis de Lolme was typical. Writing in the 1780s, he reformulated Montesquieu's contrast as a distinction between private independence and political influence: "To concur by one's suffrage in enacting laws is to enjoy a share, whatever it may be, of power; to live in a state where the laws are equal for all and sure to be executed (whatever may be the means by which these advantages are attained), is to be free."[18] Passages registering an analogous distinction between sharing in legislative power and protection from the arbitrary acts of political officials can be found in the eighteenth-century works of Joseph Priestly, Adam Ferguson, Jean-Charles Sismondi, and others.[19] All these writers had a clear awareness of what Constant would later describe as the difference between ancient and modern liberty. Nevertheless, the claims to originality advanced at the beginning of "De la liberté des anciens comparée à celle des modernes" were not entirely unjustified.[20] The abstract dichotomy between ancient and modern liberty was not unprecedented, but Constant used it in ways that were new.

TWO CONCEPTS OF LIBERTY

Ancient liberty was "active and continuous participation in the exercise of collective power." Modern liberty, by contrast, is "the peaceful enjoyment of individual or private independence."[21] A hedonistic slide from "exercise" to "enjoy" signaled the humanly debilitating consequences of modernization. Indeed, Constant's distinction between ancient and modern liberty cannot be studied apart from the notion, also inherited from Montesquieu, that European history is a singular blend of progress and decay. He made these assumptions about the human consequences of modernization:

> The liberty of ancient times was whatever assured citizens the largest share in exercising social power. The liberty of modern times is whatever guarantees the independence of citizens from their government. As a result of their character, the ancients had an overriding need for action; and the need for action is easily reconciled with a vast increase in social authority. The moderns need peace and enjoyment. Peace can be found only in a limited number of laws that prevent citizens from being harassed. Enjoyments are secured by a wide margin of individual liberty. Any legislation requiring the sacrifice of these enjoyments is incompatible with the present condition of mankind.[22]

Because of the common belief that negation implies deprivation, "negative freedom" is a very misleading translation of la liberté chez les modernes.[23] Modern liberty, as Constant conceived it, is just as much a capacity for positive action as ancient liberty had been.[24] The difference lies only in the character of the action and the field where it unfolds. Modern liberty too must be strenuously exercised, not merely enjoyed. Constant distinguished between two types of "positive" freedom in order to investigate the essential *relation* between them, the way in which they are not only compatible but even mutually enhancing.

The distinction was initially historical. Each type of liberty was originally bound to the institutions and life of a specific society. Ancient liberty, in its unalloyed form, was only possible in a sparsely populated, territorially compact, religiously homogeneous, and slaveholding warrior's republic.[25] Modern liberty was the innovation of large-scale, caste-free, internationally open, religiously pluralistic, and intensively commercial societies.[26]

Although intrigued by the contrast between public participation and private security, Constant did not allow it to obscure the radically progressive nature of modern liberty. In antiquity, "freedom" was a privileged status from which men could be excluded by the chance of birth.[27] Essential to modern liberalism was the demand that freedom be distributed to all individuals regardless of family origin.[28] The relative importance which Constant ascribed to public and private spheres was a direct function of the modern demand of citizenship for all.

Constant's emphasis on a linkage between political ideals and social contexts was not merely a subsidiary feature of his theory. In explicit contrast to the natural law and contractarian traditions, he refused to justify his commitment to the liberal state by adducing ahistorical traits of human nature. Once again following Montesquieu and other eighteenth-century (particularly Scottish) examples, he deliberately supplanted the contract myth with a theory of social change.[29] The liberal state is desirable not because it mirrors human nature or respects eternal human rights, but because it is the political arrangement most adequate to solving the problems of European society in its current stage of economic, scientific, and moral development.

Constant's conception of social change was also vital to another striking thesis of the 1819 lecture, an idea elaborated at greater length in *Conquête et usurpation* of 1814: the modern appeal to classical republican ideas is an anachronism that can serve only as a rhetorical justification and partial concealment of political fanaticism and terror.[30]

A similar thesis had been propounded by C. F. de Volney in 1794. Volney, too, lamented that "we have fallen into a superstitious adoration of the Greeks and Romans."[31] Cults of antiquity which sprang up during the Revolution and glorified selfless, Brutus-like tyrannicide suggested this insight to many observers.[32] The myth of ancient republics lent a deceptive aura of legitimacy to the abusive acts of the Committee of Public Safety: "it is in the name of liberty that we have been given prisons, scaffolds and countless harassments."[33] The enormous power of government was justified by an ideology that, invoking ancient community, denied the modern distinction between state and society. During the Revolution, in other words, the ideal of ancient liberty was a pretext for oppression.[34] Constant conceded that many of the would-be "imitators of ancient republics" were propelled by generous motives.[35] They meant to abolish arbitrary government, seigneurial privileges, and the abuses of the church. Their tragic mistake was to have chosen the classical city as an image unifying their diverse complaints against the *ancien régime*.

The French Revolution was not the first occasion on which anticlerical and antiaristocratic activists appealed to classical republican ideals: "Since the renaissance of letters, most of those who attempted to rescue mankind from the degradation into which it had been plunged by the double curse of superstition and conquest [Roman Catholicism and landed aristocracy], believed it necessary to borrow institutions and customs favorable to liberty from the ancients."[36] Though the image of classical republican freedom may have been a useful rebuke to the old regime, it was not an adequate guide to the future. The myth of the ancient city could serve as a weapon for assaulting Catholicism and the inequality of ranks, but it could furnish no clue about how to replace them.[37] Necessarily, attempts to resurrect anachronistic forms of liberty were political hoaxes on a grand scale.

THE PROBLEM

In modern times, citizens can no longer experience political participation as an intrinsically rewarding form of action.[38] But Constant also said that his contemporaries must learn to couple political participation, which he described as a path to self-perfection, with individual privacy and independence.[39] Which statement are we to believe? Was he simply being incoherent? Our perplexity is justified. But it can be dispelled if we examine how the distinction between ancient and modern liberty was used during two separate phases of Constant's career.

The 1819 lecture contains long sections authored twenty years earlier in response to exceptional political events. By 1819, the political scene had radically changed. Constant's former left-wing enemies had vanished, only to be replaced by equally intractable right-wing foes. In response to this altered landscape, he reelaborated his distinction in a new direction. No longer threatened by pseudodemocratic fraud, he turned sharply against the civic passivity that served the interests of the ultras. But he left the passages written years earlier untouched. No wonder present-day readers feel off balance! Despite these findings, we cannot dismiss the 1819 lecture as a jumble of conflicting insights. Struggling to understand the complexities of politics after the Revolution, Constant was right to cling tenaciously to both sides of his polemic: the atrophy of political life can be just as perilous as a total repoliticization of society.

THE ORIGINAL FORMULATION OF THE DISTINCTION

A good deal has been written about the two concepts of freedom and the corresponding democratic traditions.[40] What has perhaps been neglected is the history of the distinction itself, especially the context in which it was originally elaborated and the problems to which it served as a practical response.

The original version of the "Ancient and Modern Liberty" lecture can be found in chapter 3 of Mme. de Staël's *Circonstances actuelles qui peuvent terminer la Révolution,* a manuscript heavily influenced and perhaps even coauthored by Constant around 1798. Constant and Mme. de Staël wanted to convince the Directory that, instead of merely playing off the Right against the Left, it should appeal directly to a constituency of its own.

In times of political uproar, civic privatism can prevent individuals from assuming uncompromising postures associated with *l'esprit de parti.* The Directory never totally succeeded in its attempt to arrest the civil war. Thus, from 1793 until 1799, active participation in French politics meant being drawn pell-mell into a fratricidal battle: "Even the slightest criticism inspires hatred in the exalted parties. This hatred compels every man to ally himself with a number of his fellows and, just as men travel only in caravans in places infested with brigands, so in countries where hatreds are unleashed, they align themselves with a party in order to have defenders."[41] Constant's vindication of political absenteeism was intended as a reply to Rousseau's glorification of political participation. He lauded citizen withdrawal and indifference in situations of civil war when participation was largely a vehicle for partisan hatred and revenge.[42] Civil war had demonstrated the value of apolitical behavior in a country "where two opposed parties combat each other with furor."[43]

Constant and de Staël urged the Directory to draw electoral support from just those individuals who had remained aloof from the fighting in the previous years. The "inert" and "immobile" masses of the nation had views that were admirably moderate because deeply apathetic. They were indifferent to royalty but not enthusiastic enough about the Republic to want it to disrupt the nation's tranquillity. They were unconcerned about the fate of the *ci-devant* privileged caste, but they did not detest the old nobles intensely enough to have them persecuted. They knew that the persecution of even a few embroils everyone, not merely the persecutors and the persecuted.[44]

This majority "wants nothing but its own well-being." The desire for peace and prosperity may have signaled a descent from the heights of antique virtue; but it had politically beneficial side-effects. Moreover, a commitment to peace was exactly what one would have expected from most Frenchmen: "Party spirit almost never exists except among individuals thrown outside the circle of domestic life. And two-thirds of the population of France and of all the countries of Europe are composed of men who are occupied solely with their pecuniary fortune." In order to win the loyalty of these survival-minded masses, the Directoire should respect their indifference to politics. It must "never count, in such a nation, on the sort of patriotism that propelled the ancient republics." Instead of trying to win electoral support by stirring up enthusiasm, by asking citizens for heroic sacrifices of their particular interests to the general good, the Directory must acquiesce in individual contrariness. "Liberty today is everything that guarantees the independence of citizens from the power of the government." To syphon away votes from royalists and Jacobins, the Directory must offer private security to its citizens.[45]

De Staël's and Constant's aim in 1798 was to convince the Directory that the stability of the Republic required an abandonment of all the enthusiasm-promoting techniques employed earlier by the clubs, the militant *sectionnaires,* and the Convention:

> Among the ancients . . . in order to capture public opinion, it was necessary to rouse the soul, to excite patriotism by conquest, by triumphs, by factions, even by troubles that nourished every passion. National spirit must no doubt be cultivated as much as possible within France. But we must not lose sight of the fact that [today] public opinion is based on a love of peace, on the desire to acquire wealth and the need to conserve it and that we will always be more interested in administrative ideas than in political questions, because these touch our private lives more directly.[46]

The majority of the French can have a moderating influence because they are largely indifferent to citizenship and distracted from public affairs. Justly wary of the intoxicating effect of patriotism, the Directors should heed the following maxim: "The sphere of each individual must always be respected."[47] To politicize modern individuals totally is next to impossible and would be a mistake in any case. In 1798, distinguishing between ancient and modern liberty meant praising apoliticism and urging the government to honor the primacy of private life.

THE LECTURE OF 1819

Twenty years later, in 1819, Constant delivered his lecture at the Paris Atheneum. With the shift in the political situation, the argumentative thrust of his distinction between ancient and modern liberty also changed. In the France of 1819, there was no cult of Sparta which Constant might have felt compelled to discredit.[48] There was simply no threat of a resurgent Jacobinism by this time.

Constant's interpreters have systematically distorted his distinction between ancient and modern liberty by mislocating it exclusively in the context of 1793–94. The Terror—which Constant had not witnessed first-hand, for he only returned to France in 1795—provided an important motive for his rethinking of eighteenth-century liberalism. But the Directory, the Empire, and the ultra-dominated Restoration all influenced his thought in decisive ways. The Directory taught him the insufficiency of "limited" government, while Napoleon and the Bourbons helped revive his underlying republicanism, temporarily suspended in the convulsions of civil strife between 1793 and 1799. By 1819, Constant had broken with Guizot and other moderates and was sitting on the far left of the Chamber. Needless to say, his ultraroyalist enemies never celebrated Rousseau as a prophet of unlimited popular sovereignty. As Catholics, they had only the faintest sympathy for pagan antiquity. They struggled fiercely to narrow the existing franchise, doing everything in their power to discourage the involvement of ordinary citizens in public affairs. Referring to a Chamber dominated by the ultras, Constant said: "the legislators are trying to put the nation into a sleep that tyranny finds convenient."[49] Battling the ultras, liberals strove to awaken the nation from its privatized slumber.

Constant began his lecture with a "demonstration," following Montesquieu and Rousseau, that the representative system was "a discovery of the moderns."[50] He used the contrast with the direct self-government of the classical city to highlight the uniqueness of representative government. But he did not reduce the modern rupture with the past to this contrast.

At the opening of the lecture, in a section that did not appear before 1819, he opposed representation to oligarchic usurpation, not to democratic participation. The representative system was a discovery of the moderns: it was a technique invented by the Third Estate for putting limits on that "oligarchy which is the same throughout the centuries."[51] The assertion that representative government was the "only system" allowing modern men to attain freedom and social peace was clearly meant as an attack on the ultra program to reverse the relatively liberal Electoral Law of 1817.

Reminiscent of the regime of the ancient Gauls, the system the ultras wished to impose on modern France also resembled the constitution of ancient Sparta. A small elite, the Ephors had possessed religious as well as political functions. They had powers to check and limit the Spartan kings. But they also enjoyed executive authority. They could easily become threats instead of restraints. They were, in fact, not democratic representatives at all, "not . . . men invested with a mission comparable to that which election today confers on the defenders of our freedoms." The feudal aristocracy of priests and warriors idealized by the ultras resembled the Ephors in many respects. Under the *ancien régime*, "the nobility possessed privileges that were both insolent and oppressive. And the people were without rights or guarantees."[52]

Shrewdly structured, this argument was calculated simultaneously to entice and to befuddle the antidemocratic sentiments of the French Right. Every royalist had to applaud the concession that modern France could never be governed by direct popular self-rule. But the reason why the government established by the Charte was unlike that of the turbulent classical republics was *also* the reason why it was distinct from the Catholic, monarchical, and aristocratic system of the old regime.

Constant replaced Montesquieu's contrast between modern monarchies and ancient republics by a new contrast, discomfiting to the ultras, between representative and nonrepresentative regimes. Such a contrast had the embarrassing effect of aligning the Catholic Bonald with the most radical proponents of pagan democracy.[53] Taunting the Right, Constant juxtaposed absolute democracy with absolute monarchy.

The parallel drawn between the organization of the ancient city and the social program of the ultras was not merely negative. More was involved than a shared denial of the modern principle of representation. In both cases, Constant discerned a bias against voluntariness, against entrusting social choices to unsupervised individuals. With one eye fixed on the Catholic ultraroyalists, Constant mentioned the power of ancient Roman authorities to meddle in matters of divorce and marriage. Reflecting on the ultra education program, he also remarked that modern theocrats agreed with ancient republicans: a government should "take possession of the generations being born" and shape them to its own pleasure. When he said (also about Rome) that "les lois règlent les moeurs,"[54] his real target was

the ultra—not merely Jacobin—idea that the state should assume the duty
of policing private morality.

In mounting his attack on the French Right, Constant also focused
on religious toleration. There were obvious differences between ancient civic
religions and the modern alliance between throne and altar. Both could,
however, be contrasted with a liberal decision to make religion a private
matter: "the ability to choose one's own cult, an ability that we regard as
one of our most precious rights, would have seemed a crime and a sacrilege
to the ancients."[55] It is not altogether surprising that "the gallant defenders
of doctrinal unity cite the laws of the ancients against foreign gods and
support the rights of the Catholic Church with the example of the Athenians."[56] Distant from antiquity and inhospitable to the vision of the *Social
Contract*, modern Frenchmen cannot reconcile themselves to the regimental
designs of the theocratic Right. These and other parallels between the ancients and the ultras were innovations of 1819. They did not appear in
Constant's earlier discussions of the distinction between ancient and modern
liberty. They thus betray the immediate political objectives of his lecture.

In their interpretations of the Revolution, Jacobins and royalists agreed
that the Terror had been necessary to the demolition of the old regime. Ever
since his early pamphlet, *Effets de la terreur* (1798),[57] Constant had rejected
this shared premise of the Left and Right. He had sought to disconnect
liberty from an incriminating association with bureaucratic murder. An
obvious way to disjoin freedom from the Terror was to split "freedom" in
two. One form (call it ancient liberty) could be found guilty, while the other
(call it modern) would be acquitted. Mme. de Staël had this strategy in mind
in the *Circonstances actuelles* of 1798 where, together with Constant, she
initially worked out the distinction between ancient and modern liberty.
Throughout the Restoration, moreover, Constant's need to outmaneuver
the ultras led him to stress the politically harmless aspects of modern freedom. He wished to convince those who were weary of disorder that liberty
was not a timebomb. He thus wrote of "la liberté légale," "la liberté paisible,"
"la liberté régulière," and "une liberté constitutionnelle qui ne donne d'a-
larmes à personne."[58] He tended to discuss freedom in minimalist terms:
"by liberty I mean the strict execution of the Charte."[59]

But, although Constant no longer felt threatened by the Jacobins in
1819, he was becoming increasingly exasperated with the ultras. His desire
to appease their fears was evaporating quickly. This militant turn helps
explain his new insistence that freedom from politics, even if it never func-
tioned as a pretext for revolutionary tyranny, was by no means harmless.
By 1819, moreover, the distinction between ancient and modern liberty had

become Constant's way of exposing the dangers inherent in his own commitment to civic privatism. His initial intention may have been to describe modern liberty as innocent: it had had no role in inspiring the Terror. At the end of his 1819 lecture, however, his theoretical instincts and a changing political scene drew him toward criticizing modern liberty precisely because of its encouragement of apathy. Thus, the concluding thesis of the 1819 lecture was this: "Because we are more distracted from political liberty than [the ancients] were able to be, and in our ordinary condition less passionate about it, it can happen that we sometimes neglect too much, and always mistakenly, the guarantees that it ensures us."[60]

CONSTANT'S CAUTIOUS RENEWAL OF THE APPEAL TO ANTIQUITY

The final section of "Ancient and Modern Liberty" comes as a surprise. After having devoted twenty dense pages to his claim that modern peoples are exclusively attuned to private independence and freedom from politics, after having plainly said that "we can no longer enjoy the freedom of the ancients," and that "the liberty suitable to the moderns is different from that which was suitable to the ancients," after all this, Constant abruptly changed his emphasis: "Therefore, Gentlemen, far from renouncing either of the two types of freedom about which I have been speaking to you, we must, as I have demonstrated, learn to combine the one with the other."[61] The two freedoms should not be confused; but they must be combined.

In the body of the lecture, composed in previous years and geared to different situations, Constant made clear that "the perpetual exercise of political rights" and "the daily discussion of the affairs of state" offer "only trouble and fatigue" to modern nations.[62] But in the conclusion, written in or around 1819, he wrote: "political liberty, granted to all citizens without exception, allows them to examine and study their most sacred interests, enlarges their spirits, ennobles their thoughts and establishes between them a sort of intellectual equality that makes up the glory and power of a people."[63] The citizenship being praised here is only a part-time affair. Nevertheless, we cannot escape the impression that we are witnessing a dramatic alteration in Constant's tone as well as a reversal in his theoretical stance. His endorsement of civic involvement is unmistakable. That Constant, at the end of this lecture, did not denigrate political participation is obviously pertinent to the question of how antidemocratic was his liberalism. But it is not easy to integrate these final pages with the earlier part of his argument.

On closer inspection, it turns out that two distinct paradoxes preside over the jolting conclusion of "Ancient and Modern Liberty." First, there is an inconsistency between Constant's pessimistic and his optimistic assessments of popular influence on the government in a modern state. Modern citizens are said to have no influence on their governments. But their active participation is also described as decisive. Second, there is a flat contradiction between Constant's claims that: (1) in modern societies, political liberty is a means, while civil liberty is the end—that is, participation is valuable *only* as a guarantee to ensure private security from government harassment (this distinguishes modern from ancient participation); and (2) active civic involvement is valuable in itself, offering an opportunity to soar above petty individual concerns and further self-perfection.

Viewed separately, both paradoxes seem quite baffling. Taken together, each not only illuminates the other but also helps to explain the structure of the lecture's conclusion.

Consider the contrast between the pessimistic and the optimistic assessments of popular influence on modern governments. Constant's pessimism here echoes Rousseau's remark that the English are free only once every several years and solely during the few minutes it takes to vote; otherwise they are slaves.[64] "Among the moderns . . . even in the states which are most free, the individual, although independent in private life, is not sovereign except in appearance. His sovereignty is restrained, almost always suspended; and if he exercises this sovereignty at fixed but infrequent intervals, during which time he is still surrounded by precautions and obstacles, it is only to abdicate it."[65] Constant accepted Rousseau's claim that total citizenship and direct democratic self-government are impossible in a large country. But he refused to echo Rousseau's contemptuous dismissal of representative government on the British model.

Constant decided to adapt himself, without undue agony, to the new political and extrapolitical possibilities available in a society incapable of direct democracy. From a realistic point of view, the marginal contribution of the average modern individual to any political outcome is close to zero: "the individual's influence . . . is lost in a multitude of influences."[66] Hence, we should expect most men to turn their backs on citizenship and devote themselves to more rewarding, creative, and enjoyable forms of conflict or cooperation. From Constant's perspective in 1819, however, there was a serious flaw in a way of thinking that encouraged men to channel all their energies into private life. French history had by that time unambiguously demonstrated that civic absenteeism can serve the cause of tyrants and oppressors. The standard liberal argument that commercial life provides an effective counterweight to excessive political authority had been thrown into question. "The progress of industry . . . creates for each individual a sphere within which are concentrated all his interests; and, if the individual looks outside this sphere, it is only by accident."[67] But when modern citizens become too absorbed in their private financial business and fail to keep watch over the political scene, the ambitious few will amass uncontrollable quantities of power.[68] Once this has happened, private wealth itself will be insecure.

Economic independence is a precondition for political influence. Political liberty presupposes civil liberty. Constant also affirmed the inverse claim: without effective political influence, economic independence and decentralization cannot be guaranteed. This second proposition is not quite a political argument against capitalism; but it is an insight into the troublesome political consequences of business-mindedness and the spirit of commerce.

The historical experiences behind this liberal distrust of apoliticism were manifold. Just as important to Constant as the ultra program to limit the franchise was the atrophy of political life under the Empire. In an article also written in 1819, Constant described Napoleon's reign: "Military power borrowed sophisms from metaphysics in order to destroy all real elections, all public deliberation, all participation of the people in the administration of general or local interests."[69] Napoleon had encouraged a withering away of active citizenship in order to consolidate his power.[70] He had initially gained popular support for his *coup d'état* because many citizens were weary of the pseudorepublican antics of the Directory.[71] Thus, the postrevolutionary urge to escape from politics and delimit the political sphere had nourished an invasive dictatorship. Constant experienced the pang of enforced depoliticalization in his own person when he was ejected from the Tribunat in 1802. It is inconceivable that, having suffered this humiliation, he would have afterward viewed privatization as simply and exclusively a public good.

Constant's argument here might be interpreted as a democratic rethinking of a dilemma faced earlier by French aristocrats. In the eighteenth century, the "resurgent nobility" realized they had made a poor bargain when they sacrificed their political power to Richelieu and Louis XIV for the sake of cozy privileges and immunities. Without power, their new rights were insecure.[72] Private independence can only be guaranteed by political responsibility.[73] Constant echoed this point, with one major difference. He wished political rights distributed "to all citizens without exception."[74]

To provide his argument with a form more arresting to modern readers, Constant resorted to a financial comparison.[75] A rich man may, in order to gain time for other activities, hire a manager to handle his fiscal affairs. In any such arrangement there comes a point when "saving time" will be carried too far. A manager left completely unsupervised may defraud the owner. In the long run, delegating one's power is not necessarily an efficient way to save time. Like businessmen, citizens must keep themselves carefully informed in order to judge whether their delegated business is being handled honestly and intelligently: "The peoples who recur to the representative system in order to enjoy the liberty that is suitable to them must exercise a constant and active surveillance over their representatives. They must reserve to periods which are not separated by long intervals the right to dismiss these representatives if they have betrayed their vows and to revoke any powers they have abused."[76] Not so enjoyable as the firsthand despoiling, exiling, imprisoning, and executing available to the ancient citizen, this dismissing and revoking preserved some of the responsibilities of ancient citizens within modern constitutional government. From an individual's viewpoint, the importance of his own civic participation seems negligible and almost imaginary. In the aggregate, however, a participating and well-informed citizen body can certainly prevent the return of a Napoleon or, more likely in 1819, the gradual confiscation of all political power by the ultras.

There may be no contradiction in Constant's argument. But there is a practical problem. The liberal dilemma is how to motivate individuals to participate, how to galvanize them into civic activism, given the scant rewards each individual might expect from time expended on political affairs: "the danger of modern liberty is that, absorbed in the enjoyment of our private independence and in the pursuit of our particular interests, we will renounce too easily our right to share in political power."[77] Civic privatism is a danger because individuals will be more impressed by the short-term gains than by the long-term dangers of apoliticism. Rational calculation leads citizens to see that they can personally have no "real influence" on political events[78] and thus may inadvertently encourage them to expose their polity to dictatorship.

Constant understood that his instrumental argument for civic involvement (that private rights can only be guaranteed by popular power, that independence will only be ensured by participation) was not sufficient to rouse men from the civic sedation administered first by Napoleon and more recently by the ultra party. Recognizing the insufficiency of this instrumental argument for citizenship, Constant overturned the previously worked-out logic of his lecture—a logic reflecting his radically different concerns of 1798—and introduced an Aristotelian and almost romantic justification for participation. Even apart from its terrible consequences, privatism cannot satisfy individuals. True, it could make people happy. Individuals might reach *bonheur* simply by abandoning their strenuous ideals and sinking into passivity. But happiness is not enough: "No, Gentlemen, I call to witness this better part of our nature, the noble restlessness that pursues and torments us, this ardor to extend our understanding and develop our faculties. Our destiny does not call us to happiness alone, but to self-perfection; and political liberty is the most powerful and the most energetic means of self-perfection granted us by heaven."[79]

Except for "torment" and "inquiétude," this passage faithfully echoes the classical thesis that man is a fundamentally political animal. In startling contrast to the body of the lecture, it implies that the more time modern citizens lavish on public affairs, the freer they will feel.

In 1798, when the distinction between ancient and modern liberty was first elaborated, Constant was still haunted by the experience of the Revolution. Political "participation" suggested violent crusades and involvement in plots for revenge. He thus viewed civic fermentation with an acutely nervous eye. By 1819, the ultra threat had caused Constant and his liberal allies to reverse their earlier position and speak warmly of "pure, profound and sincere patriotism," a sentiment capable of ennobling the spirits of "tous les citoyens, sans exception."[80] Not merely a means to civil liberty, political liberty was also seen as an integral part of civil liberty. Indeed, "the greatest possible number of citizens" must be given influence over public affairs and admitted to important political functions. Inclusion in such tasks will give citizens "both the desire and the capacity to perform them."[81] This was the sort of thinking that eventually led liberals to espouse universal suffrage as the indispensable basis for representative government.

The strikingly democratic conclusion to "Ancient and Modern Liberty" remains puzzling until we understand how the underlying logic of the argument of 1798 was adapted to meet the demands of Restoration politics. The lecture is a palimpsest. It is so complex because it was composed twice, the second version superimposed on the first after an interval of twenty years. By 1819, Constant's original fear of convulsive and compulsory patriotism had partly yielded to his hope that enhanced participation might advance liberal causes while keeping the ultras in check.

CIVIC PRIVATISM AND ITS PROBLEMS

The foregoing analysis of the two layers of "Ancient and Modern Liberty" fails to do justice to the theoretical content of the lecture. After all, it was Constant's conscious decision to weave his new and old concerns into a

single pattern of thought. "Ancient and Modern Liberty" gains its importance from his crucial insight that both the loss and the revival of civic spirit
contain a potential for tyranny. The right to be distracted from politics is
precious but not harmless. Overprivatization and overpoliticization are symmetrical dangers. The pluralistic and voluntary pattern of life to which
modern citizens are accustomed makes them intolerant of societies in which
there are no sharply etched limits to the political. But every time we draw
such boundaries, we seal off important areas of social life from responsible
public surveillance and control. Napoleon craftily used civic privatism to
escape accountability.[82] The liberal boundaries of the political are simultaneously indispensable and fraught with risk.

This idea was not a palinode or sign of Constant's irresolute vacil-
lation. It was an insight into the complexity of politics in France after the
Revolution. Ultimately, Constant's success at keeping such ostensibly conflicting ideas simultaneously alive is what makes his thought about this
period so suggestive.

Unusable and even dangerous as a constructive principle, ancient liberty is helpful as a reminder of the central peril of modern liberty. Aware
of this danger, Constant was careful to refer to participation in sovereignty
as a form of liberty. Montesquieu had warned against confounding the
sovereign "power" of a people with its "liberty," and de Lolme adopted
this same distinction between freedom and power.[83] Constant's decision to
deviate from those who had defined liberty by contrasting it with the exercise
of sovereignty was not casual. He insisted from the start that the influence
of citizens on legislation was a form of freedom. He did not allow active
political rights to stand on the sidelines as a mere alternative to freedom.
This refusal to set popular power aside may also illuminate the ending of
the 1819 lecture, the apparent contradiction between the notion that political liberty is exclusively a guarantee and the idea that it is also a vehicle
for self-perfection. By calling popular power a form of freedom, Constant
prepared the way for his conclusion: freedom from politics is not coextensive
with liberty. True liberty is an "optimal mix" of public and private, participation and nonparticipation, citizenship and independence, activism and
distraction, cooperation and eccentricity.[84]

Those who accept Isaiah Berlin's portrait of a privacy-addicted Constant cannot explain why he devoted the last fifteen years of his life to public
service. To be sure, the politics to which he gave himself unstintingly was
not a cozy town-meeting communalism. It was a radical, reformist activism.
If it was politics with the aim of limiting politics, it was nonetheless politics.

Anti-utopian but reform-minded participation was crucial for Constant. In the *Commentaire sur l'ouvrage de Filangieri* of 1822 he was un-relenting about the importance of political citizenship. England was a powerful nation despite its absurd commercial laws:

> The political institutions, the parliamentary discussions, the lib-erty of the press which [England] has enjoyed without inter-ruption for one hundred and twenty-six years have counteracted the vices of its laws and its governments. Its inhabitants maintain their energy of character because they have not been disinherited of their participation in the administration of public affairs. This participation, while it is almost imaginary, gives the citizens a feeling of their importance that fosters their activity.[85]

Spain, by contrast, reveals the dismal fate of a country where individuals lose interest in themselves because they are deprived of any chance to in-fluence their own fate: Spain's "decadence dates from the destruction of its political liberty and the suppression of the *cortes.*"[86]

Participation in politics was not to be limited to the periodic *surveil-lance* and *contrôle* of the legislators by the electors. It was not to be merely a means by which private citizens could defend their security, goods, and *jouissances.*[87] Constant argued that concern for the public good was also creative of energetic characters and even national identity. Politics could be an engrossing passion. For Constant, it was precisely that. He merely wanted to ensure that it was voluntary, not obligatory. A voluntary politics of reform, based on ideals of civilized humanity, is certainly one of the central possibilities made available in a modern and free society.

We should not, however, allow Constant to paint a more glamorous portrait of active involvement in modern politics than he painted of ancient liberty itself. Constant admitted that he was sometimes bored with public service, and he never gave flattering accounts of his reasons for persisting in office. In a revealing letter written in 1800, when he was first appointed to the Tribunat, he distinguished sharply between personal happiness and the goal of active participation, just as he was to do at the conclusion of "Ancient and Modern Liberty." He had pursued a public career, he said:

> not for happiness—is there any such thing in life?—but as a task, as a chance to fulfill a duty, which is the only way to lift the burden of doubt, memory, and unrest, the eternal lot of our wretched and transitory nature. Those for whom pleasure has charms, for whom novelty still exists, and who have preserved the happy ability to be interested in themselves, do not need a vocation; but those who have lost their physical and moral youth

must have a route to follow, an official mission to do good in
order not to sink into discouragement and apathy.[88]

Constant was only thirty-three when he wrote this letter. Decrepitude was
his society's, not his personal, plight. Victimized by an excess of civilization,
modern men were incapable of happiness. The best they could hope for was
to quell their nagging *inquiétude*. Living in a disillusioned age, Constant
decided to christen such escapism with the name of "self-perfection." While
theoretically dubious, such idealizations of citizenship were politically effective in his battles against Napoleon and the ultras.

MODERN IMITATORS OF ANCIENT REPUBLICS

Heir to the counterrevolutionary tradition, Hippolyte Taine argued that the
Terror was a logical consequence of Enlightenment thought.[89] This conservative thesis has been so widely influential that its implausible character
often disappears from sight: if eighteenth-century liberalism led "logically"
to revolutionary dictatorship and murder, then only the illiberalism of the
old regime could sustain social freedom.

Constant had a different view. The Terror, "eighteen months of bloody
tyranny,"[90] did not result from an excess of freedom. On the contrary, "the
evils of the Revolution stemmed precisely from the Revolution's having
suspended all liberty."[91] The liberty suspended during the Terror, moreover,
was *liberty* in the singular; it had little or no resemblance to the aristocratic
liberties which had been sharply curtailed during the consolidation of French
absolutism. It was a constitutionally regulated liberty, including civil rights,
religious tolerance, legal equality, and the political influence of the Third
Estate. Unlike Taine, Constant saw no difficulty in criticizing the "years of
delirium"[92] with categories inherited from the Enlightenment. The 1793–
94 phase of the Revolution was marked by intolerant fanaticism, secular
priestcraft, and a conflation of the social and the political. The Jacobins
claimed to be establishing a new republic based on virtue; but they actually
recreated a despotism based, as Montesquieu said all despotisms were, on
fear.

Constant never accused the Terrorists of an overexuberant commitment to reason and equality. Rather than pointing an accusing finger at the
Enlightenment, he focused on the revolutionary appeal to classical republican ideals,[93] an appeal that served as a pretext for oppression, misleading
the public and to some extent deluding the oppressors. In so doing he relied
explicitly on an Enlightenment mistrust of ancestor worship.[94]

From the time of Marsilius of Padua, republicanism had been closely associated with anticlericalism. The immediate prerevolutionary generation in France may have been unprepared to foresee or even recognize misuses of republican rhetoric because of its enlightened loathing of the established *infâme*. The image of the ancient city had acquired a certain immunity from criticism because it had proved so useful in attacking the church. In order to outbid the great mythical powers of the old regime (divine-right monarchy as well as the church), the Jacobins conceived "Liberty" as a countermyth, seeing themselves as mere functionaries of this superhuman, redemptive force. This sacralization of liberty was an understandable response to the provocation of abusive but religiously sanctioned institutions.[95] The massiveness of this Catholic and aristocratic provocation may explain why it was left to a Swiss Protestant to formulate one of the first nonreactionary critiques of democratic pretense and ideology. Perhaps only a theorist who had not suffered from the bitter annoyance of orthodoxy could have retained enough distance from ancient liberty to make this critical turn in a convincing way.

Lacking any practical experience of self-government, Frenchmen were unprepared for the Revolution; or rather, even the most experienced among them were prepared solely by their classical education. Robespierre and Saint-Just, who had resurrected the Roman institution of emergency dictatorship in the crisis of 1793, were the most notorious modern imitators of ancient republics. They were not squeamish about using violence against their real or imagined enemies: "These men thought they could exercise political power as it had been exercised in the free states of antiquity. They believed that even today everything must yield to the collective authority and that private morality must fall silent before the public interest."[96] Robespierre's addiction to Plutarch and Rousseau should not be overestimated. But his admiration for the ancients certainly contributed to his self-image as a great moral legislator and founder of a new order.[97] The idea of the *polis* as a school of virtue provided a chance to misdescribe the Revolution and stress the paramount need for self-sacrifice on the part of all citizens: "Let us raise our spirits to the heights of republican virtues and ancient examples."[98] "Sparta," he rapturously noted, "shines like a lightning flash in the immense darkness." "I speak of public virtue," he added in another speech, "which worked such wonders in Greece and Rome and must produce even more astonishing good in republican France."[99]

Characteristic of the ancient city, according to Constant, was the absence of inalienable rights.[100] Rights were not absolute but contingent upon service to the community: they could be legally revoked by the assembled populace.[101] Seeking justification for the violations of judicial procedure required by revolutionary justice, Jacobins were understandably attracted to the ancient model for a morally impeccable revocation of rights. The "Spartans of the Convention"[102] also followed Rousseau in praising the absence of partial associations within the ancient city. Loyalty to family or church should never interfere with allegiance to the *patrie*. Robespierre could encourage the denunciation of family members for uncivic attitudes and chide wives whose husbands had been guillotined for harboring unpatriotic feelings.[103]

Frenchmen had to be political animals, strictly obedient ones, so long as revolutionary government was in effect: "When popular governments become perverted, that is, when they are popular in name only, they defy public opinion with more effrontery than other governments because they have at their disposal a terrible weapon which these others do not possess: they can accuse a man who criticizes them of treason."[104] The Law of Suspects defined "treason" so vaguely as to included boredom and indifference as crimes against the state.[105] Likewise, attendance at local assemblies and the assumption of public office was obligatory, not voluntary. If you married a foreigner, said "monsieur" instead of "citoyen," or went to church, some zealot might accuse you of having harmed the public good.[106] This fervid assimilation of the social to the political and the private to the public was justified by appeals to the ancient city, in which no line had been drawn between state and society.

Citizenship had to be total: "love of the *patrie* . . . presupposes a preference for the public interest over all private interests."[107] But Robespierre did not merely denounce conflicting interests. He refused to admit the legitimacy of conflicting *opinions* about the common good. He remarked that there were only two parties in the Convention, the pure and the corrupt. A coarse dichotomy between base self-interest and noble virtue dominated his vision of political life. Patriots, he notoriously suggested, should be concerned with virtue not with material well-being.[108] The same simplistic dualism supported his near-hysterical attacks on the single vast conspiracy of the egoistical and demon-driven aligned against the Revolution.[109] It also underlay his project for the reeducation of Frenchmen deformed by centuries of superstition and oppression.[110] Like a good Plutarchan legislator,[111] Robespierre was less concerned about granting a share of legislative authority to the people than with restoring their moral health: "the Legislator's first duty is to form and preserve public morality." His central aim was to instill purity of soul into citizens by means of the Revolution: "We want an order in which all low and cruel passion shall be repressed and in which laws shall awaken all the benevolent and generous passions."[112] Men can be inwardly refashioned by governmental edict. Vice can be legislated out of existence.

Robespierre had an absurdly exaggerated idea of the capacity of law to make men morally pure. Constant admired the American revolutionaries, who aspired only to a system in which ambition counteracted ambition. Robespierre aimed at creating an order "in which the only ambition is to deserve fame and serve the country."[113] Instead of rechanneling private vice for public benefit, he wished to eradicate vice and enthrone virtue in its stead.

It was this unbelievable attempt to "improve" men against their will and to resurrect a virtue-based polity on the ancient model that produced the most gruesome atrocities of the Terror. Modern citizens simply cannot be forced to identify themselves unreservedly with the public entity: "The partisans of ancient liberty became furious when modern individuals did not wish to be free according to their method. They redoubled the torments, the people redoubled its resistance, and crimes followed upon errors."[114] You cannot fight the *Geist*. The gravest error of the Jacobins was not to have adapted themselves to the general spirit[115] of the age: "When punishments that reason reserves for great crimes are applied to actions that some members of society consider a duty, and that the most honest of the contrary party regard as indifferent or excusable, the legislator is obliged, in order to sustain his first iniquity, to multiply indefinitely secondary wrongs. In order to have a single tyrannical law executed, he must compile an entire code of proscriptions and blood."[116] Totally out of touch with the realities of modern France, Robespierre became a murderous tyrant despite his benevolent intentions.

By the end of the eighteenth century, the most common complaint against the old regime was that it was a holdover from a bygone age. At mid-century, the word *revolution* had already begun to change its meaning from cycling back to going forward.[117] As the Revolution got underway, attacks on the old regime were conducted less in the name of an ancient constitution and more in the name of a desirable future. In this context, it was a skillful *coup de théâtre* to stamp the most progressive party with the epithet "anachronistic." Indeed, Constant's diagnosis of the Revolution was part of his strategy of tarring the two extremes of French politics with the same brush and thus of staking out a broad middle position for himself and his allies. It also allowed him to attack the Terror without abandoning the liberalism of the philosophes.

THE PSYCHOLOGY OF REVOLUTION

Constant's most penetrating insight into the leaders of the French Revolution was that their Rousseauism went deeper than it first seemed. Rousseau admired Sparta but was pessimistic about chances for reviving ancient frugality and virtue in a corrupt modern world. Robespierre has sometimes been depicted as an optimist who tried to do what Rousseau declared impossible. But in fact Rousseauist pessimism permeated the speeches of Robespierre from 1792 until his execution in 1794. His last speech concluded with a typical suggestion that the Republic of Virtue was too good for this world: "The time has not yet come when men of good will can serve their country unmolested."[118] This half-admission that his own goals were impossible to achieve is the most Rousseauist element in Robespierre's writings. Such a half-perceived discrepancy between extravagant goals and modest historical possibilities is precisely what Constant had in mind in this sardonic commentary: "Nothing is stranger to observe than the speeches of the French demagogues. Saint-Just, the cleverest among them, composed all his speeches in short, compact sentences, meant to jolt awake worn-out minds. Thus, while he appeared to believe the nation capable of making the most agonizing sacrifices, he recognized by his very style that it was incapable even of paying attention."[119]

In diagnosing the Revolution, Constant regularly returned to this *dédoublement révolutionnaire*. Saint-Just's audience was not asleep; it was frazzled and distracted. It suffered from *l'arrière-pensée* and other signs of excessive civilization which Constant later explored in his novel. Recall this warning of Adolphe's: "woe to the man who, in the arms of the mistress he has just possessed, conserves a fatal prescience and foresees that he can abandon her."[120] Adolphe's torment stemmed partly from his inability to throw himself into any action with complete abandon. His painful lack of illusions was startlingly mirrored in a psychological portrait Constant painted of the revolutionary crowd. Although modern individuals can become enthusiastic about certain abstract ideas, they are unfitted for feeling enthusiasm toward particular men. Adolphe and the French people share "une déplorable prévoyance":

> The French Revolution was most remarkable in this respect. Whatever has been said about the inconstancy of the people in ancient republics, nothing equals the mobility we have witnessed. If, during the outbreak of even the best-prepared upheaval, you watch carefully the obscure ranks of the blind and subjugated populace, you will see that the people (even as it

follows its leaders) casts its glance ahead to the moment when
these leaders will fall. And you will discern within its artificial
exaltation, a strange combination of analysis and mockery. People will seem to mistrust their own convictions. They will try
to delude themselves by their own acclamations and to reinvi-
gorate themselves by jaunty raillery. They foresee, so to speak,
the moment when the glamour of it all will pass.[121]

Constant attributed the savagery and violence of the Revolution to this lack
of conviction, to this mobility: "Insurrections among the ancients were much
more sincere than among ourselves." Bloodshed was a tactic used by
eviscerated men to compensate for a deficit of powerful passions: "An
artificial and contrived insurrection requires, apart from the violence of the
insurrection itself, the extra violence needed to set it in motion. . . . During
the Revolution, I saw men organizing sham insurrections who proposed
massacres in order—as they put it—to give events a popular and national
air." Void of conviction but unable to tolerate a rudderless state of mind,
modern men became "prétendus républicains," pseudozealots more odious
and frenzied than authentic zealots. Their hypocrisy was repellent: "Great
sacrifices, acts of devotion, victories won by patriotism over natural affections in Greece and Rome served among us as pretexts for the most unbridled
outbursts of individual passions. Noble examples were parodied in a miserable
fashion. Because, in earlier times, inexorable but just fathers had condemned
their criminal children, modern imitators put their own quite innocent enemies to death."[122]

Constant's general understanding of modern European societies influenced and was influenced by his analysis of the Revolution. Although he
considered the Revolution an important episode in the advance toward legal
equality, he never neglected its chilling cruelty. And while he focused intently
on modern misuses of communitarian rhetoric, he never denied the genuinely
progressive outcome of the Revolution. He thought that the disaster of the
Jacobin experiment at legislating public morality revealed the utter futility
of trying to reverse the course of social change. The morals and manners
of a skeptical, secular, and commercial society leave much to be desired.
Legislative command, however, cannot recreate otiose forms of civic virtue
and communal belonging.

Because Constant wished to counter Rousseau's pernicious influence
on the revolutionary generation and to deromanticize the classical city, he
often emphasized the brutal features of ancient liberty. Despite this tendency,
he was careful to say that the Greeks and the Romans provided the most
stunning examples in human history of political freedom. Ancient repub-

licanism, while harsh, was not despotic.[123] It is *only in modern society* that ancient freedom becomes a ploy for justifying oppression.[124] Because there were no significant boundaries of the political in the ancient city, total citizenship was not experienced as a violation of the individual or as a restriction on his chances in life. During the French Revolution, by contrast, the ludicrous demand for *certificats de civisme* revealed how threatened authorities felt by the lukewarm commitment of citizens to civic life.[125] Political absenteeism was perceived as treason, as an illicit evasion of the molding-power of a self-appointed legislative elite. The pluralism of modern society, including the "line" between state and society, first made the ideal of ancient liberty into a possible pretext for political tyranny.

Freedom in Context

Les anciens n'avaient aucune notion de ce genre de liberté.
—Condorcet

AVING deciphered the paradoxical conclusion of "Ancient and Modern Liberty" and explicated its central theoretical claim, we can now look more closely at the historical assumptions underlying Constant's analysis of liberal freedom. What cultural and organizational transformations have caused radically different kinds of freedom to flourish in the ancient city and the modern state? Why did subjective rights, difficult to imagine in antiquity, become self-evident in modern European societies? Constant believed that modern liberty was a normative counterpart to the sharp disjunction between state and society, a distinction which emerged in Europe after the Reformation. That is the sociological basis of what Max Weber himself called "Constant's brilliant construction."[1]

A CONTEXTUAL THEORY OF INDIVIDUAL RIGHTS

One of the major obstacles to a historically oriented approach to constitutional rights is a dim but widespread conviction that rights somehow inhere in the human personality.[2] Yet this mysterious "inherence" is as impervious to theoretical analysis as the related and equally obfuscatory notion of a "presocial" individual. According to Constant, rights to freedom, dignity, equality, and property do not have as their object an inborn quality discoverable in discrete individuals. Constitutional rights are valued not

53

because they mirror human nature, but because they help to solve one of the fundamental problems of modern society. Rights counter the threat posed by the expansionistic tendency of the modern political sphere. Historically, they developed as a response to the danger that political officials might destroy the newly emergent autonomy of multiple channels of social cooperation. Not indestructible human nature but a relatively fragile and distinctively modern communicative order was the object of rights. Modern liberty cannot be interpreted as a purely negative principle, as a quest to desocialize man or to eject him from social life. Constant associated modern liberty with the option of freedom from politics, but not with anything so unthinkable as freedom from society.

Constant also believed that "commerce," irrationally stigmatized under the old regime, was "one of the principal bases of liberty."[3] But this did not mean that his liberalism was a form of bourgeois ideology.[4]

DEROMANTICIZING THE ANCIENT CITY

Rousseau whitewashed many cruel aspects of the classical city. To rectify this romantic falsification, Constant echoed Volney's description of the Spartans, the Romans and even the Athenians as "half-savage peoples, destitute and piratical."[5] Daily contact with slaves had anesthetized ancient citizens to that "sympathy for pain" which modern men perceive as a natural moral sentiment. This Graeco-Roman numbness was to be expected since "the pain of a slave is a means for his master." Slavery enhanced the slaveowner's appreciation of his own freedom precisely because "slaves . . . were counted as nothing in the social system of antiquity." The brutality and lack of compassion resulting from slaveholding were not transcended when citizens entered the public forum. Indeed, an atmosphere of violence (immortalized in the Melian dialogue) pervaded political life. In sum, Constant subscribed to Hume's view that slaveholding had a decisive impact on the tone of Greek and Roman life: "a cruel and severe turn was given to their morals."[6]

But Constant explained Condorcet's dictum that "the ancients had no idea of individual rights" without relying too heavily on postulates about the backwardness of ancient morality.[7] He concentrated on institutional factors that prevented the concept of individual rights from flourishing in antiquity. He did not view ancient liberty as a context-free alternative. Instead, he depicted it as the parochial counterpart to a historically obsolete social organization. Because of the small size and the restricted population of their cities, "each citizen . . . had politically a great personal importance." Participation in the exercise of public sovereignty was a palpable joy to ancient citizens not so much because their *moeurs* were glory-directed and Homeric, but for the banal reason that their cities were tiny. The immediate pleasure of being a large fish in a small pond was so intense that it could console citizens when their lives were otherwise regimented by the all-embracing power of the collectivity.[8] They were lured into ranking politics as the noblest human activity by a curious fusion of individual and group pride and by a sense of their own personal importance in this field.[9] They were willing to sacrifice their undistinguished private lives to. the public good, not because they were disinterested saints, but because they saw in politics a chance to leave a personal imprint on the course of history.

Besides size, there was another peculiar characteristic of the *polis* that prevented the Greeks from anticipating the modern ideal of freedom from politics. Once again, the crucial variable was not moral belief but institutional structure. Speaking of the ancients, Constant said: "Their *social organization* led them to desire a liberty utterly different from that guaranteed us by our system."[10] The most striking thing about the organization of the ancient city was the way each individual's existence was "englobed within political existence."[11] It was not just a matter of cramped quarters and nosy neighbors, although Constant was not prone to dismiss such factors as irrelevant. More important to him was that most spheres of life seemed to have political connotations or overtones. Man was a political animal because his total status was encapsulated within a relatively homogeneous political sphere. Art, religion, and even sports were integrated into civic life. They offered adornments, not alternatives, to citizenship. Commerce and industry presented clearly demarcated, extrapolitical opportunities for action; but the moral code of a slaveholding society attached considerable disrepute to economic activity. As a result, freedom *from* politics *to* engage in productive tasks never seemed an attractive possibility to Greek citizens. It was a genuine alternative, but it could not be formulated as a publicly defensible ideal. The only nonpolitical but still respectable activity which the Greeks perceived as existing outside politics (and which thus was thought to set a limit on the onmicompetence of political authority) was philosophy.[12] But classical philosophy, based on an ascetic moral code, was associated with a sanctimoniously aloof *vita contemplativa* and contrasted to all forms of *vita activa*. With this rarefied experience available to so few, it is not surprising that the ancients never developed the modern ideal of freedom from politics in order to engage in a rich variety of social opportunities, challenges, and *jouissances*.

Constant's argument drew heavily on the Greek political theorists' failure to develop the modern distinction between state and society. Talk of "the political" and "the extrapolitical" as distinct spheres of social interaction was a historical innovation of modern theory. The modern constitutional doctrine of individual rights was not meant to protect the atomized individual. Rights were calculated to defend the "line" between state and society. The contract myth long concealed this fact by encouraging theorists to conceive rights as shields behind which presocial individuals might escape from the influence of society. According to Constant's theory, by contrast, private rights shelter forms and channels of social communication from arbitrary encroachment by political officials; they contribute to the protection of society against the state, not to the defense of isolated individuals against society. Even though the ancients were well acquainted with contractarian theories, they had no idea of rights in Constant's or Condorcet's sense because they lacked any systematic conception of freedom from politics.[13] They lacked it because they had no idea of any "line" separating state from society. What they did not perceive to exist, they could not have perceived as a potential object of transgression. The Greeks did not conceive of individual rights because they did not acknowledge any sharply demarcated boundaries of the political which citizens might consider worth defending.

This was what Constant meant by his seemingly radical claims that, in antiquity, "the individual was entirely sacrificed to the collectivity" and that "all the Greek republics except Athens subjected individuals to a social jurisdiction of an almost unlimited scope."[14] Certainly, ancient citizens were placed under enormous pressures by the "severe surveillance" of moralistic neighbors.[15] "Each citizen was on view." Everyone was "circumscribed, observed, repressed in all his movements." Although a citizen could participate in punishing others, "he could, in turn, be deprived of his estate, despoiled of his rank, banished and put to death at the discretion of the group of which he was a part."[16] Constant emphasized diffuse social presure to conform, the tradition of rule by unpredictable popular decrees, and the custom of ostracism in order to explain the ancient claim that the city was "prior" to its citizens. The general absence of individual rights or personal independence in antiquity was due less to moral primitivism than to the social organization of the *polis*. No healthy extrapolitical institutions existed to shelter individuals from the encroachments of officials or neighbors. The part could not be defended against the whole because, by modern standards, the necessary partitions were lacking. The striking lack (to us) of social compartmentalization was not even perceived by the Greeks or Romans as a problem in their polities.

The ancients believed that everything of human value, except that marginal and otherworldly affair called philosophy, took place within the political sphere. Nothing to speak of lay beyond politics. This belief was due to the centripetal and relatively undifferentiated character of the ancient city. Because the political sphere was so all-pervasive and because trade and industry were considered more or less defiling, the choices accessible to most individuals outside politics appeared meager. The res publica "contained everything that a man held dear."[17] Citizens found their happiness in citizenship because they had no place else to go. Just as there were no reliable *shelters* against political authority, so there were no attractive *alternatives* to political participation. That, in a nutshell, was Constant's sociology of ancient freedom.

But Constant did not restrict his attention to internal factors. Equally important for explaining the total engulfment of the ancient citizen in his city was the peculiarly belligerent international scene in which cities had to eke out of their survival:

> As an inevitable consequence of their small size, the spirit of these republics was bellicose: each people chafed continuously against its neighbors and was irritated and menaced by them. Driven by necessity against one another, they endlessly fought or threatened to fight. Those who did not want to be conquerers could not lay down their arms under pain of being conquered. All purchased their security, their independence, their entire existence at the price of war. Thus, war was the unfailing interest, the almost habitual occupation, of the free states of antiquity.[18]

It was no accident that the ancients identified civic virtue with military valor and individual liberty with the independence of their cities. If a *polis* lost a war, its citizens might well be sold into slavery or perfunctorily butchered. A general willingness to subordinate private concerns to public safety, to see the city as prior to the citizen, was encouraged by this state of affairs: "Among the ancient nations, each citizen saw not only his affections but also his interests and his destiny enveloped in the fate of his country. If the enemy won a battle, his patrimony was ravaged. A public defeat precipitated him from the rank of a free man and condemned him to slavery."[19] Being free meant owning slaves. Military defeat and spoliation of slaveowners posed an immediate threat to liberty. A man's material well-being and honor, as well as his survival, depended on his community's success in war. It is hardly surprising that uncooperative individualism was discouraged. In an obvious sense, "free riders" seemed like traitors.

This brings us to a *third* concept of liberty, distinct from both private independence and public participation: the freedom of a city from the hegemonic ambitions of its neighbors. Constant sometimes described the community's search for autonomy and grandeur in the international arena as the essence of ancient freedom.[20] The classical Greeks and Romans were often willing to sacrifice personal influence on the outcome of public debate for the sake of the international independence and envy-provoking stature of their city. The freedom of the whole was prior to the freedom of the parts.

THE DELUSIONS OF TELEOLOGY

Early modern critics of ancient teleology expressed skepticism about the possiblity of knowing nature's intentions. In politics, teleological arguments ordinarily justified normative conclusions on the basis of factual premises. Because certain inborn capacities (for example, language or reason) are unique to man, man is morally obliged to develop these capacities to the greatest possible extent. Hobbes, the archenemy of teleological politics, mocked this form of argument: man is the only creature capable of absurdity, yet men are not ethically required to maximize their potential in this regard.[21]

Central to Constant's theoretical project was a similar attempt to demystify Aristotle's teleological theory of ancient politics. He followed Hobbes and Montesquieu[22] here, but (because he wrote *after* Rousseau) he did so in his own way. In "Ancient and Modern Liberty," Constant made clear that he could not accept Aristotle's view of total citizenship as a glorious triumph of the best in man over a sniveling desire for mere life. He granted that the ancients offered noble examples of political liberty. But he did not think that this nobility was produced by heroic efforts.[23] It was caused, rather, by a bizarre set of institutional and cultural factors reinforced by a perilous international situation.

The ancients preferred political participation to individual independence not because they were political animals or had higher standards than their modern counterparts, but simply because in the ancient city firsthand participation was the most efficient way to further particular (that is to say, not particularly noble) interests. Politics was the only interesting thing ancient citizens had to do. Constant mischievously reduced their participatory preference to a mean-spirited cost/benefit calculation. If modern individuals have come to have different goals than the ancients, that is because, for reasons of social organization, their payoff schedules have been reversed: "The ancients, when they sacrificed [individual] independence to political rights, sacrificed less to obtain more; while in making the same sacrifice, we would be giving up more to obtain less."[24] The ancient ethics of collectivism and democratic participation did not represent the victory of duty over interest. Rather, the idealization of group solidarity resulted automatically from the meager human possibilities available in the ancient city. In modern Europe, as a plethora of new possibilities became accessible to citizens, ethical commitments began to shift. This moral transformation was a personal response to an unplanned and uncontrollable change in social structure.

Consider in this light one of Constant's blandest accounts of classical republicanism. Ancient liberty "consisted in exercising collectively, but directly, many parts of sovereignty as a whole; in deliberating on the public square about war and peace; in concluding treaties of alliance with foreigners; in voting laws; in pronouncing judgments; in examining the accounts, the acts of the administration of magistrates; in making them appear before the people as a whole; in condemning them or absolving them."[25] Described in this way, ancient politics sounds like the self-management of a genteel debating club. No wonder that "the exercise of political rights constituted the amusement and occupation of everyone."[26] This amusement, however, was less innocuously delightful than it first appears. It, too, was colored by the cruel and severe turn of ancient morality: "As a member of the collectivity," the ancient citizen "interrogates, destitutes, condemns, despoils, exiles, and executes his magistrates and his superiors." The outrageous trial and summary execution of the generals in command at Arginusae was a prime example here. It shows what sort of "live and repeated pleasure" political participation must have been.[27]

It bears repeating: as an inevitable result of their bellicose way of life, all ancient cities had to have slaves.[28] Slavery, in turn, led to a sense of cultural disgrace being attached to productive work as well as to trade. The importance of slavelabor to *polis* life provides the setting for one of Constant's most humorous attempts at a demystification of ancient politics. Because of the episodic nature of ancient warfare and the stigma attached to economic chores, citizen-soldiers were constantly faced with great "intervals of inactivity."[29] Politics was dull business compared with combat and pillage, but it was the only reputable way in which ancient citizens could kill time. Bored and nervously afraid of boredom, they filled up the intervals between wars (Constant wrote here of a *remplissage obligé*) with council meetings, debates, deliberations, legislation, scrutinies of ex-magistrates, trials, and the machinations of party faction. "Without this resource, the free peoples of antiquity would have languished under the weight of painful inaction."[30] In other words, contrary to Aristotle, politics was not desired for its own sake. Participatory self-government in the *polis* cannot be explained teleologically. It was neither an expression of man's political nature nor a fulfillment of his highest inborn potential. Less nobly, it was an improvised solution to the hoplite's awful problem: a surfeit of leisure time and the terrifying threat of ennui.

Constant deliberately aimed to set Aristotle back on his feet, to replace the flattering teleological explanation of the Greek commitment to political life with a mundane and nonteleological analysis. Aristotle had argued that the *polis* was prior to the individual, that political science studied everything of human value, and that citizenship was man's highest good: "we must not suppose any one of the citizens to belong to himself, for they all belong to the *polis,* and the care of each is inseparable from the care of the whole."[31] Politics is the only realm where men can perform beautiful or memorable deeds and where they can make full use of *logos* (reason and speech), given by nature to man alone. Constant rejected this analysis: ancient politics was not a realization of man's innermost essence but rather an ad hoc strategy for soothing his nagging uneasiness. "Uneasiness" was Locke's word, translated by Constant's *inquiétude,* which had its own peculiarly nineteenth-century connotations.

No acorn-to-oak teleology is invoked in "Ancient and Modern Liberty." From a post-Copernican perspective, it is less cogent to conceive nature as a preprogrammed seed or Aristotelian *entelechia* than as a threat or a problem. Institutions are valued not because they allow a seed to grow, but rather because they counter a threat or solve a problem. Instead of mirroring nature, such institutions thwart it. A negative orientation toward nature is already implicit in Hume's classical discussion of justice and the right to private property.[32] Property does not express nature's dearest wishes; but it does help to solve the social problem of insecurity about the future. That is why we need the institution. That *is* its justification. Writing under the influence of Hume and Montesquieu, Constant tried to explain the origin and self-perpetuation of classical citizenship in a strictly nonteleological and thus anti-Aristotelian fashion. Ancient liberty was prized not because it expressed human nature but because it solved a dire social problem.

Having witnessed the antics of Napoleon, Constant was unimpressed by the ancient ideal of marital glory. In modern societies, "the idea of citizen-soldiers is especially dangerous"[33] because it contaminates civic life with the military spirit. In his "Sketch of a Constitution" of 1814, he made an energetic case against the republican glorification of citizen-soldiers.[34] The ancients were driven toward the code of military valor by dint of circumstances. The warrior's ethic also had a sleazy side; it encouraged citizen-soldiers to plunder the innocent and seize property. Among the ancients, "a successful war added in slaves, tribute, and lands to both public and private wealth."[35] Material gain and self-interest may have been the prime motivation for ancient political participation in general.[36] Constant scrupulously avoided any mention of noble deeds.

The habit of war reinforced the political esprit de corps characteristic of the ancients. It also made a teleological account of ancient politics plausible in the first place: "In order to succeed, war requires common action. . . . A people profits from the fruits of war only as a collective being. . . . The aim of war is perfectly precise. It is victory or conquest. This aim is always before the eyes of those concerned. It unites them and chains them together. It forges their efforts, their projects and their wills into an indivisible whole."[37] Mobilization for combat created political unity out of individual diversity. It channeled private energies toward an overriding common purpose. Social teleology was thus a philosophy of war. Aristotle had claimed that the aim of the individual citizen should conform to the aim of the whole political community.[38] A shared *telos*, Constant added, was originally imposed upon ancient citizens by military discipline.[39]

Another example of Constant's attempt to turn Aristotle right side up is his covert reference to the statement, also found in the *Politics,* that citizens with sufficient wealth will naturally hire stewards and, released from demeaning chores, occupy themselves with politics.[40] Constant mockingly agreed: "Poor men handle their own affairs; rich men hire agents. This is the story of the ancient and modern nations."[41] His meaning was exactly the opposite of Aristotle's. Because modern society is so wealthy, citizens can now deputize agents to handle their political "affairs" (the word itself is freighted with connotations of drudgery and small-minded connivance) while they pursue their economic "speculations" (which is meant to sound lofty). Constant did not simply invert the ancient subordination of economic to political life. He identified one of the main impulsions behind the classical republican commitment to firsthand, full-time participation in politics as the cruel poverty of the ancient city. Here, again, men were not drawn into politics by some uplifting final cause; they were shoved onto the Pynx from behind.

Another piece of evidence that Constant was trying to demystify the teleological conception of ancient politics and thereby deromanticize the classical city, was his vaguely Hobbesian, mechanistic description of citizenship in a *polis*: "Men were, so the speak, nothing but machines. The laws regulated their springs and directed their wheels."[42] This emphasis on the nakedly constraining elements in ancient political life undercut attempts to interpret the ancient/modern distinction on the basis of Aristotle's own good life/mere life dichotomy. The propelling motives Constant detected at the source of ancient politics were bodily fear, interest, uneasiness, vanity, avarice, and unreasoning patriotism—all combined with moral obtuseness toward the plight of slaves.

Constant spoke about ancient citizenship as "a vast career in which men were flushed with their own force and filled with a feeling of energy and dignity." But he was careful to qualify this assertion by adding that antiquity was an age in which the faculties of men developed in a direction "traced in advance."[43] The Greeks and Romans noticed the preprogrammed nature of their freedom.[44] But since antiquity was an age of illusions, they misinterpreted their lack of autonomy as a sign that destiny was calling or that their unique *telos* was unfolding. Constant dispelled this ancient mirage. The final cause inwardly felt by ancient citizens was in reality an exogenous compulsion: a combined effect of poverty, the exigencies of war, the lack of shelter from political surveillance, the paucity of attractive alternatives to political life, and the need to discipline slaves. The Aristotelian interpretation of this external compulsion as a message from nature testified to the comforting self-intoxication of the most sober of the Greeks.

To deglamorize the ancient city, Hume emphasized its susceptibility to bloody factional strife. Madison echoed this point: "such democracies have ever been spectacles of turbulence and contention."[45] Constant touched upon factionalism and internecine conflict in his early manuscripts of 1800–06,[46] but he made no mention of it in the lecture. The reasons for this omission are not difficult to discover. In 1819, Constant was being assaulted by the ultras as a wanton factionalist. He was repeatedly accused of seeking to introduce discord into the state. Since he believed the right of opposition to be the essence of representative government, he carefully avoided any censorious commentary on ancient factionalism. To evoke the traditional association of political participation with civic disorder could only abet the cause of his opponents.

THE SOCIAL BASIS OF MODERN FREEDOM

According to Thomas Hobbes, "there was never any thing so deerly bought, as these Western parts have bought the learning of the Greek and Latine tongues."[47] He was thinking chiefly of the republican doctrines of Aristotle and Cicero that, in his eyes, fired the English civil wars. Constant deliberately echoed Hobbes's claim, but he did so with a characteristic difference: "As a necessary result of the education they received, the men whom the flood of revolutionary events brought to power were imbued with opinions that had become false."[48] The crucial innovation lies in the word *become.* The massive and irreversible process of historical change dominated Constant's thinking as it never had that of his contractarian predecessors.[49]

What characteristics of modern, post-Reformation Europe gave birth to a new concept of freedom and made classical freedom obsolete? First of all, no modern nation is "surveyable at a glance," as Aristotle insisted all good polities must be. Nor is it possible for all modern citizens to look at one another and know each others' characters intimately.[50] These are trite observations. Yet changes in scale and population had an immense impact on the firsthand experience of democratic citizenship. Even in the freest modern societies, the marginal contribution of the average individual to political decision-making is infinitesimally small: "The political importance that befalls each individual diminishes in proportion to the size of a country. The most obscure republican of Rome or Sparta was a power. The same is not true of the simple citizen of Great Britain or the United States. His personal influence is an imperceptible fraction of the social will that imparts a direction to the government.[51] Given this new situation, the incentive for modern individuals to devote their time to politics is remarkably feeble. Each citizen's "part of sovereignty" has evaporated into "an abstract supposition." Today "the mass of citizens" is called upon to exercise sovereignty largely "in an illusory manner."[52]

Described in this derogatory fashion, modern citizenship seems signally unattractive. But large size and dense population also allow for anonymity. In an ancient republic, the most obscure citizen was a power with which everyone had to reckon—that is to say, he was not obscure. Ancient citizens were on perpetual display. This had now changed: "In our day, large states have created a new guarantee, that of obscurity."[53] The value of obscurity was in fact integral to Constant's picture of liberal freedom. To evade professional and amateur spies, modern citizens must be able to come and go unobtrusively. Consider the original formulation of this point in the *Circonstances actuelles:*

> celebrity was as dangerous [in antiquity] as it is in our day. But the guarantee of obscurity did not exist. . . . There was not then, as there is in our large states, a mass of men, peaceable egoists who, mocking those poor fools who get themselves talked about, are able with the help of their individual means, the size of the country and the current organization of commerce and property, to carve out their destinies at a distance from public events.[54]

In antiquity, freedom (at least in theory) was associated with political visibility and with each citizen's readiness to serve the public safety at a moment's notice. In revolutionary France, freedom was associated with shelters, hideouts, disguises, and escape routes—anything that might interfere with the power over citizens exercised by grudge-bearing neighbors or by governmental spies and their potential informants. Thick walls symbolized the freedom which Montesquieu had defined as security. Security, in turn, hinged upon guarantees made to individuals and subgroups of noninterference by other persons, that is, on the establishment of a "free space" within which they might act as they chose. This "space" would be neutral with regard to content.[55] It would permit pleasure, friendship, self-sacrifice, self-indulgence, creative thought, bizarre whims, religious devotion, or material acquisition. It was meant to exclude only those acts which obviously violated the "free space" of others.

Constant viewed barriers separating people not merely as signs of entrepreneurial self-reliance, but also and more importantly as barricades against *l'esprit de délation*. Emergent French individualism had at least as much to do with the all-corrosive distrust characteristic of civil wars as with the spirit of capitalism. Indeed, individualism and anticapitalism were quite compatible, though this was not a position Constant himself chose to adopt.

The spatial metaphors of "barriers," "walls," "spheres," and "separate domains" are essential to the modern understanding of freedom and individual rights.[56] These images have a long, complex genealogy. It would be simplistic to reduce them to parochial correlates of the capitalist economy. The Greeks and Romans made a primitive but significant contribution to the modern idea of subjective rights against the state with their notion of the household as a sort of private enclave split off from the general political domain. The opportunities this inclosure contained, however, were not honorable or various enough to encourage many to see freedom from politics as a particularly attractive ideal. Another important source for the idea of an inviolable zone, shielded by rights, was the Christian contrast between the *imperium* and the *sacerdotium*.[57] This dualism carried the implication (fully exploited only after the Reformation) that secular officials must stay out of all questions concerning personal salvation. As free cities arose in medieval Europe, free citizens saw liberty from baronial control symbolized by and embodied in town walls.[58] The lesser magnates of Europe, in turn, fought tenaciously to preserve their privileges, immunities, and exemptions against the steady advance of the consolidating monarchies. They, too, helped promulgate the ideal of unassailable redoubts, barriers to fend off invasions of power-wielders into the "private" sphere.

Taken in isolation, neither increase in size nor the rise of capitalism can explain the emergence of a new concept of freedom in modern Europe. What must be studied is the social organization of modern states in all its complexity. When Constant referred to the "increased complexity of social relations,"[59] he meant the proliferation in modern society of two types of institution: walls, partitions, and shelters that enabled citizens to escape from (or to deflect) diffuse social pressure and the harassments of officials; and nonpolitical organizations that could engender new chances for individual and cooperative goal-seeking, opportunities more alluring than those available within the narrowly defined political domain itself. The idea of freedom from politics became widespread against a background of institutions that made such freedom plausible and enticing. Such institutions gave citizens "the possibility to exist isolated from public affairs."[60] If politics was conceived primarily as authority, then sheltering institutions were crucial. If politics was conceived primarily as participation, then opportunity-generating institutions were required. Modern citizens are less dependent on their states for these two organizational reasons: they get less relative satisfaction from political involvement, and they have an easier time eluding the police. The crucial point is that modern liberty cannot be described in a privative fashion. It is not freedom *from* society, but rather freedom *in* society.

Liberal freedom cannot be adequately defined, in the Hobbesian manner,[61] as a mere absence of obstacles. Equally essential is the presence of possibilities. Possibilities, in turn, are creatures of social institutions; they cannot be generated out of the prodigality of the individual soul. Institutions prepattern the horizon of possible experiences and actions. Hobbes located freedom in an empty space, beyond law and the interference of other men. It is unconvincing, however, to conceive laws and fellow men simply as obstructions to freedom. Rules (such as grammar) often *create* social possibilities that would not otherwise exist. Similarly, social interdependence can increase freedom, can give men otherwise unavailable chances not only to secure cooperation for preexistent ends, but also to learn and acquire new ends.[62] The Hobbesian claim that freedom is nothing but the absence of obstacles engendered the following mythology: without language, institutions, rules, and social interdependence, freedom is unbounded; for the sake of "order," we sacrifice some of our freedom. But this is an unsatisfactory approach to the problem. Accessible possibilities are constitutive of freedom. Freedom expands and contracts as does the horizon of those accessible possibilities which are important culturally and personally. Institutions, language, and rules for social cooperation, do not represent mere obstacles to freedom that must be accepted for the sake of self-preservation. They are enabling, not disabling. They are *creative* of possibilities and thus generative of freedom as well.

To cross the frontier from the public into the private does not entail forfeiting possibilities created within society. Constitutional rights do not protect the presocial individual but, rather, social pluralism and the "line" between state and society. The possibilities to which Constant's modern liberty refers are life chances made available within and by modern European societies. In these societies, it has become an anachronism to identify human self-determination in general with democratic self-government, for the simple reason that the polity and civil society are no longer coextensive.[63] Autonomy must be *both* political *and* extrapolitical.

POLITICAL USES OF PROPERTY AND COMMERCE

The ideal of individual rights, as Constant described it, could arise only within the cultural and institutional context of modern society. To see in greater detail that Constant did not view "rights" in the contractarian manner, as timeless ideals, we need only consider his most frequently cited definition of modern liberty:

> [Modern liberty] is, for each individual, the right not to be subjected to anything but the law, not to be arrested, or detained, or put to death, or mistreated in any manner, as a result of the arbitrary will of one or several individuals. It is each man's right to express his opinions, to choose and exercise his profession, to dispose of his property and even abuse it, to come and go without obtaining permission and without having to give an account of either his motives or his itinerary. It is the right to associate with other individuals, either to confer about mutual interests or to profess the cult that he and his associates prefer or simply to fill his days and hours in the manner most conforming to his inclinations and fantasies. Finally, it is each man's right to exert influence on the administration of government, either through the election of some or all of its public functionaries, or through remonstrances, petitions, and demands which authorities are more or less obliged to take into account.[64]

The right to dispose of one's own property is only one aspect of modern freedom. Behind the plausibility and utility of this right lies a massive and irreversible change in the structure of the economy. While Constant did not view commercialization as the sole factor behind the emergence of modern liberty, he considered economic modernization an indispensable stimulant to its development.

Only after slavery and serfdom were abolished did it become true that "free men must exercise all the professions and must supply all the needs of society."[65] It is no great mystery that, in a caste-free age, all professions have come to seem honorable, and that the traditional disgrace associated with productive work has been dispelled. Deprived of breathing robots, free men necessarily began to view economic life as a culturally respectable alternative to politics.

Tocqueville thought that the spirit of commerce not only diverted individuals from taking part in public affairs but also made them more dependent on government.[66] Constant adopted the more standard Smithian view that commercial life universalizes the ideal of the masterless man and helps accustom men to shifting for themselves. It habituates people to providing for their own needs without the intervention of political officials, creating citizens impatient with the meddling and bungling of their government. When the state tries to conduct or supervise our affairs, it often does so less intelligently and more expensively than people would have done themselves.[67] Distrust of fatherly commands is natural among individuals trained by commerce in self-reliance. Modern commerce provided a barrier against political regimentation. To reinforce this point, Constant drew a sharp distinction between the modern institution of moveable stocks and the traditional institution of landed property.

Modern pluralism, providing the social basis for liberal politics, is quite distinct from the corporatism that underlay the illiberal politics of the feudal regime. After 1789, France ceased to be segmented legally into estates, guilds, towns, monasteries, and other closed communities: "The Revolution had this advantage: its violence broke down the artificial compartments where men had been enclosed in order to make them easier to govern."[68] Economic stratification remained. But vying with class structure was a new set of fundamental divisions, not between corporations, but between activities. Politics, science, family relations, religion, and the market became a series of disjoined, though interrelated, realms. No individual was encapsulated inside any single sphere of activity. In this increasingly open and mobile society, everyone began to participate in a variety of dissociated "roles." It was this structural transformation that ushered in the egalitarian revolution. In contrast to the old pluralism of corporations, the new pluralism of abstract sectors made it increasingly difficult to ascribe unique social niches to individuals on the basis of birth.

Paradoxically, the radical transition from medieval to liberal pluralism occurred by virtue of an intermediate stage of political centralization. As every textbook informs us, centralizing powers broke down feudal barriers to commerce. It was only after the consolidation of modern European states that individual rights became a widespread political idea.[69] Earlier, the only universally recognized rights were "status rights," rights attributable to individuals on the basis of their family's inherited location in a social hierarchy.

Constant's discussion of moveable stocks and landed property throws light on the political consequences of modern pluralism. Each form of wealth provided the basis for a different kind of citizenship.[70] Land cannot be conveniently expatriated. By a skillful deployment of soldiers and threats of confiscation, political officials can put irresistible pressure on landowners.[71] On the other hand, moveable stocks, *la richesse mobilière,* can be smuggled out of the country. Modern commerce and the circulation of goods thus erected "an invisible and invincible obstacle to that unlimited action of the social power." When citizen-merchants are threatened, "they transport their treasures far away." As a result, liquid assets build a wall against governmental coercion: the transactions of merchants "cannot be penetrated by authority."[72]

Moveable stocks and bills of exchange not only provide a shelter behind which citizens may successfully hide. They also serve as a source of power, because governments are reluctant to embitter generous sources of credit. If "money is hidden and sent away," a government will not be able to raise the loans it needs. In Constant's view, "commerce is favorable to individual liberty" because it allows citizens to control officials by threatening to withdraw financial cooperation.[73] If Athens was the one ancient city that tolerated at least some elements of modern freedom, this was because the Athenians used bills of exchange and other "antisocial" devices usually associated with advanced economies.[74]

In the wake of the industrial revolution, the coupling of liberal politics with capitalist economies brought liberalism into disrepute. Marxists have repeatedly argued that a commitment to liberal political ideas was simply a mask for prior class interests generated in the economy.[75] This accusation is historically implausible. What made the nascent capitalist economy seem a source of hope to early modern theorists was a *prior and independent* commitment to liberal political ideals. Liberals viewed trade and industry as effective means for their pursuit of noneconomic ends. During the Restoration, the political meaning of ownership was self-evident: "The purchasers of national lands represent the most important of the [interests] created by the Revolution. They are less defenders of completed sales and laws that have been passed than defenders of the division of properties. This division provides the foundation for the new organization of France. In the near future, within this century, it will be the foundation stone of the European order."[76] Far from being a mere economic good, serving material interests, property was charged with political significance. Purchasers of national lands were precommitted to opposing the illiberal politics of the émigrés.

Anticlerical and antimilitaristic reformers naturally sought allies among the commercial classes. Constant's own strategic alliances, in any case, were secondary to his political aims. Under the Consulate, for example, he fiercely attacked Bonaparte for suppressing freedom of debate and jury trials even though most businessmen supported the government's repressive policies. Neither brigands nor the leaders of popular uprisings should ever be brought before military courts.[77] Liberal proceduralism must never be sacrificed for the protection of property. It was crucial, however, to forbid confiscation. This was the most obvious political dimension of private economic rights. "Confiscation was a habitual practice under the old monarchy."[78] It was a very pernicious form of punishment because it provided an irresistible incentive for false accusations. To outlaw spoliation was to enforce popular sovereignty against the self-serving schemes of public officials. Constant even defined arbitrary government by reference to confiscation: "Here is arbitrary government: a man wishes to take the property of another; he denounces him to a minister (an accomplice or a dupe), has him indicted and condemned, his fortune confiscated, and a part of it given to him. What is known as theft under a legal regime is called a salary under arbitrary rule. The thief, rather than being hanged, is rewarded."[79] Property rights are politically motivated: they provide a barrier against a certain style of governance. Rulers who are forced to respect private property will find it somewhat more difficult to act as ravinous preditors.

Cooperation in the marketplace can have a cordializing effect: it can teach religious sectaries how to avoid irrational bloodshed and even how to pool resources in common ventures. Commerce can be considered antisocial only if civil war is the essence of social life.[80] In early modern Europe, a man's concern for his neighbor's salvation might lead him to slit his neighbor's throat. Indifference to certain aspects of one's neighbor's life, the deeroticizing of some communal bonds, actually increase the available chances for creative social interdependence.

De la conquête is an extended elaboration on the psychological contrast between commerce and war. Only advocates of the martial virtues can denigrate commerce as a form of base corruption. According to the "civic virtue" tradition, earning one's living by trade was dishonorable in comparison with invasions and cannonades, rape and plunder. Constant dissented from the civic virtue tradition: commerce was not the worst thing men can do to one another. A nation of shopkeepers, however tawdry, was preferable to a nation of warriors.

The importance of the concept "self-interest" in liberal thought should be understood in relation to the problems plaguing modern European states. The chief antonyms of "interest" were religious passions, hereditary privileges, and martial reflexes.[81] Seen in this context, "self-interest" did not appear particularly mean-spirited or egoistical. Commercial habits, as well as commercial classes, were enlisted as recruits in an ongoing liberal campaign against rapine, revenge, tyranny, and general social insecurity.

Writing before the industrial transformation of Europe, Constant did not live to see "commerce" lose its progressive connotations and become associated with misery and massive social dislocation. Nevertheless, he was careful to distinguish the right to property, which he called "a social convention," from rights to religious toleration, freedom of opinion, and freedom from arbitrary arrest, which he considered more fundamental.[82] In the seventeenth century, Locke had ascribed quasi-sacral attributes and a presocial origin to private property. With this countersacralization he hoped to outbid the prestige of divine-right kingship. No longer facing an authority rooted in a living religious tradition, Constant explicitly repudiated this mythical view of ownership. It was absurd to "represent property as something mysterious, anterior to society."[83] Property law is a creation of social life and can be justified only by its beneficial consequences. In the present stage of economic development, the abolition of property would not have created a perfect society, as Babeuf believed. It would instead have led to a cataclysmic shortage of food. Private property allowed for social cooperation without legal castes. There was no obvious alternative. Only if "our discoveries in mechanics" could create "a total exemption from manual labor" would the erasure of all distinction between ownership and nonownership be compatible with the maintenance of civilized life. As a result, Constant hoped for a diffusion, not an abolition, of property.[84] In the meantime, constitutional arrangements must prevent the state from adopting radically confiscatory policies.

Despite this warning, Constant was anxious to stress the contingent character of property rights: "Property, in its character as a social convention, falls under the competence and jurisdiction of society. Society possesses over it rights that it does not possess over the freedom, the life and the opinions of its members."[85] Among all the rights of man, in other words, the right to property was the only one Constant held to be discussable.[86] Economic liberalism was primarily a useful weapon in the arsenal of political liberalism. Political freedom might also serve the cause of economic freedom. But the principal relation was the inverse: limited government was a precondition for self-government.

ESCAPE ROUTES

The identification of freedom with asylums and escape routes was part of the unintended legacy of the revolutionary age.[87] Constant's idea of modern freedom gave this bequest a systematic form. Not only merchandise but threatened individuals could learn to vanish at the appropriate time. They too could slip across the border.[88] In antiquity, a war-ravaged international scene made such escapes difficult if not impossible. Expatriation was a brutal punishment in classical times; in modern times it has become a pleasure, a grand tour.[89] The Latin word *hostis* meant both "stranger" and "enemy," which suggests how uninviting trips abroad once were.[90] The attractiveness and easy accessibility of neighboring countries limits the power of the modern European state over its citizens.[91] Like the monetization of economic life, international escape routes "offer to victims of injustice a sanctuary within reach,"[92] making the abstract split between state and society into a palpable experience.

Escape routes were creative, not merely protective. The marvelous achievements of late eighteenth-century Germany in philosophy and literature were made possible by competition among principalities offering asylum: "The division of Germany into a multitude of tiny sovereignties has, for more than a century, served as a guarantee of civil liberty in that country where, in other respects, almost all the institutions were feudal and despotic. The most unlimited freedom of thought and expression concerning matters of religion and politics fled from one principality into another, and found everywhere compensation and protection."[93] The border between sovereign states, although only one sort of boundary, may well have been the prototype for Constant's idea of liberating escape routes, of partitions that fostered social creativity by providing citizens a sanctuary from fear and persecution.

To summarize: besides size, the most important difference between the ancient city and the modern nation is the emergence in the latter of a sharp state/society distinction. Both institutional and cultural changes have contributed to this general transformation. The boundaries of the political are now part of every citizen's daily experience. Politics can no longer pretend to contain everything a man holds dear. It is no longer plausible to stigmatize freedom from politics as a form of utter deprivation. The possibilities available inside the narrowly political sector of society have dwindled considerably. They cannot sustain the total life-engagement of the mass of citizens. Simultaneously, options accessible in extrapolitical spheres of society have been "infinitely multiplied and varied."[94]

But the state/society distinction not only provides new forms of *vita activa* alongside politics. It also gives citizens a set of instruments with which to fend off the pretensions of powerful officials. This double function makes the state/society distinction an indispensable precondition for the emergence of modern freedom. Such freedom includes the liberty to be "distracted from political liberty," the freedom of citizens to stray off on unsupervised itineraries.[95] Social coordination is possible, but not obligatory. A citizen's concern with the public good, however important, is likely to be intermittent and must remain voluntary.

Another important feature of modern liberty is reflected in an individual's right "to come and go without obtaining permission and without having to give an account of either his motives or his itinerary." Adolphe complained bitterly about the petty despotism of Ellénore, who always demanded a detailed account of his comings and goings. When she died, however, and he finally became independent, he was forlorn. The liberal guarantee of freedom did not entail a guarantee of happiness. Perfect independence may leave a citizen writhing in agony. To escape is not to arrive. In one of his more revealing letters, Constant admitted that he had been "agitated" and excruciatingly unhappy even "in the midst of the most profound repose."[96] Despite this unhappiness, he consistently praised constitutional government because it guaranteed repose.

THE POLITICAL DIMENSION OF INDIVIDUAL FREEDOM

In modern societies, freedom from politics is a positive good, not a mere deprivation or lack. Constant absorbed this insight and went beyond it. He did not give a dogmatically apolitical definition of the freedom available in modern societies. Politics should no longer be mandatory as it had to some extent been in classical Greece and under the Terror; but it *should be* possible, and it *is* desirable. Constant concluded his catalogue of rights with a sentence worth repeating. He did so in a completely natural way, not as if he were groping with an awkward afterthought: "Finally, it is each man's right to exert influence on the administration of government, either through the election of some or all of its functionaries, or through remonstrances, petitions, and demands which authorities are more or less obliged to take into account."[97] To those whose knowledge of Constant is confined to the stylized distinction between positive and negative liberty ("Constant . . . prized negative liberty beyond any modern writer"),[98] it must come as a surprise to read his reiterated assertions that "political liberty is indispensable" and that "France knows that political liberty is as necessary as civil liberty." Even more emphatically: "Citizens will interest themselves in their institutions only if they are called to cooperate within them by voting. Now, this interest is indispensable for the formation of a public spirit, a power without which no liberty can endure."[99] As such statements demonstrate, the idea of a deep wedge between liberalism and democracy does little to illuminate Constant's position. He did not banish the notion of liberty from the political realm.[100] His position on this matter should have been difficult to misunderstand: "Those who wish to sacrifice political liberty in order to enjoy civil [or private] liberty with greater tranquillity are no less absurd than those who wish to sacrifice civil liberty in the hope of assuring political liberty and extending it further."[101] Political rights were constituent of, not merely a precondition for, the liberty to be pursued in modern society. Important offices cannot be widely shared among all the citizenry, but the function of shaping policy through public discussion and elections can be. Indifference to citizenship is undesirable not because civic life is beautiful, but because solutions to common problems can only be discovered and implemented politically. In modern societies, democratic citizenship is not the only kind of freedom available to most people most of the time. It remains, however, an essential component of freedom as well as one that is an indispensable precondition for most other forms of freedom. In sum, the mythical opposition between liberalism and democracy cannot be established on the basis of Constant's contrast between ancient and modern liberty. On the contrary, he drew the distinction sharply in order to emphasize the tight interdependence of public influence and private security.

TWO FUNCTIONS OF REPRESENTATION

On the trail of both Montesquieu and Rousseau, Constant claimed that the representative system was "a discovery of the moderns."[102] One of the aims of the 1819 lecture was to explain why representative government "was almost entirely unknown to the free states of antiquity."[103] That British-style representation was unanticipated in republican antiquity is not altogether surprising. Modern citizens treasure representation for a modern reason: it provides an institutional framework for satisfying their desire not to participate continuously and exclusively in politics. Representative government is the political acknowledgment of the modern split between state and society. It extends the division of labor into government. Eighteenth-century proponents of representation, such as Tom Paine, invoked territorial expanse and the size of populations in its defense. Constant preferred to focus on time.[104] Just as ancient participatory democracy was the improvised response to a surfeit of free time, so modern representative democracy is an answer to the scarcity of time:

> Just as the liberty we now require is distinct from that of the ancients, so this new liberty itself requires an organization different from that suitable for ancient liberty. For the latter, the more time and energy a man consecrated to the exercise of his political rights, the more free he believed himself to be. Given the type of liberty to which we are now susceptible, the more the exercise of our political rights leaves us time for our private interests, the more precious we find liberty to be. From this, Gentlemen, stems the necessity of the representative system. The representative system is nothing else than an organization through which a nation unloads on several individuals what it cannot and will not do for itself. Poor men handle their own affairs; rich men hire managers. This is the story of ancient and modern nations. The representative system is the power of attorney given to certain men by the mass of the people who want their interests defended but who nevertheless do not always have the time to defend these interests themselves.[105]

Unlike commercial agents, elected deputies represent the unity of the nation, and they must do so in public, not behind closed doors. But the commercial analogy, false to this extent, allowed Constant another provocative reversal of Aristotelian theory. According to the *Politics,* democracy was one of the perverted constitutions, since it granted the franchise to unworthy individuals. The best form of this inherently mediocre regime was a democracy of farmers: "being poor, they have no leisure, and therefore do not often attend the assembly."[106] Constant inverted this idea. Not having to attend the assembly because we are absorbed in private interests has become a privilege and a sign of wealth.

Constant praised representative government for disencumbering citizens from time-consuming political chores. In a complex commercial civilization, in which all individuals depend on people they can never know, the concept of "autonomy" must be defined with care. If autonomy requires individuals to have a personal say in every decision that affects them, there can be no autonomy in modern society. Indeed, to live effective lives, individuals must now more than ever husband their resources, including time, and focus on specialized tasks. They must permit important decisions to be made for them and without their direct participation. That is an unavoidable consequence of the division of labor. Indeed, liberal freedom is the only kind of autonomy possible in a society based on the division of labor, a society that has created a permanent scarcity of time by generating more possibilities than anyone can successfully exploit or enjoy. The division of labor, however, allows independence and interdependence to increase simultaneously. Citizenship in a modern society cannot be the center of an individual's life. But it does not vanish into thin air.

Constant also had political reasons for stressing the limited and voluntary nature of popular participation. Modern states will never be popular states, "because there is nothing less popular, that is to say, nothing that puts the mass of the people less into action than representative government, which accords to the people only the right to vote, a right exercised for a few days and followed by a period of inactivity that is always rather long."[107] In passages such as this, modern citizenship seems exiguous indeed. But a first impression is deceptive. During certain phases of the Restoration, Constant wrote in this manner, but only for strategic reasons. He had to calm the fears of moderate conservatives opposed to a widening of the franchise. In the same book from which the above passage is drawn, Constant also stressed the way representation mobilizes the cooperation of citizens in determining their collective fate: "representative government is nothing but the admission of the people to participation in public affairs."[108] In fact, Constant always insisted upon *both* dimensions of representative government. Representation simultaneously includes citizens in political life and frees them from political life. It enhances both independence and involvement: that is its utility and its strength. On different occasions, Constant emphasized one function and deemphasized the other; but his balanced view was that representation served both purposes at once.

THE ECONOMIC BASIS OF POLITICAL FREEDOM

One of the most disruptive and therefore attractive aspects of Constant's thought is the way in which it questions the association of liberalism with a hysterical fear of civic activism. Constant listed "the right for each citizen to exert influence on the administration of government" as an essential component of liberty in modern society. Citizens should not be coerced, but they should be willing to keep abreast of political events and to exercise "a constant and active surveillance" of their deputized representatives.[109]

Reconsider, in this context, Constant's argument that commerce provides an effective barrier against misgovernment.

Of all imaginable countervailing mechanisms, commerce seems to be the most suspiciously in tune with the fiscal interests of the middle class.[110] Constant was probably as naive about the future of commerce as he was about the future of nationalism. He certainly did not foresee the politically troublesome consequences of capital flight. But his theory cannot be reduced to bourgeois ideology.

Most recent treatments of liberal freedom neglect the right to exercise influence on the government through the election of representatives as well as through the traditional method of petitioning and resisting. Such voluntary influence is quite different from involuntary conscription. It is nothing like being dragooned unwillingly into civic responsibility and having one's total status engulfed in the political sphere. Modern citizenship can never offer the same intense everyday enjoyment as did participation in an ancient republic. Nevertheless, public influence on political decisions is a crucial part of modern liberty, if only because it is a guarantee against the emergence of an authority so powerful that it can eventually violate individual independence when and where it wishes. Commerce was a useful weapon in the politics of *guarantisme*. To the extent that political participation is a countervailing power, it is in principle replaceable. Commerce was a force that might aid public opinion in one of its main tasks. It was another mechanism for controlling the government. In modern contexts, public opinion needs to be buttressed in a way that ancient public opinion did not. The same factors that permit the obscurity of modern citizens, the private screens that block the prying eyes of police informants, also inhibit surveillance of government officials by the public. Obscurity cuts both ways:

> In a republic where all citizens were maintained by poverty in
> an extreme simplicity of manners, where they inhabited the same
> city, where they did not exercise any profession which deflected
> their attention from the affairs of state and where they found
> themselves constantly spectators or judges of the employment
> of public power . . . the arbitrary authority of the censors was
> contained by a type of moral surveillance exercised against
> them.[111]

In small, relatively partition-free societies, "morality found support in an immediate public, spectator and judge of all actions in their tiniest details and most delicate nuances."[112] In modern societies, men are busy in their nonpolitical hideouts and unapprised of events unfolding on the public

scene. When modern governments are granted discretionary powers analogous to those possessed by the Roman censors, they inevitably run wild,
unlimited as they are by the pressure of public scrutiny.

Public surveillance of modern officials is insufficient and Montesquieu's intermediary bodies have been destroyed. It is thus necessary to
introduce auxiliary mechanisms, such as the separation of powers, to inhibit
excessive state authority. *Commerce is just another one of these auxiliary
counterweights*. It can obstruct abuses of power by political authorities
because it is nothing like a feudal corporation. Industry enchains the enemies
of political liberty. Credit is incompatible with arbitrary power. Constant's
underlying argument was this: the abolition of private property and the
placing of all commercial activities under the control of the state could only
benefit the unpropertied classes if the enfranchised poor could, in turn,
control political authorities through full-time public surveillance. But that
is impossible under modern conditions, in societies based on a far-reaching
division of labor.

Meaningful participation in politics is itself dependent upon the state/
society distinction. Privacy is a support for publicity. In the industrial-
bureaucratic age, there can be no democracy without individual rights, no
political liberty without civil liberty. To detach men from their economic
independence by offering them "total" citizenship is but a shrewd dema-
gogical ploy.[113] When private independence has been destroyed, rulers will
hasten to despoil citizens of their political rights as well. If a government
annihilates private property, it can do anything it desires to its defenseless
citizens: "the arbitrary treatment of property is soon followed by the arbitrary treatment of persons."[114] Under modern conditions, the only guarantee of political influence is a sure foothold or bankbook out of the reach
of the state. The ultra attack on the purchasers of national lands was a
direct threat to representative government. The possibility of meaningful
discussion depends upon the right of opposition, and the right of opposition
(in turn) can only be guaranteed if the livelihood of citizens is independent
of political officials. Furthermore, creative debate in the political arena can
only occur if a unanimity of goals is not imposed upon individuals by their
community. Constant wanted to limit politics in order to create a certain
kind of politics: a politics of dissent and disagreement. His argument for
capitalism was not acquisitive but democratic: only a decentralized economy
will enable modern citizens to discuss political issues freely and exert influence on their elected officials.

This thesis brings us full circle. At the end of the 1819 lecture, Constant
asserted that private independence can be guaranteed only by political par-

ticipation. In the body of the lecture, he made the inverse claim: individual independence is not an alternative to self-rule, but a precondition for self-rule. The modern distinction between state and society makes democracy possible even in a large country. Viewed as a whole, Constant's argument was this: civil liberty and political liberty are mutually interdependent. The abolition of one will eventuate in the abrogation of the other. Contrariwise, an increase in one form of freedom does not logically imply a decrease in the other.[115] Indeed, each presupposes and vitalizes the other, and neither can survive in isolation. That is why Constant, in summarizing his position, urged his fellow citizens to integrate public action and private independence in a new pattern. Ancient and modern liberty should not be merely balanced but *combined*.

THREE

Rousseau and the Masks of Virtue

L'égoïsme sent le besoin de prendre pour étendard un principe.

THE dim myth that liberalism must always remain blind to the distortions of ideology and false consciousness[1] is exploded by even a casual reading of Constant's writings. Among the most highly charged words in his theoretical vocabulary are *voiler, déguiser, couvrir, travestir, revêtir, alléguer, donner le change,* and *feindre.* Indeed, Constant often writes as if, in an age of public opinion and fierce ideological strife, political thought is less impressive for the light it sheds on the social scene than for its capacity to disseminate darkness. That is the implication of a sharp distinction he draws between interests and opinions. "We hide our interests and display our opinions," he tells us, "because the former divide men and the latter unite them." The way opinions "unite" men, he goes on to say, is by fraud and deception: "A person can only guide *himself* by the calculation of his own interests, while if wants to engage others to cooperate with him he is obliged to put forward an opinion that will deceive them concerning his genuine aims."[2]

POLITICAL PRETEXTS

Like the philosophes, Constant was fascinated with political hoaxes and deceit.[3] He was disturbed most acutely by the way morally compelling ideas (ideas to which *he* was committed) could be misused, by the way they could be invoked to whitewash and legitimate atrocities. His careful analyses of the Revolution, the Empire, and the Restoration were quite dissimilar in most respects. In each case, however, he attended closely to "all those formulas destined to serve as pretexts for oppression."[4] This was a rich field of study since "the vocabulary of hypocrisy is inexhaustible."[5]

From La Rochefoucauld, among others, Constant inherited the notion that "the name of virtue serves self-interest just as usefully as do the vices."[6] One might even argue that this maxim (which was indeed a centerpiece of seventeenth-century French moral psychology) provided an insight inspiring all Constant's theoretical work: the mask of virtue fits almost any face.

Despite his growing sympathy toward religious ideas, for example, Constant clung to an eighteenth-century concern about the way in which genuine belief may "serve as a pretext" for entrenched clerical power. Under European absolutism, an important role was played by "a hypocritical theocracy, apeing conviction, parodying fanaticism, absolving the breach of promises, offering to justify tyranny in order afterwards to seize it and turn its agent into its slave. This theocracy was even more contemptible in its impostures than execrable in its fury." Primitive religions were used to justify pillage and conquest: "Peoples covered themselves with religious pretexts in order to attack each other with open force." In the modern age, the plea of anticipatory self-defense can be "a deft hypocrisy" useful for justifying an essentially aggressive war. "Authority, proud of its immense treasures, invents a thousand pretexts to spend them gloriously."[7] While there are countless pretexts *for* war, a war apparently declared for self-defense can also *be* a pretext:

> War will always be a method by which governments can enlarge
> their authority. It will be a distraction that despots offer their
> slaves to make them less conscious of their slavery. It will be a
> diversion used by the favorites of despots to prevent their mas-
> ters from examining too closely the details of their vexatious
> administration. It will allow demagogues to inflame the passions
> of the multitude, to plunge it into extremities that favor their
> violent counsels or their interested views.[8]

Concern with the power of falsehoods to legitimate atrocities permeates all Constant's writings. Even in *Adolphe*, the "austere principles of morality"[9] are invoked to justify and conceal society's petty malevolence against an unlucky woman. Returning to politics, the "pretext of a pretended necessity" or "the fertile pretext of extraordinary circumstances" can always be in-voked to justify misrule. Similarly, "reasons of utility can be found for any command and any prohibition." Scientific theories attributing a physiological superiority to the white race provided a "pretext" for the unbelievable cruelty of colonial powers. The illegalities of the Directory even led Constant to write of "my aversion to most of the measures taken under the pretext of consolidating the Republic." In 1820, the assassination of the Duc de Berry served the ultras "as a pretext to clamp irons on an innocent nation which recoiled in horror at that dreadful crime." Indeed, the entire Bourbon Restoration was "a terrible regime of lies, oppression, ruse, and deception." More generally, "the veil of the laws" and "the appearance of justice" can cloak and legitimate arbitrary government action. During the Revolution, "many retroactive laws were prefaced by metaphysical treatises wherein the very idea of retroactivity was obscured." In describing both the republican Directors of the Year VII and the royalist ministers of 1822, Constant used the phrase "un arbitraire hypocrite sous les formes constitutionnelles."[10]

For our purposes, the most important application of this general thesis occurs in Constant's retrospective commentaries on the French Revolution. These analyses invariably revolve around the following quite painful insight: "It is *in the name of liberty* that we were subjected to prison, executions, and countless harassments."[11] Freedom became "the plaything and pretext of every party."[12] Some historians have argued that revolutionary *fêtes*, costumes, and nomenclature were "too absurd to be dishonest."[13] But Constant thought that deceitful guile played just as important a role as autointoxication in the outbreak of the Terror.[14] The Jacobins confiscated the name of the people just as priests throughout history had confiscated the name of God. A passage from *De la religion* makes it clear that Enlightenment analyses of clerical fraud provided models for Constant's dissection of Jacobin imposture: "Among almost all ancient peoples, certain corporations made themselves masters of religious sentiments for their own profit. They usurped the right to speak in the name of invisible powers and, mendacious interpreters of these powers, ordered men drunk with terror to perform barbaric acts."[15] As an heir of the Enlightenment, Constant's concern was to expose the essentially unchanged strategies for oligarchic self-legitimation.

He explained one of the guiding premises behind his *Principes de politique* of 1802–06 in the following way: "There is no despotism in the world, however inept in its plans and however oppressive in its measures, which does not know how to allege an abstract goal that seems both plausible and desirable." Virtue may be held up as a deceptive mask: "The wielders or usurpers of authority can borrow the name of liberty to legitimate their encroachments because, unfortunately, words are infinitely plastic and obliging." This "flexibility of language supplies [political men] with many excuses." Throughout his writings, he returned to consider the numerous slogans that served as pretexts for oppression: "Men invested with authority always show a disposition to cloak themselves in mystery." He devoted much of the *Commentaire* to analyzing the "charlatanism" of "the masters of the world."[16] Novel about the despots who ruled France in the wake of the Revolution was the nonchalance with which they concocted self-justifications in the language of democracy and popular consent.[17] For example, the revolutionary appeal to classical republican ideals was often a self-serving excuse for personal revenge and private ambition. But even though "counterfeit liberty"[18] was an illusion, it had quite tangible political effects. One of Constant's main concerns was to explain how it worked.

Seekers and wielders of power can further their particular aims by systematically misdescribing the world, for example, by concealing their private interests behind "the pretext of the public good."[19] This is the ideological function of political theory. If men can lure others into accepting such public misdescriptions, into mistaking a decoy for the real thing, they will have disabled opposition and perhaps even gained outright support: "Reasons alleged publicly in favor of abuses are usually nothing but attempts to deceive and disarm public opinion." Pretexts generate popular compliance, and thus prolong misrule, by "falsifying opinion," that is to say, by softpeddling abuses, deflecting attention from controversial decisions, and obscuring who benefits and who suffers.[20] For Constant, there is nothing particularly mysterious or heroic about the "unity" of theory and practice. If you can dupe the public, you can literally get away with murder.

According to Goethe, Constant's most impressive trait was the tenaciously "practical" bent of his mind.[21] Constant liked to remark that "what seems absolutely convincing in theory is often impossible in practice."[22] His practicality and impatience with abstract speculation were visible in the question he doggedly asked of all political doctrines: cui bono? He always wanted to know if the theory in question could be employed as a deceptive mask or pretext and, if so, to whose advantage it would turn. He posed this very question about Rousseau's idea of popular sovereignty. This theory, Constant believed, legitimated revolutionary persecutions and trials for *incivisme*. But Rousseauism was responsible for the Terror only in the sense that it provided a convenient subterfuge behind which private hatreds, fears, whims, and interests could operate in a relatively unimpeded manner.

> This theory [Rousseau's theory of popular sovereignty] justified
> the horrors of our revolution, those horrors of which freedom
> was simultaneously the pretext and the victim. I do not mean
> to suggest that the countless crimes of which we were witnesses

and objects did not have the particular interests of the men who captured power as immediate causes. But these men had only been able to seize illegally the control of public force by covering with a veil the interests that guided them. They adduced principles and advanced apparently disinterested opinions that served as party–banners.[23]

Popular acquiescence in the 1793–94 phase of the Revolution was partly the product of fear. But it was also the result of a successful Jacobin propaganda campaign. The Committee of Public Safety had gulled important segments of the Parisian populace into believing that the heroic sacrifices demanded by the Terror actually served the common good. They fobbed off their particular and often arbitrary decisions as expressions of the general will. Thus the alibi of liberty (allied with "the pretext of public safety")[24] helped perpetuate the sickening Reign of Terror.

The central importance of pretexts in Constant's political writings has not been adequately appreciated. Its neglect has kept alive a number of fallacies about the essential structure and thrust of his thought. Constant's complex attitudes toward democratization and (not unrelatedly) toward the theories of Rousseau, can only be understood in light of his almost obsessive concern with public hypocrisy and fraud.

CONSTANT'S ALLEGED HOSTILITY TO DEMOCRATIC GOVERNMENT

It is common to describe the political alternatives in the postrevolutionary period as aligned along a single spectrum running from democratic to antidemocratic. Jacobins, it is often said, were "very democratic," the ultras were "very antidemocratic," and the liberals were "not very democratic."[25] But what did *democracy* mean between 1789 and 1830? Two things it did not mean were Athens without slaves (all citizens participating incessantly in direct self-government) or the system established only later, in which a variety of organized parties could compete for the right to govern through elections based on universal suffrage and held at regular intervals. Direct self-rule was unthinkable in a large modern state; and the time was not yet ripe for the emergence of a plurality of organized parties with a legalized opposition appealing to the universality of citizens. No individuals or groups actively advocated either system. To try to categorize theories and theorists according to their attitude toward either type of democracy is a futile exercise.

Jacobins distinguished themselves from the Girondins by a greater willingness, at least prior to the trial of the Herbertists, to use sans-culotte control of Paris streets to achieve their goals. But their attitude was no more "democratic" than that exhibited by the minority of bullies who intimidated the sectional assemblies.[26] It might be assumed that the question of universal suffrage would separate the sheep from the goats, the true democrats from the enemies of democracy. But the significance of universal suffrage cannot be established without an inquiry into the content of the vote and the nature of the institutions surrounding it, particularly the right of organized political opposition and freedom of the press. Ceremonial plebiscites make a mockery of universal suffrage. For a brief period in 1815, after the second fall of Napoleon and while France was occupied by foreign armies, some ultras favored a very broad suffrage because they believed that the Catholicism of the peasant majority (who were considered to be indifferent to republican politics) would solidify the counterrevolution. This was a strategy conceived to subserve party interests; but it did not reveal any hidden commitment to popular sovereignty on the part of the extreme Legitimists.

Issues can only be obscured by a casual application of the democratic/ antidemocratic scheme to theories, groups, and ideologies in the period between 1789 and 1830. The fundamental norm of liberal democracy is respect for opposition, a respect institutionalized in the legal inviolability of deputies. To the extent that men are ruled by conformism and intolerance, belief in the value of dissent and disagreement runs counter to a deep impulse in human nature.[27] It certainly ran counter to the experience of French deputies from 1791 to 1830.

The normative foundations of later democratic politics were first laid in the miniature format of the British Parliament. The Commons initially represented only a miniscule portion of the population. But if the improbable arrangement of government by discussion had not first evolved in the sheltered atmosphere of an upper-class club, would a subsequent process of "inclusion" have produced a system of a democratic kind? This is by no means certain. Universal suffrage did not lead to democratic government under the Convention, but rather to a dictatorship of the Committee of Public Safety. That may have been inevitable in a society without mass literacy. Under the Restoration, it is true, liberals did not plunge ecstatically into a battle for universal suffrage. Elections must be *organized* in a democratic manner, however, before universal suffrage can produce democratic politics. It is thus unwise to interpret liberal reticence about universal suffrage as a sign of some fundamental hostility toward democracy.

What kind of evidence is adduced to support the view that Constant opposed democratization?[28] First of all, he consistently argued that "the will of the majority is legitimate only if it does not violate any of the rights of the minority."[29] Second, during the early years of the Restoration, Constant agreed that voting rights should be restricted according to a relatively stringent property qualification. This accommodation to a widely accepted distinction between "active" and "passive" citizens has been construed as elitism and an ill-concealed expression of class bias.[30] Finally, Constant argued that Rousseau had done great harm to France by bringing the image of the ancient republic to the center of modern consciousness. His polemic against Rousseau and his outspoken repudiation of the classical concept of politics are consistently interpreted as attacks on democracy in the name of individual freedom.

To what extent does criticism of Rousseau imply a blanket repudiation of democracy? Does Constant's rejection of Rousseau's concept of popular sovereignty mean that he considered democracy dangerous to freedom? I have only come across one passage in which Constant wrote about the fear of democracy, and in it he scoffed at those who were afraid. The passage occurs in the chapter on England in the *Commentaire* of 1822, a chapter in which Constant expressed his sharp dissent from those Anglophiles at the center of the Chamber continuing the tradition of Mme. de Staël. Because of radical changes in the class structure, he wrote, even aristocrats who formerly spoke out as tribunes of the people were now "afraid of the democratic principles which are making progress."[31] Constant showed absolutely no sympathy for these nobles overtaken by time.

As a tireless advocate of representative government, Constant believed that all citizens should be admitted to participation in public affairs.[32] His target was the pretext of popular sovereignty invoked by a small political elite to legitimate its oppression of the majority of citizens. By rhetorically identifying itself with the people, the revolutionary government had been able to avoid effective control by the people.[33] To make way for a government that could be criticized and influenced by public opinion, Constant took a deflationary approach to democratic rhetoric.

TWO VIEWS OF ROUSSEAU

Constant was of two minds about Rousseau. On the one hand, he portrayed the most celebrated and reviled of his fellow Swiss as a metaphysical obscurantist and a political menace: "I know of no system of servitude that has consecrated more fatal errors than the eternal metaphysics of the *Contrat social*." Rousseau's thinking was "an absurd mixture of monarchist principles and republican opinions." The claim that the *Contrat social* furnished "the most terrible auxiliary to all forms of despotism" recurs with persistency throughout Constant's writings.[34] "Like Bossuet," he wrote in the last year of his life, "Rousseau became the private tutor of tyranny."[35] What disturbed him was the impression that "every time laws against freedom have been proposed, the authority of Jean-Jacques Rousseau has been invoked."[36] Such declamatory indictments, strung together in this way, do not speak particularly well for Constant. They incriminate him with having fathered the most banal of all misinterpretations of the *Contrat social*, the one that decrees it a "prototalitarian" defense of "democratic tyranny." At his most heated and least cautious, Constant appears to corroborate this suspicion: "It would be easy to demonstrate, by countless citations, that the crudest sophisms of the most ferocious apostles of the Terror, in the most revolting of circumstances, were nothing but the perfectly just consequences of the principles of Rousseau."[37] The perfectly just consequences![38]

Despite these vituperations, Constant also venerated Rousseau and in many respects considered himself a devout Rousseauist.[39] For example, he always referred to the author of the *Contrat social* as "that sublime genius," "one of the most resplendent geniuses of the eighteenth century," and as a man animated by "the purest love of liberty."[40] He frequently alluded to the "glory" that Rousseau won in defending "courageous truths." Among the many great publicists of the eighteenth century, Rousseau was "the first to have popularized the sentiment of our rights." His writings awakened "all generous hearts and independent minds."[41] Moreover, Constant's admiration extended beyond the person to the doctrine. He endorsed Rousseau's belief that all laws must be general: they must make no mention of particular persons or cases,[42] and he consistently defined "the sovereignty of the people" as "the supremacy of the general will over every particular will," defending it on that basis. He characterized popular sovereignty as a principle that "cannot be contested." He was quite emphatic on this point: "there are only two powers in the world. One is illegitimate: that is force. The other is legitimate: that is the general will." Constant's intellectual affinity with Rousseau was in fact pervasive. While altering the emphasis, he employed the same ancient/modern pattern of analysis popularized by Rousseau; and he accepted the basic claims of the *Discours sur l'origine de l'inégalité:* modern men are afflicted by a fundamental self-division; they lead a largely artificial life, existing more in the opinions of others than for themselves. He vowed "never" to associate himself with the opponents of "this great man."[43]

But how was it possible for Constant to reconcile such drastically conflicting attitudes toward Rousseau? How could he view Rousseau both as an ally and an enemy? Constant was no doubt aware of an acute inner conflict in his own thinking about this matter. I feel strongly compelled to attack Rousseau, he tells us, but whenever I do so "je suis en défiance avec moi même."[44] This was not the only time Constant felt misgivings about his own misgivings. But the tension that marked his attitude toward Rousseau deserves special attention. It provides an essential clue for understanding ing the basic thrust and pattern of Constant's mature political thought. Above all, it suggests why Constant's commitment to individual rights against the state cannot ultimately be described as antidemocratic and why his embrace of modern liberty cannot be dismissed as an expression of fear of lower-class involvement in politics.

ROUSSEAUIST AND ANTI-ROUSSEAUIST ELEMENTS IN CONSTANT'S THINKING

The gulf between Constant and Rousseau is wide and easy to define. In the former's writings, we find no trace of Rousseau's attack on the arts and sciences,[45] just as we find no romanticization of nature and no hymns to rustic paradise. They differ substantially on a whole range of political issues: representation, civil religion, the theory of social change, the value of natural inequalities, the structure of the best government, the value of commerce, pluralism, civility, patriotism, cosmopolitanism, and the autonomy of civil society. Constant emphatically rejected the perverse suggestion that there can be no genuine political freedom without slavery.[46] Accepting Rousseau's claim that modern commercial society creates a thick network of interdependencies, he did not despair, because he also believed that such a society provided workable strategems for warding off mutual interference. Unlike Rousseau, moreover, he could not be *totally* sure that he preferred sincerity to hypocrisy or truth to lying. He was never tempted to heroize the social delinquent with a pure heart. Indeed, there seems to have been no form of moral purity he found particularly attractive or convincing. Although, or rather because, he was an active social reformer, Constant never chose to depict himself as engaged in a one-man war against modern vice and degeneration.[47] He was as aware as Rousseau of the existence of evil: he campaigned with unrelenting fierceness for the suppression of the slave trade. But he never considered himself an embodiment of goodness and virtue, finding moral exhibitionism repugnant, not refreshing. One of the central themes of *Adolphe* is the odiousness of men who try to shirk their sins by confessing them.[48] The essential evasiveness of self-revelation may be what made Rousseau's *Confessions* unpalatable to generations of Protestant readers.

More important to our concerns is the contrast between Rousseau's and Constant's attitudes toward Sparta. Rousseau admired Sparta because its legislator did not leave the people "a moment of respite that they could call their own." The total identification of each individual with his community transformed Spartans into "beings more than merely human."[49] Constant ordinarily expressed distaste for Spartan life. He agreed with Rousseau that "Sparta was precisely the opposite of a free state as the moderns conceive of it."[50] But he considered this to be a defect of Sparta, not a failing on the part of its modern critics. Echoing a famous passage in *De l'esprit des lois,* he contemptuously described that city as a warriors' monastery. He especially disliked what Rousseau most admired: the extent to which every individual's existence was "englobed within social existence" and political absenteeism and indifference were viewed as crimes against the state. Man should be a citizen, but only partly so: freedom requires simultaneous access to distinct public and private realms. Rousseau interpreted this sort of social dichotomy as a sign of weakness and corruption. He also believed that genuine loyalty to one's community required fierce prejudice against outsiders. For Constant, any patriotism that implied xenophobia was self-discrediting.[51]

The anti-Rousseauist strain in Constant's thought is undeniable and important. Nevertheless, it has frequently been exaggerated. As a result, the important ways in which Constant had an irreducibly ambivalent attitude toward Rousseau have been neglected. The need to achieve a more balanced view can be driven home by citing the posthumous *Du polythéisme romain,* where Constant compares the Spartans favorably with his own contemporaries: "Among all peoples, the Spartans [were] the least afflicted with vanity, the most disposed to forget themselves in order to fix their sights on a common goal, the most exempt from that narrow and personal restlessness which adopts a thousand paltry goals and scurries in all directions to attain them." The theoretical affinity between Rousseau and Constant becomes even more apparent when we recall Rousseau's nostalgia-repudiating claim that "the ancient peoples are no longer a model for the moderns."[52] This statement is striking to a student of Constant because it seems virtually indistinguishable from the central thesis of the 1819 lecture, a work that is typically read as a no-holds-barred attack on Rousseau. Despite important differences, Constant was, at least in *some* respects, in profound agreement with Rousseau. To explain the authentic duplicity marking Constant's attitude toward him, however, we must examine the way in which he simultaneously accepted and modified Rousseau's claim that classical republicanism was no longer a plausible model for modern political life.

The aspect of Rousseau's thought with which Constant felt the most comfortable was, without any question, his attack on the stratified and organic old regime: "The *ancien régime* was a mixture of corruption, weakness, and arbitrary power." But Rousseau, in his onslaught against aristocratic hierarchy, relied much too heavily on the counterimage of the egalitarian and organic *polis*. As Constant noted, this appeal to antiquity was common in the eighteenth century, an age "when our philosophes, impelled by the desire to undermine European institutions (institutions which I certainly do not wish to justify) found it safe and convenient to attack them by drawing indirect comparisons. In order to render these comparisons more striking and conclusive, they searched in remote places for subjects to praise."[53] Constant was just as uncomfortable with classical as with feudal organicism. He would not have invoked the *polis* in order to denounce the old regime. Here lies an important though incomplete answer to our question: Constant inherited Rousseau's problem while rejecting his solution. He shared Rousseau's revulsions but could not accept his aspirations.

Rousseau, however, did not really view this Spartan utopia as a "solution," and Constant knew it. Sparta was irrecoverable. It could be invoked only as a stinging indictment of French society. The idea of complete subordination of a citizen to his city could function in this way because total membership was thought to rescue an individual from all "personal dependence." Paradoxically, Rousseau conceived engulfment in an impersonal *polis* as a form of negative liberty. Reduced to essentials, it meant freedom *from* the personal domination of a landlord or equivalent old-regime superior. In a very important sense, Rousseau's freedom was individual independence.[54]

While Constant wholeheartedly accepted Rousseau's attack on the inequalities of the old regime, he was repelled by the utopian counterimage Rousseau held up as a rebuke to aristocratic and Catholic France. He was repelled for two reasons: he found Sparta in some respects more cruel and humanly suffocating than eighteenth-century Europe; and he thought that Rousseau's censure of the old regime was misdirected. Rousseau did not limit himself to the ordinary enlightened criticism of traditional abuses. He proceeded to a much more questionable attack on various new elements in eighteenth-century French society: secularism, cosmopolitanism, and the relaxation of traditional prejudices against commercial life. Constant did not view these new trends as progressive in any naively onward-and-upward sense. He thought they encouraged the spread of materialistic and what he called "egotistic attitudes; but he also recognized theircontribution to the destruction of caste structure, as well as to the cordializing of bolld feuds, martial habits, and religious hatreds. Thus, he could not spurn them as mere signs of moral depravity.

The parallels and similarities between the two theorists are impressive. Constant's distaste for Rousseau's Spartan utopia was strongest during the early part of his career, when he was still reacting to the tragedies of 1793–94. In the manuscripts of 1800–06, just as in all the works published after 1817, Constant's fierce antipathy toward the old regime was unmistakable. "No one has fought against heredity more intensely than I," he quite accurately reported. He referred to the institutions of the old regime as "this cruel and bizarre ensemble." The eighteenth-century peasantry were "helots defrauded of all rights, burdened with all labors, and condemned to all deprivations." Noblemen routinely labeled commoners *hommes de rien*, which tells you all you need to know about the old regime.[55] Remarks such as these help to qualify the half-truth that Constant belonged to a great liberal tradition running in an unbroken line from Montesquieu to Tocqueville. The important thing to recall about Montesquieu is that he defended constitutional government in the name of the same heredity-based society which Rousseau hated: "The immortal author of the *Spirit of the Laws* often showed himself a zealous partisan of inequality and privilege."[56] But, disregarding for a moment the exceptional years of 1813–15, Constant devoted his political life to abolishing the vestiges of the old regime.[57] His constitutionalism was as hostile to hereditary prerogatives as it was to Robespierrist or Bonapartist dictatorship. His defense of limited government contained not the slightest trace of nostalgia for gothic Europe. Liberal freedom bore no relation to aristocratic privileges.[58] Constant's constitutionalism was meant to serve an heredity-free society. In this respect, if not in others, he was in full accord with Rousseau.

Constant's genuinely divided attitude toward Rousseau can also be illustrated by his interpretation of the doctrine of popular sovereignty. His emphatic endorsement of it was a rejection of the inflated sovereignty of absolutist kings: "The universality of citizens is sovereign; that is to say, no individual, no faction, no partial association can arrogate itself the sovereignty which has not been delegated to it."[59] Though Constant affirmed this negative side of Rousseau's principle, he was well aware that there was another, much less palatable, side to the idea of popular sovereignty. Rousseau ascribed, or seemed to ascribe, to the assembled citizenry the same sort of unlimited discretionary authority claimed by absolutist kings. In this, he echoed Hobbes: "It is of the essence of sovereign power to be illimitable; it is either omnipotent or it is nothing."[60] The crucial misstep in Rousseau's theory of popular sovereignty was this naive transfer of "the mystery of authority" from the king to the people or the nation as a whole. Rousseau saw democratization not as a transformation in the nature of sovereignty but as a mere shift in the location of sovereignty. According to Sieyès—and Constant quoted him approvingly in this context—the second-rate Rousseauists of the Revolution repeated Rousseau's fatal mistake. The unconscious grip of vestigial royalism on the popular imagination explained the tendency of revolutionary orators to hedge the first French republic with a semblance of divinity. This inverted echo of monarchial ideas was almost inevitable:

> Rousseau and the writers who most loved freedom were mistaken when they ascribed to society a power without limits. But their error came from the way they formed their ideas about politics. They saw in history a small number of men, or even one man alone, possessing immense power and perpetuating great wrongs. But their anger was directed against the wielders of power rather than against the power itself. Instead of destroying this power, they only dreamed of shifting its location.[61]

As a repudiation of the king's monopoly of political power, the principle of popular sovereignty need not and indeed cannot be contested. To the extent that it is a surreptititious continuation of the absolutist tradition, however, this principle must be criticized and revised. Bestowing political power on the nation does not require that this power be unlimited. A geniune democracy will not replicate the royal whimsy expressed in *tel est mon bon plaisir*. For sovereignty to be democratic, it must be organized within the framework of a liberal constitution.

ROUSSEAU'S INAPPLICABLE THEORY

Constant believed that the fundamental pattern of Rousseau's thought was self-correction. Rousseau typically proceeded "by tearing down with one hand what he has built up with the other."[62] Rousseau would first build up an image or an ideal: he would make a very forceful argument for unlimited popular sovereignty or Spartan regimentation. But he would then embroider his positive assertions with a sequence of caveats, provisos, and disabling clauses that rendered them completely harmless because inapplicable to the real world. Almost all those who have tried to explicate Rousseau's system have made the mistake of thinking him simply "inconsistent." But the deeper coherence of Rousseau's thought lies precisely here, in the care he took to construct "une théorie inapplicable." Rousseau designed his idea of unlimited popular sovereignty as a denunciation of monarchical, aristocratic, and clerical Europe. But when he turned to look at the monster he had created, he was "terrified." To rescue himself, "he declared that sovereignty could neither be alienated, nor delegated, nor represented. This was to say, using imprecise language, that sovereignty could not be exercised. [To declare that sovereignty could not be alienated] was, in fact, to annihilate the very principle he had just proclaimed."[63] Far from being a weakness, this sort of palinode revealed Rousseau's true genius. "I love to see the human soul revolt against itself," Constant wrote elsewhere. Rousseau's inconsistencies revealed his commitment to liberty and an underlying awareness that even his own most precious ideas might be hideously misused.

Because Rousseau did not consider Sparta a feasible ideal, he suggested banishing the words for *patrie* and *citoyen* from every modern language.[64] He insisted that the unwieldy size and large populations of modern states, the abolition of slavery, the degeneration of morals due to the influence of commerce, and especially the inappropriateness of Christianity as a civic religion all conspired to make the ideal of total citizenship impracticable in present-day societies. The situation had changed so drastically that ancient peoples no longer *could* be a model for the moderns.

By stressing Rousseau's self-subversion, Constant inadvertently revealed a central pattern within his own thought (see chap. 8). Attempts at a rapprochement, however, should not be exaggerated. Instead of revealing Constant's ambivalent view of Rousseau, they may make Constant seem uncritically Rousseauist. By overemphasizing the continuities between the two theorists, we risk obscuring the reason why Constant authored the string of damning indictments cited above.

To right the balance, we need only show that the *absence* of a constructive side to Rousseau's thought was itself a serious fault in Constant's eyes. While Rousseau was surely "the most eloquent enemy" of the old regime, and while he was impatient with the moral corruption around him, he never set his considerable imagination to the task of conceiving untried solutions to urgent social problems: "By his prodigious force, he grasped the columns upon which human existence somehow rested; and he tore them loose from their ancient foundations. But he was a blind architect. He was unable to construct a new edifice out of the scattered rubble."[65] Though a devastating critic, Rousseau was unwilling to make suggestions about improvements for the future; he offered a grim diagnosis without giving any thought to a cure. Indeed, his pessimistic image of contemporary society mocked all attempts at reform. He could sustain his marvelously uncompromising tone because he took no responsibility. This self-righteousness, this self-exculpating form of impracticality, was one reason why Constant (despite his Rousseauist commitments) felt the need to distance himself so unequivocally from Rousseau.

LACONIC CITIZENS

In one sense, it is impossible *not* to have several contradictory responses to Rousseau. Being of two minds results quite naturally from an encounter with the contradictory sides of Rousseau's own thought. What I am thinking of here is not the disparity between Rousseau's two ideals: stern citizenship and bucolic independence, Sparta and Clarens. I am referring instead to an antinomy within the *Contrat social* itself. This antinomy or "contradiction" is an important element in my story. It helps to explain how Constant could have been simultaneously attracted and repelled by Rousseau's political thought.

In the *Contrat social*, Rousseau explained his concept of civic membership in differing ways. Indeed, the relation between part and whole, particular and universal, individual and community was described in two conflicting languages: the language of contract or voluntary consent and the language of organicism or involuntary socialization. Sometimes Rousseau tries to combine or fuse these two ways of talking about membership. For example, his basic argument suggests the unintentionally comic metaphor of a body politic whose limbs willingly covenant to become members of an organic whole. But the very absurdity and strained quality of this image reveals the tension between two distinct ways in which Rousseau conceived of civic belonging.

Spartan children signed no social contract. Being "denatured" by a heroic Legislator is nothing like entering into a voluntary partnership. But Rousseau's major political treatise is in some sense a contractarian work. This paradox is expressed most sharply in Rousseau's two dissimilar (and not clearly related) accounts of how a people is initially founded or comes into being. At one point, he suggests that a people is founded by consent, compact, or convention. Harassed by the state of nature, individuals assemble and *decide* that it is in their common interest to join forces.[66] In another and equally famous passage, Rousseau says that a people is founded by a Legislator. This semidivine figure molds the moist clay of presocial individuals and stamps a common identity on them from the outside.[67] In other words, Rousseau sometimes emphasizes the autonomous and voluntary side of association; at other times, the heteronomous and involuntary side. these two aspects of membership (freely willed partnership and socialization by a semidivine Legislator) both have venerable pedigrees going back to antiquity. But in the *Contrat social* they jostle and grate upon one another uncomfortably.

This complexity, I think, helps to explain what is ultimately dissatisfying about the usual contrast made between a liberalism that promotes "the minimal state, individualism and laissez-faire" and a more radically collectivist position that is "democratic, Rousseauesque and *étatiste*."[68] According to this dichotomy, Constant and Rousseau belong to opposite camps. Such pigeonholing is inadequate. Indeed, we should probably abandon the notion of two neatly distinguishable democratic traditions: one liberal, the other radical; one individualist, the other collectivist; one Lockean, the other Rousseauist. There are important individualistic and liberal elements in the *Contrat social* itself. Not surprisingly, it was these aspects of Rousseau's thought which attracted Constant. Rousseau shifted away from the language of organicism toward the language of individualism, contract, and consent whenever he attacked the heteronomous features of the old regime. Hereditary monarchy and the aristocratic system thrived on the idea that men must passively submit to their natural superiors. The ideal of "prescribing laws to oneself" provided a potent alternative to the nonvoluntary or hereditary aspects of the traditional social order.

Constant unhesitatingly embraced this negative aspect of Rousseau's thought as the basis for his own theory. But Rousseau also lapsed frequently into organicist language and imagery. Whenever he did so, Constant's basically anti-Spartan sentiments came to the fore. Rousseau stressed the heteronomous, Legislator-stipulated features of civic membership when concentrating on his utopian vision of Sparta. Arguably, the passive and involuntary aspect of citizenship became central to Rousseau whenever he offered political participation as a hypothetical cure for the terrible bifurcation of modern man.[69] Constant was neither insensitive to nor complacent about self-dividedness. He recognized that it could be painful, but he also stressed its potential benefits (as in his analysis of Rousseau's war against himself). Certainly he never imagined that such a personal disease could be cured by political authority or community.

Putting these questions aside for a moment, let us examine more closely the Spartan ideal. Spartanization was not a voluntary process: the citizens' "common will" was a product of their common indoctrination as children. In no sense can they be said to have prescribed to themselves the *polis*-founding regimen. But Spartans were also closed-lipped and laconic. They were not disputatious. They were shy of words and public speech.[70]

Reflecting on this aspect of Spartan life (and expanding on his distrust of "cabals"), Rousseau wrote that the general will predominates because citizens "have no communication among themselves." Indeed, verbal exchange is an ominous sign. It suggests that Legislator-produced unanimity has broken down: "Long debates, disagreements, and tumult indicate the ascendance of private interests and the decline of the state."[71] Thus, when speaking in his organicist mode, Rousseau denigrates the significance of public speech in political life. Language bears the same taint as money: it is a storehouse for eccentric choices, alternatives open to the socially unsupervised discretion of individuals. A common language, far from guaranteeing moral consensus, makes permanently available the chance to say no, to disagree and dissent. Rousseau was more of a nonconformist than Constant; but he found the very thought of personal choice and deviance profoundly disturbing. The liberal idea that public disagreement plays a creative role in self-government does not appear in the *Contrat social*.[72] Indeed, the right of opposition played no more important a role in Rousseau's Spartan utopia than it had in the ideology of absolute monarchy.

ROUSSEAUISM AS A POLITICAL PRETEXT

We are now in a position to understand the meaning of those harsh denunciations of Rousseau. Nothing was further from Constant's mind than the suggestion that Rousseau was responsible for the outbreak of the French Revolution. Of this subject he had a much less bookish view: the Revolution was caused, in the long run, by the gradual diffusion of property and *lumières* and, in the short run, by "a deficit of sixty million." The most succinct statement of the charge he wanted to level at Rousseau was this: "In our day, the subtle metaphysics of the *Contrat social* is only proper for furnishing weapons and pretexts to all sorts of tyranny."[73] This brings us back to the pivotal concept of political pretexts.

Consider what at first may seem like a serious confusion in Constant's analysis of sovereignty. On the one hand, society as a whole has *no right* to exercise unlimited popular sovereignty over the lives of its individual citizens. On the other hand, society as a whole is an "abstract being" and not a political agent; it is thus objectively unable to exercise sovereignty of any sort. But why did Constant deny society a "right" that society could not possibly exploit?

The apparent confusion here stems from preconceptions about nineteenth-century liberalism that we bring with us to the study of Constant. Because of the influence of Tocqueville and Mill, we have a tendency to

assume that Constant, too, was worried about the tyranny of the majority
and about the intellectual dangers of leveling conformism. But Constant
was a *niveleur*. He was untroubled by the thought of democratic mediocrity
swamping aristocratic excellence. In the first volume of the *Commentaire*,
published in 1822, he distinguished his own position sharply from Guizot's:
"The time when it was said that everything must be done for the people
and nothing by the people now has passed."[74] Eventually, all citizens should
participate in determining goals and policies, even though they will never
be able directly to enact and execute laws. In the same passage, representative
government is defined as nothing but the admission of the people to participation in public affairs.

Constant never viewed direct popular self-rule as a threat to individual
liberty, because he did not believe direct popular self-rule could exist—at
least not in modern Europe. His statements about the conflict between
private rights and democratic power were therefore formulated with caution: "The *abstract recognition* of the sovereignty of the people in no way
augments the sum of individual liberty. And if we *attribute* to this sovereignty a latitude that it must not have, liberty can be lost despite this principle
or even through this principle."[75] The peril Constant discerned lay not in
the existence of self-government, but rather in shrewd dictators capable of
manipulating a sham democracy: "Nothing is more horrible than the despotism of a single man or several men, reigning with the authority and in
the name of all." Jacobins had shown that the semblance of popular sovereignty could be misused to legitimate not the tyranny of the majority but
the seizure of power by a few.

Rousseau's impracticality again became an issue at this point. He may
have stipulated that sovereign lawmaking or law-ratifying power cannot be
delegated, but in the real world, we cannot avoid "a practical organization
of authority." Executive power will tend to follow a version of the iron law
of oligarchy: if you try to grant such power to "society as a whole" it will
"necessarily pass . . . into the hands of a few men, often into a single hand."[76]

The "community as a whole" is a cloud-enfolded abstraction. If you
try to alienate your rights to such a mirage, you will soon discover that you
have actually handed yourself over to particular men "who act in the name
of all." Rousseau ascribed various "attributs préservateurs" to the "abstract
being that he calls sovereign." Because conditions are equal for all partners,
he argued, no one has an interest in rendering conditions more onerous for
others. By giving yourself to all, you give yourself to no one in particular.
Every citizen has acquired the same rights over his associates as he has

granted to them over himself. You gain the equivalent of what you lose with more force to conserve what you have.

All this sounds quite reassuring until it comes to a practical organization of authority, to the unavoidable *delegation* of communal power to government agents: "Whether we desire it or not, actions performed in the name of all are in the hands of a few men. Thus, it is not true that in giving yourself to everyone you give yourself to no one in particular. On the contrary, you give yourself to those who act in the name of all."[77] In giving yourself away entirely, you do not enter into "a condition equal for all" because "a few gain exclusive advantage from the sacrifices of the others." It is not true that "no one has an interest in rendering the common condition onerous for others" because there exist "associates who are outside the common conditions." Finally, if you give up your rights to the mythical "sovereign community," you will not get back the equivalent of what you lose. Indeed, you will help establish a force that may confiscate whatever you have.[78]

Constant was not seriously afraid that individual privacy and independence might be sacrificed to *l'autorité sociale*. The "authority of society" did not exist except as a pretext. During the Revolution, predictably enough, the loss of private security was not accompanied by any gain in popular power. In fact, direct democratic self-rule was never a genuine possibility. Thus, Constant could never have viewed it as a real threat.

Constant did not believe that the Terror resulted from a sincere desire to make democracy perfect. The sincerity or insincerity of the Jacobins was of secondary importance in any case. The pertinent question was this: which small group of men would seize the state and for whose benefit? There was never any chance that the community or a majority of it would actually wield power. How could it? Consider the following passage in which Constant made this crucial turn: "A people that can do anything it wants is dangerous, nay, more dangerous than a tyrant; or rather, it is certain that a tyrant will seize the right accorded to the people." Except for the very special case of religious freedom, Constant never feared a genuine tyranny of the majority in France. What worried him considerably, on the other hand, was the tyranny of a few hiding behind a façade of majoritarian rule. Not the people, but those who illicitly usurp the name of the people are the true "candidats de tyrannie."[79]

The Rousseauist ideology of popular sovereignty also allowed rulers to evade accountability by deflecting ascriptions of personal agency: "Since the general will can do anything, its representatives are all the more formidable because they portray themselves as docile instruments of this sham will."[80] The very idea of a superindividual "public will" makes it possible for individual power-wielders to pose as passive transmitters, and thus to conceal their own personal responsibilities. Constant distrusted anti-individualism for this reason: he was fiercely opposed to rhetorical sleights-of-hand that might camouflage executive, legislative, or judicial discretion. "No group," he said, "can claim *le privilége des ténébres.*"[81] Later, but in the same spirit, he was to focus on dispelling the royal shadow that concealed the responsibility of ministers.[82]

A further source of Constant's individualist bias should be mentioned here. "By invoking the limitless extent of society's authority," the self-selected representatives of the general will were able to legitimate crimes "that no tyrant would dare do in his own name." The *toute-puissance* ascribed to the people as a whole "only exists to justify the encroachments of a few." The *Contrat social* is a pernicious book because it makes available to republicans and pseudorepublicans a language of justification that rad-ically overlegitimates political authority. Rousseau's language seems like a form of inverted royalism because it contains the following implication: political decisions or actions can be legitimized *by their source alone* without reference to their content or consequences. Constant believed that "the legitimacy of authority depends on its object as much as on its source."[83]

Why did Constant say that society has no "right" to act in a certain way, *even though* he also believed that society had no capacity to act in such a way? To deny society the right of total sovereignty over all individual citizens was to discredit a language of justification, to make it unavailable for rhetorical misuse. The main task Constant assigned to political jour-nalism was to dispel the pretexts of oppression. His arguments against Rousseau, as a result, do not constitute evidence for the antidemocratic nature of his basic position.[84] The Revolution did not "veer off course" because the people as a whole took their destiny into their own hands. Nothing of that sort ever happened. Democracy as a pretext, not democracy as a reality, was the target of his attack.

Napoleon's deployment of democratic "opinions" was another prime example of this general maxim: private interests seek weapons in publicly plausible opinions. "Bonaparte always recognized the sovereignty of the people, at least in principle. He often invoked it to justify the excesses of the power he had in fact seized but which he pretended was delegated to him by the people themselves." In order to counter Napoleon's incantatory appeals to the doctrine of popular sovereignty, Constant continued, "this theory had to be attacked in order to destroy a dangerous weapon that was in the hands of a man who had abused it too often."[85] Changing metaphors, Constant went on to predict that "if you tear the flag, the army will disband." If you can convince the world that the people as a whole has no right to unlimited sovereignty over the lives of individuals, demagogues and dictators will no longer be tempted to invoke popular sovereignty as a pretext for their own acts. Thus you will disarm potential despots who draw legitimacy from a source which, "even if it were real" (which it is not), would have no power to sanction anything of the sort.[86] Constant, who never doubted Rousseau's brilliance, subtlety, and passionate love of liberty, was anxious to remove the *Contrat social* from the justificatory arsenal of the wielders of power. This simple interpretation reconciles the extreme bitterness of Constant's attacks on Rousseau with the equal ebullience of his praise.

Constant's severe criticisms of Rousseau should be understood as part of his overall response to the age of ideology and ideological struggle. The French Revolution introduced a new rhetorical opportunity into politics: tyranny could be simultaneously justified and concealed by a fraudulent appeal to democratic ideals. Confronted by this portentous innovation, liberal theory was obliged to focus increasingly on the gulf between seeming and being, appearance and reality. Predictably, Constant aimed at discrediting inspired doctrines that served to veil the realities of political power. As a provisioner of pretexts, Rousseau fell victim to Constant's endeavor to disarm the enemies he encountered at the outset of his career.

THE MASK OF CONSENT

It seems fair to mention that, according to Rousseau himself, centralized executives have a tendency to confiscate all political power in the long run.[87] Constant went beyond Rousseau only in the pervasiveness of his concern with the democratic veil behind which such an antidemocratic slippage of authority may occur. Also new, perhaps, was Constant's idea that sovereign lawmaking or law-ratifying power is subject to an even more subtle form of oligarchical usurpation.

From Diderot and others, as well as from Rousseau, Constant inherited the notion that consent is the sole valid source of political legitimacy.[88] From Robespierre and Napoleon, he learned that consent can be faked and even manufactured by the government itself. When he spoke about a "parody of liberty," and "a fraudulent simulacrum of liberty," he did not simply mean to say that both Revolutionary demagogues and Napoleon justified their acts by invoking the *name* of liberty. He was also referring to the production of "an artificial consent," or the "simulation of consent," or the "appearance of the will of the people." This is what he meant when he said that the Revolution inflicted upon "sacred principles . . . wounds perhaps difficult to heal."[89] Rousseau's fantasy that, in an ideal state, citizens "as subjects" would obey the very laws they had voted on when assembled "as the sovereign," provided Constant with an occasion to reiterate his principal quarrel with the *Contrat social:* "The people, Rousseau observes, is sovereign in one respect and subject in another. But in practice these two respects are confounded. By oppressing the people as subjects, it is easy for men in power to compel the people as sovereign to express whatever *will* is dictated to them."[90] The self-appointed "representatives of the general will" are especially dangerous "because they have in their hands the means of force or seduction necessary to assure that [public opinion] manifests itself in the manner they find convenient."[91] A dictator may pretend to follow orders while surreptitiously writing the orders himself.[92] The very idea of government by consent was challenged by "derisory appeals to the people, whom one oppresses even while feigning to consult them." The most common mechanism for simulating popular consent is the plebiscite: "There exists, I know, artificial means for surrounding violations of the constitution with an appearance of legitimacy. The people are encouraged to pronounce themselves . . . and they are compelled to sanction unprecedented measures." Plebiscites are the homage tyrannical vice pays to democratic virtue.[93]

These passages bring us close to the nerve-point of Constant's thought about the Revolutionary and Napoleonic periods. He never equivocated about his principled devotion to public opinion.[94] But he also never forgot the obvious lesson of his age: that public opinion is subject to "une contrefaction mensongère."[95] Even the leading revolutionaries inadvertently bore witness to this fact.

Under the influence of Rousseau, Robespierre often called himself and his colleagues *précepteurs* of the people, rather than (potentially corruptible) representatives of the people. Constitutional government might conserve freedom, but revolutionary government aimed at founding the Republic and creating the new republican man. Constant, disturbed by the rhetorical abuse of ancient republican ideals in modern contexts, was also anxious to reject an important aspect of ancient political life itself, a dimension which Rousseau had gone out of his way to publicize and promote. Every enduring regime was initially founded by a semidivine Legislator who imperiously charted its future course. This point also bears repeating: what Constant repudiated most emphatically about the classical paradigm was not republicanism or popular sovereignty, but moral education and soulcraft. His polemic was aimed against those who "confer on the legislator an almost unlimited mastery over human life."[96]

The *Contrat social* was adduced as a pretext for tyranny only because second-rate Rousseauists ignored Rousseau's own saving inconsistency. By eliminating his apparent contradictions, the revolutionaries showed that they were the truly "bad logicians." They bowdlerized Rousseau's thought. They erased the crucial element of self-erasure: "They adopted Rousseau's principle, while separating it from everything that rendered it less dangerous."[97] Only by ignoring his strictures against a Legislator's creating classical republican citizens in a large country and against imposing new customs on an old civilization could Robespierre and others invoke Rousseau as a justification for their own acts:

> In his treatise on the government of Poland, Jean-Jacques Rousseau wisely emphasizes the obstacles encountered when new *moeurs* and habits are introduced into a nation. . . . Unfortunately, only Rousseau's absolute principles, his Spartan fanaticism, and everything that is inapplicable and tyrannical in his theories have been borrowed. His most enthusiastic partisans and admirers only embrace his defective side.[98]

Rousseau's theories were used as a pretext for Revolutionary crimes, but only because they had been half understood. It was no accident that Rousseau was half understood, however, since "many chapters of the *Contrat social* are worthy of scholastic writers of the fifteenth century."[99]

THE MASK OF SPARTAN VIRTUE

Constant followed Rousseau in his aversion to the heredity-based old regime and in his belief that ancient citizenship cannot be revived *de nos jours*. His denunciations of Rousseau were essentially strategic. They were acts of political prudence. He wanted to make it unlikely that rulers would employ Rousseau's language, and especially his emotionally charged doctrine of popular sovereignty, to obfuscate the realities of unequally distributed political power.

Constant's obsession with masks and pretexts itself is exactly what one would have expected from a careful reader of Rousseau. In the *Confessions,* we learn that La Rochefoucauld painted society as it truly is. Rousseau loathed the prevailing tartuffery, and wrote caustically of "vice that assumes the mask of virtue."[100] His description of a corrupt state, in the *Contrat social,* is even more striking: "the basest interest shamelessly adopts the sacred name of the public good . . . and one falsely passes under the name of laws iniquitous decrees whose only goal is the interest of individuals."[101] These remarks should help us renew our sense of Constant's indebtedness to Rousseau. They also make it possible to pose afresh the question of what separates the two.

Rousseau defined freedom in the stoic or Spinozistic manner as a coincidence of needs and capacities. A man is free when his desires are matched by his ability to satisfy them. With the material improvement of European societies, needs began to proliferate out of all control.[102] Rousseau invoked the harsh and repressive discipline of Sparta to express his abhorrence of this development which, he thought, could only engender new forms of servile social interdependence. He pessimistically suggested that freedom is impossible in large societies based on commercial exchange and the division of labor. Unwilling to follow Rousseau in such a moralistic repudiation of the modern age, Constant chose to redefine freedom. He conceived it, in a much more radical way, as a function of available opportunities, without any necessary reference to happiness, human wholeness, or the satisfaction of genuine wants.

Constant divorced freedom from its classical association with welfare and self-realization. He defined it not as the accomplishment of one's aims or the unfolding of one's authentic self, but rather as the genuine availability of numerous important possibilities: "freedom, as the human mind understands it, consists precisely in the ability to choose between alternatives."[103] For a person to be free, social institutions and norms must offer a variety of attractive alternatives and, equally important, the individual must be personally capable of evaluating and exploiting them.[104] "Freedom" means that valuable possibilities exist and are accessible, not that one correct or rational action has been chosen. From Rousseau, Constant learned that a plethora of choices is unlikely to increase psychological contentment because, even if other resources are plentiful, time will always be scarce. Unlike Rousseau, however, Constant believed that freedom and frustration were intimately related.[105]

On the issue of pretexts, Constant parted company with Rousseau because of his intense focus on the classical republican rhetoric and symbolism misused by modern demagogues. While Rousseau was quite sensitive to the possibility of political fraud,[106] he did not particularly concern himself with the risk that Spartan virtue might be held up as a public mask. He did not foresee the sickening future of democratic incantations. This is hardly surprising. Before the Revolution, misgovernment was seldom camouflaged by appeals to popular sovereignty or the community of equals. One reason why Constant seems to be a more practical thinker than Rousseau is that he belonged to a disillusioned generation. The experiences of the Revolution and of that Rousseauist king, Napoleon, had riveted his attention on the rhetorical abuses of his own egalitarian and democratic commitments.

Constant's primary concern was for masks of *virtue*—that is, for the misuse of intrinsically admirable ideals as pretexts for oppression. What stunned him about the Reign of Terror was the way in which his own most precious convictions were coimplicated in hideous acts of cruelty. He was acutely conscious of the deceptiveness of all political theories, including his own. That is why descriptions of his position as "critical liberalism" or "skeptical liberalism" suggest themselves so readily. By describing freedom as a "pretext" for the Terror, however, he also *limited* the responsibility that proponents of freedom had to assume: "No one deplores more than I do the crimes that have soiled the name of liberty. But because a word has been horribly abused, does it follow that this word has lost its original meaning?"[107] In sum, Constant's analysis of despotic appeals to Rousseau, far from reflecting a simple anti-Rousseauist strain in his thought, shows the profound ambiguity of his view of Rousseau. His intense worry that the language of democracy might be abused is potent evidence that his liberalism was fundamentally democratic in inspiration and intent.

FOUR

Political Psychology in the Early Writings

Une république naissante est une superbe chose à considérer par ses effets; mais il ne faut pas l'observer avec un microscope.

ASKS, partitions, and escape routes were important in Constant's writings from the start. As stratagems for deception and disengagement, they were treated with greater sympathy than might have been predicted from his clinical analysis of political pretexts. More distrustful of masks of virtue than Rousseau, Constant was also able to be more tolerant of masks for protection and other antisocial gestures than could believers in the possibility of total sincerity or social harmony. Further complicating his attitude toward deceit, absenteeism, and social compartmentalization was the experience of espionage and surveillance in a society ravaged by civil war.

THE SOCIAL BASIS OF DISTRUST

Constant arrived in Paris on May 25, 1795, two days after the Army of Paris crushed the sans-culotte uprising of Prairial and shortly before the invading émigré troops were routed at Quiberon. The political scene was not pacified by the regime's apparent victories. Constant found a country stricken with fear, frightened by an ongoing cycle of revenge and counter-revenge.[1] The brilliant but immature works which he published between Robespierre's execution and Bonaparte's seizure of power revealed how difficult it was for France to recover from the Terror. The country's basic

104

problem was not the spirit of democracy but what, following Camille Jourdan, Constant called "l'esprit de délation," the proclivity to file police reports about one's acquaintances. Despite its rhetorical exaltation of fraternity, the Revolution had done little to promote communal bonds. Indeed, "after a political crisis, everyone is guilty in the eyes of his neighbor." Even when the Jacobin machine had been largely dismantled, many surmised that they had "an informer for a neighbor."[2] The Directory introduced a police spy into Mme. de Staël's household,[3] and such undercover surveillance was typical of the time. Half a century earlier, Montesquieu had described the corrosive impact of spying and anonymous letters of denunciation on social order. Echoing Montesquieu, Constant concluded *Des Suites de la contre-révolution de 1660 en Angleterre* of 1799 with an impassioned attack on the "mob of informers" still spreading conspiracy theories, blackening reputations, and poisoning the political atmosphere in France.[4] These "délateurs perpétuels" were undermining all sense of common nationality and turning France into "a confused assemblage of mistrustful strangers" where individuals feared being associated too closely with their fellows. "Playthings of a small number of indefatigable *dénonciateurs,* a thousand voices, disastrously docile, carry everywhere suspicions, hatreds, mistrust."[5]

Pervasive social distrust, the fundamental problem inspiring theories of the social contract, was not natural but artificial. It was the work of spies and informers spawned by civil war. Distrust could not be subdued, moreover, in the Hobbesian manner, by delivering unlimited power to the police. On the contrary, social trust could only be recreated by a constitutional restriction of police authority. An unlimited executive was, in practice, but a pliant instrument in the hands of mendacious informers. A central challenge facing liberals was to recreate the trust necessary for self-government by neutralizing falsehoods spread by informants and spies.[6] But how could trust be recultivated in such a dire situation?

The problem was an enduring one. Into the Restoration, Constant continued to detect *dénonciateurs* and *délateurs* behind arbitrary police measures.[7] "Spies are not . . . reticent by nature. They live by furnishing scraps of information, false or true."[8] Citizens could not be expected to behave lawfully so long as their government continued to subsidize secret accusations, unfounded reports, and absurd rumors. Such dark practices were incompatible with representative institutions, legal opposition, freedom of the press, and government based on public discussion. In a spy-ridden country, the most natural response to an inquisitive neighbor was not a free exchange of information, but a counterlie, the purveying of protective untruth.

During the Consulate, Constant wrote to a friend: "It is difficult to know how to write today under the eyes of so many readers. I believe that personal letters are more widely read than printed books."[9] In response, he devised a secret code for discussing delicate political subjects in his personal correspondence, thereby acknowledging that masks are essential props for maintaining freedom in an atmosphere of mutual suspicion: lying may breed apprehensions; but it is also a legitimate strategy of self-defense. Furthermore, small enclaves of trust can be preserved, even in a poisonous climate, by imaginative combinations of withdrawal and deception.

Jacobin enforcement of ideological conformity set the stage for this positive evaluation of deceit, making the liar into something of a popular hero.[10] The postrevolutionary appreciation of masks, partitions, and escape routes, however, was no sudden innovation. A calculated disjunction between the visible and the clandestine had given seventeenth-century Protestants a chance to preserve their property as well as their beliefs. In the eighteenth century, numerous philosophes benefited from a lack of total candor. Although Montesquieu attacked secret accusations, he was flexible enough to publish the *Persian Letters* anonymously. Similarly, Voltaire made a shrewd use of pseudonyms. He also praised lying as a reasonable response to a government that persecuted heterodox belief: "to lie for your friend is the first duty of friendship."[11] In the same spirit, he decided to live near the Swiss border. The possibility of easy exit from French territory made outspoken reformist campaigns compatible with something less than sublime personal courage. Even unused, a potential escape route was an effective shield. During the Terror and in response to the Law of Suspects, disguises, concealment, and the falsification of names became widespread.[12] Mendacity was often the only way individuals could resist the regime's self-styled attempt to imitate the *polis* by absorbing the social into the political. Sales were made confidentially in violation of the official Maximum on prices and wages. The nonjuring clergy celebrated mass in secret.[13] Children, expected to denounce their parents for love of the state, were never fully converted by ancient examples. In such circumstances, most people learned to treasure the resource of hypocrisy. Lying was legitimated as a strategy for eluding the thousand-eyed Jacobin machine.

THE CONTROVERSY WITH KANT

Constant's constitutionalism assigned a central role to "publicity," freedom of the press, the publicity of court procedures, and parliamentary debates. But the postrevolutionary experience of police espionage also reinforced his belief in the social value of obscurity. The French civil war and its attendant *esprit de délation* is the proper context for understanding Constant's famous exchange with Immanuel Kant.[14] Politically, Constant and Kant had much in common. Both were antimilitarists committed to the principles of constitutionalism, the separation of morality from politics, religious tolerance, absolute freedom of the press, and the disestablishment of hereditary privileges.[15] Both believed the state should have jurisdiction solely over external acts, with no say about inner motives. The state they both advocated was meant to abstain from radical attempts at moral education, since no citizen can be legally required to perfect himself ethically or promote the happiness of others. Such a state must guarantee freedom while leaving happiness up to individuals.

Despite these important parallels, Kant and Constant disagreed about the moral status of deceit. Their philosophical differences mirrored their divergent situations: the political fugitive, the spy, and the malicious purveyor of false rumors were imposing figures in revolutionary France, but not in placid Königsberg. In 1795 Kant published *Perpetual Peace,* in which he argued: "Although the saying that 'honesty is the best policy' embodies a theory which, unfortunately, is frequently contradicted in practice, the equally theoretical statement that 'honesty is better than any policy' infinitely transcends all objections and is indeed a necessary precondition for any policy whatsoever."[16] These were noble sentiments. Indeed, they were too noble, too good for this world. Revolutionary governments in France had introduced "the death penalty against anyone spreading dangerous news, the death penalty against anyone offering asylum, the death penalty against anyone corresponding with his father in a foreign country."[17] Was honesty better than any policy in dealing with such hysterical and abhorrent laws?

Frenchmen had learned to fear that terrible moment when "at night the doors to their homes were broken down." Voluntary informing could provoke nocturnal arrests. The police also knew how to solicit denunciations.[18] Writing about seventeenth-century England but thinking of the French Republic, Constant reported an appalling feature of persecution under Charles II: "No rebel could escape being suspected by his neighbors. The duty of every faithful subject was to communicate his suspicions to the government. To fail in this duty was to participate in treason." Under James II, this grim engulfment of the private by the public was accompanied by even more gruesome atrocities: "A woman, known for her charity, had given asylum to a fugitive. The wretched fellow denounced her: he was pardoned and she was burned alive."[19] Under the shadow of similarly terrifying experiences, Constant wrote: "I have sometimes asked myself what I would do if I found myself trapped in a small town where it was forbidden under pain of death to give asylum to citizens accused of political crimes."[20] In such circumstances, would it be possible to cooperate truthfully with the authorities? What was the meaning of "truth" among fanatics and murderers? Surrounded by police spies and under a persecutory government, can anyone doubt the humanity of furtiveness and perjury? These questions underlay Constant's quarrel with Kant.

In *Des réactions politiques,* published in 1797, Constant commented on Kant's maxim declaring it a duty always and inevitably to tell the truth:

> The moral principle ... that "it is a duty to tell the truth," interpreted in a strict and isolated manner, would make all society impossible. We have proof of this in the direct consequences that a German philosopher has drawn from this principle. He goes so far as to claim that it would be a crime to lie to murderers who asked if your friend, whom they are pursuing, had taken refuge in your house.[21]

In a situation of intense mutual distrust, selective lying can assume a modest community-building function. In 1797, France was still rent by reciprocal hatreds and the desire for revenge. How much men revealed depended upon with whom, and about what, they were speaking. No one could assume that police informers chose *their* maxims on Kantian grounds. Morality demanded tactical adjustment to the ghastly immorality of others. Without some commitment to candor, the basis of all moral life would be undermined. But if no distinctions are made between various addressees, undiscriminating truth-telling "will destroy society."[22] Numbed to context, veracity might shred even the delicate fabric of trust and mutuality left intact by the Terror. The value of honesty is not unconditional. It is relative to the situation in which you speak. In a civil war, stealth is indispensable not only for individual freedom but also for the maintenance of humane relations. Mendacity does not necessarily shelter rapacious egoism against a harmonious collective will. Under the shadow of the guillotine, lying screened a pluralistic community against a bloody-minded authority and its agents, professional or amateur.

In his rejoinder, "On the So-called Right to Lie from Philanthropic Motives" (1797), Kant revealed himself as insensitive to the highly charged political context that gave rise to Constant's criticism.[23] This was perfectly predictable. In Constant's view, moreover, Kant came uncomfortably close to offering a *sauve qui peut* morality, an ethics of clean hands. By disregarding the foreseeable consequences of his acts, a Kantian agent could hope to remain "innocent as a dove."[24] In France, that meant escaping the harsh retribution applied to accomplices in the evasion of revolutionary justice. Constant was appalled at the thought of purchasing one's moral purity and legal inculpability at the cost of the murder of an innocent friend.[25]

Kant's essay also revealed little understanding of Constant's pragmatic argument: if principles are too rigid and one-sided, even men with good intentions will be forced to abandon them.[26] Kant believed that conflicts might arise between duties and inclinations or between conditional and unconditional duties; but his system explicitly excluded the possibility of conflict between unconditional duties.[27] Here Constant demurred. We have an absolute duty to tell the truth, but we also have an absolute duty to aid our innocent friends. Kant resolved this normative dissonance by ignoring half of our commitments. Constant gave both sides the attention they deserved. The effectiveness of principles will be undermined if potential conflicts between principles are not taken into account. It is necessary to make moral rules more supple, adaptable to concrete situations, and susceptible to compromise. By declaring honesty an "absolutely" binding duty rather than a relatively compelling one, Kant showed his disdain for moral opportunists and trimmers. Constant showed precisely the opposite: his moral theory was a response to the particular problems that plagued France during the revolutionary age. It also embodied a recognition that moral norms were, and would remain, unharmonious.

INDIVIDUALISM AS A RESPONSE TO CIVIL WAR

The violence of sectarian hatreds in France made social estrangement in general, not lying alone, seem politically beneficial. This again was nothing new. Reflecting on civil war and religious persecution, Enlightenment liberals had noted the healing power of mutual indifference. Commercial relations, however chilly and impersonal, were preferable to sectarian hatred, militaristic bravado, and the blood feud. Early liberals hoped that acquisitive instincts, loosed from religious prohibitions, might eclipse the powerful human desire for revenge. Attitudes which, from our perspective, appear antisocial and selfish were originally seen as preconditions for creating civilized mutualities of a noneconomic kind.

Constant's early works, though written in response to a series of political crises, also reflected a consistent set of political ideals. He aimed, first of all, to put an end to civil war, to arrest the cycle of revenge and retaliation, hoping that the Constitution of the Year III might provide a legal framework for settling conflicts without spasmodic resort to force. He strove to rehabilitate Montesquieu's ideals of limited government and political moderation even though intermediary bodies—for which he felt no sympathy in any case—had been legally abolished or transmuted, as had the nobility, into conspiratorial groups fomenting extremism and violence. On the other hand, France's need for limited government was counterbalanced by its need for effective government. Under the Directory, brigandage was rampant, taxes went unpaid, conscription was evaded, legislative and administrative decisions were ignored, generals in the field made foreign policy without consulting the government, and an armed struggle raged intermittently in the West and the Rhône valley. France was almost a sovereignless nation, exposed to all the cruelties of private violence and vigilante law. In such a crisis, Constant was bound to attribute positive value to sovereignty, centralization, and nation-building. Indeed, he sought a government that was simultaneously limited and strong. He believed these qualities to be perfectly compatible. Lamentably, the Directory exhibited the opposite traits: it was simultaneously ineffective and intrusive, paralyzed and oppressive, impotent and tyrannical. It was trapped between "the alternatives of violence and weakness."[28] It could outlaw Catholic burials and the sale of fish on Friday; but it could not subdue highway murder-gangs.[29]

Finally, Constant hoped to establish a parliamentary system in France even though representatives feared that they might be imprisoned or killed if they peaceably relinquished power to their opponents. To do this, he knew that it was necessary to domesticate the country's sectarian factions into political parties. The hurdle France faced seemed psychological, a matter of attitude or personal intransigence. Democracy would be impossible so long as each side viewed itself as pure and virtuous and denounced its rival as the incarnation of evil. Limited government might cordialize this revolutionary mentality. From the liberal perspective, a "party" can be defined as a cordialized faction—a faction that has ceased to view politics redemptively, as the whole of life, or as the sole arena in which all problems must be resolved.

Standing in the way of Constant's ideals was *l'esprit de délation* and the attendant climate of fear and distrust. For individuals, truancy and deceit were reasonable responses to unpredictable police surveillance and civil war. Neither strategy, however, went to the root of the problem. Neither made any contribution toward building a relatively neutral and representative authority that might have a chance to restore civil peace, averting national disintegration without recourse to arbitrary rule. Self-protection was a necessary but not sufficient condition for effective self-government. In other words, a protracted political crisis brought Constant to acknowledge the inherent limits of the Enlightenment individualism he otherwise admired.[30]

This was the corrosive, long-term legacy of the Terror: the habits of protective individualism prohibited a recovery of social trust. Confronting this problem, Constant the individualist explicitly associated individualism with corrosive egoism:

> Revolutions destroy the equilibrium between obligations and sacrifices. What in calm times is nothing but a simple and easy duty becomes an effort of courage, an act of heroic devotion. In a sea-storm, where anyone unable to grasp a plank is threatened with death, a furious egoism seizes everyone. Each unlucky individual, battling against the floods, fears to be embraced by his fellows and dragged to the bottom of the sea. Similarly, in the immediate dangers of political convulsions, men jettison everything that previously held them together. They are afraid that a friendly hand, clutching for support, will pull them down. They isolate their fate in order to defend themselves unencumbered.[31]

In the wake of the Terror, France was marked by a desperate self-centeredness and a profound suspicion of common bonds. This was understandable; it was not altogether wrong; but it also contributed to making the country ungovernable. How did Constant propose to alleviate the atomized, terror-stricken scene?

PSYCHOLOGICAL SOLUTIONS TO THE PROBLEM OF DISTRUST

After 1799, when the Directory collapsed unmourned, Constant turned to questions of constitutional design. He interpreted checks and balances, the person/office distinction, and other institutional machinery, as strategies for dealing with the animosities engendered by Revolution—strategies more constructive and reliable than selective lying. Only a liberal constitution could permit France to recover from the politics of vengeance. In these later constitutional writings, moreover, it was no longer a question of how discrete individuals might survive the storm. The problem of personal survival yielded to the problem of limited and effective popular government. Constant tried to ascertain, with mixed results, what legal institutions could provide a framework for peaceable public disagreement and thus for some form of national self-government.

This attention to constitutional design, pervasive in Constant's writings between the fall of the Directory and the renewal of the Charte in

1815, was largely absent from the pamphlets composed under the Directory. He showed some initial concern for constitutional architecture around 1799, but this interest blossomed only in his years of forced retirement. Between the occasional pamphlets of 1795–99 and the later constitutional writings, there was a continuity of problems but a discontinuity of solutions. During the earlier period, Constant simply accepted the framework established by the Constitution of the Year III and theorized about the psychological moderation of individuals which, he hoped, might make this system function more effectively.

There was nothing particularly "modern" about his approach. According to ancient theorists, the stability of regimes depended as much upon personal qualities as upon institutional arrangements. The stability and balance of a whole was traditionally said to depend on the stability and balance of its individual parts. Most modern liberals, by contrast, denied that the nature of the polity must mirror the nature of its citizens. Hume and Montesquieu, among others, defended the radical view that a stable whole may be constructed out of unstable parts.[32] The virtuous traits of individual persons, such as generosity and moderation, are irrelevant to the virtue of a constitutional state. Kant, with his usual penchant for extreme formulations, wrote that even a population of devils could coexist peaceably under constitutional rule.[33] After 1800, Constant converted fully to this "modern" position, emancipating his political proposals from optimistic assessments of human knowledge and character. Under the Directory, however, he was still hoping to identify states of psychological moderation capable of quelling the internecine struggles that afflicted French politics. These hopes were disappointed. Thereafter, he turned his attention toward impersonal constitutional machinery that might guarantee political moderation, no matter what psychological dispositions characterized individual politicians or citizens.

PUBLIC APATHY AS A COUNTERVAILING POWER

The psychological focus of Constant's early writings was already apparent in his first sequence of articles, the "Letters to a Deputy of the Convention," published in June 1795, one month after his arrival in Paris.[34] A proposal had been floated in the Thermidorian Convention to bypass the electorate and stipulate by law that five hundred of the outgoing Conventionnels would sit as delegates in the new seven-hundred-and-fifty-member legislative councils. This self-perpetuating Decree of Two-Thirds (passed later that summer) manifestly violated the basic principle of representative government, a principle enshrined in Article 2 of the Constitution of the Year III.[35] According to Constant, the decree also revealed the extent to which "reciprocal distrust" had become the ruling spirit of French political life. Lacking confidence in the people, the Conventionnels also suspected each other: "You have repeatedly accused and defended, exonerated and condemned the same men. To have been protected by a colleague is not for any of you an assurance that he will not soon become indifferent to you or even turn into an informer."[36] From bitter experience, the representatives of the nation had learned to doubt guarantees of legal inviolability.

Fear of insurgent royalism eventually convinced Constant to relax his republican principles and support the decree. Initially, however, he viewed the proposal diagnostically, as a symptom of an impossible situation. Though promptly disavowed, his basic argument is typical of all his Directorial writings. If it became law, he asserted, the Two-Thirds Decree would inevitably increase mutual distrust within the assemblies. It would also exacerbate public distrust of the government: "The Convention will be lost precisely by presenting itself thus as a group of accused men who fear judgment and who, to render it impossible, occupy the judge's seat. It will be lost by conserving its power in this manner, not as a means to the public good but as a shield."[37] Self-fulfilling prophecies have an uncanny ascendancy in political life. Distrust justifies itself. People actually acquire the motives attributed to them publicly.[38] By expressing mistrust of the electorate, the Conventionnels would force citizens into a defensive posture that, from the government's viewpoint, could only be described as suspicious or untrustworthy. But how was it possible to interrupt this cycle of mutual consternation and alarm?

Constant suggested that the Conventionnels should simply take a chance. They should forgo the Decree of Two-Thirds and show that they thought the electorate loyal and republican. If you pretend to trust someone, your false front will ensnare him into a pattern of trustworthy behavior. Appearance will become reality. The young Constant attributed miraculously curative powers to public hypocrisy.

In these same "Letters," he also introduced a supplementary and perhaps inconsistent argument against the self-perpetuation of the Conventionnels. Fear had led deputies to overestimate the danger they faced. There was no objective reason to distrust the French people: they were much less hostile than it initially seemed. At the height of the Revolution, Frenchmen were driven by exorbitant longings and fervent passions. In such a situation, no government could safely rely upon the people's will. By 1795, however, everything had changed. The basic characteristic of the popular mind had become "the sentiment of exhaustion." After six years of upheaval, "the nation is weary of tumults." Battle fatigue, "la fatigue nationale,"[39] had two redeeming features. It served simultaneously as a source of loyalty to any peacekeeping regime and as a countervailing power to restrain wild excesses on the part of factions.

The suggestion that popular exhaustion might help stabilize authority recalls again the influence of the *politiques* on Constant's thought. In the wake of the Terror, a lack of popular enthusiasm was an essential precondition for good government. It would be counterproductive, in a bitterly polarized society, for any regime to enjoy zealous support from a particular faction. The spirit of contradiction alone would cause this party's avowed enemies to hurl themselves against the government with unprovoked vehemence. Sectarian passions must not be rekindled. The most desirable, because the least dangerous, form of public loyalty will be tepid support. The very best regime will be uninteresting, uninspiring, barely acceptable.

The idea that civic apathy fosters democratic stability was destined to enjoy a lengthy career. Around this same time, significantly enough, Constant defined *apathy* as "the disease of honesty." Political apathy was one of those gentle or mild passions traditionally invoked to counteract fanatical zeal. The inertial drag of public fatigue might hamper the criminal aspirations of private sects and government agents. One of "the foremost officials" of the Directory told Constant that "since the love of royalty had been a fanaticism among the French, the love of the Republic had to become a fanaticism in turn." But this man was completely deluded: "as if fanaticism was not destructive of the very good that we expect from liberty."[40] Against the rage for persecution and retaliation, the young Constant hopefully invoked political affectlessness and indifference. Political moderation might be guaranteed by a psychological mood.

Such naive confidence in public lassitude plays no role in Constant's later thought. Indeed, in reaction to Bonaparte and the ultras, he came to see popular "apathy" as a stepping-stone for despots. Already in 1799, he began to associate France's plight with the "deep sleep" into which public spirit had fallen.[41] Liberal politics, as he conducted it, was a campaign to rouse France from civic sedation and paralysis. Exhaustion, passivity, and lack of zeal had seemed politically desirable under the Directory; but their destructive side-effects became clearly visible after the 18th Brumaire. Spiritless citizens left their state exposed to seizure by strong men and well-organized extremists.

Later on, Constant reformulated this view with an eye to parliamentary government. Looking back at the National Convention, he noted the endemic weakness of all centrist parties. Because moderates are usually paralyzed by ambiguity, fanatical sectarians can, in periods of violent upheaval, easily gain a disproportionate influence within assemblies: "A tightly unified minority, having the advantage of attack, frightening or seducing, arguing and threatening in turn, sooner or later dominates the majority. Violence unifies men because it blinds them to whatever falls outside their common purpose. Moderation divides men because it leaves their spirits open to all sorts of partial considerations."[42] A fanatic is a man who cannot be distracted. A liberal is a man who cannot take his own side in an argument. In a crisis, there is no doubt who will seize control. The liberal mind is easily sidetracked, hypersensitive to the other point of view, and susceptible to bouts of apathy. Psychologically, French "liberals" could not abide mandatory goals. They rebelled spontaneously at the Jacobin attempt to resurrect a form of ancient citizenship in which erratic private purposes vanished before the Monumental Aim of the state. Because they were individualists by nature, however, they found concerted action more irksome than moral protest.

Although liberal ambivalence and contrariness were personally attractive, they were debilitating politically: "moderate men, not being swept along by a dominant passion, readily lend an ear to individual concerns." During revolutions, the inability to be passionately single-minded may be the political equivalent of cowardice.[43] It may ensure that a party of "violent men" will never have to face coordinated opposition. Constant eventually came to believe that apathy, although a sign of personal honesty, was just as destructive to liberal government as fanaticism.

But let us return to 1795. Constant reversed his initial opposition to the Two-Thirds Decree because he was an anti-Kantian. Abstract principles, such as popular sovereignty and majority rule, must be adjusted to the *circonstances actuelles*. When a majority of the active citizens is anticonstitutional and divided into warring sects, no government can passively acquiesce in voter preference or public opinion. Many unsavory individuals were retained in office by the Decree. Constant, however, knew he could not be politically efficacious if he insisted on keeping his hands clean in a Kantian sense. To prevent an anticonstitutional party from using the electoral system to overthrow the constitution and renew widespread persecution, he was willing to employ what resources were available, and that included men whom he did not personally admire.[44] Whether this was a wise bargain remained to be seen.

THE VANITY OF POLITICAL JOURNALISTS

The political inadequacy of psychological moderation was already obvious by 1796, when Constant published his first major work, *De la force du gouvernement actuel de la France et de la nécessité de s'y rallier*. This long essay, which established Constant's reputation as a pamphleteer, suggested the liberal dilemma on its title page. The government of France was beset by a tempest of destructive forces. The Bourbons were intransigent. Their return would entail vengeance, foreign armies, and a shocking redistribution of national lands. The Republic, on the other hand, could not survive without the enthusiastic support of moderate citizens. That boded ill for the Directory. For how could a politically apathetic populace display loyalty to this or any other regime?

The opening chapter of the pamphlet is addressed directly to "the men who attacked the Convention." Constitutional monarchists were Constant's primary audience, though he sometimes turned to address the government directly. Behind the scenes, "absurd sectarians of despotism and theocracy" also intrigued against the Convention, encouraged in their abortive plots by British subsidies. But Constant was not thinking of "pure" or conspiratorial royalists here. He was concerned instead with a fairly moderate group of constitutionalists who sympathized with the Constitution of 1791. These ex-feuillants, such as Suard, formed a distinct group within the motley coterie surrounding Mme. de Staël. In Constant's opinion, they made it almost impossible for France to recover from violent upheaval: "Marching backwards toward the future, they contemplate only the past: their memories are nothing but resentments." In the preface, Constant apologized in advance for "harsh words" about "men who merit esteem."[45] He was able to provide a convincing portrait of these writers because he was intimately associated with them by personal history, temperament, and friendship. He had lived with the Suards on his first trips to Paris in 1785 and 1787. It was in Suard's journal, the *Nouvelles politiques, nationales et étrangères*, that he had published his ill-considered criticism of the Convention the previous spring. When he reversed himself on the Two-Thirds Decree, he naturally broke with Suard and his circle.[46] Not surprisingly, his analysis of these publicists exhibited some of the inwardness of self-examination. At one point he contrasted them approvingly with rigid fanatics of both extremes, portraying them as "weak, indecisive, divided, and speculative,"[47] like a party of Adolphes.

Similar to Constant himself, but unlike the pure royalists who remained abroad or in hiding, these moderates eagerly returned to public life after the defeat of the last Jacobin uprising in May 1795. The harassment they directed at the transitional Thermidorian regime in the summer of 1795 contributed to the launching of the unsuccessful royalist coup of Vendè- miaire. Relatively untouched by the spirit of revenge, they nevertheless failed to understand how thoroughly France had changed:

> These men played a small role and did great harm during the last phase of the Revolution [the summer of 1795]. They arrived here with all the subtle finesse . . . all the comeliness of *bel espirit* that had secured their success under the old regime. And with such weapons they wanted to fight against the new men, violent and energetic, who had learned to face more than danger, and whose characters had been formed by the most terrible revo- lutionary education.[48]

A single political principle will have dramatically different consequences in distinct historical settings. That is the essence of Constant's relativism. Anal- ogously, what concerned him both in *De la force du gouvernement actuel* and in *Des réactions politiques* was the danger of transplanting a style of criticism from a ceremonious court culture to a volatile situation ruled by newsprint and new men.

Abusive and arbitrary under the old regime, the royal government had also been lumbering, cushioned, and complacent. The harassment of the government by adversary philosophes and journalists, the unmasking of scandals and the exposure of misrule, served as an effective countervailing power. It inhibited excesses by injecting an element of healthy edginess or "inquiétude salutaire"[49] into a regime that tended to be smug and self- satisfied. Before 1789, gadflies moderated the government by souring the pleasures accompanying abuses of authority.

Such a role satisfied the vanity and self-importance of the would-be Voltaires. What they ultimately resented about the Revolution was that it had preempted their position in the forefront of an audacious opposition: "They had assigned themselves roles in a play that should have been of general interest," but the Revolution "swept them cruelly from the stage." Resentment at being upstaged, not antirepublican fervor, ultimately ex- plained their bitter attacks on the Convention: "These men are not royalists, but what they love about royalty is the proportion established between the weakness of government and their own individual power. A vacillating authority, indecisive ministers, a timid and unsteady administration all read their works, feared them and threatened them. They were given exactly the amount of persecution that made for glory. *Voilà*, precisely the enemies that suited them!"[50] Their new enemies, the governing authorities of the Directory, did not suit them. But why not?

THE INSECURITY OF NEW MEN

Constant often described Machiavelli and Montesquieu as the two greatest publicists of the modern age. He rejected, however, the idea advanced by several hostile critics that his book of 1796 was marked by "beaucoup de machiavélisme."[51] The critics were nevertheless right: both the problem Constant saw and the solution he proposed bore the imprint of Machiavelli.

The Directory exhibited all the defects traditionally associated with a new regime. According to Machiavelli, governments that spring up rapidly have shallow roots and will be destroyed by the first storm that strikes. Original in Constant's treatment of this theme was his emphasis on psychological factors. It was the skittishness and insecurity of first-generation rulers that made them such unsuitable targets for journalistic attacks.[52]

Criticism and demasking, countervailing forces under the old regime, became incitements to misrule under the Republic. Cutting ironies, hindrances to arbitrary rule in a court culture, were now dangerous provocations. "Revolutions make nuances disappear." Badgering critics softened the abuses of the old regime: "They are, by contrast, not only useless but essentially dangerous during revolutions and under newly founded regimes. They can do nothing against an irresistible impulsion and nevertheless, by the obstacles they create, they make the government believe in the necessity of additional precipitousness."[53] Rather than harnessing power, they unleashed it. It was a mistake for adversary philosophes to continue their blunderbuss tactics in this jittery situation. To increase the anxiety of uneasy men, far from moderating their behavior, is to exacerbate their inherent nervousness and drive them toward authoritarian acts. If you harass a new man with principles, you may incite him to violence.

In principle, the press had a "right" to criticize the government. As in his controversy with Kant, however, Constant insisted that abstract principles must be adapted to fit complex circumstances. He was not unaware of dangers inherent in a relativist position: "If one is not careful there will always be circumstances that can be invoked against principles."[54] On the other hand, unlike Kant, he emphatically believed in *l'empire de circonstances* and in the imperative need for political actors to adjust themselves to it.

Not merely a "right," freedom of the press was an indispensable means for limiting government power. While Constant underscored this point in the *Force du gouvernement actuel,* he also focused explicitly on the problems of incendiary journalism, on the way a free press may adopt a confrontationist stance, cleverly cornering officials, allowing them no chance to save face. This was a dangerous game. A few years later, speaking of liberty of the press, he said that "the good it does is mixed with a great deal of evil." The need to write something every day, even when they have nothing to say, leads journalists to construct an eye-catching but largely fictive world.[55] Do they have a "right" to do this, even when it increases government persecution and citizen suffering? Constant, it should be added, battled consistently for absolute freedom of the press. While the annoyances of journalistic hyperbole and distortion were real, they were, he believed, always outweighed by the evils of censorship.

The scope existing for dissent under the old regime was a product of the pillowed contentedness of self-confident ruling groups. What obsessed Constant was how to revive governmental toleration of dissent in a France ruled by edgy new men. A change in political psychology dictated a reassessment of political tactics: "Allowing others to speak is that which men in power learn with most difficulty. But this is what they most need to know. Now, a ceaseless buzzing of malice, insinuation, and bitterness forms an almost insuperable obstacle to acquiring this knowledge."[56] The message seems to be this: if citizens speak out, then the government will never learn to let citizens speak out! But the point is a serious one. Political opposition, when banned publicly, will withdraw underground. A conspiratorial opposition, in turn, will compel the government to employ informants and spies: the Directory did so, successfully infiltrating, for example, the circles of Babeuf and Pichegru. But a regime which makes lavish use of spies spreads distrust, eroding an essential precondition for representative government. Attempting to break this chain of suspicion, Constant strove to teach journalists to teach the officials of the Directory to tolerate dissent.

In so doing, he returned to the self-fulfilling character of public professions. If you bludgeon authorities with criticism, you will cause them to be more abusive by "making them accustomed to blame."[57] As the title indicated, the basic argument of *De la force du gouvernement actuel de la France et de la nécessité de s'y rallier* was precisely that the government was terribly weak, needed support, and could not tolerate criticism. Its inability to abide harsh commentary was due to a paranoid style typical of new men. Maistre was belaboring the obvious when he taunted Constant with the weakness of the contemporary government of France.[58] This was Constant's own point: "More than once a biting insinuation has retarded the revocation of a bad decree, a wounding allusion has provoked an unjust measure, an imprudent reminder has made men who were already repentant intractable about their mistakes." The new men of the Directory, yet to master the difficult science of tolerating dissent, were subject to a chronic anxiety. Quick to panic, they were unable to assess realistically the threats they faced: "Fear enlarges its objects, rendering terrible what would only be contemptible."[59]

Old-style gadflies, transplanted into the new order, were dangerous because the threat they posed was magnified ridiculously in the fearstruck eyes of inexperienced rulers. Referring to antigovernment journalists such as Suard, and implicitly to the recusant author of "Letters to a Deputy," Constant wrote: "Their carping, which would in no way trouble the security of an established government, takes on—as a natural result of the mutual suspicion and mistrust that is inseparable from new men and institutions— the appearance of a conspiracy. Rulers mistake maneuvers for attacks, fencing foils for real swords. They mistake men who merely want to show off for men who intend to inflict real harm."[60] Constant was later to discern this same paranoiac inability to distinguish real from imaginary threats in Napoleon. The only way to deal with such a ruler, he came to believe, was to overthrow the regime. In the *Force du gouvernement*, he had taken a milder line. He argued, with childlike naiveté, that liberal-minded pamphleteers could assuage the apprehensions of new rulers simply by striking a more conciliatory pose. What led him to entertain such a fantastical hope?

In the *Force du gouvernement*, we find a skeptic preaching faith, a relentless doubter recommending an attitude of uncritical acceptance. This is disturbing. The Directory was never a particularly attractive regime. Many of its policies were motivated by an obsessive hatred of priests and Catholicism, and it tended to identify the desire for peace with royalism and treason.[61] So why was Constant, for four consecutive years, loyal to such an illiberal government? The answer is not particularly mysterious. Without support in the country, the Directory had only two strategies for governing: it could play off returned royalists against ex-terrorists released from prison, or it could call up the army.[62] For the Republic to survive as a constitutional regime, and that was Constant's hope, it had to discover some method for garnering support from a coalition of moderates. It had to overcome the skepticism of Parisian elites. Constant traced the regime's illiberal measures to its lack of public support. As a result, he threw himself, quite unrealistically as it turned out, into a campaign to build the sort of consent among elites that would allow the Directory to abandon its policies of persecution and annexation. His support of the coup of Fructidor, which he soon came to regret, resulted from this same belief that a continuation of the government in place was the least intolerable of all the other possible and likely evils.

As a political writer, Constant came into his own under the Consulate and during the Restoration. Only in the face of stable and consolidated governments was he free to step forward as a reformer, skeptic, and unmasker of authority. Intellectually and politically, he thrived on distrust of men in power. Under the wobbly and stalemated Directory, this was not a reasonable position to adopt. Concerned with satisfactory results rather than pure intentions, he quickly recognized the uselessness of pouring criticism into a mounting sea of recriminations. The confusion and impotence of the regime made a mockery of "countervailing" powers. Enlightenment liberalism was to some extent inappropriate to the *circonstances actuelles*. Thus, Constant simply bit his tongue, and wrote pamphlets easy to misconstrue as essays in self-promotion.[63]

HYPOCRISY AS MORAL EDUCATION

From Machiavelli's *Prince,* Constant learned that public façades can moderate the cruelest extremes of misrule. To sustain the public pretense of acting for the common good, a prince must curtail the number and range of his abusive acts. Constant fastened upon this insight: not merely an homage vice pays to virtue, hypocrisy is also a mechanism for transforming vice into virtue. Characteristically, he modified this Machiavellian insight by emphasizing a psychological or Pascalian dimension.

Men are not mentally strong enough to be consistently dishonest. Because public actors tend to become what they pretend to be, the appearance/reality schema may obscure the nature and course of political life: "We enter seriously into roles we must play ceaselessly and adroitly; and we become by habit what we at first wanted to seem by hypocrisy."[64] This statement echoed an idea that Pascal, in turn, had borrowed from his Jesuit enemies: outward religious ceremony, scrupulously observed, can eventually produce genuine inward belief. Within Constant's own works, the same idea is echoed in *Adolphe* ("we are such mobile creatures that we end up feeling the sentiments we feign") and in the *Commentaire.*[65] Much more optimistic than his later works, however, the *Force du gouvernement* suggests that man's pliant adaptability can help solve the elemental problem of French politics: the vicious cycle in which suspicion breeds suspicion.

Although an individual may once have been implicated in an extremist movement, that does not mean he is unalterably an extremist. As Hume wrote, "man is a very variable being." Montesquieu reformulated the same insight: man is an "être flexible." Having no fixed essences, people cannot be essentially royalist or Jacobin. After 1789, in fact, the career open to talents seemed the most natural of social arrangements. Not Talleyrand alone but all those actively involved in politics led many successive lives. But recall the rest of Montesquieu's definition: man is that flexible creature "who, in society, conforms to the thoughts and impressions of others."[66] Appearance in the public eye reshapes reality in conformity to itself. If we assume that a one-time zealot is basically an extremist, we may freeze him into a pattern of behavior which he wishes to renounce.[67] Most men are psychologically too feeble to be consistent dissemblers. They are much too changeable to be thoroughly evil. "We are such versatile creatures that when we look within we see ourselves vacillating at every step. By what absurdity then do we judge ourselves so unlike our fellows? Let us profit at least from our instability, from our fickleness, from all the faults of our feeble nature. Let us not credit ourselves with a coherence and profundity of crime incompatible with these faults."[68] The theme of inner instability permeates Constant's autobiographical works. What is unique in this early period is his suggestion that political profit may be drawn from man's *mobilité ondoyante*.

Moderate French journalists should deploy a very special version of the "noble lie," one differing radically from the Platonic prototype, because the appearance/reality distinction is unsuitable for understanding political life. Lies can be "noble" precisely because they set in motion a process whereby they became truths. Once again, the notion that hypocrisy can be a subtle instrument for moral education is not exclusively modern. Aristotle argued that men become good by habitually performing good acts.[69] The adage *laudando praecipere,* to teach by praising, also goes back to antiquity. Here, too, Constant rethought an old precept in relation to the Revolutionary crisis. In the following passage he is ostensibly speaking about "crime." From the context, however, it is clear that he is referring to "the violent and uncouth men" who ruled France under the Directory. "So long as [crime] is strong, we must not demask it. We must lend it a mask. . . . By disguising its ugliness, we diminish it, because its ugliness is often nothing but the result of the idea it conceives of its own appearance."[70] In revolutionary situations, masks and disguises can be virtuous. Liberal journalists must not unmask the potentates of the Directory but lend them masks.

This advice, while artfully paradoxical, was not particularly realistic. Political crimes cannot be controlled by white lies. Nevertheless, Constant's position should be compared with Rousseau's plea for total sincerity: "Until now I have seen only masks. When will I see the faces of men?"[71] Constant made a subtler appeal. The authenticity of brutal men made him long to look upon benevolent façades, however, ungenuine. Moreover, falsehood could be a form of moral education. This suggestion reflected the young Constant's general hope that political moderation might have psychological roots.

His initial confidence in the morally reformist powers of hypocrisy may have been sparked by the conversion of leading Conventionnels in the aftermath of the 9th of Thermidor. The men who initially overthrew Robespierre were actually hardened Terrorists.[72] While intent on saving their own lives, they seem originally to have had no plans for relaxing the severity of the revolutionary regime. Nevertheless, they soon revealed that they were versatile creatures. Unexpectedly celebrated as popular heroes who had emancipated France from an unwanted dictatorship, Tallien, Fréron, and others quickly adapted to the expectations of their fellow citizens: "After the Ninth of Thermidor, the Convention slowed the revolutionary movement despite itself. . . . The love of popularity drew the Thermidorians along: Tallien, Fréron, and others. All the youth of Paris had lined up behind them, but instead of following, pushed them."[73] The leading Conventionnels refashioned their personalities in conformity with a public misperception. They became antiterrorists, but only because they inwardly assumed a flattering mask that had been foisted upon them.

In the *Fragmens* of 1800–03, writing in favor of direct elections and against the plan to have a Senate appoint members of the lower House, Constant continued to ascribe educative powers to public hypocrisy. One of the great advantages of representative government is "to establish frequent relations between the different classes of society." Regular elections require that "the powerful classes" exercise "des ménagements soutenus" toward the lower classes: regular elections "force wealth to dissimulate its arrogance and power and to moderate its action." Moreover, we "should not disdain this motive for benevolence, which may initially be nothing but a calculation but which by force of habit will soon become a virtue." Constant saw two advantages to hypocrisy. If men are authentically vile, public dissimulation will be preferable to forthright self-expression. He remained deeply committed to this argument against Rousseauist candor: "free governments oblige [individuals] to hide their vices." "Hide from us your shameful passions!"[74] is a phrase that appears often in his speeches aimed at the ultraroyalists.

The second advantage Constant ascribed to hypocrisy is the same one he advanced a few years earlier in the *Force du gouvernement*. Given time and repetition, appearance becomes reality, lies become truth, masks become faces. This argument, while fascinating, is also disturbing: it seems incompatible with a distinction between public and private spheres, a dichotomy central to Constant's understanding of modern liberty. A second inconsistency between the *Force du gouvernement* and Constant's later thought follows directly upon the first. In *Conquête et usurpation* (1814), Constant drew a sharp distinction between two sorts of tyranny: consolidated despots frankly oppress their subjects, while revolutionary dictators not only oppress the people but also force them to proclaim aloud how fortunate they are to be blessed with "freedom." The mask of liberty is an irritating pretext, not a moderating force. Hypocritical regimes are the most pernicious and destructive kind, since "illegalities committed in the name of liberty alienate the people from liberty itself."[75]

In chapter 7 of the *Force du gouvernement actuel*, Constant openly rejected what later became his considered view: "Republics are frequently reproached with disguising oppression and prostituting sacred names to the most ghastly of tyrannies. This is doubtless a great evil. But those who see only an evil in this abuse, seem to me to be looking exclusively at one side of the question."[76] Behind this claim lay a storehouse theory of hypocrisy. "Republican forms," even when they are pretexts and shams, "tend to preserve a tradition of liberty." Despotic forms, by contrast, consecrate and perpetuate slavery. They ensure that "the servile spirit" outlasts real servitude: "If the horrors of Robespierre had been perpetrated in the name of divine right or of implicit submission or even in the name of order and tranquillity (which is the usual pretext invoked by monarchies) the 9th of Thermidor, encountering only ideas of divine right and implicit submission, would have halted the massacres, but it would not have revived liberty."[77] Just as Adolphe's counterfeit love for Ellénore soon became real love, so Robespierre's false devotion to liberty will turn genuine under the Directory. The analogy is not comforting. Adolphe's authentic spurt of feelings quickly ran dry. Similarly, the Directorial regime soon disappointed Constant's political hopes. Hypocrisy did not successfully reform those violent men. Turnabouts, disavowels, and recantations illustrated human versatility while worsening the problem of social mistrust.

Early disappointment weakened Constant's reliance upon the psychological mood of civic apathy as a source of political moderation. He retained the idea in a marginal role but could no longer give it pivotal importance, convinced as he was that public dispiritedness smoothed the path for tyrants. His experiences during the Directory also led him to doubt the morally educative function of public hypocrisy. Looking back, he found that the tendency of appearance to become reality, of masks to become faces, could be politically disastrous as well as helpful.

Doubts about the educative function of public hypocrisy eventually led Constant to claim that the greatest harm the revolutionaries inflicted on France was to oppress it in the name of popular sovereignty. Despite this important shift, the pamphlets written between 1795 and 1799 provide an essential clue for understanding a dimension of Constant's mature thought. Throughout his life he sustained a divided attitude toward sincerity and hypocrisy. What he consistently valued about hypocrisy, however, was less its educative power than its capacity to protect the individual from political surveillance and control.

BENTHAM AND DISTRUST

Although a persistent critic of utilitarianism, Constant obviously admired Jeremy Bentham.[78] What struck him most forcefully was Bentham's concern with "the mask of patriotism and the public good," with "wilful falsehoods that allowed unauthorized persons to steal power."[79] The tensions peculiar to French politics, however, prevented Constant from becoming a full-fledged convert to Benthamism. Individualism was not a solution to the problem of mutual distrust. Bentham made a strong argument in favor of paid informers and government spies, an argument which must have seemed absurd from Constant's perspective. He also suggested, ludicrously enough, that citizens should have their names tatooed on their wrists, a practice that would have eliminated the sort of anonymity and disguise that saved many lives during the Revolution. Furthermore, Bentham denied that the desire to punish the guilty might interfere with the need to protect the innocent— a normative dissonance no Frenchman would have been tempted to belittle.[80]

Unlike the author of *De la religion*, Bentham was numb to the allure of "mystery," even outside of politics. Characteristically, his cold passion was to purge legal language of all metaphor, obscurity, and imprecision. While also committed to clarity of thought and expression, Constant doubted that legislation could be freed from all residual ambiguity.[81] Scientific language could not eliminate controversy. Not only the jerry-built common law, but also highly rational statute law (no matter how well written) had to be interpreted, and no interpretation could be definitive.

The doctrine of natural rights and the principle of utility had this in common: both promised ordinary citizens leverage against customary authority. But Bentham disliked talk of natural rights. He complained not only that "rights" were metaphysical qualities, but also that they could be interpreted in any number of ways and even be politically abused.[82] To this argument, Constant replied intelligently that "utility," too, admitted of diverse interpretations: "Utility is not susceptible to precise demonstration. It is the object of individual opinion and, as a consequence, of discussion and indefinite contestation." Bentham's principle could also be politically misused: "Reasons of utility can be found for any command and any pro46bition."[83] Thus, or so Constant argued, Bentham's case for preferring "utility" to "rights" was much feebler than he believed.

Constant's central objection, however, was that utilitarianism is a self-defeating theory.[84] To defend an institution on the grounds that it increases utility actually decreases the utility of the institution in question. Bentham's defense of religion was a classic example.[85] Religious belief may have politically beneficial side-effects. But these side-effects, however desirable, do not provide good reasons for people to entertain religious beliefs. Indeed, a government which sought to justify religion by pointing to its social usefulness would be undermining religion and thus eroding the very good it was attempting to produce.

Focusing on the problem of social distrust, Constant argued that the doctrine of natural rights might be preferable to the principle of utility, even on utilitarian grounds. Rights are neutral goods. They protect each faction in turn, making political compromise possible and self-government likely for the first time. Because "rights" cannot be overriden on any pretext, they allow trust to grow. Bentham's efforts to redefine *utility* would not alter the ordinary understanding of the term. Utility will always suggest the possibility of trade-offs. Under utilitarian maxims, as popularly understood, zones of security can be invaded if potential benefits are substantial enough. While the idea of "rights" suggests the existence of obligations and immunities independent of all calculation, the idea of "utility" suggests that no barriers are truly inviolable.

In times of confusion and upheaval, the doctrine of natural rights provides a politically desirable element of predictability: "Say to a man: 'It is your right not to be arbitrarily robbed and killed,' and you will give him a totally different feeling of security and guarantee than if you say to him: 'It is not useful for you to be arbitrarily robbed and killed.' "[86] Political theories must be judged by their unintended psychological effects. In France it was socially useful, and indeed indispensable to self-government, that certain rights be affirmed unconditionally, with no attempt being made to "demonstrate" their social usefulness. This argument may seem Kantian. It was not. It was purely contextual and consequentialist.[87] As such, it was quite compatible with Constant's objection to Kant's moralistic rigidity, his refusal to bend his maxims to fit the messy situations in which they had to be applied.

As a psychologist and a stylist, Bentham was undoubtedly less engaging than Constant. But psychological subtlety and literary flair are not always political virtues. Although Constant's early pamphlets were brilliantly suggestive and liberal in purpose, they failed to achieve common sense. Politically, they could be used only as propaganda, as a call for citizens to rally uncritically around the government in power. Frustrated with the psychological focus and fawning appearance of his early works, Constant shifted his energies, after 1800, to a dryer, more constructive, more Benthamite task. When the Constitution of the Year III collapsed to be replaced by a military dictatorship, he turned his attention to legal carpentry.[88] Anticipating an eventual return to representative government, he took up the challenge of constitutional design.

Constitutional Design

On peut supprimer les discussions publiques; mais on ôte aux nations leurs organes, on les détache de leurs intérêts, on frappe de stupeur le corps politique.

S a liberal constitutionalist, Constant aimed not only at restraining sovereign power but also at organizing and even constructing sovereign power.[1] The *séparation des pouvoirs* is an example of the division of labor.[2] It is creative not merely obstructive, since specialization fosters efficiency, personal responsibility, and sensitivity to a wider variety of social problems. A clear delineation of functions encourages cooperation and allows for mutual vitalization. Constant favored legally enforced tolerance for similar reasons. Toleration both restricts the sway of the intolerant and creates conditions favorable to public debate, to the genesis of a democratically legitimated authority. In fact, the fundamental premise of his constitutional theory was that limited government subserves self-government.

Relentlessly practical, Constant wrote profusely about the mechanical details of constitutional design. Not satisfied with simply defining a good political order, he made specific proposals for bringing it about.[3] He turned directly to questions of constitutional architecture in the *Fragmens d'un ouvrage abandonné* of 1800–03; but his first published constitutional brochure was the *Réflexions sur les constitutions* of 1814. While the manuscript composed during the Consulate contained a sketch for a republican constitution, the brochure of 1814 registered Constant's acquiescence in a constitutional monarchy. The two treatises, however, were almost in-

128

distinguishable in structure, argument, and intent. Numerous passages were transcribed unchanged from the earlier to the later work. In the *Fragmens,* moreover, Constant wrote that "there is no doubt: when a monarchy exists, one must handle it with care, and profit by the power of public opinion to spread enlightenment and prepare the people for liberty."[4] When the Bourbons were restored, he took his own advice. Unwilling to make himself politically irrelevant by impracticable republicanism, Constant compromised with the Charte.[5]

The *Principes de politique* of 1815 was published during the Hundred Days and styled as a commentary on the *Acte additionnel.* It was Constant's last full sketch of a constitution. Thereafter he battled within the established framework, struggling to compel, by political arguments and maneuvers, a liberal interpretation of the Charte. Throughout the Restoration he remained republican in spirit. He wished to turn France into what Montesquieu said England already was: "a republic disguised as a monarchy."[6] Most important of all, his proposals can be understood only if the positive as well as the negative aims of liberal constitutionalism are taken into account.

PURPOSES AND PRECONDITIONS

Aristotle's *Politics* begins with the claim that the goal dominating the lives of citizens should be identical with the goal of their city.[7] Modern liberalism repudiated this identification of the "highest" aims of the individual with political goals. When the purposes of the state are idealized, private citizens may become resources at the disposal of public officials. Classical liberals thus frequently described the objectives of the state in uninspiring ways.[8] Security and prosperity were the aims they cited most often. They expressly conceived these goods as being subservient to the purposes of individual citizens who, on the basis of politically secured social cooperation, may seek salvation, comradeship, bliss, love, amusement, or knowledge. Locke, for example, defined the overriding purpose of government as the protection of property, while he thought that the purposes of individuals were much richer than this.[9] Men will seek the entire heterogeneous array of goods made possible by the security of possessions. True, liberal man is a part-time citizen; shared or communal goals are included among his personal aims. But individuals also pursue less standardized objectives.

Constant, too, rejected the teleological focus of Aristotle's politics. The state he fought to establish was not meant to embody or nurture man's noblest inborn purpose. It was empowered, first, to secure conditions under which individuals might elaborate and pursue their private plans and, second, to guarantee the right of public dissent. "Politics" must facilitate compromise and solve social problems; but it has no business expressing man's essence or enforcing an orthodox standard of moral health.

Constant's constitutional writings can best be understood in light of the antiteleological and problem/solution patterns of analysis found in both Montesquieu[10] and Hume.[11] Constitutional government could put an end to civil war without resorting to Bonapartist methods of arbitrary arrest, censorship, and oppression. A limited government will moderate the fears and vindictiveness motivating all parties. Constant did not aim for the creation of human perfection or the cultivation of virtue. He deliberately resigned himself to less controversial goals: peace and representative government. His objective was to build a neutral framework for self-government among resentful individuals and rival sects.

Liberalism is often accused of having abandoned the ancient quest for the "good life" in favor of a materialist pursuit of mere comfort and survival.[12] But this is a travesty of the liberal idea. Liberals simply decentralized the pursuit of the good life. Self-realization could no longer occur solely in the political arena; it was partly displaced to extrapolitical spheres of society. Disencumbered in this way, "politics" became responsible for social order, the prevention of mutual harm, and the creation of background conditions for individual autonomy and collaboration among rival sects. Equally important, liberalism aimed at organizing public opinion, through public debate and popular elections, into a sovereign political force. Within the political domain, rules became more fundamental than values. Procedures were fixed and held in common, while ideologies were open to question and subject to peaceful contestation. But liberals did not aim at extirpating moral commitments or all sense of common endeavor; they merely reapportioned moral exhilaration so that it was no longer channeled exclusively into political affairs.

The Greek word *politeia* meant not only constitution, but also citizenship, the body of citizens, the daily life of the city, administration, a term of office, a course of policy, and the general structure of the *polis*.[13] Such a "constitution" was commonly referred to as the "life" or the "soul" of the city.[14] Greek constitutionalism was thus focally concerned with the study of civic participation and the moral adherence of the individual to his community. Liberal constitutionalism was more skeletally conceived.[15] It focused on rules for political compromise and cooperation, not on the salvation or improvement of souls.[16] Within limits imposed by the pluralism of modern society, however, Constant also had an idea of public purpose, even an idea of national purpose. A well-designed constitution might be a source of life in the community, a means of involving citizens rather than merely protecting them.

ELEMENTS OF A LIBERAL CONSTITUTION

In both the *Fragmens* and the *Réflexions,* Constant advocated a constitutional system that stipulated direct popular elections, integral renewal and inviolability of representatives, two chambers, an executive veto, the right of dissolution, a responsible executive liable to dismissal, an independent judiciary, trial by jury, a ban on retroactive laws, absolute freedom of the press, and an institutional barrier between the army and the police. The legislature was to have the right to initiate new laws and repeal old ones; and it was to control the purse strings of government, voting every year on taxes and on support for the armed forces. Equally important, it was to scrutinize all executive actions such as treaties with foreign governments. By constitutional stipulation, all such acts were to be countersigned by a minister. Constant also proposed the establishment of a "neutral power" whose main purpose would be to resolve deadlocks between the executive and legislative branches of government. In the 1790s, France had been a laboratory of abortive constitutional experiments. Constant aimed to avoid earlier mistakes.

To say that Constant's legislative ambitions were modern is to say that they were modest. Unlike Rousseau's Legislator, he did not aspire to change human nature, to create "citizens" in the emphatic sense, by impressing human clay with a strenuous set of moral ideals. Apart from an important exception to be noted later, his constitutional program consistently repudiated moral education. Its purpose was neither to make men good (as if the rival factions in French politics could agree on what it meant to be "good") nor to infuse them with love of their *patrie* (the march back from Moscow had somewhat soured that dream). Constitutionalism was principally meant to establish the preconditions for representative government and prevent the recurrence of civil war.

Constant disconnected the stability and moderation of the liberal state from the *moeurs* of its citizens and public officials: "guarantees resting on personal virtues are precarious and insufficient."[17] His primary emphasis fell not on the desirable traits of individual personalities, but rather on abstractly conceived "rouages constitutionnels."[18] Averse to crafting souls according to some controversial ideal of happiness or perfection, he advised constitution-makers to acknowledge the permanence of human imperfection. Men have to be accepted as they are: capable of heroism, but often vacillating, ambitious, cowardly, vain, and sometimes even villainous.[19] Unlike the great political theorists of antiquity and their Jacobin heirs, Constant now denied decisive *political* importance to the contrast between virtue and vice, probity and corruption.[20]

Despite the horrors of 1793–94 and the oppressive laws passed by the chambers of the Restoration, Constant remained firmly committed to the supremacy of a popularly elected legislature. Dismayed at the First Republic's obstructionist and anarchic assemblies, many well-meaning republicans had acquiesced in the executive-led coups of 18 Fructidor and 18 Brumaire. But this had been a grave error. Freedom cannot exist without the political dominance of an elected assembly.[21]

A vigorous defender of legislative supremacy, Constant also believed that partisans of democracy often overestimated the representativeness of even the best representative assembly. "Why do the most exaggerated partisans of democracy among us believe that 750 men in a single chamber legitimately represent thirty million?" Representative government is indispensable, but theorists should not veil its deficiencies behind rhetoric and myth. A liberal constitution must freely acknowledge that "the majority of representatives is always a fictive majority in comparison to the numerical majority that can be found among those who are being represented."[22]

Election is vastly preferable to heredity as a method for recruiting political officials, but "the authority of ignorance and vice" can be established in either way. Indeed, the "primitive discord" between governors and governed may be unavoidable in a large country. When a deputy is elected, he immediately acquires an interest distinct from that of his constituents.[23] Although unable to eliminate this disparity of interests, the "constitutional art" can seek to minimize it: "We can hinder this inconvenience by creating diverse sorts of governors, invested with powers which restrain each other, so that their own interests cannot triumph and they will approximate the will of the governed."[24] The Declaration of Rights of 1789 had proclaimed that the core of any constitution was the division of powers.[25] As a student of Montesquieu, Constant accepted this premise.

In the *Fragmens,* Constant argued that "the function of the legislative branch is to express the national will." But a representative assembly can express the national will only in the form of absolutely general laws. Special edicts, exceptional laws, and *lettres de cachet* are strictly forbidden. Indeed, legislative supremacy implies the rule of law. The executive can encroach on private freedoms, but solely on the basis of general laws (which neither name names nor single out distinct classes of individuals for special treatment). Retroactivity is also strictly forbidden. In this system, legislators are "governors in principle, but governed in application," while members of the executive are "governors in application and governed in principle."[26] By this allotment of functions, elected representatives are encouraged to assess pending legislation from the standpoint of citizens, not from the standpoint of the bureaucracy and police.

At the Tribunat, Constant argued that the persecution of suspect classes weakens the central government's capacity to control its own agents.[27] When a directive to dispossess or incarcerate a certain group of individuals is transmitted down the ranks, subordinate officials interpret it as they please, using it as a pretext to gain personal advantage or avenge personal wrongs. One of the principal purposes of limited government is to prevent local officials, who are practically unknown to the central authorities, from wielding unsupervised discretion over punishment and confiscation. In criminal matters, Constant attributed a purely negative role to the Tribunat: "the only justification for examining a law is the assumption that the authorities may abuse it." His pedagogical aim was to teach Bonaparte's government that persecution was a source of weakness and that criticism of its policies was not a personal insult. Even if they had complete confidence in the central government, the Tribunes were obliged to examine every proposed bill under the assumption that, in the future, it might be abused by unknown officials for unknown ends. This worst case approach was not a slur on the government's motives, and would actually enhance its capacity for centralized control.[28]

Within individuals, opposite and rival interests must compensate for a lack of superior talent and the self-forgetting virtues: "One must try to build political institutions that combine the interests of the diverse wielders of power in such a way that their most obvious, long-run, and assured advantage is to remain within the limits of their respective spheres of competence." No procedure can be made "idiot-proof." Similarly, it is impossible to create rules that no one could benefit from violating. While carefully weaving checks and balances into his constitutional scheme, Constant was skeptical and practical enough to insist that no constitutional arrangement could make the interests of governors and the interests of the governed coincide: "One must not . . . delude oneself about the efficacy of these means, nor flatter oneself that these two interests can ever be completely amalgamated."[29] Within limits, however, a durable constitution can ensure that authorities have a manifest interest in obeying the law.[30]

In the eighteenth century, partisans of democracy—such as Thomas Jefferson and Tom Paine—tended to favor a single chamber and no independent executive. But France's experiment with unicameral government had meant "the despotism of a faction." The Convention had been "an assembly subjugated by some of its members, but concentrating all the powers." It was "enslaved and dominated by factions," and its "will, decorated by the name of law, was not counterbalanced, repressed or arrested by anything."[31] The logic of factionalism, which allows extremist minorities to control moderate majorities, ensures that a single chamber, combining all the powers, will lose touch with the electorate, immunizing itself against public protest.[32] Thus, Constant advocated bicameralism, as well as a separate executive, not merely to prevent tyranny but also to increase the chance that government policy would correspond to the national will.

Initially, Constant's defense of bicameralism seems ambiguous: did he introduce a second chamber for liberal reasons ("to counterbalance another assembly" and to ensure that legislation would be passed only after thoughtful discussion),[33] or for conservative reasons (to protect a privileged class against the threat of confiscatory democracy)? The question can be answered historically: his case was strictly liberal, not at all conservative. In 1814–15, Constant repeated verbatim the arguments for bicameralism he had advanced in the antiaristocratic *Fragmens*. When he introduced the idea of a chamber of Peers into the *Réflexions* and even into the *Acte additionnel*, against Napoleon's advice, he was making a concession to what he saw as political realities. He was not repudiating his commitment to legal equality. By 1818, when he reissued the *Réflexions*, Constant conceded that his attempted conciliation of the émigrés had been ill-considered.[34] In the *Mémoires sur les Cent-Jours*, he approvingly reported Napoleon's devastating remarks about the absurdity of a hereditary chamber in France.[35] True, he never openly attacked the house of peers, even after this date. The Charte had stipulated that the upper chamber was to be hereditary, and he was committed to seeking reforms within the framework of the existing constitution. Throughout the Restoration, moreover, the upper House happened to be a more liberal body than the chamber of deputies on many issues, considerably dampening liberal opposition to the peerage. In any case, Constant's arguments for the *pouvoir de la durée*, advanced publicly in the chaotic years 1814–15, all stem from the republican *Fragmens* where they were applied to an upper house the members of which were elected for long terms of office. Thus, they cannot justify describing him as an "aristocratic liberal."

In ancient republics, the powers of government were not clearly interrelated because they were largely "confused."[36] Similarly, the Jacobin dictatorship had exhibited a disorienting overlap of jurisdictions, an unclear chain of command, and a blurring of distinct functions. There was little specialization of portfolios within the Committee of Public Safety; its range of competences was never disentangled from that of the Committee of General Security; and representatives on mission, such as Fouché or Carrier, commonly acted without authorization from the central government.[37] In other words, authority was not only too concentrated: it was bewilderingly and contradictorily dispersed. Constant's proposal for the division and interrelation of powers was meant to solve both problems.

The separation of powers does not require the executive and legislative branches to be sealed in airtight compartments. That had been the great failure of the Constitution of the Year III: designed to prevent tyranny, it had produced an irresolvable deadlock between the branches. Constant, as a result, elaborated complex proposals for the interrelation and mutual influence of the executive and the legislature. For example, in the republican constitution of the *Fragmens,* the legislature was not only to pass and repeal laws, but also to elect the executive, while the executive shared the power to initiate legislation and wielded an absolute veto against all laws passed by the assemblies. The legislative authority to withhold taxes, while useful for inhibiting expenditures in peacetime, was of no use at all for curbing executive actions in moments of crisis.[38] Thus, a more direct form of ministerial responsibility was required: "a minister who is inept or suspect to the majority of the national representatives cannot remain in power. In England, the minister loses his place *de facto* when he finds himself in the minority."[39] In other words, Constant suggested that the executive was "responsible" in this sense: ministers must retire if they lose the confidence of the elected assemblies.

In the *Réflexions,* he adjusted realistically to the return of the Bourbons, granting the king the right to appoint and dismiss ministers. Article 56 of the Charte declared that ministers could be accused only for acts of treason or embezzlement.[40] But executive responsibility toward the elected chamber and thus "toward the nation"[41] remained one of Constant's essential preoccupations throughout the Restoration. At the beginning of 1830, before the dynasty was overthrown, he wrote: "Ministers whose laws have been rejected cannot govern. . . . Thus the faculty of rejecting laws and of accusing ministers are the means given by the Charte to the chambers to obtain a new ministry. . . . It is in the interest of the king not to keep ministers who do not have the public confidence."[42] Constant's underlying position did not change. Ministers, though officially "chosen" by the monarch, could not be his agents: the king was not an "active power" and thus could have no agents. Instead, ministers were responsible, and not merely for defalcation and malfeasance in office, but also for violating the will of the assembly.[43] They could be dismissed for having lost legislative confidence; but they could not be personally punished.

The doctrine of ministerial "responsibility" follows from legislative supremacy and belies compartmentalizing interpretations of the separation of powers. While the Charte was unclear about the king's duty to choose his ministers from the party that controlled the chamber, a parliamentary system of this sort evolved by tacit consent between 1816 and 1829. During the transitional years of the early Restoration, Constant's remarks about responsibility were more tentative than either of the statements cited above. But his reticence can be explained politically.[44] Throughout the Restoration, "vive la Charte!" was the rallying cry of the Left. Liberals recognized that a strict construction of the constitution was a powerful weapon in their struggle against the ultras. The Right was reticent to express publicly its contempt for the Charte. Thus, the opposition was able to "box in" the government and resist the most extreme reactionary measures.[45] In this context, it is easy to see why *De la responsibilité des ministres* of 1815 contains a somewhat blurred defense of parliamentary government. Committed formally to Article 56, Constant tried to "reinterpret" the penal responsibility of ministers for treason as an adequate basis for political responsibility. This reform-minded attempt to stretch the meaning of the Charte, while piously respecting its language, naturally resulted in some obscure and waffling formulations.

In *La monarchie selon la Charte* (1816), Chateaubriand had proposed an advanced parliamentary regime for France: ministers were to govern only with support of a majority in the chamber. But this scheme, which sounds progressive in the abstract, was meant to guarantee the ascendancy of the reactionary Chambre introuvable over the relatively moderate ministry of Richelieu. In principle, Constant supported a parliamentary (and not merely constitutional) regime.[46] But the unpromising wording of Article 56 and the reactionary composition of Restoration assemblies combined to force him into public hesitations and vagueness on this point.

While the executive should act within a legal framework established legislatively, it should not be reduced to the passive instrument of an all-powerful assembly. Indeed, the abysmal collapse of the first French Republic was traceable to two technical flaws in constitutional design. While guarding carefully against a tyrannical concentration of powers, neither the Constitution of 1791 nor that of the Year III (1795) had provided legal means for ending a deadlock between the legislature and the executive. Specifically, they failed to incorporate either an absolute veto or a right of dissolution.

For example, if the Directory had been constitutionally permitted to pro-rogue the Councils and call new elections, the "deplorable *journée*" of 18 Fructidor would never have occurred. The right of dissolution would have deprived Barras of his "pretext" for closing the legislature and arresting its unobliging members—his claim that the Councils were not acting in ac-cordance with the national will.[47]

Committed to legislative predominance, Constant also warned against hobbling the executive with constitutional obstructions.[48] "In rendering a government too weak, you reduce it to a position where it is forced to employ illegitimate means." Under the Directory, delegates would have been safer if executive power over the Councils had been gently constitutionalized rather than being obstinately forbidden: "The inviolability of the legislative branch will always be a fiction without the right to dissolve the representative assemblies." Inflexible checks on executive influence can be destabilizing. There are certain actions which any executive must undertake. If the path to necessary goals is cluttered with checks and roadblocks, hindrances and regulations, the government will soon acquire the habit of violating con-stitutional rules. Then the rules which are truly essential (for instance, the protection of basic rights) will themselves fall victim to unfortunate pre-cedent: "Man finds it amazingly easy to fail in his real duties once he has emancipated himself from artificial duties."[49]

A quite specific psychological theory underlay this warning against an over-restricted executive. After a government breaks its own laws, it inevitably panics.[50] Then the routine of tyranny begins: "If the Directory had been able to dissolve the Councils legally, it would neither have purged them by force nor proscribed their members. It would have used its con-stitutional right and, having used it without becoming guilty of usurpation, would have avoided that state of fear, violence, and suspicion; it would have avoided that convulsive, rash, confused, and disordered state which usurpations always entail."[51] The Directors, "reigning in the name of a constitution they had overthrown,"[52] became the panicky victims of their own illegality. From the Councils' standpoint, less would have been more: legislative supremacy would have been better served by fewer constraints on executive power.

A parallel argument appeared in Constant's defense of representative government. Free national elections would democratize government, chang-ing it from a remote and alien force to an arena in which national debates could occur. But such a promise did not appeal to all moderate parties in France. To undermine the most credible claim of the Right, Constant reassured his readers that political freedoms, too, were a safety-valve. For example, the disorders accompanying elections in England were greatly exaggerated:

> I certainly saw elections accompanied by brawls, commotions, violent disputes. But, the men elected were always distinguished either by their talent or their wealth. And once the election was over, everything returned to its accustomed regularity. The voters of the lower class, recently obstinate and turbulent, became once again hard-working, docile and even respectful. Satisfied with having exercised their rights, they yielded that much more readily to their superiors and to social conventions, because, in acting this way, they knew they were obeying only a reasonable calculation of their own enlightened self-interest. The day after an election, there remained not the slightest trace of yesterday's agitation. The people had resumed their labors, but public spirit had received the healthy shock necessary to reanimate it.[53]

In England, twenty thousand men could gather together without a policeman in sight and without posing any danger to public order. In France, by contrast, such gatherings always "bristle with guards and bayonets." Such defensive precautions are counterproductive, ensuring that Frenchmen "have never contracted the habit of repressing [them]selves."[54] Constant employed this argument not because he yearned for lower-class deference but because he was struggling to outmaneuver the antiliberals. His central argument was that further liberalization would bring not anarchy but peace.

CONCESSIONS TO HUMAN IMPERFECTION

The "constitutional art" must acknowledge personal aspirations and convert them into supports of, rather than threats to, the established government. Political offices must offer "to ambitious men more methodical and thus less stormy careers."[55] Constant insisted that deputies should be able to become ministers. "This open entry," he wrote, "is perhaps what has preserved the English constitution."[56] Even a remote chance of being raised to the executive will make legislators treat the office of minister gingerly and with enhanced respect. An ambitious deputy will not want to destroy a weapon he may someday wield. Talented place-seekers, whose personal characteristics will not be radically improved by a new legal order, must be provided with routes to power which they may tread without subverting the constitution itself.[57]

A similar appreciation of safety valves led Constant to favor the opportunity for indefinite reelection to the chamber. This system, he wrote, "encourges the calculations of morality"[58] without actually requiring men to become moral. It artificially guarantees that the interests of the delegates will coincide with those of the electorate. Such "impersonal" devices were suitable replacements for that noble but unreliable quality, personal uprightness: "The guarantee of the citizen's most precious rights must be found in the laws: it must not be sought at random in the probity of men, whose very virtues are but fortunate accidents."[59] Constitutional tactics are more reliable than moral fiber.

Self-interest and ambition were not the only human weaknesses upon which constitution-makers must keep their minds apprehensively focused. For Constant, fear (justified or unjustified) was the greatest threat to the durability of limited government. "In politics, fear is the most hostile of all the passions."[60] Constitutions must be constructed to keep this destabilizing emotion under control.

During the revolutionary and Bonapartist regimes, judges had to have "the courage of the most intrepid warriors" to deliver verdicts according to their convictions.[61] Human nature is not equal to such a task. The independence of the judiciary, achieved through lifetime appointments, is a concession to the fact that most judges will not possess superhuman daring and fortitude. The opposite mechanism is invoked to neutralize the fears of ministers and representatives: the person/office distinction. It is a great vice in any constitution to offer rulers no alternative between clinging to power and being executed. The person/office distinction is meant to ensure that when ministers are dismissed and legislatures prorogued, individuals vacating office will remain untouched as private persons. Only the certainty of a civilian afterlife for ousted personnel will make possible the introduction of self-correcting mechanisms into government. Viewed in this light, the celebrated "impersonality" of the modern state appears to be a concession to anxieties generated by the revolutionary experience. A durable constitution must be compatible with the politician's instinct for physical survival.

Next on Constant's list was the problem of vanity or *amour-propre,* a peculiarly French flaw, he thought, and one with dire consequences in an age of public opinion. Reflecting on the revolutionary assemblies, he revealed a central ambiguity in the liberal idea of publicity: "nothing is more costly to a nation than reputations to be made."[62] This concern with new men, with first-generation politicians intent on winning fame and currying favor, surfaced repeatedly in Constant's writings from his analyses of the Directory to his attack on Napoleon in *Conquête et usurpation:* "One had imposed on unknown men the necessity of making themselves known, and violence always succeeds better than wisdom."[63]

The chance of speedy notoriety provided a powerful incentive for eye-catching gestures. But what institutional devices might counter this relish of public acclaim, the *besoin de faire effet?* Besides suggesting that various external checks be clamped upon the elected chamber, Constant also proposed the British system that forbade written speeches in Parliament. This rule was meant to create a "majorité silencieuse" in the Assembly, since those unable to make effective impromptu speeches "will take refuge in reason as a last resort."[64] Men cannot be expected to act rationally on their own, but institutions can be devised that will channel their nonrational drives, such as *amour-propre,* in the direction of reason.

Another natural result of vanity was the exorbitant proliferation of laws. Constant considered "the regulative and legislative mania" to be an ailment endemic to representative states.[65] He worried that the very office of legislator encouraged men to pour forth legal regulations:

> The multiplicity of laws flatters in legislators two natural tendencies: the need to act and the pleasure of believing oneself necessary. Every time you give a man a special vocation, he will prefer to do more rather than less. Those charged with arresting vagabonds on the highways are tempted to pick fights with every traveler. Spies who cannot discover anything, invent something. As soon as a country establishes a ministry to look out for conspirators, one hears ceaseless talk about conspiracies.[66]

Elsewhere, Constant reformulated the same point: "Regulations are not made for the advantage of the governed, but to prevent governors from appearing useless," and "laws are always wanted since they cause their authors to be spoken about."[67] He conceived the executive or royal veto as a safeguard against the craze for legislation associated with the *amour-propre* of elected representatives.[68]

Finally, knowledge was a scarce resource. Constant took this eternal human infirmity into account when limiting the aims of constitutionalism. Similarly, one of his principal arguments against censorship was that censors are human and, being human, always need more knowledge than they have. Men are chronically underinformed and therefore make grievous mistakes. When arguing in favor of strict judicial formalities, Constant always claimed that "forms" are the best way to compensate for this human fallibility, the tendency to misinterpret evidence and leap to hasty conclusions: "Formal rules are the best means of ascertaining the facts."[69] Procedures compensate for cognitive imperfections bequeathed by nature to the human mind.

GOVERNMENT BY DISCUSSION

A liberal constitution is not only an obstruction and a safety-valve: it is also a mobilizer. It can serve as a stimulant as well as a depressant, enlisting the energies, imagination, and knowledge of citizens in formulating policy and solving common problems.

Representative government, including the election of local officials, was abandoned by the Committee of Public Safety in 1793 and was never convincingly reestablished by the Directory. Napoleon had eliminated the last vestiges of the representative institutions created by the Revolution. Except for a brief period between 1814 and 1816, when France was occupied by foreign troops and the Right controlled the chamber of deputies, the ultra party opposed genuinely representative government and shared the Jacobin and Napoleonic unwillingness to face the electorate.[70]

These self-enclosed and unrepresentative regimes were unable to tap the creative resources of the nation. According to Constant, "Representative assemblies alone introduce life into the body politic."[71] His vitalistic language reflected his commitment to legislative supremacy as well as his dissatisfaction with a mechanical separation of powers. The *Réflexions* concur with the *Fragmens* on this question. Representation is a mechanism for social learning. The "primary condition of representative government" is "the liberty and independence of all discussion in the legislature."[72]

Truly absurd about the Constitution of the Year VIII (1799) was the separation between the Tribunat and the Corps législatif: discussions were held in one chamber while decisions were struck in the other. But decisions should obviously be made on the basis of discussions.[73] Political opposition, which Bonaparte considered a source of weakness, was actually a source of strength.[74] Against centuries of religious and political dogma as well as against the profoundest psychological impulses of men in power, Constant argued that public disagreement was a creative, problem-solving, community-building force. The principal function of the Tribunat was not to oppose the government, but rather to gather, from all parts of France, suggestions for improvement and reform on questions ranging from local administration to agricultural techniques. Federalism was not only a system for dispersing power but also, and more importantly, a method of decentralized experimentation. The entire nation could learn from successes and failures in different regions. For example, all of greater France could imitate Geneva's very successful system of public education.[75] For such mutual learning to transpire, however, there had to exist a forum for "national discussion," and this could be no other than the Tribunat. Moreover, since the executive branch was overloaded with tasks and severely underinformed, it needed all the help it could get. Far from obstructing government, the Tribunat should help it avoid self-contradictory legislation, providing necessary facts as well as imaginative policy suggestions.[76] Exposing its proposals to public debate, in sum, a government can improve the quality of its governance. By silencing its critics, it will only weaken itself. Constant's speeches in the Tribunat repeatedly stress this point: liberalism seeks not to eliminate government but to create intelligent government.[77]

Freedom of debate can remedy the biases of both the electorate and the elected assembly. Free discussion, carried out in public among nationally chosen delegates, will facilitate creative collaboration between particularistic and universalistic perspectives on public policy.[78] The problem of every assembly is that it is compact: it tends to develop an exclusivist esprit de corps, to detach itself from the needs of the nation. There is no guarantee that delegates indifferent to regional interests will be especially devoted to national interests.[79] Periodic and direct elections are essential. They will disrupt the assembly's tendency to corporative self-encapsulation and ensure that local concerns are heard at the national level. Secluded in Paris, political elites risk becoming ignorant of the needs of their country. Expert knowledge about which grievances need redressing can only be found among those who suffer such grievances first hand.[80]

Although ultimately sovereign, the electorate is scattered: each local constituency, although intensely conscious of its own perspective on national problems, is ignorant of the views of other groups in other regions. Only within a national assembly can acquaintances be made. Mutual partisan readjustments will produce a "general will," which Constant defines as an intelligent bargain between individual wills: "What is the general interest except the compromise that takes place between particular interests? What is general representation except the representation of all the partial interests that must negotiate about the objects common to them?"[81] Only representatives meeting face to face can hammer out a common will.

Delegates must pledge to introduce their own constituency's opinion as an initial baseline for further bargaining: "The representative of a section must be the organ of this section. He must not abandon any of its real or

imagined interests until after he has defended them. He must be partial
to his section, because if each delegate is a partisan for his constituents,
the partiality of each, reunited and reconciled, will have the advantage of
the impartiality of all."[82] If the national will emerges gradually and "from
the bottom up," its name will not be confiscated so easily by an autocratic
faction. Responsibility to constituents is indispensable. Nevertheless, delegates must not be saddled with imperative mandates which make a mockery
of parliamentary discussion and render mutual compromise and learning
impossible.[83] Parliamentary debate *is* a learning process, not merely a bro-
kerage of pre-given interests: "Laws must be the result of a multitude of
ideas. Men who are different because of their habits, their relations, and
their social situations must pool the contributions of their multiple reflections; and the variety of the discussion will throw light on the advantages
and disadvantages [of the proposed legislation]." A free market of ideas,
mobilizing decentralized knowledge, gives truth a fair chance to prevail over
error: "Liberty is precious above all because it ensures the examination and
evaluation of opinions, and because it leads in this way to the rectification
of ideas."[84] Public discussion may not guarantee the triumph of truth; but
it is the best means available for preventing errors from becoming permanently ensconced. Much more consistently than other regimes, representative government is able to recoup its own mistakes. Mechanisms for self-
correction thus assume high priority in all liberal constitutions.

The principle of representation stipulates that "each representative
vote for general national interests" and that he "can, as a result, sacrifice
to them the partial and momentary interests of his constituents." Consid-
eration of the general good is what distinguishes a national representative
from a mere proxy or business agent for particular interests. Immediate
recall could be parochial not democratic. A system whereby localities could
at any time unseat delegates willing to compromise their special claims
would be "the most dangerous form of federalism." It would enshrine "the
egoism of locality,"[85] mocking national unity and preventing the mutual
adjustment and learning among delegates which is the essence of representative government.

The transformation of special pleading into national self-government
does not occur by means of an invisible hand. It goes on in public, as all
genuine representation must, and it requires delegates to aim consciously
at promoting what they judge to be the public good. Within the Assembly,
decisions are reached according to the principle of majority rule. Unanimous
decisions are not merely unlikely, they are positively undesirable: "the essence of a representative constitution is that the minority and each of its

members can express its opposition in any manner and with complete in-dependence."[86] The minority accepts the legal bindingness of the majority's vote, but (by the right of opposition) it continues to debate the wisdom of legislative decisions and to protest morally. The constitution is thus more than an instrument for protecting citizens from misuses of state power: it creates a mechanism for public learning and governmental self-correction.

The driving force behind discussions in the legislature is "public opin-ion," a strong echo of ancient liberty surviving in modern citizenship. In the early modern age, "the discovery of printing furnished men with a new means of discussion and a new cause of intellectual ferment." The vast extent of modern polities meant that the press was the only feasible means of publicity and debate. Paraphrasing the antimercantilists, Constant as-serted somewhat optimistically that "*laisser écrire* is all that is needed for the human mind to achieve the highest degree of activity, insight, and justice."[87]

A free public debate on all important political issues will involve citizens in the governance of their state. Even more strikingly, it will help forge the unity of the nation: "The liberty of newspapers will give France a new existence. It will identify the country with its constitution, its gov-ernment, and its public interests. It will cause a confidence to be born that has never before existed." Through a liberal constitution, France will be-come more of a unified national community. Constant applied the classical vitalistic metaphor to this subject as well: "public opinion is the life of states." Full freedom of the press will establish throughout the country "a correspondence of thoughts, or reflections, of political knowledge."[88] This nation-building aspect of constitutionalism reveals another neglected con-tinuity between absolute monarchy and the liberal state.

Against all the censorship-based regimes France had known, Constant insisted on the need to create, organize, and sustain popular sovereignty through public discussion carried out in the medium of an absolutely free press. He conceived public discussion as a positive expression of sovereignty. It was not a force alien to freedom, or merely a tool in the service of freedom. It was an embodiment of freedom; it was freedom in action.[89]

NEUTRALITY IN CONTEXT

In the 1730s, Voltaire had described the English monarch as "un pouvoir mitoyen" arbitrating between Lords and Commons; and he added that the absence of such a mediating power had resulted in civil wars between ple-beians and patricians in ancient Rome.[90] In the *Fragmens* and again in the

Réflexions, Constant elaborated on this idea: the English monarch was not an active power at all, but rather an aloof arbitrator, a *pouvoir neutre.* He reigned but did not govern, making no substantive decisions but resolving deadlocks and reestablishing a situation in which decisions could be made. Under the Republic sketched in the *Fragmens,* members of the proposed "neutral power" were to be popularly elected to lifetime office and given land to guarantee their independence and prestige. In the *Réflexions,* Constant quietly rewrote the job description of his *pouvoir modérateur* to accommodate Louis XVIII,[91] now referring to a constitutional monarch as "the judicial power of the other powers." Such a king was to be an impartial conciliator, "a moderator elevated above the sphere of agitations."[92] Dampening conflicts between the Houses and the ministers, he must ensure that, when necessary, the two branches act decisively and in concert.

Rhetorically, Constant aggrandized the monarch; but the powers he granted his neutral king were basically harmless. He did not treat "monarchy" as a form of government, but rather as a cog in the constitutional division of functions. While making superficial concessions to royal (or imperial) self-importance, he aimed at reducing Louis XVIII (or Napoleon) to the role of a figurehead. To call him a neutral power was to neutralize his will. Not that the ceremonial trappings of monarchy were unimportant. For instance, they might have reconciled the Bourbons and their followers (or Napoleon and his) to a constitutional and parliamentary regime.

Writing about neutrality, Constant stressed the need for an intermediary force between the ministers and the chambers. But a larger issue lurked in the background. When, following Voltaire, he discussed the chaos of Roman political life resulting from the lack of a neutral power, he ascribed to neutrality a much wider significance. The king's neutrality symbolized the general impartiality of the state itself, an impartiality that in turn was meant as an essential condition for the maintenance of public discussion and debate. When he referred to "civil dissensions" in Rome caused by "the opposed interests of two enemy classes,"[93] he was obviously thinking of France. The groups to be balanced were much broader than the executive and legislative branches of government.[94]

Morality is a field of battle, not a source of social harmony. Unable to create moral unanimity in a divided nation, the state can relax social tensions by adapting a stance of relative impartiality, by keeping questions of personal morality distinct from questions of legality. Like money, formal procedures can neutralize morality in embattled contexts. During the Restoration, Constant advocated the divorce of the legal from the moral in the following way: "The Law of 9 November does not require citizens to melt with pity when walking over the tombs in the Vendean valley. Deafness to the cries of 1793 or to the cheers of 1814 may be a physical infirmity or a moral wrong. But it does not fall within the jurisdiction of the correctional police."[95] Antiliberals, both ultra and Jacobin, believed the state responsible for correcting the moral obtuseness of citizens. They thought that "the government can interfere actively in all individual relations and make laws to command and encourage the virtues."[96] For the sake of national cooperation, Constant disagreed. He insisted on distinguishing the aim of legislation from that of morals.[97] Many important laws must have a moral basis; Constant's relentless struggle to abolish the slave trade shows he knew this. But the moral content of the law must be relatively unobtrusive if the constitution is to be a framework for compromise and discussion and not just another stake in civil strife.

Moral conflict is perhaps too tepid a description of the reciprocal hatreds and fears that boiled beneath the surface of French life after the Revolution. No government in this period could hope to embody fully the moral ideals of all French citizens. The prevailing ideals were much too discordant. As a result, a pragmatic constitution maker had to abandon the attempt to create a society-wide consensus about "the highest good" upon which to base political authority. The liberal slogan was thus "Let Authority be Neutral."[98] Constant strove to abstract as far as possible from controversial moral questions and to establish a constitutional order on a practical compromise. Constitutionalism required a bare minimum of moral agreement; but this could be an abstract consensus focusing on procedural matters and leaving ample room for maneuver, ad hoc compromise, and nonviolent dissent.

Interpreted philosophically (i.e., in a context-free manner), the liberal pretension to "neutrality" rings hollow: Constant suggested that the constitutional state could be a purely formal arrangement, taking no stand on matters of content. He pretended that it might be meticulous about means but oblivious of ends. But a strict form/content or means/ends distinction is untenable. Every formal rule includes certain kinds of content and excludes other kinds. Means shape the ends. A commitment to the rules of peace and personal security excludes feudal self-help, prohibiting the sanguinary escapades of the bellicose. Rules instituting religious toleration prevent ecclesiastical persecutions and douse the enthusiasm of zealots.[99] Liberalism, judged from this perspective, was either naive or dishonest: it was not, and could never have been, "neutral."[100]

Intriguing conceptually, this argument is historically unconvincing. Protestants living in sixteenth-century France had no trouble understanding the meaning of an edict of toleration. They would not have been impressed by a theoretical demolition of the form/content or means/end distinctions. Viewed in context, "neutrality" is a coherent and even an indispensable concept; it picks out a very important feature of the modern constitutional order: procedural impartiality. To reveal the cogency of this idea, we need only enter the following caveat. Neutrality can be established only *relative* to specific factions or individuals. Impartiality means nonpartisanship, even-handedness toward identifiable parties.[101] Formal rules tolerate certain content and prohibit other content. But a single formal framework may be compatible with a broad spectrum of action and belief. While no instrument can be pliantly adapted to every conceivable function, there *are* multipurpose tools. The rules of the liberal state, as envisaged by Constant, left room for diversity in ideology and behavior. He espoused a constitution that was neutral relative to moderates of both Left and Right. Admittedly, his liberal regime would not be neutral toward the rabid irreconcilables of either extreme.[102] It was not meant to be.

Jacobins and ultras who yearned for a conflict-free society with moral unanimity enforced by the police were thwarted by a liberal peace based on a degree of mutual indifference and tolerance for disharmony. Constant was nevertheless right to insist that peace was a *relatively* nonpartisan ideal. The aims and ideologies incompatible with a liberal constitution had been discredited by twenty-five years of civil war. History had exposed the utopian character of moral unanimity. A peace that secured the right to dissent by encouraging a degree of mutual indifference appeared neutral with respect to most historically plausible goals.

Louis XVIII was obviously attracted to the role of a neutral power. Not wishing to reign over two nations, he pursued a policy of conciliation. By refusing to attend the meetings of his ministry, he kept (to some extent) above the battle. Charles X, by contrast, refused to submit to the discipline of neutrality. Sawing wood, he believed, was more attractive than ruling in the manner of an English king. Charles attended the meetings of his cabinet and was so closely identified with the ultra faction that Polignac's defeat led to a collapse of the dynasty. In the context of Restoration politics, in other words, *neutrality* was not a timorous slogan denoting evasiveness or the straddling of fences. Neutrality was militant, or became so. As the power of the ultras increased, Constant was driven into an aggressive response. He began to wage a fierce campaign of public sarcasm against a government that chose to sacrifice the interests of the nation to the interests of a small faction.

Militancy does not preclude diplomacy. During this same period, Constant often formulated his arguments in a conciliatory and nonpartisan style. The phrase "I will attempt to abstract from my own opinions and even from my wishes" recurs again and again.[103] Moreover, his general mode of argumentation led him to stress facts and avoid moral posturing. An often repeated exhortation is thus "Attachons-nous aux faits." Facts were instruments of peaceful change: "men can acknowledge facts without their *amour-propre* being wounded." In the Tribunat, he had argued that "one of the greatest obstacles to the regeneration of our country is that we do not know enough facts." Later, in attacking the slave trade, he assumed that he could win his case simply by revealing facts, by reading aloud detailed documentary reports on how slave merchants brutalized their human cargo. A similar fact-mindedness characterized his argument against protective tariffs: "I would like to examine this material from a point of view that dispenses with all declamations, and thereby begin with a principle that appeals to all interests."[104]

In the same practical and antimoralistic spirit,[105] Constant made extensive use of conditionals. He typically addressed a royalist minister in the following manner: given that your goals are such and such, you had best adopt the following means. There was no question of convincing his opponents to embrace nobler moral aims. Conversion to a life of virtue was not his goal. Instead, he consistently argued, "You are subverting your own purpose."[106]

Abstraction from controversial moral questions was a central strategy in Constant's politics of constitutional design. His arguments themselves were meant to be as neutral or nonpartisan as procedural legality. They were built to appeal to nonliberals, so long as they were not hell-bent on vengeance. Just as the solution to civil war is civil peace, so the cure for *l'arbitraire* is proceduralism and limited government. No matter what your beliefs, you will be pleased to know that if you do not break the law the police are unlikely to arrest you: "the true principles of liberty have this advantage: they protect all parties in turn."[107]

Having endured the atrocities of terror and counterterror, what values might Frenchmen share? In an attempt to formulate a thin theory of the common good, Constant focused on the idea of security. The principal victim of anarchy and arbitrary rule was the security of citizens (and Constant defined *citizen* in a universal manner, as a category to be awarded blindly, never according to party allegiance or family background). This explains why he sometimes followed Montesquieu and defined freedom *exclusively* as personal security. "In 1800," he wrote, "the dominant idea was: liberty has done us harm, and so we want no more liberty."[108] In response, he strove to depict freedom as harmless, to sever its connection with terror. Moreover, since he preferred to focus on reforms that were incomplete but possible (rather than ideal but unattainable), he occasionally deemphasized the right to vote and participate in public discussion, concentrating instead on a less dangerous freedom: the right of citizens to be left alone by their government. But these were realistic political maneuvers, designed to awaken a minimal consensus in a faction-racked country. They did not express a truncated idea of freedom or antipathy to democratic ideas. This is demonstrated by other passages in which Constant emphatically endorsed a broader sharing of political rights.

THE RESTRICTED SUFFRAGE

What can be learned about Constant's liberalism from his support in 1814– 15 of *le suffrage censitaire*? Is it really helpful to view this, as virtually all commentators do, as a sign of class bias, of a fear of democracy built into the foundations of his theory?

Concealing one's wealth to avoid taxation is an old tradition. The restricted suffrage was a useful technique for inducing wealthy citizens to divulge their incomes and pay up accordingly. By limiting the vote to those who officially paid a substantial tax, governments could hope to raise much-needed revenue from a secretive people. Representation for taxes: it was a quid pro quo. It, too, had a venerable ancestry reaching back to medieval times.

This fiscal concern is wrongly neglected in most discussions of the limited franchise. But what other issues were involved? In 1829, nearing the end of his life, Constant wrote:

> In matters of government, the most absolute equality of rights
> distributed among all individuals assembled together in the body
> of the nation must be and soon will be, in all civilized countries,
> the prime condition for the existence of every government . . .
> and all those who possess these rights will be authorized
> to cooperate in their defense, that is to say, to participate some-
> how in making the laws that determine the action of the
> government.[109]

This sounds like a plea for maximizing the number of electors, not for limiting suffrage on the basis of a high property qualification. Similarly, in the *Commentaire* of 1822, Constant condemned England for its disastrously narrow franchise.[110] Yet there were more than a half-million electors in

Britain at this time compared to a scant ninety-thousand in France.[111] Unlike Royer-Collard and Guizot, Constant unambiguously affirmed the sovereignty of the people.[112] Earlier, in the *Fragmens,* he had defined *liberty* as rule according to the national will.[113] In the *Principes* of 1802–06, he wrote, "Citizens will take no interest in their institutions unless they are called to participate in them by voting."[114] Virtual representation is meaningless, and assemblies have no right to decide which delegates to seat.[115] The right of dissolution, exercised by the neutral power, was essentially democratic: new elections would resolve governmental deadlock in favor of either the ministry or the assembly.[116] The Constitution of the Year VIII (1799) had arranged for "representatives" to be appointed from above. With this in mind, Constant wrote: "There exists only one guarantee against the corruption, dependence, servility of legislative assemblies: popular elections. The more direct and pure they are, the more they ensure the integrity of the representatives of the people."[117] After 1817, Constant consistently argued for a lowering of the existing property qualification. Eventually, he wrote, the vote will be extended to all social classes.[118] Viewed in context, such passages appear quite radical. Nonetheless, in the early manuscripts, as well as in the *Réflexions* and the *Principes* of 1815, we also find a defense of the limited suffrage. How can we account for this discrepancy? Was Constant being inconsistent? Did his views on the franchise evolve in significant ways?

Constant gave three basic arguments for a property-based franchise: (1) an argument from independence; (2) an argument from education; and (3) an argument from fear.

Voting had to be restricted to men "who exist without the help of a salary that makes them dependent on others."[119] The ownership of property served the same function later assumed by the secret ballot, sheltering the voter from pressure exerted by those on whom his livelihood depended. A wage earner was in no position to deliver anything resembling free consent. A dependent voter will follow his *maître* sheepishly to vote: "Property owners are masters of his existence because they can refuse to give him work. Thus, only someone who possesses the income necessary to exist independent of any foreign will can exercise the right to vote."[120] Autonomy is not a natural attribute of the soul: it has specific institutional preconditions. Without a protective screen to prevent manipulation, a man's will is not his own.[121] Public citizenship presupposes private independence. A dependent situation narrows a man's vision and produces a chronic case of diminished responsibility. Because representatives are meant to "express the needs of the people,"[122] they should be elected only by citizens capable of enunciating popular needs without fear of reprisal. The necessary shield was not hereditary property, however, but property circulating freely in postaristocratic and commercial society.[123]

Constant's argument about the social preconditions of voter autonomy has a logic of its own, apart from the supposed interests of the middle class at war with upper- and lower-class enemies. Viewed *as* an argument, it is based on a distrust of manipulative pressures, whatever their source. This distrust, in turn, registers the pervasive influence of legal thinking—with its traditional concern for the independence of judges—on democratic theory. If, by 1830, Constant was looking forward to universal suffrage, it was because he had come to believe that property was not the only way to shelter voters from manipulation and intimidation.

Constant also mounted a second defense of a restricted suffrage. Citing classical (that is, aristocratic) sources, he noted that the owners of property were blessed with superior *lumières* acquired by a diligent use of leisure time. To confine the vote to the educated was progressive in one sense: enlightenment was no longer the monopoly of a single class, but was spreading rapidly. As it spread, the size of the electorate would naturally grow.[124] Nevertheless, Constant's argument of 1814–15 seems peculiarly mechanical: wage earners simply have *no time* to appreciate the intricacies of the political scene. This thesis is dissatisfying for several reasons.

In accord with his Protestant heritage, Constant frequently associated "leisure" with moral degeneration. Personally, he was a compulsive worker. In the *Fragments,* he wrote that "the nobility is cordialized by civilization. But it is corrupted by civilization as well. It has fewer active careers open to it than do the other classes, and with more leisure time, more chance to abuse it." Similarly, he contrasted Europe with underdeveloped America, where citizens were involved in the massive agricultural and industrial transformation of the landscape. Europeans, he asserted, were "exposed, thanks to the leisure provided by the security of their physical existence, to all the restlessness of a nervous vanity and to all the squeamishness of an unoccupied imagination."[125] But if leisure corrupts the soul, how can it illuminate the mind?

Ancient philosophers believed that the principal condition for the pursuit of truth was release from the pressure of needs. Modern liberals chose instead to emphasize freedom of debate open to all. In his discussion of jury duty, Constant claimed that political enlightenment resulted not from leisure but from civic participation. Reason is perfected by use. Citizens learn to appreciate political problems not because they are blessed with nothing to do, but because they are thrust into situations where they have

urgent problems to solve. Only property-owners should have a right to sit
on juries. But Constant's argument implied that public debate, not property-
ownership, fostered enlightenment.

This argument, addressed to those who adduced citizen incompetence
against trial by jury, is worth quoting at length:

> Who does not see that, for want of habit, an institution can
> initially seem ill-suited to a nation and yet become suitable and
> beneficial if it is intrinsically good, because the nation acquires
> by means of the institution itself a capacity it did not have? . . .
> The insouciance, the indifference, and the frivolity of the French
> are the result of defective institutions, and the effect is adduced
> to perpetuate the cause. No people remains indifferent to their
> interests when they are allowed to occupy themselves with these
> interests. When they are indifferent, it is because they have been
> brushed aside. In this respect the French need the institution of
> the jury precisely to the extent that they seem momentarily
> incapable of it. The people will discover [in the jury system] not
> only the particular advantages of the institution, but the general
> and more important advantage of renewing their moral
> education.[126]

Jury duty, by involving citizens, will overcome what a right-wing opponent
described as the typical French "indifference to everything regarding public
administration . . . the empire of egoism and particular interest, the tepidity
and nullity of public spirit."[127] Civic responsibility, not property ownership,
leads to political enlightenment.[128] Why, then, a restricted suffrage?

Ultimately, Constant acquiesced in a narrow definition of the *pays
légal* for strategic reasons. Universal suffrage registers the sovereignty of the
people only if elections are genuinely free, but "elections cannot be free if
they are held in moments of danger and terror."[129] Because of the bitter
divisions racking French society, "we have never had a truly popular election."[130] Constant's liberalism was a philosophy of transition: it represented
an attempt to guide France from civil war to self-government. A republican
constitution can help establish a republic, but only under specific conditions:

> In what circumstances was the French Republic founded? In the
> midst of what convulsions, what crimes, what delirium? A few
> days before the Republic was proclaimed, did not massacres
> arouse fear among the governed and remorse among the gov-
> ernors? Still earlier, was not the National Assembly subjugated
> by a troop of armed men? Had not popular leaders justified

murder and cursed all social order? Were not the men capable
of founding a republic, the truly republican spirits, already
threatened? What sort of constitution could emerge from this
frightful confusion?[131]

The Constitution of 1793, declaring universal manhood suffrage, had never
gone into effect, swamped as it was by anarchy and terror. Mass abstention
of eligible voters had been common under the Directory. In Constant's
judgment, the truly urgent question was "how to portray as an enduring
authority" a legislative assembly "which two hundred armed men suffice
to annihilate?"[132] Recreating a modicum of trust in representative institutions and designing a system in which opposition was legitimate took priority over extending the vote to all citizens.

Furthermore, restricting the franchise temporarily might be a precondition for building trust. Hopes for constitutional government and reform
in France depended on the cooperation of moderate royalists as well as of
wealthy non-nobles. Without concessions to their fear of confiscation, no
constitutional and reformist government would have had a chance to survive: "If propertyless men are placed among the number of the legislators,
however well intentioned they be, the disquietude of the property-owners
will block all their measures. The wisest laws will be distrusted and as a
result disobeyed, while a different organization would have reconciled popular consent even to a government defective in some respects."[133] Yielding
to the anxieties of wealthier citizens made it possible to establish the ru-
diments of a parliamentary system.[134] This argument was more practical
than theoretical.[135] Constant accepted a restricted suffrage in order to
reassure the comfortable and well-connected and thus to launch representative institutions and the rule of law in an unstable social environment.
Parliamentary government based on a limited suffrage closely resembles
parliamentary government based on universal suffrage. Concessions necessary to get the basic system in place were a price worth paying.

Constant's attitude, however, was militant as well as conciliatory.
While accepting the framework established by the Charte, liberals took
advantage of a deep internal contradiction in the Restoration: policy was
dictated by the nobility and the clergy, while the vote was granted to the
base-born and irreligious—so long as they had sufficient wealth. After 1814–
15, Constant fought for a gradual extension of the electorate within the
framework of the Charte. Popular support, in the form of petitions, riots,
and national agitation, showed that nonenfranchised groups recognized the

importance to themselves of the liberal struggle to obtain marginal readjustments in the electorate.[136]

POLITICAL EDUCATION

Wary of Great Legislators and concerned to defuse ideological conflict,
Constant avoided the idea that citizens should be morally transformed at
the hands of public officials: "the government is not the tutor of individuals."[137] Nevertheless, the idea of moral education through politics surfaced
at key junctures in his mature writings. The discussion of jury duty is one
example. Although "political liberty" is "always agitated," he wrote in *Du
polythéisme romain,* "by its very agitation it strengthens and aggrandizes
the souls of men." Moreover, he explicitly described his own speeches and
articles as contributions to "the constitutional education of France."[138] He
aimed to educate future citizens in fact-mindedness and to teach rulers that
criticism of government policy was quite distinct from insurrection. This
was not the kind of moral education Rousseau had in mind. The surprise
ending of "Ancient and Modern Liberty," however, contains a more ambitious reference to the idea. After devoting twenty dense pages to the thesis
that man's moral center of gravity now lies beyond politics, Constant concluded with a ringing defense of a seemingly Rousseauist legislative ideal:
"Il faut que les institutions achèvent l'éducation morale des citoyens." These
educative institutions, Constant continued,

> must consecrate [the citizens'] influence on the *res publica.* They
> must call them to participate by their decisions and by their
> votes in the exercise of power, guaranteeing their right to ex-
> amine and supervise through the free public expression of their
> opinions, and thus educating them by practice to these elevated
> functions, giving them at the same time the desire and the ca-
> pacity to perform them.[139]

Freedom and virtue remain distinct. But citizenship can, at least to some
extent, improve the mind.[140]

Constant invoked this educative argument for intensified participation
without explaining how it related to his other views, especially to his argument that the "purpose" of elections was not to cultivate personal character but rather "to establish the hegemony of public opinion by the free
and periodic renewal of its interpreters." In the passage about elections in
England, intended to assuage fears, he depicted the suffrage as an anaesthetic
that made the lower-middle class sober, deferential, and trustworthy. In the

Fragmens, he had argued in precisely the opposite manner: "You may well write a constitution, but where will be the public spirit that maintains it?" To create this public spirit, "I want direct and popular and I would even say tumultuous elections for national representatives."[141] The conclusion to "Ancient and Modern Liberty" echoed this republican claim that elections can vivify the public: politics in a school of popular self-reliance. But why was Constant, the cool skeptic, drawn toward such an intoxicating idea?

The marginal contribution of a modern voter to the outcome of a given election is negligible. Considered separately, each citizen is a supernumerary, wielding a meaningless fraction of power. On strictly rational grounds, no individual should believe it worthwhile to indulge in a ritual vote. Constant recognized this; but he also knew that mass abstention from electoral politics would allow an ultra elite to confiscate political power, a result no "perfectly rational" civic shirker would desire. An obvious way to circumvent this problem was to furnish voters with *another* reason to participate besides their exiguous personal influence on the outcome of an election: to vote is to undergo an ennobling form of civic education. As a rhetorical gesture aimed at building confidence among the electorate, Constant introduced the anti-instrumental notion that participation is not a mere means but rather an "end in itself." He even suggested that the primary purpose of citizenship is personal self-development. This sounds extraordinarily narcissistic. But Constant meant it to answer a nagging question of liberal democracy: why should any single citizen, whose "personal influence is an imperceptible fraction of the social will that imparts a direction to government,"[142] take the trouble to vote?

Repelled by the idea that individuals should be educated morally by a self-selected didactic elite, Constant nevertheless claimed that political institutions must accomplish the moral education of citizens. This claim, which registered an implicit dissatisfaction with the distinction drawn between active and passive citizens, must be interpreted politically. Against the character disqualifiers adduced by his ultra opponents, Constant invoked the universal human capacity to "learn by doing" which all individuals share. To privatized citizens tempted to neglect the political scene, he spoke of the uplifting and energizing effects of participation.

To outflank the ultras and give heart to potential civic truants, Constant argued that citizenship is a form of moral education. But can this stirring claim be reconciled with the disillusionment and antiromanticism that usually characterized his political views?

SIX

Romanticism and the Rancor against Modernity

The Greeks put us to shame.
—Schiller

CONSTANT cherished few of the exorbitant hopes inspiring political romanticism. He was not, however, a mere dry-eyed contriver of liberal constitutions. He was also a sentimentalist, a Germanophile, and a self-aware participant in the revolt against the eighteenth century.[1] He shared many of the attitudes and antipathies that roused a number of his contemporaries into an impassioned romance with the nation and its *Volk*.

Though unexplained, this paradox has not gone unnoticed: the same writer can label Constant a foremost "protagonist of the doctrine of liberal constitutionalism" while also grouping him among the "political romantics."[2] But no effort has been made to explain how the romantic and the antiromantic sides of his thinking fit together. Benefiting from intellectual exchange at Coppet, Constant was one of the first French writers on whom German romanticism exerted a decisive influence. But why was his reception of romantic thought so selective? With all his romanticizing impulses, why did he develop a basically colorless, legalistic, and even antiromantic theory of the modern state? Almost anything can be romanticized: sunsets, rainstorms, war, children, the Catholic church, Roman ruins, the noble savage, and, of course, *la patrie*. In religion and literature, Constant was generous to a fault with his romantic sentiments. In politics, however, he was sparing:

156

"we cannot create a constitutional monarchy with poetry and nostalgia."[3] It would be a mistake to suggest that his political thinking remained completely "impermeable to romanticism."[4] But his theory of the state was distinctly unromantic; and this needs to be explained.

Toward the end of the eighteenth century, there appeared in Europe antiliberal romantics such as Novalis, antiromantic liberals such as Bentham and Destutt de Tracy, and a few liberal romantics, such as Humboldt. Constant cannot be comfortably grouped with any of these theorists. His position was singular. He reconciled liberal principles with romantic impulses (when I say "impulses," I mean primarily aversions), and he did so in a unique way. The most noteworthy attitude Constant shared with Schiller, Novalis, Adam Müller, Friedrich Schlegel, and other romantics was disgust at the calculating mentality, social phoniness, and the petty egoism of self-interest. A central theme of *Adolphe* was the dessicating influence of "a totally artificial society" which "substitutes conventions for emotions." When Constant wanted to hurl a devastating insult at Napoleon, he called him "calculation personified."[5]

Moreover, the propelling insight behind the major intellectual endeavor of his career was that religion "does not have our utility as a goal." What fascinated him about religion was that "it triumphs over all interests." During the course of centuries, spontaneous "religious sentiment" (which cannot be grasped by "dry logic") outgrows and sloughs off the conventional husk of religious practices, doctrines, and institutions: *le fond* endures, but *les formes* are discarded by the wayside. In literary theory, he championed German drama against what he saw as the brittle fastidiousness of French classicism. Genuine art was closely allied with genuine religion. It, too, conquered self-interest: "In the contemplation of beauty there is something that detaches us from ourselves."[6]

Why did the repugnance Constant felt for utility, narrow self-interest, and "artificial conventions"—a repugnance which caused him to turn in relief to romantic or quasi-romantic conceptions of art and religion—not also impel him toward a romantic theory of the state? This question becomes more pointed when we recall that several typical components of such a theory loomed large in his political thinking. Throughout his career, he expressed concern about the humanly debilitating consequences of civic privatism. In a chapter on the decadence of Spain in the *Commentaire,* he argued that the apathy and degradation of Spaniards was a result of the authoritarian structure of their state: by prohibiting popular involvement in public affairs, Spanish autocracy condemned citizens to the moral "stupor" which inevitably results from an exclusive concern with "the profits

of commerce." In *Conquête et usurpation,* he echoed Montesquieu's statement to the effect that commercial life isolates citizens from one another:
"In order for men to cooperate mutually in each others' destinies, they
require something more than interest." Even "Ancient and Modern Liberty,"
usually interpreted as a one-sided defense of private independence, contains
the claim that political participation "enlarges the spirit and ennobles
thoughts." "Political liberty" is "our most energetic means for self-perfection."[7] So what prevented him from taking a further step and actively
glorifying the nation-state?

HATEFUL DIVISIONS

The political romanticism that flourished in Germany in the wake of the
French Revolution reflected a keen dissatisfaction with the role of the state
as a mere guarantor of preexistent rights or arbiter between conflicting
interests: "Our states are nothing but legal organizations and defensive
institutions." The state should be "the most beautiful artwork of man,
whereby he raises his being to a higher level," but it is now "regarded as
a necessary evil, as an indispensable mechanism for concealing man's defects
and rendering them harmless." All political romantics agreed that the modern state had degenerated into "an almost exclusively juridical institution."
The system advocated by liberal constitutionalists was insipid and humanly
dissatisfying. Romantics rejoined that the state should present itself as an
explicit *alternative* to the sordid network of rights and interests that goes
by the name of "civil society." The state is not a factory. It must rescue
men from stony isolation and mean-spirited competition. Schiller, for example, identified his beautiful state with "the pure ideal man" who transcends selfishness and repudiates the modern cult of utility.[8]

As worshipers of antiquity, some German romantics hoped the state
might elevate the individual above himself and provide an outlet for heartfelt
enthusiasm. Disenchanted with an increasingly secular and commercial society, they yearned for redemption from a fallen condition. Especially dis-
tressing about the modern age was the fragmentation it imposed on the
individual and the impediments it raised to social and personal wholeness.
Modernity wrenched asunder the public and the private, knowledge and
faith, love and power. In *Christendom or Europe* (1799), Novalis assailed
the disunity of modernity, praising the health and harmony that he imagined
to have been characteristic of the Christian Middle Ages. Modern men are
trapped by the "egoistical cares" of "commercial life" as well as by "the
restless tumult of social distractions and the negotiations of petty affairs."[9]

Contemporary attitudes appear vulgar when compared with medieval disdain for material possessions. In the Middle Ages, a Christian would swoon over a religious relic like a lover over a lock of his dead beloved's hair.[10] Maudlin touches of this sort distinguished political romantics from political conservatives. What Novalis admired about the Middle Ages and the lack he resented in modernity, was poetic color rather than social order. The Enlightenment attack on religion was essentially an assault on artistic inspiration—or so he thought.

Pleasant and dreamy reveries of this kind were less foreign to Constant than, say, to the affectless and rationalistic Idéologues. If romanticism means the pursuit of occasions for sentimental response,[11] then he too displayed a characteristically romantic attitude toward objects that evaded utilitarian evaluation: "Everything uncivilized, everything not subjected to artificial human domination, answers the emotions of man. Things fashioned for his use are mute, because they are dead. But even these things, when time annihilates their utility, reacquire a mysterious life; destruction, passing over them, restores their relation to nature. Modern buildings are silent; but ruins speak."[12] Although occasionally sentimental about ruins, Constant never sentimentalized the state. Political romantics did: political institutions must serve as a prime occasion for emotional release. A new "state" will soon unify all the nations of Europe, Novalis predicted; and Europeans will eagerly join together "to chant sacred songs."[13] The mawkish unrealism of this vision was a logical consequence of the demand that *politics* reverse the disenchantment of nature and heal the divisions of modern man and society.

When Constant criticized social arrangements, he focused on violations of rights and frustrations of basic needs. Political romantics were uninspired by needs and rights. They criticized the liberal state not for failing to reach its goals, but for aiming too low. Schiller explicitly condemned the "state based on need" and the "state of rights." Such states did not accomplish the moral vocation of man. They adjusted ignobly to the outlook of those who "know no other measure of value than the effort of acquisition and manifest profit."[14] Man's full humanity would only appear within a higher sort of state, a state that resembled ancient Athens and reflected "the unity of the ideal man." Defining freedom as the realization of the perfect man in the perfect community, Schiller declared that the French Revolution had failed because Frenchmen were personally unworthy of being liberated from the old regime. They should have been morally perfected first, and emancipated only afterward. Schiller's standard of moral perfection was located in the inward state of the individual soul, in "the wholeness of man." Only the "whole man," who unified thought and feeling, reflection and naiveté, was genuinely free. The greatest problem of modern Europe was not poverty, abuse of power, or the humiliation of caste, but specialization. Schiller thus blamed the division of labor for having "mutilated" humanity by creating one-sided individuals. In ancient Greece a man could be "a whole in himself." But this personal harmony and "completeness,"[15] along with the possibility of true liberty, was shattered in the course of modernization:

> The state and the church, laws and customs, were split apart; enjoyment was divided from work, means from ends, and effort from reward. Forever enchained to a single small fragment of the whole, man became nothing more than a fragment; the monotonous whirr of the wheel he operates ceaselessly in his ear, he never develops the harmony of his being. Instead of inscribing humanity on his own nature, he becomes a mere imprint of his occupation, his science.[16]

This "dismemberment" may have benefited society; but it has scarred the individual. Man can be restored to his "totality" only if he undergoes a moral education through art: "the goal of an education for taste and beauty is . . . to cultivate the whole of our sensuous and mental powers to the greatest possible harmony." Art will also confer a "social character" on men. Political reform is totally useless "until the division in the inner man has been healed again." When human souls are reunified through art, the perfect state will effortlessly emerge. As Schiller conceived it, the ideal state would have no law and no police force, because citizens will have beautiful and harmonious motives. While suggesting that this vision was utopian, he used it unhestitatingly when attacking modern society for those hateful divisions impeding the rise of a new Athens.[17]

The juxtaposition of Schiller and Constant highlights the chaste unromanticism of the liberal idea of freedom. For Constant, liberty did not prescribe any particular form of action. It was independent of character, happiness, self-realization, and the goals one pursues. A person can be free even if he is not beautiful, satisfied, cultivated, or virtuous. Liberty depends on the maintenance of various attractive possibilities, political and extrapolitical. To achieve such freedom is difficult, but not in itself enough to make life worth living. It is quite compatible with personal frustration. Freedom is a precondition, not a goal. It is certainly not the triumphant realization of an ideal pattern or the birth of Potential Man. Political romantics had a much more ambitious concept of freedom.

Also characteristic of political romanticism was a Rousseauist ideal of total citizenship. For total citizenship, according to Novalis, the public must swallow the private: "We see our state too little. That is a great mistake. The state should be visible everywhere. Each man should be characterized as a citizen wherever he goes. Cannot insignia and uniforms be introduced? Whoever holds this sort of thing trivial does not understand an essential part of our nature."[18] Despite his periodic outbursts, Constant never incorporated Spartan yearnings into his political vision. Committed to a curtailed sphere of state competence, he believed that politics was essential but not total. On balance, he preferred the part-time to the full-time citizen, the citizen-tourist to the citizen-soldier. He was not attracted to compulsory insignia and uniforms: the Revolution had taught him to travel incognito and convinced him that estrangments were not merely hateful. Social compartmentalization, especially the "line" between public and private spheres, created attractive possibilities both for individuals and their community.

In politics, romanticism was compatible with the glorification of heavy-handed state regulation, so long as this regulation was aimed at nurturing citizens with antique virtues. While distrusting the reactionary and Catholic tendencies inherent in Friedrich Schlegel's version of political romanticism, Constant reserved his bitterest indictments for its ostentatious impracticality. Having had a discussion with Schlegel about commerce and its consequences, he jotted the following remark in his *Journal intime:* "Schlegel is one of those people who, never having had anything to do with real life, believes that everything can be accomplished by ordinances and laws, without dreaming of the struggle that vexatious laws provoke between citizens and the authorities, or of the ensuing necessity for laws to become progressively more rigorous so that in the end they embrace all the individuals in a country."[19] Concerned with practical truths, Constant found Schlegel's political views to be childish. They registered a failure of historical understanding as well as a refusal of adult responsibilities.

Nevertheless, Constant echoed romantic thinkers when, for practical reasons, he spoke of the state as a school for the formation of character or as a context for "moral education" that lifted men above themselves and emancipated them from their self-interest.[20] For all its dryness, his constitutional vision, too, had a romantic side. In the early *Force du gouvernement,* for example, Constant criticized absolutism for having fostered "a deprivation of aims, interests and hopes other than narrow or personal ones." A lack of citizen participation was "the source of one of our greatest woes." In the romanticizing description he gave of this *malheur* we may well detect the flamboyant hand of Mme. de Staël. Psychologically, the result of civic privatism is "that arid and corrosive sentiment that consumes our existence and drains all objects of their color and that, like the scorching winds of Africa, dessicates and withers everything it touches. . . . It pursues not only the obscure subjects of monarchies but even Kings on their thrones and ministers in their palaces, because the soul is always constricted when it is driven back into egoism." In a privatized society, "one cannot forget oneself or give oneself up to enthusiasm."[21] Citizenship lends color to life. The young Constant, in other words, went beyond the ancient belief that the state should be a school for the formation of character. Exaltation and self-immolation, not maturity and self-reliance, were what citizens should seek in their state.

Although it does not provide a representative picture of Constant's views on political participation, this early paragraph was not an isolated eruption. Constant continued to use the strangely intoxicated image of "moral electricity"[22] to describe what citizens miss most in a nonpartici-patory state. Soberly rational privatized individuals may conclude that personal participation is not worth their while. To counter their calculations, Constant invoked the unmeasurable benefit of participation as an "end in itself." However, his taste for civic "enthusiasm" rarely got so far out of hand.

In light of these sporadic flirtations with civic exaltation, our guiding question can be formulated with renewed force. What hindered Constant from pursuing his occasional romantic fancies (e.g., his desire to replace convention with emotion or yield himself up to enthusiasm) in a nationalist direction? In his writings about religion and art, he repeatedly acknowledged his indebtedness to Schleiermacher, Schelling, Herder, Schiller, and others. But in his political theory, despite occasional remarks about "moral electricity," he remained a child of the Enlightenment. Why? What stopped him for plunging into a full-fledged romantic theory of the state?

ROMANTIC NIHILISM?

Before trying to answer this question, I wish to make it slightly more complicated by focusing attention on another dimension of Constant's thinking—what I choose to call, for lack of a better term, his "nihilism."[23] By this I do not mean his somewhat gloomy belief in "le néant de tout,"[24] though Constant's romantic melancholy is not irrelevant here. (It discourages total reliance on the blander and more cognitive term *skepticism* to describe the attitude in question.) I am referring, rather, to Constant's dispiriting sense of the purposelessness of life, or his utter lack of confidence in the power of reason to provide guidance about ultimate ends. In his encoded *Journal abrégé* (1804–07), Constant reserved a special number for "uncertainty about everything,"[25] and the state of mind so denoted occurred quite often. In 1790, he had been exhilarated by a story he heard according to which the clockmaker God of the philosophes had died halfway through his endeavor to fashion the world: "Thus everything that now exists was made for a purpose which no longer exists. We, in particular, feel predestined for something about which we have not the slightest idea. We are like watches without hands. Our wheels, endowed with intelligence, turn until they are worn out, without knowing why and always saying to themselves: I turn, therefore I must have a purpose."[26] This comic paraphrase of Descartes' Cogito ergo sum was profoundly Cartesian in intent, mocking as it did any appeal to purposes inscribed in nature.[27] Indeed, this waggish myth as a whole can be fruitfully contrasted with romantic disavowals of the scientific revolution. According to Novalis, again, modern science was based on "cold and lifeless" reason. By desacralizing nature, by interpreting the world in mechanistic terms, it rendered man homeless: "Out of the infinite creative music of the universe, [modern science] made a uniform rattling of a gigantic mill . . . a mill grinding itself."[28] Seeing the solution to modern social and psychological sterility in a new politicoreligious order, Novalis also predicted that a new science lending meaning and purpose to nature would soon emerge.

Anthropocentric teleology had been very reassuring. Modern science, reinterpreting nature in such a way that it no longer provided guidance about man's moral vocation, deprived political theory of its old Aristotelian crutch: "Among earlier peoples . . . nature seemed to speak to man, while for us it has fallen silent."[29] Nature was now a threat or an opportunity, but not a source of wisdom, comfort, or fatherly chastisement. Responsibility fell on human beings alone. Liberalism was in part a response to this challenge—an attempt to cope with the revolutionary surrender of a meaningful and purposive cosmic order. Constant strove to fashion a humane, stable, and self-regulating polity without ontological or theological foundations. Liberal freedom, including self-government, was conceived as a morally responsible reaction to the sudden disappearance of nature's purposes.

Belief that cosmic order imposes no binding duties on man and that human insight into reality cannot provide a satisfactory answer to the question "What for?" were important motivations for Constant's commitment to the liberal state. Thus, his writings and career support the somewhat counterintuitive claim that a certain "nihilism" can be a source of political moderation and restraint. But why did Constant's deep skepticism not lead him, as one might have expected, to some form of political irrationalism—say, to the worship of brute force or the will to power?

LIBERAL MISTRUST OF COMMUNITY

As he revealed in his *Journaux intimes,* Constant was a man who craved "distance." Reluctant to be absorbed in any situation and unwilling to be a total participant, he coolly observed and analyzed everyone, including his closest friends—including himself. Psychologically he was not a joiner. His personal remoteness helped to ensure that his rejection of utility, self-interest, and artificial social conventions would not catapult him into a romantic conception of the state.

His disillusioning experience with the French Revolution, however, was an even more decisive factor. Liberal distrust of community has often been portrayed as the logical consequence of a prior philosophical commitment to individualism; and Constant did favor "individualism" in some sense of that elusive concept. But it was not in the bourgeois or acquisitive and competitive sense. A civilization based on self-interest will be corrupt and mechanical. Its atomized citizens will be unable to pursue public goals in a coherent, cooperative manner, and they will suffer the corrosive effect of purposelessness and anomie.

Paradoxically, it was Constant's repugnance toward private self-interest, refracted through his experience of the Revolution, that made him acutely suspicious of the ideal of political community. Unlike the abusive monarchs of the old regime, revolutionary demagogues employed the idea of a community of equals as an ideology to disguise and justify their personal ambitions and desire for vengeance. To secure public support for eccentric policies, the Terrorists concealed the extent to which various legitimate interests legitimately diverged. The characteristic fraud of the Revolution was a public disclaimer of any self-interested motives. A person can best engage *others* to cooperate with him by displaying an opinion that deceives them concerning his genuine aims. That was precisely what the Jacobins did.

Germans had not suffered the Terror firsthand. Thus, Germany provided more promising soil than France for political romanticism. "At the end of the eighteenth century the influence of the Universities inspired the Prussian youth with a taste for science, a penchant for exaltation and pretensions to I know not what warlike appearance. After having read Schiller, each student armed himself with a sword and believed himself a knight of the thirteenth century or a liberator of the nineteenth." When German schoolboys settled down, as they inevitably did, to steady jobs and adult responsibilities, "they regretfully watched the world become disenchanted."[30] In Germany, neither a revolution nor heroic militarism had had a chance to disillusion young men chained to the galleys of the civil service. In France, after two decades of bitter disappointment, the public denial of self-interest could neither seem so innocent nor so thrillingly poetic.

Constant found the cure of community even less tolerable than the disease of social atomization. Moreover, in a society where rights of contract and achievement had definitely ousted those of status and ascription, the "common good" was more likely to be a *prétexte* than a reality. Schiller's "system of egoism" may have been despicable, but to conceal it behind sham disinterestedness and a mock communal spirit was more contemptible still.

ROMANTIC MILITARISM

This lesson was reinforced by Constant's experience of the Napoleonic wars. Romantic militarism is permanently enshrined in the character of Stendhal's Julien Sorel, in his penchant for sudden, unpremeditated gestures by which he threw away in an instant what he had built up through years of calculation. The romanticization of war reflected a need to escape from the drab predictability of everyday life. The adventurous citizen-soldier was a reproach to the cowering shopkeeper. Willingness to die—not to mention willingness to kill—for France revealed manly indifference to private property and egoistic survival. No admirer of the ancient city could slight the martial dimension of public virtue. Indeed, the "civic virtue tradition" was a protracted hymn to the glories of war. In the Napoleonic generation, "the brilliant dreams of military glory intoxicate[d] the imagination of youth." Napoleon was "le calcul personnifié" because he managed to exploit these archaic and spontaneous popular longings for the sake of his own carefully planned, self-aggrandizing goals.[31] As a result, Constant's distrust of *le calcul* led him to prefer commercialism and the division of labor to romantic militarism and the citizen-soldier.

In some passages of *Conquête et usurpation*, Constant pushed this line of thought so far as to make unintelligible Napoleon's appeal to French youth. Instead of portraying the emperor as an object of self-immolating devotion, Constant drained Napoleon's military escapades of their enthusiastic fervor. He described the French army on its way to Moscow as a force "of four hundred thousand egoists," as if no genuine devotion or self-sacrifice had been involved.[32] This was unconvincing, not to say inconsistent with Constant's own remarks about brilliant, youthful dreams of military glory. But Constant seems to have been genuinely deaf to the siren-song of nationality. His impassiveness in this regard was another reason why his inchoate romanticism never achieved political expression.

ADOLPHE AND THE CRITIQUE OF AUTHENTICITY

Constant's distrust of communitarian rhetoric was reinforced by his belief, also inherited from the great seventeenth-century tradition of French moral psychology, that even the most heartfelt passions have something about them which is phony and contrived. One of the main sources of his political antiromanticism lay in his coolness toward the ideal of total sincerity—in his hesitation to view the genuine as a readily available alternative to the artificial. He defined freedom as a function of accessible possibilities, not as an ability to achieve "what I truly or authentically want."[33]

An unsettling aspect of *Adolphe* is that both stale social conventions and spontaneous-seeming sincerity are portrayed with a clinical absence of sympathy. Those "primitive and passionate feelings that throw the spirit outside the common sphere" are treated with the same diagnostic contempt as "the common sphere" itself. The dryly chaste style of the novel did not admit self-consciously lyrical outbursts in the manner of Chateaubriand's *René*. True, Constant presented the fluctuating love between Adolphe and Ellénore as sufficiently genuine for it to stand as a moral rebuke to the society that decreed it out of bounds. But this vaguely romantic suggestion was undermined in turn by the corrosively antiromantic idea that what feels like love is actually vanity, self-evasion, pity, or possessiveness. Especially crushing is the idea that apparent impulse is in truth an automatism of the psyche. At root, the genuine may be artificial simply because "we end up feeling the sentiments we feign." It may ultimately be impossible to distinguish clearly between true and false devotion, since false devotion, practiced for a time, becomes true devotion. This sort of psychological insight, not merely enlightened distaste for zealots, prevented Constant from following Mme. de Staël too far in her celebration of German enthusiasm.[34]

The irresolvable conflict between social convention and the spontaneity of the heart is a theme *Adolphe* shared with that gospel of the early Romantic movement, *The Sorrows of Young Werther*. What distinguishes the two books is quite telling. Goethe reserved for himself all limiting commentary on Werther's tempestuous passions. Constant, by contrast, granted an illusion-shattering clarity to Adolphe. That is why Adolphe was not allowed the self-dramatizing gesture of suicide and why there could never have arisen a cult of his protagonist for Constant to repudiate, as there did for Goethe. Indeed, not even the most sentimental reader could have been tempted to misinterpret Adolphe as a hero because, unlike Werther (or René or Julien Sorel), he understood his own brokenly unheroic nature as lucidly as did his creator.

Adolphe is also unlike that other prime occasion for romantic palpitations, La Nouvelle Héloïse. The love between Julie and Saint-Preux, though unacceptable to society, was itself uncorrupted. By contrast, the love between Adolphe and Ellénore was impure at its source. Rousseau hated the artificial Parisian world where "being" was reduced to "appearance" and where a man could be "totally absorbed in his mask."[35] In order to revile this world, he embraced various images of absolute purity, such as Spartan self-sacrifice and the total candor of the unguarded heart. Constant had a more ambivalent attitude toward masks, deceit, and inauthenticity. He did not find Rousseau's ideal of total sincerity any more convincing than his ideal of Spartan citizenship, and he was skeptical of the very attempt to get behind appearances to the true essence of the self: "One can say about most men that they are still artificial even when they are alone."[36] In another famous passage from the Journaux intimes, Constant offered the following gloss on his own attempt to write a totally sincere private diary: "At the beginning, I made myself a rule to write down everything I felt. I have observed that rule to the best of my ability, but the habit of speaking to the gallery is so strong that I have not always and completely observed it."[37] Indeed, the insincerity of sincerity was one of his most persistent themes, underlying, for example, his analysis of the pretexts passionately invoked during the Revolution. But he did not view this pattern romantically, as a cause for self-torment. It was simply a fact about human beings and their condition.

Social life is haunted by the unspoken, by thoughts that cannot be shared. Adolphe is the story of something incommunicable: the end of love. Both Adolphe and Ellénore know that their love has expired; but they simply cannot speak about it to one another. The novel's plot is resolved by an inadvertent communication, the reading of a letter which should not have been read. But the limits of communication are permanent, excluding any chance for complete mutual transparency: "Between others and oneself there is an invincible barrier. It is an illusion of youth to believe that any relationship can make [this barrier] vanish: it will always reappear."[38] The state can do absolutely nothing to overcome the profound and elemental divisions between human beings.

Constant was quite caustic about the self-righteousness of intellectuals "who believe themselves great geniuses," picturing themselves soaring above the "ordinary" world. He mocked Schlegel, "praising himself for his contempt of society"; and he resorted to the insolence of the philosophes to deflate romantic pretentiousness: "Friedrich Schlegel wishes to be the leader of a new religion; but he looks more like a monk in an old and rich religion."[39] He never suggested that he was pure while his surroundings were corrupt. His incipient romanticism was held in check by an unwillingness to present the genuine, the sincere or the purely natural as realistic alternatives to the artificial, and by a belief that, in this clinically self-observant age, heroism was implausible even as a delusion.

THE POLITICS OF COMPARATIVE RELIGION

De la religion was an acknowledgment of romantic and sentimentalist impulses. But it was also, and more importantly, a strategy of containment. Political romantics rechanneled religious emotions into adoration of the state.[40] Constant aimed his polemic against the abusive sacerdotalism of the old regime and the militant atheism which had discredited the Directory, ruining France's first experiment with constitutional government. But he also polemicized against the romantic tendency to ascribe a redemptive potential to politics. Indirectly, but unmistakably, De la religion was an argument for a separation of spheres, for the public/private distinction, and for secularization in a double sense: priests were to have no coercive power and the state must never attempt to secure citizens' loyalty by mobilizing religious sentiments.[41]

In Polythéisme romain, Constant discussed "two moralities."[42] The first ignores thoughts and feelings and limits itself to forbidding external crimes. This is the morality of the liberal state. The second aims at remaking the inner man, giving him good motives rather than preventing his bad actions. Although this second morality is morally superior to the first, it must never be implemented politically. It is a strictly private affair. By privatizing the urge for moral improvement, Constant deromanticized membership in the state, deliberately diverting romantic impulses away from politics and into extrapolitical pursuits.

But this is not the whole story. While skeptical of political enthusiasm, Constant did not renounce it entirely. During the last thirty years of his life, indifference to citizenship served the purposes of power. In such circumstances, the liberal opposition looked expectantly toward a rebirth of civic spirit and the intensification of popular participation. In this battle against autocracy, liberalism and romanticism temporarily converged.[43]

The step-by-step evolution of Constant's seven-volume study of comparative religions reflects the different regimes under which it was written. The Revolution reinforced the young Constant's distrust of zealotry and his skepticism toward the ethics of self-immolation for the sake of collective goals. When he began his projected study of pagan religions in the 1790s, he was anxious to denounce priestcraft, zealotry, and intolerance. In the spirit of Helvétius, he identified rationality with calculations of enlightened self-interest. Much later, when *De la religion* began to be published in 1824, Constant still recognized the validity of his original insight: against fanatical religious impulses, it was sensible for the philosophes to have enlisted the calculative mentality and the principle of self-interest. But they went too far in this direction. In attempting to quell religious fanaticism, the philosophes ran the risk of extinguishing all noble emotions, especially the capacity for self-sacrifice that enables men to die as martyrs for the cause of freedom. Freedom always requires citizens. Sometimes it requires heroes. Religion contributes to liberty by detaching men from materialistic and egoistic wants: "a free government needs disinterestedness" and irreligious men are unlikely to be disinterested.[44]

Napoleon had not relied exclusively on romantic militarism to bolster his rule. He had also used "the arid doctrines of enlightened self-interest," especially to consolidate support outside the army. An impulse more generous than personal advantage was required to defy an authority so well armed. Skeptical about the Jacobin pretense to public spirit, Constant was also bitterly disappointed by the privatized ethics of *sauve qui peut*. Despotism and materialism were quite compatible. During the first twenty-five years of the century, "self-interest . . . has lamented over victims; but when victims were dragged to be tortured, [self-interest] took care that order was not troubled. It let heads fall, while guaranteeing property. It prevented pillage but facilitated legal murder." The age of calculation breeds despots. Self-interest incites citizens to be rebellious when the government is moderate and to be servile when the government is violent. While lauding private independence and the effort to draw boundaries around political power, Constant was equally sensitive to the danger of extinguishing public spirit before private interest. Under the Empire: "A man was egoistical for his family, as earlier for himself. He repulsed his threatened friend for fear of alarming a restless wife. He deserted the cause of the *patrie* because self-interest well understood did not wish to compromise the dowry of a daughter. He served an unjust authority because self-interest well understood did not wish to block the career of a son." Under the Roman Empire, Epicureans were slaves while the Christians, who "placed their point of support outside of egoism," were willing to die heroically for the freedom to follow their conscience.[45] In other words, although he never romanticized authority, Constant did draw a romantically tinged portrait of the persecuted citizen in his battle against authority. He never romanticized the state; but he did romanticize (to some extent) the struggle for reform. In politics, his romanticism was exclusively a romanticism of protest.

Constant developed an unromantic theory of the state not in spite of but because of his inchoate romanticism. This is the secret of *De la religion* and *Du polythéisme romain*. Unlike the rationalistic Idéologues of the Auteuil circle (for whom man was a pleasure-pain machine), Constant attacked the rule of priests because he believed that religion answered an authentic human need. When he spoke of "the mask of disinterestedness," he was echoing a seventeenth-century maxim ("Self-interest speaks all languages and plays every role, including that of disinterestedness"); but he did so polemically and politically, not with La Rochefoucauld's ironic detachment. Referring to "exaltation," "enthusiasm," and "the interior sentiment of man," he wrote, "they are sublime when they are spontaneous, but terrifying when they are abused."[46] It was because he personally shared the desire to leap beyond private interest and disrupt the monotony of everyday life that he responded so antagonistically to the rhetorical manipulation of these desires for political ends.

LITERARY ROMANTICISM AND ITS LIMITS

Something similar can be said about Constant's sympathy for romantic strands in German literature and drama. He published a French adaptation of Schiller's *Wallenstein* in 1809; and he took this work extremely seriously. In art, German romanticism promised liberation from the pruned-garden regulations expounded by Boileau. Constant associated the "jealous rules"[47] of classical French literature with the mercantilist regulations of the Colbertist state.[48] As an antimercantilist, he was naturally attracted to literary tendencies that discarded confining precepts. As a cautious revolutionary, however, he attempted to civilize Schiller's sprawling work within the conventions of French drama. This halfway house was a failure: "I destroyed the dramatic effect in many ways by condemning myself to respect the rules of our theater."[49] While frankly admitting his blunder, he did not suggest that a better solution had been available. The sharp dissimilarity between German and French theater reflected an unbridgeable moral gap between the two nations.[50]

German playwrights could glorify a single burning passion, such as love, even if it led the protagonist to repudiate all his ordinary duties as a family member. French audiences would never tolerate this intoxicated negligence,[51] perhaps because (like Adolphe) their primitive feelings were already subdued by civilization. "The Germans see in love something religious, sacred, even an emanation from the divinity." The French have a more secular view: "love is kept in its proper place in France, even by the young."[52] The unromantic strain in Constant's temper is strikingly displayed in his commentary on this dry and calculating attitude toward amorous relations:

> I am so little inclined to rebuke civilization for this abatement of a once disorderly passion that I am happy to admit that *moeurs* have improved because of it. Since the imagination is no longer exalted, each man limits himself to his wife for reason of proximity. Sometimes habit and, above all, identity of interest, also produce a moral affection. Vice becomes superfluous and fatiguing, a distraction from regular and profitable occupations. We are faithful to marriage vows because of nearness, and we are moral because we employ our activity elsewhere.[53]

Constant knew what it meant to be swept away by love; but he also knew how to attain an unanimated coolness toward such an anarchical emotion.

Constant's literary theory was another defense of separate social spheres. No work of art should be dominated by a moral aim. Voltaire was unrivaled as a polemicist against the old regime; but he debased literature by treating it as an instrument of political reform. His "boldness . . . does honor to the man, but is a defect in poetry." The characters in his plays "are destined to make triumph or discredit such and such a doctrine: one forgets their personal troubles and listens to their axioms." Indeed, "in Voltaire's hands, tragedy became a battering-ram which he directed against the tottering fortress of the old regime." Constant did not really blame Voltaire, since "circumstances were pressing." All available weapons had to be utilized against "the vicious and criminal institutions" and the "barbarous and stupid prejudices" of eighteenth-century France.[54] Admirable morally, this "use" of literature was aesthetically wrong. Art is denatured when it is made to subserve a purpose, even a politically worthy goal. As a side-effect, art can instruct men, but instruction cannot be its intended aim. This was Constant's romantic revolt against didactic literature. As a defense of the fragile pluralism of modern society, it, too, was liberal in intent.

As an opponent, first of Napoleon then of the ultras, Constant romanticized political protest for obvious reasons. But he did not view political activity primarily as a vehicle for self-expression, individual or national. Rhetorical overstatements aside, he ultimately saw politics as an instrument. In the transition to a liberal-democratic regime, activism was instrumental to imposing public opinion on political authorities and introducing reforms. Under an established constitution, participation in public debate contributed to the solving of common problems. Constant's concept of citizenship was instrumental without being egoistic. It was neither debased nor redemptive. While participation could be personally rewarding, it was meant principally to subserve nonexpressivist social goals.

THE SOULLESSNESS OF THE LIBERAL STATE

Skepticism toward community, sincerity, and heroism, stemming from an old tradition of French moral psychology and jolted back into consciousness by the rhetoric of the revolutionary and Bonapartist periods, may well explain the rechanneling of Constant's romantic impulses. But there were independent reasons for his attraction to a minimal liberal-democratic state. His loyalty to constitutional government derived partly from his deep skepticism. Far from encouraging a commitment to any form of political irrationality, his general lack of confidence in reason's capacity to determine ultimate ends was a source of political moderation.

Constant found the constitutional state laudable for its anonymity and lack of warmth. In his writings on art and especially in those on religion, he routinely praised *le fond* at the expense of *les formes*. In his political writings he did the opposite. He did not sacrifice the spirit to the letter, but he came close to it. Adjusting rhetorically to the realities of Restoration politics, he at times implied that he cared little if the state were monarchical or republican, so long as a separation of powers compelled it to respect freedom of the press and other fundamental rights.[55] He was less concerned with the type of government, he said, than with the extent and accountability of government. This agnosticism of regimes, which was politically motivated, also steered him away from a romantic image of the state. He fought for secure barriers against authority as well as for a system in which free debate would influence public policy. He never asked for a beautified authority.

Not even the sovereignty of public discussion was meant to compensate for the drabness of everyday life. Constant emphasized procedures for solving common problems, settling conflicts and adjusting rights and duties. He deemphasized substantive goals such as the creation of moral consensus and the education of virtuous citizens. Procedures that compelled *la lenteur* were less likely to be deployed as pretexts for oppression than were weightier moral values: "In the body politic, only the forms are stable, and only they resist the acts of men. The most substantive things, that is to say, justice and virtue, can be distorted. Their names are at the mercy of whoever wants to employ them. Robespierre can invoke liberty and morality just as easily as Lanjuinais."[56] Constant's formalism was partly motivated by distrust of the disreputable motives lurking beneath rousing pretexts. Equally important, however, was his awareness of the inner chaos of the human soul. The liberal state was attractive partly because of its superficiality—a great relief from the difficulties of personal life and intimate relations. The elemental characteristic of human nature is its "fluctuating instability." Far from mirroring human nature, the state should be everything man is not: "The human spirit is versatile. Institutions must be stable."[57] Novalis understood the ideal state as a macroanthropos. That was not Constant's ideal. Individuals are indecisive, vacillating, and unpredictable. Because they have the instincts of gamblers, they will be relieved to discover no trace of their fickle selves in the state. Legalism, with its emphasis on the generality of abstract rules, is cold and predictable. A constitutional state, making no effort to heal the breach between public and private realms, will provide a welcome respite from the personal, the eccentric, and the human.[58]

Constant insisted that his political activities did not reflect his inner life. He wrote about politics "without passion." In political journalism, he said, "I will never violate a formal measuredness, which is neither in my feelings nor in my speech nor in my action, but which is eminently in what I write." Legal impersonality or the caesura between public and private realms also enabled the liberal publicist to disentangle himself from the chaos of other men's lives. Because "I fear the thorn-bush of relations with other men," he wrote, "I prefer to speak to them from a distance and about their general interests."[59] In the same spirit, he mercilessly ridiculed a royalist minister who employed the bombastic and emotionally charged style of René in what should have been a businesslike public speech.[60]

Theorists steeped in romantic and counter-Enlightenment traditions frequently declare the modern social order to be intolerable and alienating because it is "expressively dead." A recent heir to political romanticism has glossed this claim in the following manner: "Modern society . . . is romantic in its private and imaginative life and utilitarian and instrumentalist in its public effective life."[61] That is exactly what we learn from Constant, except, of course, that the implicit evaluative signs are reversed. A good society is one in which public success is judged by uninspiring standards such as peace, order, efficiency, impartiality, openness to criticism, and procedural justice.

Private life can and should embody any number of expressivist ideals: bliss, creativity, friendship, emotional sensitivity, salvation, genius, and love. But these are best excluded from the public realm, at least for the most part.

Only a basically deromanticized and soulless political system can provide the stable framework for the soul-storms and adventures of our unregulated, unpredictable private lives. To sentimentalize privacy, we must deeroticize publicity. This paradox lies at the heart of Constant's liberalism: as the legal framework of social life becomes increasingly cold and impersonal, the chances for personal intimacy, emotion, and expressivism are markedly increased, even if happiness can never be politically guaranteed.

VARIETIES OF INDIVIDUALISM

In his book on the characteristics of modern Europe, Fichte decried the "empty freedom" and the "bare naked individualism" of his contemporaries. Modern men are dominated by the unwholesome "desire for self-preservation and material well-being." They seem to believe that "there is no other motive in man than self-interest."[62] Reacting to Fichte's book of 1800, *The Closed Commercial State,* Constant compared it to Schlegel's defense of heavy-handed state regulation:

> This is the masterwork of a similar system, a project for restricting nations to their interior commerce by introducing a currency with no value abroad and too heavy to be transported, forbidding external relations, etc., etc. God bless them with their Spartan ideas in the midst of modern civilization, surrounded by needs that have become part of our existence, by bills of exchange, etc. They are madmen who, if they governed, would resurrect Robespierre with the best intentions in the world.[63]

As the Preface to *De la religion* makes clear, Constant partly accepted the romantic attack on the commercial age. But he doubted that France could spiritually afford to recognize the truth of such criticism. In any case, commerce was not the worst thing men could do to each other; and self-interest, in Smith's sense, was a defense against despotism. Attacks on self-interest could easily be misused. Constant was not naive about economic man's joyless quest for joy; but, unlike Fichte, he never translated his romantic discomfort with commercial self-interest into a glorification of the nation or the *Volk.*

Constant's position can also be usefully compared with Humboldt's quasi-romantic defense of the *Rechtsstaat*. Humboldt, unlike his friend Schiller, advocated a minimal state that did little more than arbitrate conflicts and establish a general framework of peace and security.[64] But he shared Schiller's ideal of "the whole man." The liberal state, he argued, would encourage the formation of energetic, self-reliant characters as well as foster the development of strong communal bonds.[65]

Constant never argued in this manner. In his analysis of the decadence of Spain, for example, he linked the development of energetic character to participation in *political* life. Political activities alone can sustain the development of vigorous moral personalities. He advanced this argument for practical reasons: he was fighting to widen the franchise and to intensify citizen involvement in public affairs. But the telling divergence between Constant and Humboldt ran deeper than this.

Note first that the connection between liberalism and individualism in Humboldt's thought (as well as in Mill's *On Liberty,* based largely on Humboldt) is different in important ways from the verbally analogous connection we normally associate with the name of Adam Smith. Classical political economists, in their debate against mercantilist policies, urged that the state should be limited in order to allow free and equal bartering partners to pursue their private interests. The mechanism of the market, with little or no public spiritedness on the part of citizens, will (or so it was claimed) automatically equilibrate private competitive activities for the sake of the common good. Free traders furthered their controversial program by falsely describing market behavior as a spontaneous "play" of natural forces.

For Humboldt, the individual whom the state must leave inviolate was not an entrepreneur of commercial self-interest; he was a cultivator of self-development in a wide variety of directions. Thus, the cliché that liberalism views the state primarily as an instrument for the protection of individuals, even if it were true, would be too vague to be informative. Its significance hinges upon the primary characteristics, capacities, and contexts attributed to individuals.

Constant often invoked the standard antimercantilist justification of the minimal state. But he was not committed to economic man: "I admire political economy . . . but I hope it will be remembered that man is not merely an arithmetical sign." The daily conflict, within each individual, of needs and ideals, hopes and resentments, is not susceptible to computation, let alone aggregation. Similarly, Constant denounced despotic states because they paralyze the faculties and drive citizens into "inertia" and "apathy." The Chinese polity, he wrote, "suffocates the germ of whatever is enthusiastic in our nature."[66] But Humboldt's robust language of celebration, especially his endless botanical metaphors of human blossoming, were equally foreign to his way of thinking.

Constant sometimes mentioned the stars and the ocean as occasions for romantic emotionalism.[67] But images of organic unfolding and luxuriant growth had little hold on his mind. The "individuality of energy and self-development" was too heroic for the author of *Adolphe*—the man who had defined "apathy" as "the disease of honesty." The overcited phrase from the preface to the *Mélanges* of 1829, in which he equated liberty with "the triumph of individuality," is very misleading. Much more frequently, he wrote of "the burden of my individuality" and of "cette individualité qui nous pèse." And we should not forget Adolphe's confession: "I took only the slightest interest in myself."[68] Representative government was not meant to guarantee the self-cultivation of flourishing souls. For Humboldt, the state must respect "the true end of man," which is "the highest and most harmonious development of his powers as a complete and consistent whole." For Constant, the individual whose autonomy the state must respect was not so full of himself: "on s'aperçoit qu'il n'y rien de réel au fond des âmes." In his view, the human soul was neither triumphant nor a seamless whole. "I am not a completely real being. There are two persons in me. One observes the other and knows quite well that his convulsions will pass."[69]

No sort of state and no sort of citizenship could abolish this elemental "division of the inner man."[70] Constant was never thunderstruck by Plutarch's heroes. He was fond of the emotional hypersensitivity and neurosis of his own age, even though he believed his own inner dividedness to be beyond remedy. The narrator of *Cécile* describes his feelings toward his beloved as follows: when she is here, I yearn for her departure; but when she has gone, I long for her to return. Similarly, "My heart is weary of everything it possess and craves everything it does not possess."[71] The modern individual is incurably afflicted; but his ailment, while sometimes absurd, is oddly intriguing. Above all, it is not susceptible to a political cure.

Constant failed to appreciate Schiller's and Humboldt's ideal of the perfectly well-rounded personality, not only because it was Graecophile and utopian, but also because it was pompous and boring, not to mention slyly coercive. "There is no total unity in man, and people are almost never completely sincere or completely in bad faith." Mixed motives and inner conflict, "les contradictions du coeur," make the search for personal wholeness seem as coarse as the quest for untainted sincerity. "Every individual has within himself a coalition, that is, a civil war."[72] Personal wholeness is as unattainable as the wholeness of the body politic is undesirable.[73] Indeed, a life without mental reservations is not worth living. To identify freedom with "the realization of the real self"[74] is to assume the existence of a single, identifiable essence of the individual. Constant doubted that such an essence existed. The most engrossing characters, such as Hamlet and Wallenstein, were torn by inner conflicts.[75]

Constant valued the minimal state because it opened up a space. It was a space reserved not only for the pursuit of self-interest and the efflorescence of the authentic self, but also for self-doubt and sometimes for self-excoriation. Radically dissociating political from individual stability, he treasured social peace but not personal serenity. As his daybook makes clear, he was attracted by neurotics. Nothing bored him more thoroughly than stolid psychological health.

Like Smith and Humboldt, he conceived the state partly (though not exclusively) as an instrument for protecting individuals. Fundamental differences emerged, however, when each specified which individual qualities deserved and required protection. Constant's individual was characterized by obsessive self-doubt, self-dividedness, and "a suffering part at the bottom of his soul." He was also driven by "the need for sensibility," contrasted explicitly with the Greek and Roman "need for action."[76] The state must never do what the Committee of Public Safety and Napoleon did so often: force citizens to desecrate close emotional ties.[77] Against clerical power, Constant defended "the sentimental and melancholy part of religion." Against the power of the bureaucracy and the police, he defended neither the cultural athlete nor the scheming marketeer, but rather the melancholy recesses of the individual. Every person has a right to states of disgust, regret, and boredom, and to the bitter grief at the bottom of his heart. Constitutionalism must shelter *les souffrances* as well as *les jouissances*.

But we should not overemphasize human isolation and suffering. The liberal state must also abstain from violating "gentle affections" and various forms of intimate or personal contact—"individual relations" which "are composed of delicate, fluctuating and ungraspable nuances." Viewed from this perspective, ancient fortitude was a form of emotional underdevelopment: "The moderns, fatigued by experience, have a sensibility which is more unhappy but for that reason also more delicate. They have a more habitual capacity to be moved. Egoism itself, which becomes commixed with this emotional faculty, can corrupt but not destroy it."[78] It was a troubled and self-divided sort of romanticism, not the heroic, classicizing,

Schillerian kind, that reinforced Constant's commitment to the liberal-democratic state.

BEYOND THE MONOETHICAL STATE

Romanticism helped demolish the conceptual framework that sustained the ancient concept of politics. Some classical authors identified human fulfillment with the surcease of desire, a stale perfection repellent to romantics, who admired infinite striving.[79] Modifying a Hobbesian dictum, romantics renounced the search for a satisfying finality, affirming a perpetual and restless desire for excellence after excellence that ceaseth only in death.

They also shattered the uniformity of the ancient concept of virtue, suggesting that self-development can lead in an infinite variety of uncoordinated directions.[80] There is no single standard of the good life and no orthodox unity of the virtues. Although the Spartan constitution was "the most sublime monument to political virtue," according to Schiller himself, it still "deserves our severest condemnation." The essential flaw of Spartan life was "monotony." In Schiller's words: "One virtue was practiced at Sparta to the exclusion of all the rest."[81] For all their important differences, Constant and Schiller agreed in rejecting the classical standardization of virtue. From a romantic standpoint, teleology had been much too single-minded.[82]

Citizens ought to feel relieved when they fail to recognize themselves in their state. This insight, although charmingly paradoxical, should not blind us to an important parallel between the liberal state and the liberal citizen. What makes them similar is that neither has a single fixed *telos*. Liberty is often considered the goal of the liberal state. But freedom is fundamentally unlike, say, national glory. For Constant, liberty was very similar to free time or peace. It was a "precondition for . . . ," not a final and self-justifying aim.

That deep skepticism need not fuel political irrationality is less surprising than I initially suggested. Lack of confidence in reason's capacity to establish ultimate ends can be a powerful source of political moderation, compelling men to acknowledge their limits. For individuals who are like clocks without hands, who are unsure of their purposes, what violation could be greater than a clockmaker state, a state that imposes an official timetable for achieving an overriding purpose? Motivation to constrict the competence of the state can spring from fidelity to one's own lack of a consistently highest aim. People who believe nothing with certainty may be unwilling to tolerate the finality of orthodox views.

Constant's belief that human beings were surrounded by darkness and would never have compelling answers to ultimate questions made him wary of any sort of community based on moral consensus. His sense of hopeless personal instability led him to see the good side of what Schiller deplored: that "the state remains ultimately alien to its citizens."[83] Sovereign power did not have to be utterly foreign to the freedom of citizens. But some degree of alienation must always be maintained.

The default of a political *telos* did not imply the lack of a coherent social order. Constitutionalism produced a state without an overriding purpose, but not a ruleless or anomic state. The Aristotelian tradition suggested that political communities must always be organized with a view to realizing some highest aim, such as the flourishing of man's political nature. Social order hinges on unity of purpose. Laws, from this perspective, were supposed to discourage men's base qualities and encourage their noble ones. In the same spirit, the morally educative function of law was lavishly praised in Jacobin harangues. Robespierre proclaimed the ultimate aim of legislation to be the establishment of "happy harmony," the "direction of the passions of the human heart toward objects useful for public prosperity."[84] Faced with this sort of zealotry, Constant wished to show the inadequacy of classical Legislator-paternalism to modern morality and social conditions. He did so by elaborating a distinction between "positive" and "speculative" laws.[85] In *De la religion,* positive religion was contrasted disdainfully with spontaneous religious sentiment. In his theory of law, positivity was declared a strength.

Social order is possible even without an overarching moral purpose. Indeed, fanatical purposefulness on the part of moral legislators can fire civil war. Speculative law was "any law that pretends to prescribe to each individual how he must act for his own utility." Positive laws, by contrast, do not give moral guidance; but they do allow citizens to develop stable expectations. They order social life not by directing citizens toward a morally worthy aim but by providing highly general rules that have a conditional or "if . . . then . . ." structure: "men have consented to the constraints of law in order to attach predictable consequences to their actions. On this basis, they can direct themselves and choose the line of conduct they want to follow."[86] If a certain action is committed, specified sanctions will be applied. If an enemy invades national territory, the government will be granted emergency powers. If you want to make a contract, you must follow certain specified procedures. Such "positive" laws have the advantage of providing a stable framework for cooperative action. They create social order without imposing a social *telos*. Positive laws, while not immune to misuse, help avoid arbitrary government. Abuses inevitably follow when men in power view themselves as founders of a new moral order or enforcers of an orthodox conception of the highest good.

The liberal state *is* responsible for providing a minimal framework— that is, for securing the necessary preconditions for the pursuit of various and changing goals. But while bearing some responsibility for such preconditions ("How much?" is a question of dispute), the state must not impose the goals themselves. The antiteleological core of liberal theory is expressed succinctly in Constant's claim that the state should build highways and keep them well paved but nevertheless allow its citizens to travel in a variety of freely chosen and uncoordinated directions.[87]

It is possible to justify absolute freedom of thought and expression on the ground that an airing of alternative views is the best way to ensure scientific progress. Constant's arguments, however, were not usually so robust. He was not always optimistic about the success of free competition. Against the civic privatism of the Bonapartist and ultra regimes, he insisted that Frenchmen should "not extinguish convictions that serve as the basis for the virtue of citizens."[88] But he never went to extremes: "When one is in perfectly good faith with oneself, complete conviction is a word devoid of meaning."[89] Toleration was not valuable simply because it paid off. The liberal state may accelerate the march of truth, promote life-enhancing variety, and allow unique individuals to express their artistic souls. But Constant valued a state based on absolute freedom of thought and discussion principally because it would allow men to experience honestly their own innermost vacillations, perplexities, and ineradicable lack of certainty. This was the inward side of fallibilism; this was *l'angoisse de choisir*. While he believed that "indecision is the great torture of life," he embraced that uncertainty. The constitutional state was never meant to be "a durable exaltation."[90]

A Liberal Theory of Progress

... mon âme est peu disposée à l'espérance.

REVILED as a secular version of apocalyptic redemption, dismissed as a juvenile utopian fantasy, and judged a fatal flaw of the liberal tradition, the idea of progress has, in addition, been charged with horrible political atrocities.[1] More specifically, eighteenth-century expectations of scientific and moral improvement have been blamed for the sanguinary millenarianism of the Jacobins.[2] Scholars sympathetic to the Enlightenment have responded by unearthing "pessimistic" impulses, by claiming, for example, that reminiscences of the decline of Rome checked the philosophes' dangerous tendency to acquiesce in the myth of progress.[3]

Disillusioned with progress, commentators have been consistently perplexed by Constant's short but important "De la perfectibilité de l'espèce humaine," drafted around 1805, though first published in the *Mélanges* of 1829 (2:125–48). After two centuries of abuse, the Enlightenment concept of progress has been so drained of credibility that we find it difficult to understand how an antiutopian thinker could seriously subscribe to the perfectibility of man. But our perspective is too narrow. Admittedly, Condorcet expected mankind to be emancipated from all its "chains"—perhaps from mortality, certainly from "the rule of chance."[4] By reformulating the theory of perfectibility in a rhapsodic-chiliastic fashion, however, Condorcet overextended the modest and realistic notion of social improvement found in Hume, Voltaire, and Adam Smith.[5] Constant did not allow eschatological exaggerations to discredit that original belief. His affirmation of progress was no drunken hallucination: he did not expect human beings or society to become perfect. Nevertheless, scientific discoveries, the collapse of feudal lordship, the abolition of slavery, the banning of torture, the substitution of legal procedures for blood revenge, the invention of parliamentary government, and the extension of religious toleration were all undeniable signs of moral improvement. To the extent that reforms were still in the making, the concept of progress constituted a program for militancy and a psychological disadvantage for entrenched powers. Moreover, since perfectibility is an endless process,[6] no government could claim insight into the all-justifying finale of history. Relocated in its political setting, Constant's essay on perfectibility makes the concept of progress appear reformist and soberly moderate.[7] A historical account must stress both the modest realism and the strategic utility of the idea.

HISTORICISM IN CONTEXT

Not only "Ancient and Modern Liberty," but all Constant's political writings were dominated by a consciousness of history—by an acute sense of the massiveness and irreversibility of historical change: "Human affairs take a progressive course, independent of men, and which men obey without knowing it. Even their will is swept along, since people can only will what is in their interest, and their interests depend on coexistent circumstances." Social evolution involves profound transformations. Nothing is left untouched: "The same act, performed by two individuals in different [historical] circumstances, never has the same significance."[8] Similarly, principles initially articulated in one historical context acquire very different connotations when cultural inertia transports them into a subsequent period. As Europe crossed the threshold into the modern age, political theorists invoked the pagan city against the authority of the church; but they also directed their irreverent skepticism against the teachings of ancient publicists and philosophers. This was prudent. Many classical doctrines, convincing in an earlier setting, had become anachronisms—if not sources of delusion. In the eighteenth century, Plutarch provided a confusing education for young lawyers from the provinces.

Revolutionary attempts to revive ancient citizenship revealed a weak sense of history and historical change.[9] Constant aimed at strengthening public consciousness of irreversible social transformations: it is impossible to reverse the torrential current of history.[10] Despite this impossibility, it has been "an error common throughout the centuries" for rulers to imagine they can stem this flow. Some philosophes had suggested that, by the mid-eighteenth century, the Bourbon monarchy was out of date. In the wake of the Revolution, Constant followed a similar strategy, advising would-be imitators of ancient republics that "The state of mankind in antiquity was so different from what it is today that nothing applicable in one of these states is admissible in the other." In 1813–14, he warned Napoleon against resurrecting the savage spirit of conquest in a refined age of commerce. After 1817, he warned the ultras against attempting to reestablish primogeniture or return coercive power to the church. It was a persistent theme: "in politics, anachronisms are especially disastrous."[11]

The leading figures of the Scottish Enlightenment had a notable impact on Constant's thinking about society, law, and the state. Judging from the sheer quantity of references, the influence of Hume and Smith seems to have been decisive. But lesser Scots such as Adam Ferguson and William Robertson also stimulated Constant's interest in social change.[12] Historicism, the belief that principles of justice and legitimate authority are valid solely in relation to specific historical contexts, is sometimes said to be but a step removed from the spineless abandonment of all principle.[13] Like *progress*, historicism is associated with acquiescence in the politics of fanatical extremism. The implausibility of this charge is nowhere more apparent than in the case of the historicism Constant learned to appreciate while still a young man in Edinburgh. Far from being a source of immoderation, this historicist style of thought was designed to furnish a grounding for limited government. The distinction between state and society served such an aim. The state was conceived as an "active" power, embodying man's potential to intervene purposefully in the world. Civil society, while a dynamic and evolving system, was "passive": its development could not be adequately comprehended by means of categories used to describe the goal-directed acts of individuals and groups. Individuals, including political officials, behaved in a purposive manner, but the aggregate and long-run outcome of their actions was only incidentally related to their imagined goals. Social change had a logic of its own: the logic of unintended consequences. It could be grasped intellectually; but it could not be adequately understood as the intentional achievement of aims proposed in advance by human planners.

The original assertion that civil society possessed a large degree of autonomy had a polemical function. It served an antimercantilist campaign to restrain the excesses of the Colbertist state. Only a very few theorists—

Godwin, for example—believed that society might dispense with government. Everyone else recognized that social order must be maintained, property protected, contracts enforced, national territory defended from invasion, and taxes collected to finance these minimal but necessary functions. The antimercantilist claim was merely this: dirigist governments cannot, by sheer force of will and good intentions, radically improve society. They cannot autocratically perfect society or successfully accelerate the slow pace of social improvement. Indeed, an overambitious government is likely to *damage* its society, derailing the spread of enlightenment and the progress of opulence. This simple historicist model, based explicitly on the state/society distinction, may be vulnerable to criticism. But its connection with the ideals of political moderation and limited government cannot be doubted.

A related but distinct aspect of Constant's thinking about social change was his theory of progress, or what he, following eighteenth-century precedents, called "perfectibility." His ideas about progress were somewhat anomalous because he combined a belief in the moral advance represented by modernization with an austere lack of illusions about his own age. History is the story of advancing equality: old forms of privilege and hierarchy have been gradually extinguished and men are moving, in a somewhat halting fashion, toward the irrelevance of family background for an allocation of chances in life, an irrelevance called "the career open to talents." While Constant asserted that this unplanned process was a moral advance, he left unclear the relation between perfectibilism and the idea that modern Europeans were tortured by self-doubt and incapable of firm conviction. Moral advance was real enough; but it was impossible to overlook the ambiguities of progress. Unlike either Condorcet or Condorcet's conservative critics, Constant embraced "the modern" coolly, without jubilance or hesitation.

Both the idea of progress and that of social change in general served important strategic functions in liberalism's two-front war against the Left and Right. Constant used his theory of history as a framework for making concessions to both revolution and reaction, Jacobins and ultras. The idea of a slow but irreversible transformation of society was designed to dedramatize ideological conflict. During the Restoration, moreover, ultra attempts to reverse the gains of 1789, led Constant to display prominently his belief in moral progress, even though it did not seem completely consistent with other views he held about modernization, views that can only be characterized as intermittently resigned and pessimistic. Constant's historicism subserved his campaign for restraint, while his theory of progress subserved his campaign for reform.

HISTORICAL PESSIMISM

In an unpublished version of the preface to *Adolphe*, Constant offered the following description of what he saw as the psychological debility attendant upon "excessive civilization":

> In *Adolphe* I wanted to paint one of the principal maladies of our century: this fatigue, this incertitude, this lack of force, this perpetual analysis that places an *arrière-pensée* alongside every feeling and thus corrupts it at birth. . . . We no longer have any force. We do not know how to love or believe or will. Everyone doubts the truth of what he says, smirks at the vehemence of what he affirms and foresees the end of what he feels.[14]

The *vieillesse sceptique* of modern civilization had been a relatively frequent theme among the philosophes.[15] Accounts of it abound in Constant's writings: "The progress of civilization polishes human character by weakening it." Moreover: "All kinds of enthusiasm are spent . . . the world is old . . . material life has become softer, more independent, more secure—and all this kills enthusiasm. The type of happiness available to ancient peoples is no longer within our grasp. We live in an age of cold and egoistical reason." In contrast to classical Greeks and republican Romans, modern Europeans were "fatigued by experience." Similarly, postrevolutionary Paris was a city where "nobody believes anything" and where "nothing that is said influences even the person who says it."[16] The impossibility of complete conviction was the *idée maîtresse* governing Constant's analysis of the spirit of modern society.[17] It underlay, for example, his ambivalent appraisal of political hypocrisy.

A mad professor wrote Napoleon claiming to have discovered the secret of the universe. Constant remarked: "Such a firm conviction and one that seems in such good faith is an extraordinary event in the France of 1809." To believe anything unreservedly was to be a lunatic. In one of his sunnier moods, Constant celebrated "the triumph of reason" in the modern age. But such statements must be read in light of the observation that "reasoning only leads to doubt"—an idea pivotal to Constant's understanding of the contrast between ancients and moderns.[18] The energy of modern European culture was sapped by self-doubt.[19] "The ancients had an entire conviction about everything. We almost never have anything but the hypocrisy of conviction." Or, as he wrote somewhat later, "We almost never have anything but weak and fluctuating convictions, the incompleteness of which we struggle in vain to conceal from ourselves."[20] After 1820, as the government fell increasingly into ultra hands, Constant came to invest this inner failing with ominous political implications. He adopted the typically eighteenth-century view of China as a stagnant culture,[21] but applied it shockingly to Europe: "China, with which Europe acquires every day a more striking resemblance . . . has many formalities but few convictions. . . . China is the sad result of despotism and excessive civilization. It is, for the European nations, what mummies were in Egyptian festivals: the image of a perhaps inevitable future which we seek to conceal from ourselves but toward which we march with giant steps."[22] In this prophecy of Europe's impending mummification, a cautious "perhaps" is the only chink of hope.

Constant invoked a wide spectrum of social and cultural factors to explain the disparity between robust ancient citizens and puny modern individuals. "Commerce and industry," he wrote, "have changed the face of the earth."[23] But economic growth was not the sole motor of moral change. Transformations in religion, new techniques of war, and demographic shifts, as well as a dramatic revision in the received attitude toward slavery, all conspired to destroy greatness of soul, courage, loyalty, generosity, sangfroid, contempt for death, and the capacity for selfless devotion.[24]

In seeking for partial explanations, he revealed a special fondness for the paralyzing force of self-observation. He dwelt at length on the tendency of the mind to fold back upon itself: self-awareness undermined heroic élan and provoked a general *affaiblissement morale*. Ancient poetry was "simple and seamless." The enthusiasm of classical poets was "true, natural and complete." By contrast,

> Modern poets are always haunted by some sort of *arrière-pensée*
> that . . . defeats enthusiasm. It seems that they fear to appear
> naive and gullible. Rather than surrendering themselves to an
> irresistible movement, they reflect on their own poetry along
> with their readers. The first condition for enthusiasm is not to
> observe onself with too much wit and cunning. But modern
> individuals observe themselves even in the midst of their most
> sensuous and violent passions.[25]

By focusing on this sort of passage—and examples could be multiplied—we could easily make Constant appear an "evolutionary pessimist" in the manner of Rousseau.[26] Too much reflection transforms men into depraved or at best anemic animals. Having lost all "simplicity of character," a modern individual "allows himself to be swept away by the perpetual need to talk about himself," and "presents himself as someone always intent on playing a role."[27] While ancient citizens were healthy, natural, and whole, their modern bourgeois counterparts suffer from a crippling malady called self-dividedness.

This grim story of etiolation and defeat was certainly an important dimension of Constant's philosophy of history; but it was only one side of the coin. As already indicated, Constant was equally impressed by scientific and especially moral progress. Here is the anomaly: European history registered both moral advance and moral degeneration: we are becoming perfect even as we decay. At certain times Constant sounded very much like Rousseau, lamenting the moral degradation that accompanies material improvement. At other times he resembled Condorcet, praising man's forward march toward bliss and moral faultlessness.

In the optimistic "De la perfectibilité de l'espèce humaine," Constant wrote that "only the progressive perfection of our species establishes assured communication among generations."[28] But he also had a bitterer view of the subject:

> In the epoch of our excessive civilization, relations between fathers and children have become extremely difficult. Fathers live in the past. The future is the domain of their children. The present is nothing but a neutral terrain, theatre of a great combat in which some strive ceaselessly to hasten the collapse of what others would like to retain. In sum, each day the torrent of affairs, pleasures, and aspirations separates the generation taking possession of life from those whom life abandons.[29]

Perfectibility did not sweeten these embattled and embittered relations between generations.

The ambiguities in Constant's thought about progress cannot be resolved by chronological segmentation. Optimism and pessimism, Condorcet and Rousseau, are mixed together promiscuously from his earliest to his latest writings. The fundamental question is therefore: how could Constant combine these two contradictory perspectives on social evolution? How did he reconcile decrepitude with perfection, self-doubt with self-realization?

DISCREDITING THE GREAT LEGISLATOR

Let us bracket for a moment the question of "progress," returning to a more general question: what role was played by the theory of social change in Constant's political writings? This procedure is justified by his odd habit of defining *progress* agnostically, as nothing more than change. Consider this: "Everything relating to man and his opinions ... is necessarily progressive, that is to say, variable and transitory."[30] Such noncommittal definitions help explain how he was able to reconcile "perfectibilism" with historical relativism and even pessimism; they suggest that he sometimes conceived of *perfectibility* less as a guarantee of improvement than as a euphemism for the dual possibility of either perfection or perversion.

But what was the political function of the liberal theory of social change? Napoleon pursued military adventures in an age of *doux commerce,* when his fellow citizens craved for peace. Constant tendered him this historicist advice: "Obey the times!"[31] Stop your wars! They clash with the dominant beliefs and habits of the age! Our highest moral duty is to adapt pliantly to the general spirit of the times. This seems to be a dubious moral imperative; in Napoleon's case, as we shall see, it was painfully ineffective and indeed redundant. But how could an inveterate protester and opponent of established powers describe conformism, at least in some circumstances, as an unfailing path to reason and moderation?

Constant's theory of social change was meant to reoccupy the place previously filled by the discredited myth of the social contract. State-of-nature theory was "trivial and burlesque."[32] Instead of starting with an unreal and ultimately unimaginable choice situation, political theorists should begin with existing social problems and make recommendations on that basis. They must not place a heavy moral burden on supposedly unchanging traits of human nature. What now seems natural and transhistorical may well appear arbitrary and contingent to later generations facing radically different problems: "Because man is not stationary, he can only guess tentatively what is not inherent in his nature—what he does not carry with him but merely uses en route as a supplementary and temporary resource." Constant had political reasons for occasionally invoking "rights" that transcended specific cultures and historical situations. The ultras blamed Louis XVIII for having imported a "monstrous English charter" into France; and a superficial relativism seemed to support their cause.[33] But, in general, Constant leaned heavily toward a historical relativism of moral principles. The progress of civilization "has created for man new relations with his fellows and, as a result, a new nature." The "epoch of commerce has given man a new nature."[34] Man is not merely in history, but of history.

Constant did not justify the constitutional state because it mirrored human nature, sheltered timeless rights, or elicited the voluntary consent of socially uninfluenced individuals. Rather, he valued public debate, representative government, the responsibility of ministers, majority rule, the whole machinery of checks and balances, bicameralism, an independent judiciary, trial by jury, freedom of the press, religious tolerance, and all the other characteristics of the modern liberal state, because of their historical appropriateness. Compared to the available alternatives, they were the political arrangements most adequate for solving the problems of European societies in their present state of scientific, moral, and economic development. The suitable criteria for judging political actions, policies, and institutions lay not in the philosophical abstraction "man," but in the concrete, problem-riddled realities of contemporary European nations. The most obtrusive and urgent problems afflicting French society during this period were polarization, factional hatreds and ideological intransigence: "hates subsist. . . . memories divide us."[35] This was a problem that any legitimate government had to solve.

To argue that society evolved according to a logic and rhythm of its own was to say that important and durable social changes are largely unaffected by the positive interventions of political authorities. Social development is essentially and not just incidentally unintended; it will never follow a pattern laid down by political fiat or choice. But Constant was a social planner; liberal constitutions are social plans. So why did a designer of liberal constitutions wish to deprecate political management and innovation?

Constant's manner of criticizing the Jacobins was somewhat different from the antimercantilist polemics of Adam Smith. In *The Wealth of Nations*, the idea that society develops according to a logic of its own was meant to discredit and discourage the interventions of a hypertrophic state—a state that endeavored to orchestrate individual actions, but not to "improve" souls or save citizens from themselves. Classical political economy represented an attack on presumptuous *étatisme*, not revolutionary, but Colbertist. The wisely orchestrated society was an illusion. Constant agreed; but unprecedented circumstances led him in a somewhat different direction. With luck, it might be possible to establish a procedural framework for resolving conflicts and making decisions without resort to force. The autonomy of social change did not rule out clever constitutional design; what is excluded was the imposition of moral orthodoxy by a self-selected didactic elite. Above all, historicism signaled Constant's break with philosophes such as Helvétius who expected to legislate vice out of existence.

The corrosive doubts of the Enlightenment were ultimately incompatible with a religious faith in the fatherly administration of society's moral affairs. Constant remained unswervingly loyal to the skepticism of the philosophes even when rejecting their ideal of moral legislation. Political authorities should shelter society from internal disorder and external invasion and implement the policies chosen by a majority of citizens, but they cannot single-handedly impose moral harmony, create the new man, or substantially accelerate society's voyage into the future. The state may *attempt* to remake society according to an ideal moral blueprint, but it will probably injure the autonomous motion of cultural and economic development. Historically, "the action of authority, ancient or modern, has always run in the direction opposite to . . . the destination of mankind."[36] Geared to throw doubt on the very possibility of Great Legislators, Constant's "theory" of historicism was in large measure a political stance.

It was Montesquieu who had first argued that "there is in each nation a general spirit upon which power itself is founded. When it shocks this spirit, it shocks itself, and it necessarily comes to a halt."[37] There is no use fighting the *Geist*. The idea of the "general spirit" of an age or country provided a sociological rather than merely philosophical or anthropological grounding for the liberal commitment to limited government. The limits of politics were not to be found in natural law, in the purity or fallenness of man, but in the logic of social change. Only a "philosophical" neglect of political context and political purpose could lead to the assertion that this sort of historicism undermined all hope of resisting tyranny.

Filangieri did not share the wild dream of transforming the modern bourgeois into an ancient citizen, but he nonetheless lapsed into "the grave error of considering the customs of peoples as derived exclusively from the will of legislators." The Italian philosophe naively believed that the Spartans really did repudiate luxury and commerce solely because Lycurgus outlawed by fiat all such customs, and that they really were bellicose merely because Lycurgus single-handedly fashioned their characters for war: "In the same way, [Filangieri] attributes the industrial spirit of the Athenians to the appeal their Legislator made to industry, without realizing that when industry becomes indispensable to the existence of a people or when a people has reached the industrial epoch of its social condition, there is no need to promote industry by means of authority and laws."[38] Societies naturally evolve toward industrialization. Deliberate planning and political choice can do little to accelerate major shifts in economic, scientific, or moral life. Wise lawmakers will therefore be diffident and restrained. They will know how to obey the times, tempering their decrees and moderating their aspirations in the face of social processes that run their course beyond human design and control. The myth of an all-powerful Legislator obscured the autonomy of civil society and encouraged destructive attempts by modern political authorities to reshape, by violent means, economic and moral life according to anachronistic fantasies.

With his usual skepticism, Constant also examined the possible abuses of historicist thinking. The political aim of historicism—to induce a sense of reticence in overly zealous wielders of legislative authority—would be thwarted if governors decided that they, and they alone, understood what was demanded by the current phase of social development: they could then justify their most abusive acts by adducing the standard of historical appropriateness. Enlightened rulers, they might say, have a right, indeed a duty, to keep benighted citizens on schedule. Filangieri himself was an historicist. Like many philosophers, he believed that a proper "proportion" should exist between promulgated laws and a society's current stage of growth:

> Such a "proportion" is certainly indispensable. But, with his metaphor, Filangieri always seems to attribute to the Legislator a talent for judging and determining this proportion. Here lies his mistake. I reject with all my strength the hypothesis that there exists a class of men miraculously gifted with a supernatural sagacity out of all proportion to that of their contemporaries. This hypothesis serves as an apology for all kinds of oppression. Sometimes it justifies the refusal of the most opportune reforms; at other times it justifies the equally disastrous attempt to impose premature reforms and innovations.[39]

Constant's thinking about social change was guided by his political goals. Thus, historical appropriateness ceased to be a standard for political rationality the moment it became a *pretext* for governmental coercion.

DECENTERING THE POLITICAL

The guiding purpose behind Constant's historicism also sheds light on his rejection of the primacy of politics. The idea that politics enjoys a mysterious "priority" over other aspects of social life goes back to Aristotle and survives vestigially in Rousseau's belief that the *legitimation* of authority is identical with the *foundation* of society. Constant's claim that social development is autonomous, that it follows a logic of its own apart from the decisions of political legislators, was meant as a recommendation rather than as a simple description. Politicians in a liberal regime should recognize that many things lie beyond politics. During the 1820s, the ultras dominated the French state. This was another—though not the sole—reason why the liberal opposition avoided celebrating the supremacy of government over society.

What does Constant's historicism—and its affiliated distinction between state and society—tell us about his rejection of the primacy of politics? To understand what is at stake here, we should recall that some of Constant's most loyal followers have, in responding to Marxism, *reaffirmed* the primacy of the political.[40] They usually introduce two observations as grounds for refurbishing the classical paradigm, for depicting politics as the ordering center or uncommanded commander of social life. First, in totalitarian regimes, the seizure of state power has had a profound impact on the destiny of society as a whole. Constant would have found this easy to understand. The dictatorship of Robespierre signaled a deplorable *morbus Graecus;* a ruthless and unpredictable political machine sent waves of panic throughout French society. Less drastically, Colbertist economic policies stifled the vitality of French commerce and industry. The political abolition of the Spanish Cortes eventually led to the atrophy of Spain's intellectual and economic life.[41] The rule of the ultras, too, was a source of endless grief. Constant knew well that politics could be prior in *this* sense: a bad regime can wreck society. Examples of negative priority, however, did not convince him that politics was the center or essence of society. In fact, these examples had the opposite effect, leading him to deny even more emphatically the priority of politics over other social domains.

Harkening to the classical tradition, present-day liberals such as Raymond Aron, insist upon the primacy of politics for a second and more general reason. They first assert—and it is quite easy to prove—that the political system is *indispensable* to other sectors of society; and then they decree that indispensability means primacy. Their inferential leap, however, is less than totally convincing: one part of a system can be indispensable to the other parts without being in any sense "prior" to them.

This dispute among liberals, however, is in large measure verbal. By denying the Aristotelian primacy of politics, Constant was mainly concerned to reject the conceit that modern politics should become the whole of life. (If politics were the whole of life, parties would be uncompromising factions and governors unstoppable tyrants.) But he also stressed that politics—conceived either as authority or as participation—was a crucial and indispensable element in social life. He never doubted that political decisions had a lasting impact on social organization. He knew equally well that a collapse of sovereign authority could shred the fabric of society. His constitutional schemes were meant to provide a framework within which Frenchmen could cooperate and learn from one another as well as disagree. Opposed to the monoethical state, he nevertheless aspired to give France a "constitutional education" through his numerous articles and pamphlets.[42] But he did not seek to impose moral orthodoxy by coercive means. The tasks he assigned to constitutional design were relatively modest and were, in any case, thrust upon his generation by an unplanned confluence of circumstances.[43] If his legislative efforts were effective, this was because he had adjusted himself to his historical surroundings. He cooperated with social forces that not only merited support but also had an energetic life of their own independent of him and beyond his control.

Constant's politics were antiextremist, aimed, in the first instance, at limiting the scope of political mastery and lessening the intensity of political animosities. He fought for a popular but not a beautiful government. Unlike the ancient *politeia,* his modern constitutional order was not meant to generate or contain all valuable human possibilities. Its principal task was to protect chances in life produced by extrapolitical institutions. Constitutionalism acknowledged the autonomy of society. The role of the liberal state was limited; but it was also crucial.

On some occasions, Constant's historicism led him to overstate his case and belittle, at least rhetorically, the importance of politics. But he always did so with a practical purpose in mind: he was battling to inculcate a sense of the limits of politics in both faction leaders and public officials. Disencumbered of its politically motivated exaggerations, his position was this: politics is indispensable without being any more primary than ideology, economic structure, cultural traditions, religious ideas, class relations, the system of education, and so forth. Social influence flows in many directions. Political actors cannot impose any form they wish on their changing social milieu, since the "general spirit" of a nation is widely diffused, psychologically and institutionally anchored, and resistant to centralized manipulation.

Politics is not the master of society; but neither is it society's servant. Liberal egalitarianism implied that social and economic power should never be translatable directly into political power. Legal equality—especially the equal right to vote—selectively diminished the relevance of society for politics. But while a political regime may be to some degree autonomous (that is, independent of social and economic power), it cannot assume total responsibility for society. Extravagant hopes for the society-shaping role of government are unrealistic and will become, should the delusion persist, hideously destructive.

BETWEEN RIGHT AND LEFT

Jaunty optimism was not in Constant's nature: "the future is always doubtful."[44] In fact, his idea of perfectibility had to battle against a grim sense of history:

> Ignorance of the events menacing us has often been considered the greatest benefit we owe to nature. The past already renders life sufficiently hard to bear. No one arrives one-third of the way through his career without having to grieve about ruptured

bonds, extinguished illusions, and disappointed hopes. What would it be like if man, his heart blighted by these gloomy memories, was pursued by a terrible foresight; if, near the tombs of the departed, he saw in his mind's eye the tombs open that must engulf those who still remain; if, wounded by the ingratitude of a perfidious friend, he recognized the traitor-to-be in the new friend who replaced the old one? The fleeting and imperceptible present would then be trapped between two terrifying phantoms. The instant which is not yet and the one which no longer exists would conspire to poison the present. But men escape from the past because they forget it and think they possess the future because they are ignorant of it.[45]

How can Constant combine this bleak outlook with his cheerful claim that the system of perfectibility "explains the enigma of individual and social existence"?[46] One answer lies in the astonishingly sharp disjunction he managed to sustain between his private and public lives.

Against the grain of his personal and, one might even say, metaphysical pessimism, Constant found himself drawn toward the idea of progress because, like the more general concept of social change, it was an effective weapon in his political struggles. Already in the eighteenth century, "progress" had been deployed as a framework for social reform. Turgot's concept of progress certainly set the stage for his activities as a reformer.[47] The socially beneficial consequences of economic growth provided antimercantilists with a new argument against political despotism. When entail is abolished and land can be freely sold, property will be diffused, a complex division of labor will develop, and general prosperity will ensue.[48] Misgovernment does not merely violate traditional rights. It impedes progress (for example, an increase in total food production) from which all citizens might benefit.

After the Revolution, liberals used the concept of progress in their two-front war against Jacobins and counterrevolutionaries. Both Left and Right were addicted to conspiracy theories. Constant emphasized long-term and unplanned change to counter their common tendency to ascribe either the outbreak of the Revolution or its failure to the treachery of individuals. An invisible hand displaced the intriguers of palace and Masonic lodge. In her *Considérations sur la Révolution française,* Mme. de Staël gave this argument a personal twist, invoking the massive inexorability of historical change to exculpate her father from charges of ministerial incompetence.

Constant referred to the ultras as "stationary spirits." They were "in open war against their century." His counteroffensive stressed the irrever-

sibility of social change. The ultras viewed the Revolution as a mere pa-
renthesis in French history: after God had fully punished the country for
its sins, the old immutable order would be restored. Speaking of the demolition of the principle of heredity, Constant responded: "each step in this
direction has been *sans retour*."[49] One of the main themes of *Adolphe* had
been the futility of trying to rekindle youthful enthusiasms once they have
flagged. After an old religion has collapsed, he also wrote, it can never be
reestablished.[50] He genuinely believed in the unalterable direction of social
change; but he stressed it publicly for political reasons. Late in his life, he
wrote: "I have thought it best to treat the past civilly, first because the past
is not all bad, and second because civility will induce the past to retreat
more compliantly." Acquiescence in change did not presuppose contempt
for the past. It was, in any case, impossible to turn the clock back: "the
necessary course of the human mind is stronger than the wills of men."[51]
This did not imply that the present was necessarily superior to the past.
That was Constant's face-saving concession to conservative forces. When
he stressed irreversibility, rather than moral improvement, he did so because
of its neutrality. It might soften the resistance to change even among those
whose social ideals clashed violently with his own.

If *irreversibility* was neutral, *progress* was not. The ultras had been
very displeased by the concessions to progress inserted into the preamble
to the Charte, for progress was an anticlerical idea.[52] To the ultras it seemed
demonic, not neutral. According to Constant, the Catholic church was "a
church fiercely proud of its immutability," and its priesthood was "a corporation that saw its own interest in keeping religion stationary." He devoted some of the most political sections of *De la religion* to a polemic
against "sacerdotal immobilism." But his argument was tactical, not doctrinaire. The "stationary principle," inspiring religious conservatism, was
unwittingly self-destructive. Since the force of history is stronger than the
wills of men, only change is genuinely conservative. Institutions unable
to adapt to new situations have no chance to survive. For example: "If one
refuses to change a doctrine inherited from a period when men knew nothing
about the laws of nature, one turns every new scientific discovery into an
attack on this doctrine." The refusal to acknowledge intellectual progress
is self-defeating: "Religious beliefs that lag, hostile and isolated, behind the
general development of culture, transform allies into enemies. They find
themselves, so to speak, besieged by enemies they have unnecessarily created."[53] A few years later, Tocqueville would try to reconcile the heirs of
the theocrats to democracy by describing it as an irresistible, providential
force.[54] Constant had deployed the concept of inexorable social change in

this same manner, disguising moral improvement as an irreversible process beyond moral approval or disapproval. It was a kind of impartial power—an immutable fact. Recognition of this brute fact might sober up "the men who wish to reverse the course of centuries."[55] They might be brought to accept liberalization, even if they sorely regretted the old regime. As a practical reformer, it is worth recalling, Constant always preferred to rely on facts rather than on philosophical abstractions or moral homilies. There might never be a moral consensus between constitutionalists and ultras; but the nonpartisan fact of social change could become a neutral ground upon which compromise might be reached. Factions cannot be eliminated from a free society; but they might be civilized, at least to some extent.

History will always be a laborious process of gradient climbing. This image was Constant's way of encouraging the Left to drop its extravagant ambitions and discover the virtues of patience: "the good is only accomplished by degrees," while "impatience makes the world worse."[56] Change is inevitable, but it cannot be forced. It was ludicrous to restart the calendar at the Year I—the roots of the past cannot be so easily yanked up. Moreover, no group can claim special insight into the end of history since there is no end of history: perfectibility excludes eschatology. Progress is slow, uneven, endless, and, above all, inadvertent. It is seldom the result of virtuous intentions. Turgot had explicitly argued that the polishing of manners and the enlightening of minds were the unintended consequences of "self-interest, ambition and vainglory."[57] A by-product view of social improvement was totally incompatible with the Lycurgus-like pose struck by Robespierre and Saint-Just. Constant embraced this aspect of the Enlightenment theory of progress. It exploded the myth that citizens might be perfected through governmental edict.

Jacobins and ultraroyalists were guilty of symmetrical errors. The former—despite their admiration for antiquity—vaulted impatiently ahead of the age, while the latter lagged intransigently behind. Guilty of anachronism, neither heeded the historicist advice: "Obey the times! . . . Do not be obstinate in maintaining that which collapses, nor too anxious to establish that which seems ready to announce itself . . . consent to many things happening without you, and confide to the past its own defense, to the future its own accomplishments."[58] The idea of inexorable change, be it noted, could only serve liberal goals because it incorporated the idea of moral progress. Constant's interpretation of the Revolution as a watershed in mankind's moral advance revealed his personal sympathy for the ideals, though not the impatience, of the Left. History had a direction: it was moving toward justice—toward a decrease in oppression and suffering and a dismantling of the absurd old regime: "the reign of privileges is at an end."[59] The Revolution had been progressive despite its atrocities. Constant's underlying commitment to the disestablishment of privilege was never weakened by his ad hoc concessions to the conservative forces. His "philosophy of history," however, was a bargain as well a theory. It was meant to have a nation-building function in a country racked by hatreds and riven by ideological factions.

Although Constant's views on these matters were purposely eclectic, they were not devoid of all consistency. From the Left he borrowed a belief in justice and equality, ideals that served to condemn the rotten abuses of the old regime. From the Right he borrowed the idea of a slow-moving historical development, unorchestrated by human design. He combined these ideas, as did many of his contemporaries, into the idea of history as a gradual and unplanned emergence of social equality. Only someone as deluded as Robespierre could view himself as a personal founder of the new democratic order. Only someone as deluded as Charles X could hope personally to reverse the torrential course of history.

Moral relativism allowed Constant to avoid any suggestion of contempt for the unpolished past. Referring to violations of equity and justice under the old regime, he wrote: "these abuses were once useful" and "to-day's abuses were yesterday's needs."[60] Contextual justification (whereby a political institution is decreed legitimate not because it corresponds to human nature but because it helps solve a historically pressing social problem) also had a more practical advantage. It allowed Constant to discuss ultraroyalism critically, while de-moralizing the language of political contestation. Ultras were not evil; they were merely out of date: "I do not doubt their morality, but only their enlightenment."[61]

Constant was pulled toward relativism, despite his philosophical convictions about progress and decrepitude, because relativism was also an effective position for someone striving to dampen the mutual fears and hatreds that marked French political life. He was not, however, completely satisfied with this functional mode of justification. Montesquieu had already made a half-hearted attempt to justify ancient slavery on historicist lines, but "the voice of nature" had cried out against the endeavor. Constant furnished a less exclamatory argument against all such efforts: "To prove that an abuse is the basis of the existent social order is not to justify it. Every time that there exists an abuse in the social order, it seems to be the basis of that order. It is heterogeneous and isolated by its nature. Thus, in order for it to be preserved, everything must bend to fit it, which means that everything rests upon it."[62] In ancient Greece and feudal Europe, it seemed to all men of privilege that society would collapse without slaves and serfs.

The "appropriateness" of a government to its society, in other words, is an uncertain standard of legitimacy because political institutions can aggressively distort social life. Even the despicable feudal system could be justified as "the only government proportioned to the *moeurs,* customs and enlightenment of the nations that adopted it."[63] In advancing such historicist justifications, "one forgets that the worst institutions always are (or become) proportioned to the people who endure them, since when these people are too enlightened to approve of them and too weak to destroy them, the institutions debase the individuals to their level."[64] In lieu of unchanging standards, natural or divine, historical "fit" provides a useful criterion of good government; but it must be applied with caution.

Constant spoke out sharply against the oppressions once inflicted upon the nation by "the great land-owners" of the old regime.[65] But Montesquieu had not been completely mistaken to suggest that the old landed nobility preserved a "spirit of resistance accustomed to action" which shielded France from the doddering senility of Spain.[66] To stress the erstwhile usefulness of abuses, however, was not to justify them, not even for the past. But neither was it a blanket condemnation. Relativism allowed him to maintain respect for the past and conciliate conservative forces without fundamentally compromising his liberal values.

Speaking again of feudal arrangements, Constant wrote: "Those times exist no longer. Those advantages have been replaced by other advantages."[67] Historical change is less a matter of progress than of irreversible transformations, accompanied by both gains and losses. Talk of the "advantages" of feudalism may sound inconsistent with Constant's pronouncements about the upward direction of social change. Nevertheless, it represented an attractive position in its own right, with a respectable genealogy among the philosophes.[68] Historical development was a matter of trade-offs between benefits and costs. The benefits outweigh the costs; but the costs are significant and should not be slighted.

In the early years of the Restoration, before his final surge of militancy began, Constant extended a white flag toward his traditionalist enemies. But he did not aspire to suppress all discord and dissent. He intended only to soften the language of political conflict. This practical aim also informed his thinking about progress. He wished to deescalate the civil war, to compress it into the miniature format of parliamentary battles. He hoped that plans for revenge would be focused exclusively on the next election. Note the conscious effort to be impartial toward the conflicting parties in this passage:

> If mankind follows an invariable path, then we must submit to it. Only resignation will preserve men from senseless struggles and hideous suffering. If, after recognizing the necessity of a general resignation, we discover the particular kind of resignation applicable to the epoch in which we live, this discovery will corroborate and strengthen the first. Sacrifices will be enlightened. We will avoid both vain resistances and superfluous exaggerations, both mistaken efforts and false directions. We will know precisely what must be repulsed with force, suffered with patience, softened with skill, improved with zeal. I am speaking equally for those who lose and those who gain, for those who fear and those who aspire, for those who profited from abuses and for those who were devoured by abuses. All have an equal need to be instructed about the fate awaiting them. Enlightenment is necessary for all. Both conquerors and conquered must reconnoiter the field of battle: ignorance of the terrain will precipitate them into the abyss and will add the useless calamities of chance to the inevitable evils of war.[69]

Enlightenment will not eliminate strife, but it will alleviate the worst consequences of conflict. Constant wished to sublimate the civil war into "the struggle of the conservative spirit and the progressive spirit."[70] This sort of domesticized conflict would be compatible with democratic cooperation and a social truce.

PROGRESS AS A DESCRIPTIVE CATEGORY

Constant's diagnosis of *la malheureuse maladie morale* of the modern age was not obviously consistent with his announced belief in progress. But despite his ingrained pessimism, Constant was attracted to the idea of progress—intellectually attracted, not merely on political grounds. Just as historical relativism was a concession to the Right that would not offend the Left, so progress was a concession to the Left which the Right could be brought to accept. Both ideas had an arbitrating function in a situation of incipient civil war. But this is not the whole story. The anticipated endpoint of progressive development bore some relation to the facts of European history and was, moreover, partly compatible with a pessimistic diagnosis of man's moral degeneration.

Without doubting the reality of scientific and technical progress, Constant was concerned almost exclusively with moral and institutional aspects of historical change. What were the ends he assigned to the march of history? They were basically three: equality, religious toleration, and legal conventionalism.

Already in the *Force du gouvernement* of 1796, Constant endorsed Condorcet's notion that history has a preordained goal and that this goal is equality: "The origin of society is a great enigma, but its development is simple and uniform. We see mankind emerging from an impenetrable cloud that obscures its birth, advancing toward equality over the debris of all sorts of institutions."[71] He also advanced a theory of "four great revolutions" that successively demolished these institutions: (1) theocracy based on an untouchable caste; (2) slavery; (3) feudalism; and (4) the eighteenth-century nobility of privilege. History has a *telos*. It is a journey toward equality: "the perfectibility of man is nothing but the tendency toward equality."[72] Drawn to this idea because of its polemical value, he also had reason to consider it an empirical claim. He submitted this persuasive evidence for the reality of progress:

> During the struggle of the French Revolution, even the most inveterate aristocrats did not dream of proposing the reestablishment of slavery; while Plato in his ideal republic did not imagine that he could do without it. Such is the course of the human spirit that even the most absurd men of today cannot, despite themselves, retreat to positions held by the most enlightened men of previous centuries.[73]

The gradual triumph of equality seemed both a moral victory and an objective process unfolding outside human control. But what did Constant have in mind by "equality"?

He was thinking less of a positive than of a negative state of affairs. The journey to equality was defined almost exclusively as a journey away from inequality: "the destruction of hereditary privileges was an inevitable result of the progress of civilization."[74] The starting point determined the goal. The four basic stages in the advance of equality were identical with the four revolutions that destroyed decreasingly oppressive forms of social hierarchy. Inequality had conceptual priority over equality; the former gave content to the latter, specifying the relation of subordination being overthrown. In general, Constant conceived equality's progress as the increasing irrelevance of the past characteristic of modern civilization. Prestige, power, social roles, and other chances in life were decreasingly allocated on the basis of family background. "Equality" was able to serve as a rallying cry for the heterogeneous Third Estate because it was a bloodless, privative concept. It gathered the aggrieved under a single banner not by painting a picture of the ideal society but, rather, by attributing their multiple grievances to a single source: the injurious "inequality of ranks."

In the Third Estate's attack on the old regime, the ideal of equality was coupled with that of liberty. Constant followed this tradition. Just as equality signaled release from the dead hand of heredity, so freedom meant emancipation from religious orthodoxy and absolutist rule. Freedom and equality shared a negative, abolitionist connotation: their content came from the social arrangements they challenged and which, it was predicted or hoped, they would replace. "Equal rights," too, were disestablishmentarian, aimed principally at destroying the privileged-based old regime. Individuals do not have rights because of their specific family-determined location in an organic social hierarchy, but simply because they are human beings. No one is born to command or obey. Under all four regimes destroyed by the march of civilization, a person's status in the ladder of privilege was ascribed by birth. With the advance of equality, individual status became contingent—that is, independent of birth—although it obviously remained dependent on many other factors, such as talent or luck.

But what sort of *perfectionnement* did Constant have in mind? We know that it was not theocracy, not slavery, not feudalism, and not the old regime. But what was it? To this, his theory of equality gave a meager answer. A journey is usually more than the abolition of obstacles; but that is almost all we learn about this great march. Equality can open doors, but it cannot guarantee fulfillment. While furnishing a goal for history, it does not provide a sense of direction for individual lives. This was not an oversight, but the essence of Constant's theory of equality.

Progress and regression can be two sides of the same coin. In post-Reformation Europe, religious toleration and the incapacity for complete conviction seemed natural allies and mutual reinforcers. Besides his *politique* reasons for endorsing religious toleration, Constant had a deeper motive: he was unsure. The modern age is the age of reason, and reasoning leads to doubt. Complete conviction is now unattainable.

Religious toleration is supported by lack of certainty (not by dictatorially inclined atheism). The culture of permanent doubt, however, also produced Adolphe and all the wretchedness of his self-torture. Constant's ambivalent assessment of moral and intellectual uncertainty helps to explain how he could combine an optimistic with a pessimistic view of social change. He saw religious tolerance both as a release from the misery of priestly oppression and an integral component of the modern culture of insecurity.

The third goal of progress was "positive" or legislature-made law: "the destruction of the privileges of the nobility is the beginning of a new age: the age of conventional laws." Constant also presented this idea as a compromise between Jacobin utopias and the burdensome realities of the past. Conventional laws have the advantage of being "simultaneously more reasonable than force and less abstract than reason."[75] Unlike earlier law, which was purportedly discovered in nature or in God's will, positive law forced men into an acute consciousness of their own responsibility for re-forming legal codes: "In studying conventional law we must never lose sight of this first principle. Conventions are not natural or immutable but artificial, susceptible to change, created to replace truths which remain little known and to serve momentary needs. As a result, they must be amended, perfected, and above all, restricted to the extent that truths are discovered or needs change."[76] Echoing Condorcet's famous "no master save reason" passage,[77] Constant went on to provide democratic reasons for calling the present "the" epoch of conventional laws, even though there have been man-made laws in all periods:

> It is because this is the first age in which conventional laws have subsisted alone and without admixture. There have always been conventional laws, since men cannot live without laws. But these conventions were secondary things. Prejudices, errors, and su-perstitious venerations sanctioned these conventions, occupied the first rank, and characterized the preceding ages. It is not until today that men, no longer recognizing any occult power which has the right to dominate their minds, wish to consult only their own reasoning powers. Thus they refuse to subscribe to anything except conventions that result from interaction with the reason of their fellows.[78]

The natural law tradition, because it concealed man's political responsibility for legislation and adjudication, was a form of obscurantism. In the post-revolutionary age, laws are no longer validated by supposedly kerygmatic guarantees. They are legitimate so long as they remain changeable and contingent. Citizens are only obliged to obey a law if they can modify it legally. Susceptibility to revision becomes a source of legitimacy and a reason for acceptance.

In antiquity, constitutional design was often conceived as a war against change, as an attempt to stay the inevitable march of corruption.[79] Constant rejected this ancient model, conceiving constitutions as frameworks for political improvement and self-correction. While his neutral power was preservative, for example, it was not conservative: "the spirit of the preservative power is not at all a stationary spirit." It adjusts to and even encourages social progress.[80] Similarly, Constant's overriding emphasis on public debate registered the liberal commitment to scientific fallibilism. In modern science, the only remaining justification for a belief is the standing invitation for the whole world to refute it.[81] Analogously, the free salability of land strengthens the property claim of landowners.[82] Government policy commands respect to the extent that the constitution makes visible the rules which govern orderly change. This is "the age of conventional laws" because institutions are now subject to criticism and no problem can be considered definitively solved. No reform is immune to future reform. Deprived of a destiny proclaimed by God or etched into nature, citizens are charged with ongoing responsibility for the improvement and repair of their own legal order.

This routinization of precariousness is also visible in the liberal conception of political office. No longer founded on natural necessity, the legitimacy of rulers is based instead on convention and contingency. We accept the decisions of political officeholders not because they were appointed by God, but because we know they can be ousted in the next election. This parallel argument suggests that Constant's rapprochement with the "legitimate" dynasty, after 1814, was purely strategic, not at all doctrinal (see chap. 9 below). It also sheds light on the connection, within liberal thought, between conventionalism and equality. Among other things, equality means that the social allocation of authority is contingent and revocable.

LIBERAL DISILLUSIONMENTS

"The word illusion is not found in any ancient language, because the word cannot be invented until the thing no longer exists."[83] The Greeks and Romans were in many respects like "children."[84] Explosive vigor resulted from infantile illusions. The ancients deceived themselves that some men were born to miserable drudgery and others to the challenging opportunities provided by freedom. The historical destruction of this illusion led Constant to draw a close parallel between scientific and moral progress: "This tendency [toward equality] stems from the fact that equality alone is in conformity with the truth, that is to say, with the relation of things among themselves and of men among themselves."[85] The propelling force of change in history is the gravitational tug of moral truth, of the truth that differences of talent, however calculated, do not correlate positively with the status acquired at birth in traditional societies. Like Condorcet, Constant was committed to the dispelling of illusions; but, unlike Condorcet, he doubted that the advance of truth would eliminate vice or succeed in making men particularly happy.[86]

One must admire antiquity because "in those times, the faculties of man were developed . . . in a truly vast career." Ancient citizens were "flushed with their own strength and with . . . a feeling of energy and dignity." Nevertheless, all this was possible only because it occurred "in a direction traced in advance." More concretely: "Ancient peoples were unable to quit the occupations of their fathers for an occupation closer to their desires."[87] It is characteristic of the modern age that careers are no longer traced in advance. Modern individuals can choose their professions and change them in mid-life. A plethora of alternatives, while liberating, can lead to disorientation. Nevertheless, like the rise of equality (of which it is actually a subvariety), the contingency of careers and social rank represents a triumph of truth. *Triumph* is not the most appropriate word, however, since truth erodes the social preconditions that nourish triumphant personalities.

Human nature varies according to cultural beliefs and social context. The progress of European civilization has, nonetheless, brought society into closer conformity with the truth about human nature. Man is by nature a chameleonlike, mercurial, and changeable creature. In the eighteenth century, insight into man's malleability led Helvétius, Filangieri, and others to formulate masterful plans for moral reform through legislation.[88] The Revolution discredited such designs. Thereafter, the indefiniteness of human nature assumed a different function, allowing Constant, for example, to explain why modern European societies were more truthful or less caught in a web of illusions than ancient or medieval communities. Postrevolutionary France provided the chance for individuals to live honestly with the naked contingency of their own choices, their own careers, and their own positions in society. Man's *mobilité ondoyante* may have been painful.[89] While accepting it and embracing its consequences did not guarantee happiness, it was a form of fidelity to man's innate lack of any fixed essence or predestined mode of life. Here at last was an inborn potential that liberals could hope to maximize. It was, however, quite unlike a robust Aristotelian *telos;* it was merely Locke's "capacity for choice."[90] There was no guarantee that the choices would be good. Without a wired-in *telos,* an individual can evaluate imagined goals by comparing them with other imagined goals achievable with the same resources.[91] Unlike teleological theories, liberalism emphasizes the lack of natural standards for human choice. It is therefore a challenge without being a comfort.

THE PROGRESS OF HYPOCRISY

The tensions among Constant's perfectibilism, pessimism, and moral relativism were creative, not debilitating. He deliberately built pessimism and relativism into his concept of progress. The resulting ambiguities did not discredit his theory because they were treated as attributes of its subject matter. Progress is inherently ambiguous. This was the realistic core of the liberal idea of social and moral improvement. Moreover, to the extent that Constant's perfectibilism and relativism did conflict with his underlying pessimism, they can be interpreted politically, as a groundwork for reform and as strategies for maneuvering successfully between Left and Right.

Filangieri claimed that European rulers were now, for the first time, enlightened enough to see that their subjects did not desire war. In his commentary, Constant suggested that such progress was but a change in the language of hypocrisy:

> Rulers recognize the truth as late as possible. But despite their efforts, they cannot evade it forever. They have now observed that a change has occurred in the disposition of their peoples. They pay homage to it by their solemn acts and speeches: they avoid openly confessing a love of conquest, and it is always with great professions of regret that they take up arms. In this respect, as Filangieri observed, reason has penetrated even to the throne. But, in forcing power to change its language, has reason—as Filangieri likes to hope—illuminated the spirits and converted the hearts of those upon whom chance has conferred authority? It grieves me to say so, but I cannot believe it. I do not perceive in their conduct any increased love of peace, but only a greater hypocrisy.[92]

"Progress" compelled vice to change the vocabulary in which it paid homage to virtue. What follows is a catalogue of the official pretexts invoked to justify forty years of war during a period that rulers politely christened an age of peace.

Constant's ambivalent attitude toward progress recalls his obsession with the power of pretexts. Although already known in antiquity, pretexts assumed special importance in modern times. As the only illusions left to a disillusioned age, they could be extremely effective or destructive. The most ominous innovation of modern society was the emergence of a new rhetorical opportunity: the chance to defend tyranny in the name of freedom and democracy. The vocabulary of hypocrisy was enriched. Formerly, men

were oppressed by a few in the name of divine right; now they were oppressed by a few in the name of popular sovereignty.

This cynical analysis epitomizes Constant's ironic and dedogmatizing
approach. But it is not representative of his view of progress. It even fails
to record his belief that the substance of oppression changes when oppressors
adopt a democratic mask. For all his personal *tristesse,* he was not a fatalist
in political matters. He believed that constitutional government and legal
liberty were possible alternatives to the Reign of Terror. Despite his awareness of the ambiguities of progress, he directed his own political activities
toward steady reform. At the end of his life, he wrote that the two fundamental goals of his career had been "to understand the great crisis that
has been in preparation for two centuries and that erupted forty years ago,
and to encourage the movement that draws mankind as a whole toward a
better sphere of ideas and institutions."[93] Authentically ambiguous, Constant's idea of progress was both theoretical and practical, explanatory and
combative. To explore the central weakness of his historicism, we must now
turn to a more detailed study of *Conquête et usurpation.*

EIGHT

Modern Tyranny

*Le pouvoir absolu n'a pas besoin de mentir; il se tait. Le gouvernement
responsable, obligé de parler, déguise et ment effrontément.*

—*Napoleon*

TO highlight the uniqueness of Napoleon's rule, Constant drew a sharp distinction between traditional despotism and postrevolutionary dictatorship. Absolute monarchs oppress their subjects, cruelly or less so; but they never claim that their actions express the public will. A populist dictator not only oppresses the people, he also forces them to *say* they are free. Alert to every profanation of democratic symbols, Constant carefully observed Napoleon's plebiscites, showtrials, rubberstamp parliaments, and behind-the-scenes manipulation of a purportedly free press.

Progenitive of the more recent contrast between authoritarian and totalitarian regimes,[1] Constant's distinction between two kinds of tyranny has been as influential than his distinction between two kinds of liberty. To understand and evaluate the contrast correctly, we must examine the situation in which it was originally introduced.

THE ENIGMA OF 1813–1814

The anti-Napoleonic *De l'espirit de conquête et de l'usurpation dans leurs rapports avec la civilisation européenne* was hastily composed in Germany in December 1813 and first published in January at Hanover. It is an extremely puzzling work for several reasons.[2] The first three chapters of part

2,[3] grouped together with the thirteenth chapter of part 1,[4] read like a treatise of the counterrevolution. Constant seems to argue, illiberally enough, that only rulers who inherit their power can govern with moderation. He also hints that legal uniformity may be equivalent to savage tyranny. Indeed, if Constant actually held the positions attributed to him on the basis of these chapters, the coherence of his liberalism would be severely compromised. De Broglie, who blamed Constant for drifting too far to the left during the Restoration, liked to recall that in this brochure "he celebrated the legitimacy of princes and cursed usurpation in terms that an *habitué* of Coblentz would not have disavowed."[5] Was De Broglie's assessment correct?

Constant was obviously embarrassed by the conservative and Legitimist impression conveyed by his pamphlet. In the June edition he added several apologetic footnotes[6] as well as two new chapters, to correct the widespread misapprehension that he had suddenly become an anticonstitutionalist. In the first of these remedial chapters, he argued that picturesque localism must never be allowed to interfere with equality before the law,[7] and in the second he insisted that a monarch's right to rule can derive only from public consent, never from bloodline ascription.[8] While reaffirming Constant's loyalty to the principles of 1789, these belated codicils deepen the mystery. Why did a theorist who relentlessly denounced the ancien régime write a pamphlet so easy to misunderstand? From his private daybook, we know that he was collaborating at this time as a propaganda agent for Bernadotte.[9] Indeed, he initially conceived *Conquête et usurpation* as a contribution to Bernadotte's campaign to establish a constitutional monarchy in France on the English model. The first two editions of the brochure[10] included a eulogistic chapter on William III, a transparent brief for Bernadotte.[11] In the third edition, published after the Bourbons had been effectively restored,[12] he prudently suppressed this chapter.

Like Napoleon, Bernadotte was a revolutionary general and a self-made man. Thus, the suppressed chapter in his honor makes *Conquête et usurpation* an even more baffling work. As Talleyrand said, "Bernadotte was only a new phase of the Revolution."[13] So how could the opening chapters of part 2, which denounce new monarchies and extol dynastic legitimacy, support Bernadotte's claim to the throne?

Constant had initially planned to entitle his pamphlet *De l'esprit de conquête et de l'arbitraire,* but he ultimately settled upon the word *usurpation,* misleadingly suggesting royalist commitments. Why did he make this choice? In the posthumous *Du polythéisme romain,* he mocked the very concept of usurpation, dismissing it as a rhetorical embellishment. Referring to the self-serving but universal tendency to label foreign religions "magic" he wrote: "the accusation of magic in religious quarrels corresponds to the accusation of revolt and usurpation in civil wars and political strife." In 1813, however, he seemed to build his entire case around this single idea. Napoleon is tormented by his own illegitimacy since "mistrust is an element inseparable from usurpation." As "a usurper sits with fright on an illegitimate throne," the emperor's "suspicions grow out of all proportion to the number of his enemies."[14] Under the pressure of his own insecurity, he ends up attacking his own allies.[15]

Relying on the army for his accession to the Consulate and later to the throne, Napoleon had no choice but to rule by the equivalent of battalion orders, surrounded by a praetorian guard, and with a strong emphasis on military glory.[16] Only the pursuit of an adventuristic and annexationist foreign policy had gained him popular support. Compelled "to replace the prestige of antiquity by the prestige of conquest," Napoleon was even "condemned to great deeds."[17] Having acquired power illegally, he was psychologically unable to establish a stable legal order:

> Illegality pursues him like a phantom. In vain, he takes refuge both in display and in victory. The specter accompanies him into the midst of pomp and onto the battlefield. He promulgates laws and he changes them. He establishes constitutions and violates them. He founds empires and overturns them. . . . You never see a usurper who has not twenty times revoked his own laws and suspended the forms he has introduced, just as a novice or impatient worker breaks his tools.[18]

Napoleon led 860,000 young Frenchmen to their deaths because, not having been born to rule, he was personally insecure.

Montesquieu had intriguingly argued that "as the power of a monarch becomes immense, his security diminishes."[19] Constant mentioned this thesis once in *De l'usurpation;* and he returned to it frequently in his later writings: "unlimited power becomes insane."[20] In the bulk of *Conquête et usurpation*, however, he did not follow Montesquieu's lead, but focused instead on the contrast between inherited power and power that is seized. The problem with Napoleon was not that he was an excessively powerful autocrat, but rather that he was a first-generation autocrat! Revealingly, Constant festooned the opening of his chapter on the differences between usurpation and monarchy with two epigraphs, one in Greek from Aeschylus, "a new master is always harsh," and the other from his adaptation of Schiller's *Wallenstein,* celebrating the "sacred and invincible power" of tradition.[21] Not educated to the calm expectation of ruling France, Napoleon was intoxicated by the grandeur of his new position.[22]

The contrast between a hysterically anxious Napoleon and the un-
flappable Bourbons is curious not least of all because it echoes Edmund
Burke. When Constant first read the *Reflections on the Revolution in France*
in 1790, he wrote: "there are more absurdities than lines in this famous
book," and he singled out Burke's defense of nobility as a peculiarly egre-
gious absurdity. In *Conquête* itself, Constant compared those who justify
privilege by appeal to custom with "that French cook who, reproached for
making eels suffer by scorching them, replied: 'They are used to it, I have
been doing it for thirty years.' "[23] This was a sign that Constant did *not*
wish his readers to view tradition piously as an invincible and sacred power.

The opening chapters of *De l'usurpation*, however, seem to be a systematic elaboration of Burke's warning against "*new* power in *new* persons." According to Burke, the members of the National Assembly were
"snatched from the humblest rank of degradation," and thus "intoxicated
with their unprepared greatness."[24] Lacking the confidence of true gentlemen, *homines novi* are a blight on politics and civilization. Constant reiterated this aristocratic teaching. Lacking inherited skills for negotiating a
complex social environment, Napoleon was inevitably tempted to apply the
easy remedy of violence. What else could be expected from a new man, an
homme de rien?

The royalist maxim that only dynastic succession can prevent rulers
from being dazzled by their own luster is completely at odds with Constant's
ordinary view. His earlier works bristle with contemptuous remarks about
hereditary government: "the situation of princes is so contrary to nature
that it causes mediocre men to become stupid and distinguished men to
become insane."[25] His later writings and speeches reveal a firm commitment
to abolishing the ascription of power and status according to birth: "Two
great principles have always divided the world: heredity and election. . . .
As a people becomes increasingly enlightened, the principle of election gains
ground."[26] As he wrote in 1818, the destruction of the principle of heredity
had been the truly glorious achievement of the Revolution:

> The immense majority of the nation felt that it had the right to
> achieve any goal or position, but also that it possessed the nec-
> essary skills, so that the fact consecrated the right. Generals
> emerging from counting-houses and libraries, affixed victory to
> their standards. Negotiators, ignorant of the traditions of a su-
> perannuated diplomacy, represented France with dignity. Thus,
> despite sinister predictions and precisely because men did not
> perform exclusively their own professions, all jobs were done
> well.[27]

Far from being intoxicated by their unprepared greatness, the new men thrown up by the Revolution were sober, hard-working, and honorable.

THE MYSTERY RESOLVED

The anomaly of *Conquête et usurpation* can be explained historically. The pamphlet is a creation of scissors and paste, a collage containing chapters and long sections transferred from the manuscripts written between 1800 and 1806. Some of these passages did not travel well. Mechanically excerpted from republican tracts, their original meaning was occluded in the political context of 1813–14.

The *Fragmens* contains an extensive and merciless attack on monarchical government. The crimes of Louis XIV were no less heinous than those of Robespierre. While the English manage to be free under a king, the French will never be able to do so. America, disencumbered of nobility and royalty, provides the aptest model for France to imitate. After castigating Louis XIV, Constant went on to attack Napoleon for having destroyed the foundations of representative government: today "the people counts for nothing in the selection of its deputies."[28] In a subsidiary way, he also mocked Napoleon as a pseudo-king. Napoleon's revival of court ceremonial and noble titles, and later his marriage to Marie-Louise, revealed an Achilles' heel bound to attract the barbs of polemicists. By styling himself "emperor," by displaying laurels and eagles, Napoleon had meant to evoke Roman antiquity and thus dissociate himself from "medieval" monarchs such as Louis XVI.[29] The temptation to reoccupy the Bourbon throne, however, was too great to resist. It was almost inevitable that Napoleon would try to appear as "the new Louis XIV." As a result, "during the last years of Bonaparte, the imperial principles became so close to the principles of the counterrevolution that it became difficult to distinguish them."[30]

In the manuscripts, Constant attributed ill-fated French expansionism to the absence of a popularly elected assembly that might have imposed limits on Napoleon's ambitions.[31] In *Conquête* this republican explanation was suppressed, giving bizarre prominence to what had originally been a minor, offhand suggestion: Napoleon had been forced into performing spectacular military feats to compensate for his shabby pedigree.[32]

Of course, to mock Napoleon as a pseudo-monarch was to attack him on his own ground, to expose the massive confusion and hypocrisy of his crowned revolution. Since the *Fragmens* was a militantly antiroyalist treatise, Constant could argue that new monarchies are even worse than inherited ones without implying that hereditary monarchy was in any way desirable or tolerable.[33]

During the winter of 1813–14, the fate of France was sealed by a group of allied powers. None favored the reestablishment of a republic. Pressed for time and unwilling to sink into virtuous oblivion as an uncompromising republican, Constant excerpted the contrast between Napoleon and "legitimate" kings from his manuscript collection. Since context bestows meaning, this brusque relocation warped Constant's basic position and made it appear, especially in the chapters under discussion, that he had been mysteriously converted to the ideology of the émigrés.

THE AMBIGUITIES OF UNIFORMITY

The thirteenth chapter of *Conquête,* entitled "On Uniformity," also makes a troublingly conservative impression. Indeed, it seems like another sequence of eloquent elaborations on a statement by Burke: "No man was ever attached by a sense of pride, partiality, or real affection, to a description of square measurement." According to this chapter, "all disinterested, noble and pious sentiments are associated with loyalty to local customs." In an attempt to destroy the last outposts of resistance to tyranny, Napoleon and his agents increased the standardization of administrative units begun by the Revolution: "they came close to identifying cities and provinces with numbers, just as they did the legions and the army corps, so much did they fear that a moral idea might be associated with the institutions they were creating."[34]

Here again, the apparent conservatism of Constant's position can be explained historically. An earlier version of "On Uniformity" occurs in the *Principes de politique* of 1806.[35] There, Constant's discussion is straightforwardly republican, owing nothing significant to theorists of the counterrevolution. In 1800 Napoleon had abolished the election of local officials, instituting his network of centrally appointed prefects and subprefects.[36] Constant's original attack on governmental "uniformity" was therefore a defense of "popular elections," local as well as national. While chapter 13 of *Conquête* opens with an ironic dismissal of "the systematic spirit,"[37] its counterpart in the *Principes* offers the following plea for a devolution of political power from Paris down to the communes:

> Suppose there was a nation of a million inhabitants divided among a number of communes. In each commune, each individual would have interests that concerned only himself and that must therefore not be submitted to communal jurisdiction.

There would be other interests that did concern the remaining inhabitants of the commune and these interests would fall within the whole commune's sphere of competence. Each commune, in turn, would have interests that touch only its interior and others that extend to the district. The former would fall under purely communal jurisdiction, the latter under the jurisdiction of the district, and so on in succession up to the general interests common to all the individuals forming the million who compose the people.[38]

This accountantlike passage in infused with the systematic spirit. Constant's constitutionalism, unlike Montesquieu's, was meant to subserve an individualistic and anticorporatist social order. He defended the self-rule of districts and communes, while renouncing hierarchy-sustaining corporate bonds. As mentioned earlier, he defined *corps intermédiares* not as barriers against tyranny, but as "artificial compartments in which men are incarcerated to make them easier to govern."[39]

Stripped of all reference to local self-government, "On Uniformity" obscured Constant's profound commitment to a rationally codified and nationally consistent legal framework. In the *Principes* of 1802–06, he wrote that many "acts of justice," such as "the abolition of slavery," can only be imposed from above by the central government of a large state.[40] He did not believe that France had been "oppressed" by a uniform system of weights and measures, the centralization of the lycées, or the rationalization of the tax code. In 1819, wishing to leave no ambiguity on this question, Constant wrote: "Struck by the advantages for liberty which the diversity of customs produced in England, I once believed that this system could be applied to France. I spoke out against the uniformity which our successive governments had tried to impose upon us for twenty-five years. . . . I now recognize that their desire for uniformity was based on justice and reason."[41] By acknowledging the interdependence of uniformity and justice, Constant confirmed again the debt of liberal theory to the traditions of absolutism.[42] The path to liberal pluralism had been paved by political centralization, that is, by the destruction of medieval pluralism. Pledged to liberal ideas, Constant could not very well repudiate the steps taken toward legal equality by Richelieu and the absolute monarchs of seventeenth-century France.

NAPOLEON AS A REPRESENTATIVE MAN

It is worth clarifying the mystery of *Conquête et usurpation* because of the astonishing subtlety with which Constant analyzed the ambiguities of

Napoleon's regime. The central theme of Bernadotte's campaign for the throne was the utter estrangement of Napoleon from the French nation.[43] Bonaparte's Corsican origins were stressed ad nauseam. Bernadotte undoubtedly hoped that Constant would help spread this message—not the embarassing thesis that "new men" should never be called to positions of power. Indeed, Constant began *Conquête* by reiterating Bernadotte's central theme: as a warrior-king, Napoleon was an anachronism, a throwback out of place in the age of commerce. As he proceeded, however, Constant deviated egregiously from his commission: if Napoleon was an anachronism, he was also a child of his age, a product of public opinion, modern journalism, and the career open to talents.[44] This stunning ambivalence was inadvertently expressed. Political thought was the unintended by-product of political propaganda.

According to Montesquieu, "peace is the natural result of commerce." Kant agreed: "the spirit of commerce cannot coexist with war; and, sooner or later, it takes hold of every people."[45] Constant echoed this liberal thesis in *Conquête:* "We have arrived at the age of commerce, an age which must necessarily replace that of war."[46]

Looking back on the revolutionary age, every heir of the Enlightenment faced the following question: why, if this is a time when commerce replaces war, have the nations of Europe been embroiled in two decades of hideously destructive wars? Earlier, Alexander Hamilton simply denied Montesquieu's original claim.[47] But Constant chose a more varied and indirect approach. At one point, recognizing that historical periods seldom succeed one another as seamless wholes, he attributed the modern revival of the spirit of conquest to cultural lag or a vestigial "bellicose tradition."[48] Echoing the émigrés, he also blamed Napoleon's wars on the personal insecurity of a new man with new power. The theoretical cornerstone of his argument, however, lay elsewhere.

Not war but shattering defeat alienated France from Napoleon. Although polished by civilization, the country had still felt the lure and intoxication of victory. Rather than extinguishing the spirit of conquest, Constant argued, "commerce has [merely] modified the nature of war."[49] The masterstroke of Napoleonic officials was to enlist the calculations of commercial men in the adventures of imperial expansion. Commerce has irreducibly ambivalent effects on political life.[50] From a theoretical standpoint, this is the most remarkable implication of *Conquête et usurpation.* Commerce "cordializes" man, mollifying a passionate urge to inflict pain on one's enemies. But it also encourages civic privatism, a shirking of political responsibilities that, in turn, allows despots such as Napoleon to pursue bloody adventures unopposed.

Constant called commerce "civilized calculation" in order to contrast it with war, which is "savage impulse." He swiftly subverted this antinomy, however, by referring to Napoleon as "calculation personified." Indeed, the Napoleonic wars were especially brutal because they were motivated by modern self-interest rather than by an old-style quest for honor.[51] The discomfiting appropriateness of Napoleon to the commercial age showed that, even if he was something of an anachronism, he was *also* perversely in step with modern times. Breaking ranks with Bernadotte, Constant revealed the complicitous relation between contemporary France and the imperial system.

In a half-hearted attempt to dissociate Napoleon from his country, Constant wrote that the Corsican adventurer was to modern France what a leopard would be to a populous city. A civilized environment is unsuited to a creature "from another climate, another planet, or another species than ours." It bores him, and he yearns for the dangerous jungle. In a modern, urban civilization, the spirit of conquest is a wild and exotic intrusion. Its aberrant presence can perhaps be explained; but ultimately it is "a fragment of a state of things which no longer exists."[52]

This passage seems straightforward enough until we recall that Constant also attributed the instability of French politics to the predominance of Paris, a hypercivilized city where "all ambitions are agitated." A few years earlier he had described the French capital as a place where people believe nothing, not even what they say themselves. It is a city "without memory," where "every action of today is contradicted tomorrow."[53] Driven by ambition into expansionistic wars, unable to respect today the laws he had promulgated yesterday, Napoleon was perfectly at home in this urban jungle.

Napoleon and France were mirror-images of one another. Moreover, Constant did not hold himself aloof from this painful affinity. A few weeks before he began *Conquête et usurpation*, he noted in his daybook that a "mad agitation of ambition" was overtaking him.[54] Similarly, and this is one of the most bizarre twists of the pamphlet, Constant openly assimilated himself to the imperial regime by arraigning Napoleon as a "gambler" who transformed sedulous young men into "gamblers."[55] As is well known, Constant was an inveterate and compulsive gambler.

In point of fact, Napoleon was not an utter anachronism. As heir to the Revolution, he helped to institutionalize civil equality, religious tolerance, and the right to choose one's own profession. He gave France "legal codes more perfect than those of other nations." In the *Mémoires sur les Cent-Jours*, Constant described Napoleon as "a man to whom our age owes, in almost equal proportion, its misfortunes and its progress."[56] Having fashioned *la couronne ouverte aux talents*, he was himself the most visible symbol of a society making the transition from status to contractual rights. By nationalizing education and providing a system of scholarships for the lower-middle classes, he widened popular access to positions of influence and prestige. Finally, he helped to stabilize the revolutionary land settlement and temporarily arrested the civil war, giving royalists and regicides an apprenticeship in coexistence. None of this excused or justified his maniacal annexationism or his acts of political oppression. Constant's awareness of Napoleon's adherence to some of the principles of 1789, however, made it impossible to attack the emperor as nothing but a barbaric anachronism.

At its most formulaic, Constant's historicism rested on the premise that good governments will "obey the time," yielding passively to the manners and morals of contemporary society. *Conquête et usurpation* explodes this coarse providentialism. For good and ill, Napoleon *did* obey his time. The current stage of economic growth offered no political guarantees, only political pitfalls and opportunities. The individualized social world, to which Constant was thoroughly committed, provided rich soil in which a new form of despotism might root and grow. An "atomized" France was unable to depose its despot without the assistance of foreign armies. By focusing attention on the continuity between Napoleon and his age, Constant admitted that a theory of social change cannot assume the theological burden previously unloaded on foundationalist doctrines of the social contract. It may not have been Constant's intention to say anything so labyrinthine and even self-incriminating; but in the course of writing *Conquête et usurpation*, that is what he did.

Constant originally intended to use the "general spirit" of modern France as a critical standard by which to condemn Napoleon's regime. This "general spirit," however, turned out to be highly protean, capable of sustaining either war or peace, freedom or tyranny. Hastily searching for an alternative standard, Constant latched onto the royalist doctrine that inherited power is moderate. But even in *Conquête et usurpation* he used this idea as a foil, not as a flag, as a standard by which to criticize Napoleon, not as a principle for constructing a new regime. Predictably, Constant never reaffirmed the principle of heredity in any work after 1813–15.

THE ANATOMY OF TYRANNY

"There are two kinds of servitude: one that precedes liberty and the other that replaces it."[57] This sharply etched contrast between traditional autocracy and postrevolutionary dictatorship was central to *Conquête et usurpation,* making it an influential work in the history of European liberalism. Unique about despotism after 1789 was its rich display of democratic and egalitarian pretexts: "The usurper who arrives after a revolution made for freedom, or in its name, has many more means for sustaining himself than any other type of despot."[58] Like Robespierre, Napoleon relied upon counterfeit liberty and the mask of consent: "the triumph of tyrannical force is to constrain slaves to proclaim themselves free."[59] Although old regime monarchs committed gruesome atrocities in the name of the common good, they did not simulate public opinion.

Napoleon's intolerance for political opposition was his most blatant betrayal of Enlightenment principles, giving Constant sufficient reason to emphasize the "futile semblance of opposition"[60] voiced in the mock deliberative bodies of the Consulate and Empire:

> Despotism banishes all forms of liberty. Usurpation, to justify the overthrow of what it replaces, needs the *forms* of liberty, but in taking hold of them, it profanes them. The existence of public spirit being dangerous to it, and the appearance of public spirit being necessary, it strikes the people with one hand to stifle genuine opinion and strikes them again with the other to constrain them to simulate a false opinion.[61]

Despots forbid discussion; usurpers stage prescripted rituals, creating a false impression of discussion. Despots send their opponents directly to the gallows; usurpers feel compelled to mount showtrials. Rather than simply violating justice, they parody it. Such travesties of freedom resemble genuine freedom the way electrically induced convulsions in a corpse resemble life.[62] Even the mystifications of anointed kingship look honest when contrasted with the smoke-screen tactics of plebiscitary caesarism.

Hypocrisy and self-deception are more closely related than one might suppose. In the early days of the Consulate, Frenchmen were surrounded by soldiers and informers. Their enthusiastic consent to Napoleon was fortified by threats backed up with force. The typical reaction of intellectuals to this situation was acquiescence in a split between their public avowals and their private disclaimers. They overtly consented to Napoleon while covertly ridiculing him. Although public acquiescence was "a strange sort of artifice of which no one was the dupe,"[63] it was nevertheless inexcusable.

What counts politically is what one says in public. Private ridicule is meaningless. Worse yet, it provides a justification for cravenly obsequious behavior. Furthermore, the split between public assent and private mockery
is highly unstable. When public men repeat something often enough, they
end up believing it. That is only natural: we are such mobile creatures that
we cannot help feeling the sentiments we feign.

Those who submit to Napoleon in public while ridiculing him in
private are indeed the dupes of their own artifice: "Despotism reigns by
silence and leaves a man the right to keep quiet; usurpation condemns him
to speak, and pursues him into the intimate sanctuary of his thought. Forcing
him to lie to his own conscience, it deprives him of the last consolation
which remains to the oppressed."[64] Public hypocrisy spills over into private
confusion and self-deception. Prevaricating to his own conscience, a man
becomes unable to understand the nature either of his own behavior or of
the situation in which he is acting.[65] Regimes which counterfeit public
consent may be harder to depose than old-style despotisms, precisely because
they corrupt the consciences of their victimized citizens.

In his preface to the third edition, Constant wrote that *Conquête et
usurpation* reflected his frustration at living abroad during the Napoleonic
period. The most painful aspect of foreign exile was the futility of trying
to explain to other Europeans that the French were actually being ruled
against their will even though they affirmed Napoleon's sovereignty by
acclamation. Adolphe had spoken bitterly about "le joug que j'avais l'air
de choisir."[66] France, too, appeared to have voluntarily chosen its own
harsh master. So were not the French as guilty as Napoleon himself? How
could they simultaneously adore the emperor and view him as a despot?

Constant tried to analyze the "new" tyranny at a time when a decisive
shift was occurring in the criteria by which tyranny was distinguished from
acceptable forms of rule. In the old *contra tyrannos* literature, tyrants were
identified by certain objective standards. When kings violated certain codified or customary rules—when for example they upset the traditional dis-
tribution of power in society—they were considered tyrants.[67] By the end
of the eighteenth century, the situation had changed. Tyranny began to be
defined "subjectively" as a function of popular consent. The American col-
onists, while cataloguing violations in the traditional manner, considered
the relatively harmless George III a tyrant for a new reason: he was not a
monster; but rule from afar was unacceptable and unaccepted. Tyranny did
not mean misgovernment, but simply government without consent.

This conceptual shift produced a theoretical embarrassment for Constant, and the traces of his bafflement remain visible in *Conquête et usur-*

pation. He wished to make intelligible a new type of tyranny, a kind of tyranny based on the counterfeiting of democratic consent. But the new criterion for identifying tyranny was none other than the lack of democratic consent. Realistic about the difficulties of distinguishing genuine from sham consent, he balked at the magnitude of his problem. Later, confronting a form of oppression that made no pious efforts to insinuate or assert popular support, Constant invoked public opinion against every press and electoral law advocated by the ultras. When facing Napoleon and the Committee of Public Safety, this tack had been less convincing. The strangely Legitimist flavor of *Conquête et usurpation* can partly be explained as Constant's momentarily disoriented reaction to this dilemma: it was implausible to denounce pseudodemocratic dictatorship simply as government without consent.

During the Restoration, Constant saw no advantage to belittling the sort of tyranny that did not hoist a democratic flag. From the ultra point of view, "it is terrible to be imprisoned or perish on the scaffold in the name of popular sovereignty," while "nothing is sweeter than captivity or torture in the name of an absolute king."[68] Faced with such enemies, Constant deliberately neglected his contrast between consolidated despotism and usurpation. He criticized Charles X for his Napoleonic ambitions just as he had once criticized Napoleon for his attempts to imitate Louis XIV. In the *Commentaire,* he wrote quite naturally of "the war mania of princes."[69] Even monarchs who had inherited their power could be moved by the spirit of conquest. Dynastic legitimacy furnished no guarantee of peaceful intentions or acts. Chronically apprehensive about the political misuse of his own theories, Constant now buried the suggestion that hereditary monarchy was a "relatively good" form of tyranny, realizing whose cause this idea might serve.

NINE

Liberalism and the Counter-Enlightenment

On n'a pas le désir inné du jury, de la liberté de la presse, ni de voter l'impôt ou de faire des lois.

Bonald

DURING the last fifteen years of Constant's life, French politics were dominated by antiliberalism. Moving in and out of power, the ultraroyalist party consistently pursued a policy of press censorship, Catholic control of education, electoral fraud, politically orchestrated trials without the benefit of a jury, and indemnification of the émigrés at the expense of middle-class holders of government bonds. Back from a long exile, the ultras were inspired by a sense of mission. Frustrated with the compromises of the Charte and irked by the unprecedented competition for land and office, they refused to come to terms with "this entire generation, not nourished on prejudices, not interested in privileges, and asking only for equality."[1] At war with the new France, they made serious efforts to restore primogeniture and legally to enforce the dogma of the "divine presence."[2] In 1816, with Louis de Bonald taking the lead, they made divorce illegal. Viewing the Revolution as an unmitigated evil,[3] they swore to eradicate its legacy, including religious toleration and equality before the law. No compromise was possible because liberalism meant atheism and terror. Rather than pursuing a conciliatory strategy, for

220

which there were impeccably royalist precedents, the ultras chose to be harshly militant and doctrinaire.

No longer faced with pseudodemocratic dictatorship, Constant reshaped his position through contests with the intransigent Right. His own earlier militancy returned to the fore. Ultra hostility to the constitutional framework made "neutrality" impossible for liberals. Constant boasted of sitting on *le côté gauche* of the Chamber; and he described the liberal cause as that of the nation—of the people as a whole.[4] He openly referred to the ultras as "the counterrevolutionary faction," "the Jacobins of royalty," "this antinational conspiracy," "an inexplicable minority," "the inquisitors of our day," "the apostles of nonconstitutional royalty," and even as "madmen," "ferocious beasts," "men of blood and prey," "seven or eight thousand privileged individuals grown old hating their native land," "the basest canaille who ever frequented antichambers wearing gilded clothes," or simply "our enemies."[5] Their "doctrines" were "war-cries against the Charte."[6] Referring to the royalist Chamber of 1820, he wrote: "All the insolence of provincial nobility, all the ignorance of court nobility, all the fury of counterrevolutionaries, all the greed of titled beggars, as well as the determination to listen to nothing and the inability to understand anything—these are the distinctive traits of our majority."[7] Echoing Sieyès, he stated that "this party does not belong to the nation."[8] History told an unambiguous story:

> During thirty-one years, they have encouraged foreigners to invade our country, placing themselves alongside or rather behind our enemy's rifles. If they have not often fired on France—and we admit that they generally keep their distance from the shooting—they have applauded the fire of the Prussians at Valmy, the Austrians at Jemappes, the Russians at Zurich, the English at Waterloo. They have slandered us in our success and insulted us in defeat. Eight years ago, when our unhappy countrymen armed themselves to defend their humble cottages, these men wrote . . . that the neck of French peasants should be decorated with the Order of Merit for bandits, that is, with the noose. If they require it, I will cite the journal, issue, date, and paragraph. I refrain from doing so now only to see if they have the audacity to deny it.[9]

Constant's daily skirmishes with these extremists, waged on the floor of the Chamber and in the pages of the liberal press, covered a broad range of issues. Beneath the taunts and the polemics we can discern an incisive criticism of the antiliberal tradition.

THE SOCIAL NATURE OF MAN

Arguably, the permanent structure of antiliberal thought was fixed during the Restoration. The premier spokesman of ultraroyalism, Louis de Bonald, advanced an argument of stunning simplicity: liberalism is defective at its foundation. It is founded on a demonstrably erroneous theory of the person, on the myth of the presocial individual. Liberals typically conceive society as a voluntary compact between preexistent persons. They assume that a socially uninfluenced individual can, before learning a language and being socialized into a culture, identify his pregiven needs and negotiate contracts to ensure their satisfaction. As Bonald triumphantly and voluminously explained, this idea is implausible. Social relations are not secondary and optional, but primary and necessary: "society constitutes man." People only come to recognize their needs, indeed they only come to have identifiably human needs, through socialization: "man only exists through society."[10] Because the elemental building-block of liberal theory can bear no weight, the entire edifice of liberal politics must be demolished to be replaced by a system celebrating the priority of society over the individual.

Although it will never cease to be repeated, this antiliberal argument is deeply confused and in fact self-contradictory.[11] More importantly, it is wholly ahistorical and based on an impoverished understanding of the issues at stake. Liberalism was a theory of politics, not a theory of man.[12] Constant's writings provide a guide to self-government, not a guide to life. His principles and his proposals were perfectly compatible with the truism that man is a social animal. He said it explicitly: "man . . . is sociable because sociability is of his essence."[13] Too trite to be an insight, the "social nature of man" has no political consequences whatever.

It was misleading for Bonald and Maistre to denounce liberalism as an "antisocial" doctrine dedicated to the loosening of communal bonds and ultimately to the atomization of society. Constant valued some social attachments above others. He preferred voluntary relations to relations ascribed by birth. The theocrats considered his preference "antisocial" because they identified "society" with a hierarchical system of ascribed relations. Needless to say, a person's relationships within a group of equals voluntarily joined are just as "social" as his relationships within a hierarchial group into which he was involuntarily born.

By confiscating the category "social" and applying it exclusively to caste systems organized around a landed aristocracy and dominated by an all-powerful Church, Bonald and Maistre believed they had clinched their case. Who could prefer the cold and isolated individual to the warmth and richness of these "communal" attachments? Their verbal victory, however, introduced a fatal confusion into the mainstream of antiliberal thought. It has enticed antiliberals ever since into identifying "the social" with "the good," and into asserting that a strengthening of "social bonds" is always and necessarily desirable. Needless to say, this position does not invite rational defense—which may explain why even today antiliberals regularly deride their critics as morally unsound.

The flimsy fiction of the presocial individual does not need to be refuted; but its rhetorical prevalence should be historically explained. Constant was a reformer and activist. His liberalism was a political program. He did not conceive it as an academic doctrine or a "theory" of man. He stressed individual independence and contractual relations, not to describe society realistically, but as part of an effort to dissolve relations of nonvoluntary subjugation and dependence characteristic of the traditional European order. All political programs are "antisocial" in a trivial sense: they suggest that certain institutional arrangements should be replaced by others. Article 5 of the Charte, establishing religious tolerance, was antisocial in this sense.[14] The civil code was similarly antisocial because it affirmed equality before the law—that is, the irrelevance of birthrank to a person's legal status. Legal and fiscal equality represented a break with the past, a dissolving of compulsory membership and inherited ties:

> The great corporations that once imparted a uniform motion to all their members have been replaced by personal activities blazing independent paths. Rather than being subjected to the family, itself based on the state, each individual now lives his own life, taking his freedom into his own hands. Conformism in life, doctrine, and belief is no longer possible. You may lament this if you wish, but resign yourself to it, for it cannot be changed. . . . As for myself, I rejoice in it. . . . The intellectual anarchy which [the ultras] deplore, seems to me an immense gain for human intelligence.[15]

Ascribed solidarities inhibit the spread of Enlightenment. They can also be incompatible with civil peace. Constant hoped, as did other liberals before and after, that individuals might progressively disengage themselves from certain emotionally charged social bonds, especially from feuding clans and fanatically intolerant sects. Other inherited attachments were less dangerous but were nevertheless obstacles to national citizenship and government by discussion. Typically, liberals encouraged individuals to extricate themselves from caste groups in which authority and obedience were ascribed by birth, and from parochial village life. The static and hierarchical "body politic" described by medieval theorists had to be decomposed before it could be rebuilt as a more dynamic and egalitarian political community in which disagreement might serve a creative function. Viewed in context, liberal individualism was not antisocial: reciprocal disengagement was a precondition for mutual involvement. Before becoming members of a nation, people must cease to consider themselves primarily as Capulets or Montagues, Catholics or Protestants, northerners or southerners. They must think of themselves as individuals, as citizens. Individualism unites. In a caste-ridden, sect-torn, and regionally compartmentalized society, atomism fosters nation-building and even democratization.

Meant to undermine the great edifices of prescribed authority and dependence surviving from feudal times, the ideal of the masterless man also registered a new opportunity for every man to express distrust of those in whose power he stood. Bonald ostensibly defended the traditional guild system because it provided its members with a sense of warmth and belonging.[16] Less poetically, Constant depicted the emancipation of the modern individual from traditional associations as freedom from surveillance by government agents:

> The defenders of masterships, wardenships, and apprenticeships are ultimately quite indifferent to the perfection of trades; and the interests of consumers they claim to serve . . . touch them very little. What attracts them about these superannuated institutions is the belief that they provide means of police surveillance over the class of workers, a class that is always feared because it is always more or less miserable.[17]

The collapse of the guild system during the Revolution did not signal the triumph of coldness over warmth, egoism over community.[18] Corporatism was the ideology of the police. Contrariwise, liberal individualism registered something more attractive than an insatiable appetite for profits. It sanctioned resistance to the corporatist organizations used to spy upon and control society. Far from being coarsely egoistic, individualism was a defense of voluntary social cooperation and trust against those noxious purveyors of distrust, the undercover agents of the state.

PERMISSIVENESS AND SOCIAL ORDER

A basic premise of Constant's antiliberal opponents was that freedom corrodes social order. When the duke of Berry was assassinated by a lone fanatic in 1820, the ultras blamed the moderate Decazes ministry for having adopted a recklessly permissive stance toward the liberal opposition.[19] To preempt this sort of attack, Constant asserted that freedom does not disrupt order: it actually helps to maintain peace, stability, and even historical continuity.

A paradoxical principle serves as the *fil conducteur* through Constant's mature writings: in matters of constraint, more is less and less is more: "prohibitive laws" often serve only to produce "disorder."[20] The ultras were wrong to believe that tightening restrictions on freedom would enhance social order. Exactly the opposite was the case: "By useless precautions, one causes and even increases disorder."[21] Constant's central argument in the *Mémoires sur les Cent-Jours* was that royalist intransigence had inadvertently rekindled quiescent Bonapartist sympathies. Revolutions were caused not by the inexorable advance of equality, but by backward-looking groups trying vainly to impede the natural course of reform. Stubborn attachment to moribund privileges intensified pent-up frustrations that were bound to explode. Coercion guaranteed upheaval. Looser constraints, a degree of freedom, flexibility, and openness to reform, were preconditions for social stability and peace.

Between 1814 and 1830, Constant relentlessly employed this same pattern of argument to a wide range of political issues. Any attempt to impose celibacy on the poor would result in general "wantonness." Social order is enhanced by generous concessions to the inherent disorderliness of human nature: "The great social secret is to furnish individuals with the means of satisfying themselves legitimately." Analogously, property will not be made secure by violently repulsing new claimants but only by making ownership legally accessible to all.[22] Criminal behavior is most effectively controlled by a loose and broad, rather than tight and narrow, definition of the legally permissible: "What preserves the majority of men from crime is their feeling of never having overstepped the line of innocence. The more narrowly this line is drawn, the more often men are exposed to surpassing it. However slight the infraction, man has lost his surest safeguard when he has conquered his first scruples."[23] An initial boundary-crossing has an uncontrollable bandwagon effect: "disobedience is contagious."[24]

Constant's liberalism during these years might be described as a philosophy of side-effects. He discriminated carefully between the proclaimed goals and the actual results of legislation. Legislators are responsible not solely for the aims they intend to achieve but also for the effects their laws will predictably bring about. The ideal purpose of a constricted definition of the legal is to encourage law-abiding behavior. But its foreseeable result may be to habituate citizens to violations of the law.

Constant often tailored his speeches and articles to his principal adversaries. The ultras were lovers of repression and admirers of the intimidation power of hangmen. Half-mockingly and half-seriously, he offered them the following paradox. Tolerance is the surest means of preserving order; freedom is the best mechanism for social control.

In his campaign against political censorship, for example, Constant emphasized prudential arguments constructed from the viewpoint of the royalist party. Given your aim—to prevent the disruption of society by incendiary journalism—the optimal strategy is not censorship but freedom of the press. Distinguishing between the intended goal of censorship and its actual consequences, he catalogued the unintended social effects of past restrictions on free speech: "The action of authority on speech has been composed of the following elements: espionage, corruption, informing, calumnies, abuses of confidence, treasons, suspicion between family members, dissension among friends, enmity between those who would otherwise be mutually indifferent, the sale of domestic infidelity, venality, lies, perjury and arbitrary acts."[25] Laws against freedom of speech are not violations of natural rights. They are practical blunders, miscalculations guaranteeing a result contrary to the one intended. They irritate but do not control. Bonald thought that a government tolerating "erroneous" opinions had abdicated its fatherly responsibility.[26] He naively believed that governmental regulation of speech and the press would engender social harmony.[27] Constant countered that in nineteenth-century France personal contrariness could be exasperated but not stilled.

The ultra belief that a government could strengthen its hand by muzzling critics was obviously erroneous: "One believes nothing affirmed by an authority that does not permit anyone to respond to it; one believes everything affirmed against an authority that does not tolerate examination."[28] By exhibiting distrust of the people, the government exacerbates the very problem it is trying to solve. Unavoidably, there will be a return of the repressed. Forbidden fruit appears sweeter: censorship encourages the circulation of clandestine literature and "attaches an excessive importance to forbidden works." In a variation on one of his oldest themes, that in politics appearance *is* reality, Constant added that the censorship of opposition is counterproductive: "in attributing an imaginary influence" to opposition writings, government censorship "greatly increases their real importance." If legislators are responsible not merely for the intended aim but also for the predictable side-effects of their laws, then the following result must be blamed on the proponents of censorship: "When men see entire codes of prohibitive laws and armies of inquisitors, they must assume that attacks repulsed in this manner are truly formidable. When such pains are taken to keep these writings out of our hands, the impression they would produce must be very profound indeed! No doubt they carry with them an irresistible power to convince!"[29] Freedom of the press, rather than being an invitation to insurrection, helps establish a new form of social stability. Far from sedating citizens, censorship heightens social tensions.[30]

According to Maistre, no government can govern if the wisdom of its decisions can be legitimately contested. The ruler is "infallible" not because he is incapable of error, but because he cannot be legally accused of it. When the sovereign decides—and an authoritative decision must always be made—discussion comes to an end.[31] Constant's response to this Hobbesian argument can easily be inferred. In 1822, he observed that English institutions were becoming increasingly fragile and could be overthrown by a revolution at any time. Nevertheless, "the opposition conserves the right to manifest itself in all its force. This still saves [the English], despite their oppressive laws. If opposition went unexpressed, it would produce a terrible explosion; and the government, lamenting its lack of sufficiently repressive means, owes its salvation to the impotence it deplores."[32] Myopic governments view opposition as a nuisance to be circumvented, if not crushed. Impatience with obstacles and intolerance for disagreement are common human instincts, intensified among wielders of power.[33] A revolutionary insight of Enlightenment political thought was that what seems like an embarrassment is actually a safety-valve and a source of strength. Even an ultra who feared freedom would be wise to sponsor a liberalization of the regime.

Constant enlisted other arguments for liberty of the press as well. Censors are fallible and governments may doom themselves to ignorance of brewing crises if unofficial channels of communication are shut down.[34] He also considered "publicity" the only reliable guarantee that legal procedures are being followed by the government, and especially by its subaltern agents. In the forefront of his writings, however, was this claim: the best way to achieve the order and stability for which the Right yearned was to build "give" and freedom into the system. He insisted that constitutions should be "short and negative," and that they should invite future reforms: "For stability itself, the possibility of improvement is preferable to the inflexibility of constitutions."[35] Rigidity is brittle; flexibility is sturdy. That was the essence of Constant's endeavor to subvert the social metaphysics of the French Right.

Relentlessly skeptical, Constant also acknowledged the limits of this style of argumentation. In the *Commentaire*, for example, he recognized that laws prohibiting the slave trade had redoubled the atrocities committed: "the result of the laws obtained and promulgated was to aggravate the fate of the unfortunate race we wished to protect." This inadvertent result was easily explained:

> Since the slave trade was prohibited, the ships engaged in it have been built to make it easier for them to escape pursuit. They lock their captives, whose numbers have increased, in a narrower space. Fearing unforeseen visits, the captains of these boats seal their booty in closed containers where the eyes of police agents cannot discover them. When discovery becomes inevitable, these containers, with victims inside, are heaved into the sea.

Here, too, legal prohibitions encouraged illegality. But against "the merchants who speculate in human blood" Constant called for "a rigorous legislation."[36] When an outrage to humanity was at issue, he did not suggest any conciliatory relaxation of the law. Against the complacency of the ultras,[37] he clearly suggested that slave traders be punished as murderers.

RELIGION, ENLIGHTENMENT, AND TERROR

The word *religion,* so Bonald believed, stemmed from the Latin for "to bind together." Against a policy of toleration he argued quite simply that religious orthodoxy is "the most powerful bond of human societies and the surest guarantee of the obedience owed to the ruling institutions."[38] Religion was the glue that prevented society from falling apart: "the fundamental constitution of all society is religion."[39] The "secret motive" behind the Revolution was the desire to destroy religion.[40] The satanic attempt to undermine the religious basis of society began with Luther. The Enlightenment was a direct product of the Reformation: "It is the same folly, having moved to another age and changed its name."[41] When the theocrats denounced "this system of individuality that began the Revolution,"[42] they were thinking less about commercialism and the loosing of acquisitive drives than about the ability of individuals to read the Bible with their own eyes. Modern society is sick, and the festering disease is individualism. To challenge religious orthodoxy, to make religion into a private experience, is to undermine all social order. Once membership in a church became as voluntary as membership in a club, the path was open to every conceivable personal heresy, and eventually to atheism. The crisis at the end of the eighteenth century was easy to diagnose: "We have just seen society shattered to its foundations because there was too much liberty in Europe and no longer enough religion." The philosophes bore a disproportionate share of the blame: "false doctrines and impious and seditious writings" had been "the true and sole cause of the Revolution and of all the crimes by which it frightened the world."[43] The cure for this modern malady was obviously less freedom of thought and a more rigorous enforcement of religious orthodoxy.

By instinct, claimed the ultras, men are wild beasts, totally unable to control their own passions. To lead a human life, individuals absolutely need the harsh discipline of priestly authority and theological dogma. Religion snaps the will. This, too, explains the conservative claim that "man is by his constitution a religious animal."[44] By unmasking clerical power and ridiculing Catholic doctrine, the philosophes loosed an uncontrollable flood of human passion on the world. They naively believed that "reason" could replace unthinking prejudice as a means for integrating society and repressing destructive emotions. By returning power and wealth to the Church, the ultras sincerely hoped to bolster the dynasty by disciplining unruly passions and tightening social cohesion.

Constant rejected these claims, arguing what may be called the anticlerical case. In the Middle Ages, when men possessed genuine faith, they nevertheless went on rampages. It was historically implausible to associate religious belief with social calm and skepticism with violent upheaval. It was unwise for the ultras to blame political crimes on atheism, "because religion itself could often be accused."[45] In the aftermath of the Reformation, moreover, religious diversity became compatible with social tranquillity, while attempts to impose religious uniformity were indirectly seditious. Peace was to be found in multiplicity.[46] The privatization of religion neutralized potential conflict, removing sectarian disputes from the political agenda and thereby increasing chances for democratic integration and political stability. By contrast, the bigoted re-Christianization campaign pursued by the ultras had a profoundly destabilizing effect, reawakening old suspicions and eventually helping to discredit the Bourbon line. The law of sacrileges "will not achieve its goal," to extirpate heresy, "but it will serve as a pretext for a thousand minor afflictions and a thousand obscure and isolated acts of cruelty."[47] Religious persecution may turn men into hypocrites; but it will not save their souls.[48] The theocratic Right was making a serious miscalculation: "by mixing religion and politics, you will eventually lead the people to religious indifference."[49] Though convinced that religion was humanly important, Constant denied that it was politically relevant. Be this as it may, modern societies cannot be integrated by religious sentiment and dogmatic conformity.[50] Stability can only be achieved by loosening the conditions of social compatibility. Toleration subserves social cohesion and also gives genuine religion itself a chance to flourish.

According to its conservative enemies, the scientific revolution was an expression of overwhelming human arrogance. Modern science, they suggested, can most accurately be understood as a Christian blasphemy, an impious attempt by men to become God. The Enlightenment confidence in human reason led directly to the Terror, to the attempt to remake society according to a geometrical plan.[51] First came Luther, then Voltaire, and finally Robespierre. The brutality of 1793–94 was the logical and necessary result of European impiety, including the Reformation and the scientific revolution. Murderous regimes arise from too much rather than too little Enlightenment. This claim, although paradoxical, is nevertheless false. It is based on a fallacy of the form post hoc, ergo propter hoc. According to Bonald, "there is not one political principle espoused in 1789 from which a rigorous dialectic could not deduce the entire Revolution."[52] Constant demurred. He understood why "the frenzy of 1794 convinced certain weak minds to disavow the enlightenment of 1789."[53] But he thought their reasoning was shallow and confused. Referring to revolutionary extremists, he wrote: "the subsequent ill-conduct of this delirious faction proves nothing against the justice of the original cause for which everyone fought."[54] The Terror did not discredit the Enlightenment. Robespierrism resulted from the cruel oppressiveness of the old regime: "Man becomes furious in chains: his fury endures even after his slavery has ended. This is not the effect of the freedom he has reacquired, but of the chains he has borne too long."[55] The violence of the Revolution convicted traditional France of its unreformed abuses: "the terrible calamities that overwhelmed France before the 9th of Thermidor were a product of oppression. Freedom of the press had nothing to do with it, or rather the absence of this freedom was very much at fault."[56] The "harmony" of the old regime was an ultra myth with no basis in fact: the old regime produced the Revolution.[57] How could the enemies of upheaval look back with nostalgia toward a self-destructive regime?[58]

Against the charge of hybris and self-divinization, Constant responded that the Enlightenment was a "limits of reason" tradition. It had been quite easy to criticize the Jacobins for violating Enlightenment ideals. Robespierre was not a particularly rational man. There was no connection between the scientific mentality and the idea that man can refashion society as a whole according to a rational blueprint. Conversely, there was nothing Promethean about a realistic assessment of the responsibilities that befall individuals. Men cannot decide how to act on the basis of unaided reason. According to Maistre, this means that they must succumb pliantly to authority.[59] Constant rejoined that not even a foot-soldier can act according to the doctrine of passive obedience: "Must a soldier shoot his Captain at the command of an intoxicated Corporal? He has to decide if the Corporal is drunk or not, and he must reflect that the Captain is the Corporal's superior. Intelligence and personal examination are thus required even of the soldier." The ultras were wrong, moreover, to trace the Terror to the spirit of insubordination: "France has not suffered so terribly from its various tyrannies because of a lack of obedience among subordinate officials. On the contrary, in 1793 and after 1793, everyone obeyed and only too dutifully. If a few miserable souls escaped, if some injustices were mitigated, if Robespierre's government was overturned, it was only because sometimes the doctrine of passive obedience was ignored."[60] Disobedience is not the most horrible human vice. Although unquestioning compliance to a murderous authority is a permanent possibility, it cannot be associated with social order.

Slaves can obey their masters; but individual reason cannot yield piously to "tradition," because the legacy of the past is fraught with contradictions and often compels men to make choices without precedent. Consider Burke's own example of the settlement of 1688. The tradition of hereditary kingship clashed with the tradition of English Protestantism. Tradition was set against tradition. Human reason was called upon to adjudicate the conflicting claims and provide a compromise solution. In this case, choice was not an expression of human pride and wilfulness, but a response to the complexity of the past and the novelty of the present. Accepting Bonald's idea that "the human will" is not a stable principle upon which to build political authority and social order, Constant noted that the postrevolutionary situation made traditionalist warnings inappropriate and without practical consequences: "Constitutions are rarely made by the will of men: time makes them. They are introduced gradually and in an imperceptible manner. There are circumstances, however, and the one in which we find ourselves is among them, that make it indispensable to design a constitution."[61] Authority depends upon circumstances beyond human control. Zero-based constitution-making is impossible. Constant accepted these ultra propositions. But he also claimed that postrevolutionary circumstances *demanded* imaginative constitutional design. History provided the basis for

political order and the twenty-five years between 1789 and 1814 could not
be cavalierly ignored. Be humble and pious toward history: make a
constitution!

The theocrats appealed not only to history but also to nature. No one
has an inborn desire for jury trials or freedom of the press. As Aristotle
said, the natural world is organized hierarchically: some elements rule and
others are ruled. This is true in all domains. Measured by nature's standard,
liberal government is an unnatural monstrosity. If the king were dependent
on the consent of his subjects, "the order of beings would be inverted."
History confirms the lessons of nature: "however one tortures our history,
one will always discover that kings have commanded and peoples have
obeyed; and if it had been otherwise, neither kings nor peoples would have
long survived in France or in any other great European state."[62] The universality and moral necessity of hierarchy is one lesson taught by nature.
The insignificance of choice is another. We do not choose our parents or
our native language. We do not choose to be born or to die. Here again,
liberalism swerves from the natural order, suggesting that citizens can
"choose" those who govern the state. The theocratic counterargument here
moves swiftly from Is to Ought, from what is true in nature and society
generally to what ought to be true in political life: "Being necessarily associated with others and necessarily governed, man's will plays no part in
the establishment of government. When peoples have no choice and sovereignty results directly from human nature, sovereigns no longer exist *by
the grace of the people,* sovereignty being no more the result of their will
than society itself."[63] Contracts can only be made within a preexistent social
order in which rules of promise-keeping are legally enforced. This prior
social order cannot, in turn, be the creation of a contract.[64] Authority comes
first, historically and morally. To subject governments to popular approval
is to invert nature and demolish the basis of all social life. Liberalism, with
its emphasis on voluntary contracts and popular consent, leads directly to
the kind of bloody anarchy and civil war that began in 1793.

Constant rejected this argument as well. The ultras gave a totally self-
serving portrait of traditional societies, praising their "organic" structure
while ignoring the unspeakable misery of "the oppressed castes."[65] In general, when antiliberals said "community" they meant "authority." Against
the masterless man, they sided with the master. Individuals should not
consult their own feeble reason but should rely on tradition: that is, they
should act as their betters direct. Antiliberalism was a "servile doctrine"
that "tends to assimilate France to Egypt divided into castes."[66] Against the
ultra drive to reestablish religiously sanctioned authority, Constant argued:

> We have demonstrated that classes are utterly foreign to the Charte. Fixed classes no longer exist. Society has been equalized by the progress of education, the development of industry, and the Charte. Anyone seeking to restore classes . . . is an enemy of the Charte. . . . If "hierarchy" refers to the chain of offices running from the mayor to the subprefect, from the subprefect to the prefect and so on, no one disputes it. But if this is a moral hierarchy to be imposed upon us by I know not what violent means, I reject it with all my force.[67]

Despite flirtations with "aristocratic liberalism" in 1814–15, Constant's attitude toward the nobility was uniformly hostile. It was, as I have said, almost indistinguishable from that of Sieyès.[68]

Constant seems to have had greater sympathy for another theme of counterrevolutionary thought, for what we can call *the atomism-despotism thesis*. As traditional social bonds are loosened and dissolved, individuals become more isolated from one another and the chances for tyranny increase. Napoleon did not exactly pursue a divide-and-conquer strategy. But France had been "atomized" by the Revolution, and individualism eased the tyrant's accession to supreme power.[69] Constant's position, however, always remained sharply distinct from that of his ultra opponents. Against the atomism-despotism pattern, he did not propose a reestablishment of intermediary bodies based on birth-ascribed membership. Instead, he advocated an individualistic cure for an individualistic disease: absolute freedom of the press would keep open lines of communication and collaboration among citizens, helping to prevent despotic government. Without a free press "a nation is but an aggregation of slaves."[70] With a free press, a society bereft of closed clans, sects, guilds, and caste groups can nevertheless avoid tyranny and perhaps even govern itself.

Antiliberals typically argue that voluntary relations are manipulative, materialistic, and egoistic. By assimilating all freely chosen social bonds (whether political, religious, intellectual, or amorous) to contractual bargains struck in the marketplace, they hope to stigmatize voluntariness and win spurious prestige for birth-ascribed relations. Unimpressed by this verbalistic maneuver, Constant saw the political cure for the dissolution of ascribed relations as residing in the freedom to establish voluntary relations, including freedom of assembly[71] as well as freedom of the press.

THE CONCEPT OF LEGITIMACY

There were no Legitimists before the Revolution. Under the old regime, hereditary succession had been a custom; by the time of the Restoration, it had become an ideology.[72] Only after Legitimacy ceased to be taken for granted could it be placarded on walls as a party slogan. Only when dynastic continuity had been broken could fealty be transformed into Bourbonism. The theoretical justification of hereditary entitlement to the throne was fundamentally restructured to suit the purposes of counterrevolutionary thought and propaganda. Insensibly and perhaps inevitably, the concept of Legitimacy assumed the uncompromising stridency and world-rescuing pretensions of that to which it was opposed.

Before the Revolution, there were two commonsensical arguments for regulating accession to the throne according to a strict law of male primogeniture: (1) an unambiguous rule for succession permitted a peaceful transferral of authority and decreased the likelihood of interregna marked by bloody contests for supreme power; and (2) by careful upbringing, an heir apparent could be inwardly prepared for the responsibilities of rule in a way impossible for neophytes raised from obscurity. Bonald and Maistre did not reject these arguments; but they slighted and snubbed them, distrusting the secular mentality they represented. According to Maistre, *le droit de naissance* had a religiously consecrated self-evidence that buoyed it above the grubby world of justification by appeal to consequences. Bonald appealed directly to human nature: "Monarchy considers man in society, the member of society, or social man; a republic considers man independently of his relation to society or natural man."[73] Legitimacy was a moral imperative, not merely a practical arrangement. In truth, it was a hand-me-down vessel into which was poured twenty-five years of pent-up émigré frustration.

As a weapon in the counterrevolutionary arsenal, the principle of Legitimacy was conceived as an anticontract, as an attack on agreement-making individualism and the hybris of constitution mongers. A careful reader of the *Contrat social,* Bonald made a choice diametrically opposed to Constant's. He accepted the organicist side of Rousseau's thought about membership while spurning the voluntary half of the formula. The "general will," he argued, is synonymous with "the will of God" and symbolizes the nullity of all claims to creativity or authority put forward by individual human wills.[74] Because human volition is sterile, authority cannot rise from contracts among individuals, but must descend directly from God.

The theocratic assault on the myth of the socially uninfluenced individual has been frequently but misleadingly associated with sociological realism.[75] In fact, theocracy is incompatible with a secular outlook; it is incomprehensible without reference to Original Sin and Divine Providence. The ultras did not justify dynastic succession in a notably logical or scientific manner. They described the sanctity of Legitimate monarchy, quite confusedly, as a denial of the very possibility of human planning and choice, an assertion that the plans and choices of the revolutionaries were sinful and could have been otherwise, and as evidence that the Revolution had been ordained by Providence as a means for punishing eighteenth-century France for its atheistic degeneracy.

According to Maistre: "the origin of sovereignty must always present itself as outside the sphere of human power."[76] In the preamble to the Charte, Louis XVIII had denied that he had been freely called to the throne by the French people. His Legitimacy was an expression of God's inexorable will, that is to say, of man's passivity—a passivity which was simultaneously inescapable *and* desirable. Legitimacy was not only a sacred truth but also an efficient device in a reflection-stifling propaganda campaign. It not only registered but also justified and promoted the total absence of discussion and comparison of alternatives, voluntary agreement, and choice. Like language itself,[77] the Legitimacy of a royal line cannot be invented by the puny will of human beings. The very thought of dynastic filiation should be enough to make men feel contrite. Inherited titles should teach subjects the nonresistance proper to man. Legitimacy was a powerful symbol of human passivity as well as of the impropriety of the category "free consent" for an understanding of human life. It was *also* an aggressive (i.e., nonpassive) public denial that real alternatives exist; just as it was a vigorous attack on the awful choices made by Frenchmen from 1789 onward. The aggressiveness of both the denial and the attack was heightened by an unpleasant awareness that these "unreal" alternatives were in fact readily accessible. It was also aggravated by a recognition that Legitimism, rehabilitated as a counterideology, had transformed its adherents into chevaliers of the faith, into mirror-images of militant revolutionary agitators. The Legitimists even shouted their own version of "crush the infamous thing."

Consider a frequently cited passage in which Maistre contrasts a properly devout veneration for Legitimacy with the Enlightenment conceit that society can be rationally constructed according to a blueprint:

> Unable to produce an insect or a blade of grass, man considers himself the immediate author of sovereignty, of the most important, sacred, and fundamental thing in the political and moral world. For example, he believes that a certain family reigns because a certain people has willed it; while he is surrounded by incontestable proofs that every sovereign family reigns because it is chosen by a superior power.[78]

This passage was published in 1814, a few months after the sovereign

Bourbon family had indeed been chosen by a superior power to reign in France. That superior power was Alexander I. Louis XVIII reigned not by the grace of God but by the grace of the Allies. The anti-Legitimist barb that the Bourbons "returned in the baggage trains of the invading armies" damaged the Legitimist cause less by recalling national dishonor than by stressing the ad hoc nature of the reinstauration. The ultraroyalist conception of Legitimacy was so doctrinaire because it represented a denial of the obvious. It was a hopeless attempt to suppress public awareness that in 1814 the reenthronement of the Bourbons had been a human choice, and (more generally) that "prescription" was now only one principle among many for justifying political authority. "Consent" and "glory" were rival principles, and widely accepted ones at that. At this time, the most striking emblems of the precariousness of Bourbon Legitimacy were probably the wall-hangings in the Tuileries, where everyone could see that the lilies had been hastily stitched *on top of* Napoleon's bees.

Recognizing the problem, Maistre claimed to detest writing books, even books of Legitimist propaganda. It made him feel disconcertingly like a fallen man, a constitution-maker or a philosophe. The need to write in defense of Legitimacy was a sure sign that Legitimacy was hopeless, its self-evidence irrecoverably eroded: "Every false institution writes a great deal, as it is sensible of its weakness and seeks to buttress itself."[79] The ultra-royalists responded in two complementary ways to the realization that Legitimacy had become a rickety basis for political authority. They were simultaneously militant and escapist. Both qualities were amply represented in 1825 at the coronation of Charles X, a ceremonial acting-out of the ultraroyalist conception of Legitimacy.[80] Taking our clue from Maistre, we can view the *sacre* as testimony that the ultras were half-aware of the moribund condition of Bourbon Legitimacy. According to Gellner, "legitimacy is sovereignty recollected in tranquillity."[81] In Restoration France, just the opposite was the case. Legitimacy was sovereignty hallucinated in anxiety.[82] Or better: the ultras responded to the awareness that their cause was lost by dreaming of a return to *le bon vieux temps* while deliberately insulting secular and liberal France.

THE SECULARIZATION OF LEGITIMACY

The *Fragmens* of 1800–03 is a distinctly antimonarchical work: it states that those who prefer monarchies to republics can only be victims of an optical illusion. Monarchies oppress quietly and torture in secret, while republics oppress publicly, theatrically, and by tempestuous uprisings. When a king is overthrown by revolution, monarchy itself is judged much more favorably than it deserves, both because present troubles make people forget past oppressions and because revolutions almost never occur except when a government is very weak. In retrospect, this weakness, which caused the regime's destruction, is seen as an inherent advantage of monarchy. Moreover, the defects of republican governments are much better publicized than the defects of monarchy, because each new set of republican officials has a vested interest in making its predecessors look incompetent.[83] Constant made an especially strong plea against any form of restoration: "To reestablish a fallen monarchy . . . is not to give a nation a calm and affable king but to deliver it . . . to all the vengeance of an authority irritated by its ancient defeat."[84] In 1814–15, adapting to the accomplished fact of the reenthroned Bourbons, he hoped to minimize the king's authority by promoting him into a "pouvoir neutre." Militancy, however, breeds militancy: after 1817, Constant became increasingly caustic in his attacks on the ultras and their ideology, ultimately dismissing Legitimacy as "the superannuated axiom of divine right."[85]

He openly discussed a change of dynasty and referred often to the English Revolution of 1688. He showed that the theocrats' fear of social "atomization" was a pretext concealing and justifying a nostalgic longing for the power, wealth, and prestige enjoyed by aristocrats under the old regime. His most convincing argument against those who hoped to found the current French government upon the traditions of the past was that "the Revolution has destroyed everything that existed and left nothing in its place."[86] Men can only build upon those aspects of the past which survive into the present. As the ultras themselves lamented, the French past had been violently swept away and, quite obviously, "the wailing of night birds cannot restore castles in ruins." Royalists refuted themselves as they tried to reanimate an ancient constitution: "this pretended constitution of France which everyone cites but no one knows [is] so thoroughly forgotten that its defenders themselves do not agree about its basic principles and fundamental maxims."[87] They were living an illusion: "[The ultras] counsel us to reside in ruins inhabited by phantoms, after an upheaval that has opposed many interests to each other, put all ideas in fermentation, and that for twenty-five years has prevented an entire generation from contracting any habits."[88] The principal advantage deriving from hereditary monarchy depends upon its being uninterrupted: "A revolution that separates an ancient dynasty from a people and that creates new interests among this people surrounds this dynasty with all the defects of novelty."[89] The Bourbon pedigree was of little value after twenty-five years of murderous war and domestic upheaval.

Accepting the value of continuity, Constant still denied that present-day France offered any possibility of continuity, dynastic or otherwise. The counterrevolution was just another form of revolution. Heredity was "an abstraction" which only a fanatical party, out of touch with history, would try to reimpose. In 1797, turning the conservative belief in tradition against the traditionalist cause, Constant had predicted that equality would soon become the prevailing custom in France.[90] By 1814, France had a new tradition embodied in the civil code.

Constant developed his basic attitude toward "the dogma of Legitimacy"[91] in this year, immediately after the first Bourbon restoration. Along with Talleyrand, Chateaubriand, and others,[92] he justified the re-enthronement in a wholly secular manner. In this particular situation, the return of Louis XVIII might help secure peace, foreign and domestic.[93] Similarly, "the constitutionalists . . . preferred Louis XVIII to Bonaparte because they believed they could see more chances for liberty under Louis XVIII."[94] Bonald thought that this was the culmination of revolutionary shrewdness: to have saved the Revolution by concealing it behind the cloak of Legitimacy.[95]

Constant admitted, along with Maistre, that "there are advantages which can develop only if an institution endures a long time." Nevertheless, the value of any such institution is contingent: it depends upon the realization of these advantages. The Bourbons were not *entitled* to rule. If they could have made peace with Europe and reconciled the émigrés to the gains of the Revolution, they would have deserved to keep the throne. Louis XVIII was a farmer holding a long-term lease on a piece of national property: knowing that he and his children would be staying on the farm for a long time, he might have been willing to refurbish the premises. A short-term leaser would probably have had less incentive to bother with upkeep or improvement. This was Constant's conditional and antitheocratic justification of Bourbon rule—his secularization of Legitimacy. The dynasty's long-term lease might encourage a commitment to maintenance and reform.

But such a justification had its limits: "No property-owner would tolerate a farmer who burned down the farm, and there are conditions so onerous that they would justify a rescinding of the lease. Similarly, a nation could not be forced to tolerate a constitution so vicious that it would be worse than the shock of change." In the modern age, it was ludicrous to defend authority by making obedience into "a sort of mystical duty." Such superstitions are out of step with history and will remain without effect. A meaningful defense of the Bourbon monarchy must accommodate itself to the "age of conventional laws," when citizens openly recognize that their form of government is man-made and changeable. The principle of descent, which removed important political decisions from human hands, was appropriate to earlier and more fragile societies unable to survive contestation. France had reached a stage of civilization in which disagreement was not only compatible with social order but might even become a creative force. A majority of Frenchmen could still support the restored dynasty, but only if attempts to suppress public awareness of political contingency were abandoned: "The axiom of the English barons, 'we do not want to change the laws of England,' is much more reasonable than if they had said: 'we cannot change them.' The refusal to change the laws because one does not wish to change them can be explained either by the intrinsic goodness of the laws or by the inconvenience of an immediate change. But such a refusal becomes unintelligible if it is justified by some mysterious impossibility.[96] Only by admitting that there are alternatives to Bourbon rule, and thus that its Legitimacy depends upon the securing of secular advantages, would it be possible to defend the dynasty to a public created by the Revolution. If "Legitimacy" refused to adapt itself to the expectations of the new generation it could not retain the loyalty of the country. That was Constant's persistent message to the Bourbons from 1814 until the dynasty collapsed in 1830.

The ultras, of course, did not adapt themselves.[97] Charles X considered himself a Legitimate monarch. That is why, in 1829, he felt free to insult the Chamber by appointing Polignac (who had originally refused to swear allegiance to the Charte) to head the ministry. Confident of the king's support, Polignac went on to exhibit "a tenacity that smacked of madness."[98] The blind arrogance of dynastic title also explains why, after promulgating the July Ordinances, Charles X just had to go hunting in the countryside. His conception of Legitimacy distracted him, beclouded his vision, and kept him consistently out of touch with reality. Legitimacy in practice spelled self-delusion. It encouraged Charles X to attempt an extraconstitutional suppression of the liberal opposition; and it made him neglect to tell the Paris police that trouble might be expected.

Napoleon acted in an irrationally self-destructive manner because he perceived himself as an illegitimate king. The insecurity accompanying his sense of illegitimacy caused Napoleon to refuse the peace overtures of the Allies in 1813. The historical irony of this émigré diagnosis is that, in inverted form, it can easily be applied to the reinstalled Bourbons: Charles X was so inflexible, his policies were so extreme and uncompromising, because he "knew" he was a Legitimate king. His stubborn fidelity to the royal prerogative prevented him from adapting himself to a parliamentary regime. The ultraroyalist concept of Legitimacy thus symbolized the inability of Charles and his courtiers to understand the perceptions and commitments of Frenchmen who had grown up after the Revolution. This was the most important meaning of the concept of Legitimacy during the Restoration. As a symbol of sectarian intransigence and self-delusion, it provided a doctrinal monument to ultra obtuseness and an ideological framework for dynastic suicide.[99]

After the July Revolution, Constant cast aside all practical inhibitions and freely denounced "a dynasty that for fifteen years has thought solely of counterrevolution." He had no use at all for "this doctrine of Legitimacy in whose name Paris streets were drenched in blood." There is no legitimate authority without the consent of the governed, and that consent cannot be merely habitual acquiescence but must be conscious acceptance arrived at through free public debate. Divine right has no prerogatives in the face of deputies elected by the French nation: "the doctrine of Legitimacy can no longer be tolerated. In the present circumstances, the will of a people, expressed through its representatives, must decide who occupies the throne." By identifying himself with "the reaction," Charles X had lost all chance to remain in power. Hoping to exclude new social forces from the political process, the ultras succeeded only in isolating themselves: "the submission of a people to a family who treats it according to its own good pleasure, the absolute power to enchain citizens, to violate what they hold dear and sacred, the power to shoot down those who try to resist—if this is Legitimacy, I detest it, and I reject it."[100] As Legitimacy refused to be secularized, it could only be deposed. The ultras had failed to grasp the fact that, in political life, more is less. Doctrinaire idealists defeat themselves.

The Public and the Private

THE importance of Benjamin Constant lies in the trenchancy and unexpectedness of his political ideas. His writings mock and disrupt conventional understandings of liberal thought. They convey a renewed sense of what liberalism was and a fresh perspective on what can be learned from it today. Constant stressed the interdependence of ancient and modern liberty and examined the potentials, preconditions, and inherent limits of republican politics in modern society. Restricted government serves the cause of self-government. That was the guiding premise of his theory. He drew an analytical distinction between active citizenship and personal independence; but he linked them politically. Public and private realms are not hostile alternatives. They mutually stimulate, disencumber, and strengthen one another.

According to its critics, liberalism assigns primacy to the private over the public, subordinating collective concern for social goods to an uncoordinated and decentralized pursuit of individual aims.[1] Liberal freedom is said to be nothing more than the protection of individuals from the misuse of political power. To shelter private rights, moreover, civic participation must be curtailed. The problem of freedom (in this view of liberalism) is solely to limit power, never to channel power toward the realization of common aims. Sovereign power cannot be a vehicle for freedom, only an obstruction to freedom.

Although erroneous, this conventional criticism of liberal thought contains a distorted echo of the truth. The public/private boundary played a pivotal role in Constant's thinking about legitimate authority and civic

241

freedom. He often expressed distrust of public life and sympathy for the private. Neither his affection for individual eccentricity nor his reticence about the so-called common good, however, registered ignoble materialism or a renunciation of social benevolence. Where, between 1789 and 1830, could anyone have found an ethos of social benevolence to repudiate? As a harsh critic of "enlightened self-interest," could Constant have defended the public/private boundary for egoistic or materialistic motives? Could his liberalism have been merely an ideology useful to the business class as it trampled down workers and wrested political power from the aristocracy? Was it his principal hope that merchants might "sleep comfortably" in their beds?[2] The answer is that *many different motives,* not merely a desire to accumulate wealth and elude confiscatory taxation, stimulated Constant's desire to constitutionalize the political realm.[3] He had many noneconomic reasons for distrusting "the public" and for sympathizing with "the private." Indeed, his attitude was even more complex than this might suggest. While suspicious of the public and cordial toward the private, he was also firmly committed to "publicity" and openly antagonistic toward important dimensions of privacy and individual interest.

"Public" and "private," be it noted, are omnibus terms covering a wide gamut of social and antisocial actions. Constant naturally had an ambivalent attitude toward *the public* and *the private* since these concepts designate many different aspects of human behavior, some creative, others destructive. As he conceived it, the public/private distinction had subtle affiliations with similar dichotomies, such as impersonal/personal, state/society, and exposed/hidden. But he never conceived the contrast according to a nostalgic and morally charged Gemeinschaft/Gesellschaft scheme. "The private" cannot be convincingly reduced to a domain of commercial deals, thereby exiling personal intimacy or religious inwardness beyond its borders. Similarly, within "the public" the authority of officials must be distinguished carefully from the participation of citizens. Beyond these political dimensions of the public, Constant was intensely concerned with the everyday, extrapolitical visibility of one's neighbors. To shelter one dimension of "the private" or limit one aspect of "the public" was not necessarily to shelter or limit the others.

THE IMPORTANCE OF PUBLICITY

A wide range of noneconomic motives inspired Constant's mistrust of the public and sympathy for the private. Nevertheless, he did not sacrifice ancient liberty on the altar of its modern counterpart. He did not assign primacy to the private over the public. Such descriptions distort elemental features of his position. No one who accepts such a perspective can explain his active celebration, throughout the Restoration, of "popular institutions," "national government," "national opinion," and "the rebirth of public spirit."[4] Ancient liberty must not be totally eclipsed by modern liberty. Instead, personal independence and political citizenship, although conceptually distinct, are in practice inseparable.

Central to Constant's liberalism was the idea of *publicity*. While distrusting publicity in some contexts, he revered it in others. Under Napoleon, his principal complaint was that "there is no public." This was deplorable since "publicity is a sacred right" or "the right of all Frenchmen." Under a liberal constitution, in fact, "publicity" is "the soul of government." To his fellow deputies, he could say: "the renunciation of publicity is the abdication of our powers."[5] In the first place, publicity was the most effective guarantee against arbitrary government: "The coercive force needed to constrain a government to obey the laws is located in the constitution, in the penalties it pronounces against treacherous wielders of authority, in the rights it assures citizens, and *above all* in the publicity it consecrates."[6] As a consequence, publicity must be given the highest priority in the constitutional order: "Power, even when full of good intentions, is always predisposed to suppress publicity; and this is always against its own best interests. Publicity alone permits authority to know what is true. The reports of its agents often contain nothing but what serves or flatters it."[7] Publicity, in the positive sense, only became important during the seventeenth and eighteenth centuries with the spread of literacy, the growth of a reading public, and the diffusion of a popular press. In 1796, Jacques Necker wrote about the profound transformations that had occurred in France over the past two hundred years. Manners and morals had changed, fear of the king had diminished, knowledge had expanded and so had wealth, "and above all an authority has arisen that did not exist two hundred years ago, and which must necessarily be taken into account, the authority of public opinion."[8] According to Constant, by the second half of the eighteenth century, public opinion had become "a mysterious force" which drew "what might be called a magic circle" around authority, giving private citizens a new ability to influence their governors' decisions. This influence was enshrined in representative government: "the Chambers . . . are responsible before public opinion, which is their judge."[9]

For eighteenth-century philosophes, publicity had been opposed to obscurity—the obscurantism of Catholic priests as well as the covert machinations of the court: "public opinion can curb only the abuses that come to its attention, and the great art of monarchy is to cloak most of its oppressive acts in thick shadows."[10] In this spirit, Montesquieu attacked secret accusations, which he described as a fatal poison in the body politic. Constant stressed the same principle: if denunciations are to be made, they must be made publicly.[11] His campaign on behalf of Wilfrid Regnault, reminiscent of Voltaire's defense of Calas, illustrates a similar commitment to publicity.

Constant was always concerned that publicity might protect famous individuals while leaving unknown citizens to the mercy of local agents.[12] In March 1817, Regnault, a *petit épicier* in Normandy, was charged with having brutally murdered the female servant of a man in his debt.[13] The evidence was flimsy and circumstantial, while the political motivations behind the indictment were obvious. An ultra named Blosseville maliciously biased the jury by spreading a rumor that Regnault had been involved in the prison massacres of September 1792. Various aspects of Regnault's "disreputable" past were surreptitiously introduced into court by the public prosecutor, while the defense attorney was never allowed to challenge this pseudoevidence on the grounds that it was "irrelevant" to the accusation. Finally, the main witness for the prosecutor contradicted himself wildly. Despite all this, Regnault was convicted and sentenced to death. Constant took up his case—successfully as it turned out. His tool was nothing other than publicity: *l'examen public* of the judicial farce leading to Regnault's conviction.

Only total publicity of charges, records, and court procedures will give a defendant the chance to correct gross errors of fact and interpretation. Constant repeatedly stressed that "publicity" is "the sole guarantee of judicial procedures." Even when resorting to the rhetorical fiction of the "presocial individual," he did so in order to affirm the primacy of publicity: "A man . . . has rights independent of all association. The most sacred of these rights is never to be brought to trial except according to procedures which are set beforehand and conducted slowly and in public."[14] The opportunity to answer accusations publicly is the essence of judicial rationality. Although still a deputy, Constant himself was arraigned at the court of assizes for moral complicity in an abortive revolutionary plot. The charges were ludicrous and politically motivated. But he was not allowed to answer them effectively through ordinary legal channels. "What recourse remained to me? Publicity. I had to use publicity and I did."[15] Besides imposing publicity on all three branches of government, Constant aimed at outlawing torture in the colonies, abolishing the slave trade, and improving prison conditions. He conceived public opinion as a civilizing force. His consistent tactic was to expose the cruelty and imbecility of officials to the light of day. This common strategy of liberal reformism makes it difficult to argue that liberals considered the private the sphere of freedom and the public the sphere of coercion.[16]

The idea of "publicity" as an arena for give and take, for controversy, debate, and the exchange of ideas, was also crucial for Constant. When ideas are tested in public, truth has a chance to prevail over error.[17] The public will always buy certain products not for their intrinsic worth but simply because other people are buying them. Analogously, a free market of ideas will not guarantee the rationality of political decisions. Nevertheless, publicity is the most effective method yet discovered for preventing errors from becoming permanently ensconced. Constant, in any case, did not believe that public opinion was merely a barrier against authority. *La discussion publique* was much more creative than this. It was a stimulant as well as a depressant. Publicity not only discouraged misgovernment; it offered a new system for making laws and setting national priorities. And publicity meant that citizens could participate in a common venture, securely, argumentatively, cooperatively, and without conformity.

Publicity is a vehicle for freedom. This simple insight undermines the conventional interpretation of liberal thought. The public was not reduced to a tool at the disposal of the private. Instead, the private was conceived as a resource in the service of the public. For example, rational discussion was thought possible only if certain issues were privatized and freed from social regulation. The "limits of reason" tradition, a by-product of religious civil war, was given renewed life by the ideological sectarianism of revolutionary France. For reason to function effectively, its horizons had to be constricted, its focus narrowed. Certain emotionally charged themes were decreed "private"—that is, beyond the jurisdiction of the community as a whole. The limits of politics reflected the limits of rational discussion.

The immediate goal of tolerance is peace. By means of mutual indifference, individuals with conflicting attachments and ideals can live peaceably side by side. "Coexistence through mutual indifference" summarizes the *politique* contribution to liberal thought.[18] The democratic movement gave Constant's liberalism another dimension. Tolerance not only allowed rival groups to coexist. It encouraged mutual learning as well as instrumental exchange. By drawing boundaries round the political realm, liberals hoped to transform sects into parties, making politics into a sphere where diverse groups might meet and hammer out common aims. If I am permitted to involve myself actively with your eternal salvation (if I consider killing you for adhering to an unorthodox religion), there will be little chance for any kind of rational discussion. The national purpose is not eroded—indeed it is reinforced—by restrictions on the discretionary power of local police. Referring to rules protecting private rights, Constant wrote: "all the branches of government, even if in perfect concert, should not be allowed to override these principles. When they are in agreement, however, these powers should be authorized to pronounce on everything that does not conflict with such principles."[19] Democratic liberals went beyond the *politiques* by assuming that the contribution of sovereignty to liberty could be constitutive and not merely instrumental. Constant understood government by discussion as intrinsic to freedom, not as merely conducive to freedom. He affirmed the sovereign power of public debate. As a result, Oakeshott, de Jouvenel, and others are quite mistaken when they portray him as an unyielding enemy of all forms of sovereign power.

An insipid community romanticism underlies much contemporary antiliberalism. Already in the nineteenth century, romantics looked with distaste on boundaries, disengagements, and moral disputes. Separations were considered antisocial and humanly alienating; divisions were thought hateful. Constant's liberalism is also important because it explodes this myth. Divisions can be creative. What initially appears to be antisocial may be a condition for new forms of social cooperation and mutual learning. Constant conceived the public/private boundary in this light.

THE LIMITS OF PRIVATE INTEREST

"Publicity" was an emphatically positive category for Constant. Similarly, he eyed "the private" with much less sympathy than is conveyed by standard readings of his thought. His polemic against "enlightened self-interest" makes this clear. His outrage at secret accusations is another case in point.[20] Basic to the establishment of the liberal state, moreover, was the abolition of private armies, such as the royalist murder gangs in the south.[21] If the government adopts a strictly hands-off policy, the strong will coerce and bully the weak. The state's monopoly on the legitimate use of force—the banning of dueling and so forth—was originally justified by the legal principle that no man should be judge in his own case. This rule, echoed in the disqualification of ex parte testimony, registers the depths of liberal antiindividualism. In fact, liberalism was a philosophy of self-renunciation. It asked individuals to give up their profoundest passion: the desire to inflict physical pain on people they hate. Constant chose to treat the individual as the primary unit of social analysis; but he did not uncritically affirm all private interests any more than he believed in the ludicrous fiction of the presocial individual. He merely wished to prevent shrewd rhetoricians from concealing personal responsibility behind a nebulous and uncriticizable "collective will."

A periodic refugee from Mme. de Staël, Constant was highly sympathetic to cabin fever: the urge to seek asylum *from* the private. His discomfort with privacy, however, also had a more explicitly political dimension. If most citizens were exclusively engaged in nonpolitical pursuits, the government might be seized by a despotic few. A privatized society is ripe for tyranny: "The art of oppressive government is to keep all its citizens separated from one another and to render communications difficult and meetings dangerous."[22] Tyranny is an inherent and ever-present danger in the age of egoism. Under Napoleon "a great calamity" had "dispersed" men of liberal views. An autocratic government will thrive on this breakdown of social communication: "these individuals live alone, ignorant of each other and in a painful sleep, interrupted by noises to which they contribute nothing. What results is a momentary annihilation of all opinion, all public suffrage."[23] The capacity of citizens to mobilize and organize resistance is the ultimate guarantee that officials will not violate the public trust. Constant insisted that community-building through politics must be voluntary and not obligatory. Negative freedom must remain an available option. If civic privatism is carried too far, however, it can undermine the very basis of private rights.

DISTRUST OF THE PUBLIC

Constant's skepticism about the public good was motivated principally by *political misuses* of the idea of the public good. During the Revolution, a handful of individuals had justified juridical murder by invoking the name of the people. Apparently devoted to freedom and virtue, the Terrorists delivered men they personally resented or feared to the guillotine.[24] Communitarian rhetoric, what Locke would have called the "specious show of deceitful words,"[25] concealed the real motives involved: paranoia, spite, whim, and ambition. Thus, Constant's distrust of the public good did not derive from an antecedent commitment to the sovereignty of the private individual or his personal advantage. Quite the contrary. Talk of the public good stimulated his distrust because he believed that individuals might be malicious or deranged. He was aware that men will don any disguise, assume any mask, to promote their own point of view. No tool is more effective for promoting private aims than the mask of disinterestedness.

Constant followed numerous liberal precedents when he stressed the nonorganic quality of social bonds: "peoples are nothing but aggregations of individuals." Society is "an abstract and fictive being" and the interest of the collectivity "is nothing but the interest of all considered together." Remnants of the political struggle to overcome feudalism, such statements are best read as polemics, not descriptions. They proved equally useful in the struggle against Jacobin demands for patriotic self-immolation. When traditional corporations are dissolved, "everything is individualized." Constant acknowledged the change; but he did not uncritically endorse the "age of egoism." Unlike the ultras, he was not aggrieved that individuals had been dislodged from the compartments in which they had been locked for centuries to ensure their subservience to a privileged elite. But his principal concern was prospective reform, not retrospective approval: "It is in vain that one deplores the misfortune of a country in which only individuals exist."[26] Worries about atomization, legitimate to some extent, should not encourage a revival of the hierarchical institutions and exclusive privileges regretted by the ultras. Earlier in his career, Constant urged antiorganicism against the Jacobins, especially against their fraudulent invocations of the common good. His point was not that the whole is equivalent to the sum of its parts. He wished only to alert Frenchmen to the dangerous megalomania of any politician who claimed to *represent* a whole that was more than the sum of its parts.

It is an important principle of liberalism that obligations arise solely from the voluntary acts of individuals. Governments overstep the bounds of legitimate action "when they impose on individuals obligations or rules of conduct that are not integral parts of engagements contractually assumed."[27] This principle, too, must be understood politically. Constant employed a consent-based theory of obligation to discredit both feudal dues and the execution of innocent individuals for crimes purportedly committed by their next-of-kin.

He also distrusted "the common good" for a second and closely related reason. Often the very idea of a public good contains an implicit or explicit denial that there are heterogeneous interests and perspectives within the body politic. This is always false to some extent. Indeed, except for times of war when the fate of each citizen is palpably linked to the fate of his nation, it is usually very false. Robespierre and Saint-Just assumed the existence of a monumental Public Good. Their "very exaggerated idea of the public interest"[28] led them to believe that virtuous citizens could never entertain conflicting aims, or even conflicting opinions about common aims.[29] If citizens were genuinely benevolent, they would necessarily agree about what to do. Anyone who dissented from Jacobin policies was accused of

treason—of failing to subordinate private interests to the good of the Revolution. In the Republic of Virtue, statesmen could expect unanimity. Not
required to sponsor ignoble compromises, they could thoroughly enjoy their
superiority to the pettiness of everyday life.

Denying the diversity of interests does not make diversity disappear;
but it does serve the purposes of specific groups who desire their concerns
and visions to prevail over the concerns and visions of others. Prevented
from admitting private motivations publicly, individuals become hypocrites.
Politics can never be purified or made completely interest-free. Nor should
it. Unanimism is coercive and one-sided—that is to say, incompatible with
personal integrity and meaningful public debate. Committed to popular
sovereignty, Constant nevertheless praised Sieyès for his willingness to speak
out against public opinion.[30] Dislike of a homogenizing conception of the
public good left him free to affirm the value of a looser notion of collective
aims so long as this notion took a debate-provoking variety of social perspectives, opinions as well as interests, into account.

A third reason motivating Constant's distrust of the public can be
summarized in Huizinga's memorable phrase "cruel publicity." *Adolphe*
registers the slow shift, accompanying the rise of modern European societies, from an ethics of shame to an ethics of guilt. Throughout the novel,
the representatives of conventional society are more concerned with what
others say about them than with their own firsthand experiences and
responses. They seem totally dominated by public space. Adolphe and
Ellénore, by contrast while frustrated by society's conformist demands,
have no trouble distinguishing what they want from what society expects
them to want. Nevertheless, individuals such as Ellénore, who failed once
or made a visible blunder, were stigmatized for life. Pilloried publicly, they
were permanently ruined. They could not withdraw to a nonpublic sphere,
recoup their self-respect, and reappear. This option was not available because the public, or the court, was the only place that mattered, and public
memory was implacable. In other words, Constant's distrust of the public
registered his revulsion at the human misery produced by cruel publicity,
by an unforgetting and unforgiving community, which could be a local
village as easily as a court. Man is a flexible creature. He should not be
frozen into his mistakes but should be allowed to correct errors and begin
anew. To affirm man's remedial and reparative powers was to reject the
ethics of traditionalism. Indeed, Constant did not view the ethics of tightly
knit communities as a morality of benevolence, but rather as an ethics of
"no second chance."

In an age of journalism, the public/private boundary assumes an additional meaning: "I have always fought for freedom of the press; but I have always detested and I still detest personal attacks." Defamation and the blackening of reputations were indignities of which Constant had first-hand experience. He spoke about this passionately: "the investigation of private lives is always wrong." To appreciate privacy, however, is not to relinquish publicity:

> The actions of an individual do not belong to the public. . . . A man's private life belongs to him: it is his personal property. . . . Why do we disdain spies? Because they violate the secrets of families and denounce them to the authorities. . . . But everything associated with public life must be exposed to publicity. Every oppressive act against the least of citizens is an attack on the community as a whole. The voice of the oppressed must be heard. . . . Newspapers are the voice of the oppressed.[31]

Paradoxically, the private can become more private as the public becomes more public.

Article 6 of the Charte declared Catholicism "the religion of state." As a Protestant, Constant wished to draw boundaries around this particular public good. Indeed, the great liberal cause from the sixteenth to the eighteenth century was secularization. Creating the conditions for commercial growth was a secondary concern. As an Enlightenment treatise, *De la religion* assailed the power of priests and called for a total laicization of politics, law, and education. In a society with a powerful church enforcing orthodox belief, public profession became a private scandal. Dodging religious censors, Diderot chose not to publish his most original works. He acquiesced in a split between the public and the private, the overt and the clandestine. For nonreligious writers, real life took place in secret. The visible was phony; the hidden, authentic. Orthodoxy and censorship led men to speak their minds not in public, but in the sheltered counterworld of the Masonic lodge. The French revolutionaries destroyed the power of the church and disarmed religious intolerance. But they still guillotined individuals for public denunciations of the regime. During the Terror, the concealer was again a hero. Religious ceremonies, political arguments, commercial deals, and even family relations were carried out in secret. Such circumstances explain Constant's dissent from Kant. They helped perpetuate liberal skepticism about the public, or at least about a coercive and intolerant public.

Under Napoleon, the public life that remained had similarly repulsive traits:

> We are the last remnants of a useless generation which is ig-

norant of how to perform military drills and which will not be replaced. When I think of the public that is now being shaped and the obstinacy with which I continue a project [his comparative study of the history of religions] the time for which has passed—as has the time for everything that does not pertain to the profession of killing or being killed—I compare myself to Ariosto's knight who continued to fight without noticing that he was already dead.[32]

A militarized "public world" meant that bitter, crippled withdrawal was the only alternative for certain people.

Private individuals are often more rational than politicians. That was another noneconomic reason why Constant distrusted the public sphere. Politicians, making decisions that have no effect on themselves personally, tend not to be very alert or anxious to choose better over worse solutions to collective problems. Even their cruelty is "metaphysical," since their bloodiest orders are executed by others in distant prisons. A private citizen "can retreat, advance, change course, correct himself freely without anyone noticing. The situation of the legislator is exactly the opposite. More remote from the consequences of his decisions and not experiencing their effects in such an immediate manner, he discovers his errors later. And when he discovers them, he is in the presence of enemy observers. He has reason to fear that he will fall into disrepute if he corrects himself."[33] Publicity is not always a congenial environment for learning. Unlike politicians, a private man lives in *obscurité*. He can therefore maintain a rational skepticism and flexibility. He can afford to be noncommittal, since he has no public image to cultivate and thus "no reason to defend a false idea."[34] Politicians will cling to outmoded and discredited views simply because they do not want to appear inconsistent or expose themselves to public mockery. That is the liberal rationale for elections. By changing personnel, by sweeping out one batch of public officials and putting in a new, we enable the political system to learn, even though single politicians suffer from a terrible learning disability associated with exposure to the transfixing light of public life. Constant's attitude toward publicity, in other words, was inherently ambiguous: it can poison the air as well as cleanse it.

He also acknowledged that there can be "une publicité déplacée." For example, brigands should not be alerted beforehand of an impending police raid.[35] He advanced a similar argument about diplomacy: "Foreign nations will not negotiate, or only in great distrust, with a people which associates only through the legislature. The publicity of its deliberations alone would destroy any alliance."[36] Sensitive information may be prematurely disclosed.

Furthermore, whenever they are in public, politicians pose. Public postures are not harmless. They can lock a statesmen into policies that he would otherwise find repellent and against his country's interests. Diplomatic negotiations are best carried on in a sheltered hideaway, where journalists cannot crash the gates and record every word. This makes possible a slow and gradual process of mutual accommodation. A negotiator cannot usually get his home constituency to accept accommodations unless he can show them which accommodations have been made by the other side. For negotiators to launch trial balloons toward each other, they must not be forced to appease their own skeptical publics at the outset, but only after they have had a chance to extract mutual concessions by making offers. To be sure, this argument must not be taken too far. It can easily become antidemocratic. But the importance of secrecy for negotiations reinforces the claim that there were multiple noneconomic reasons for liberal distrust of publicity.

Constant never denigrated citizen participation in politics. Similarly, his distrust of publicity was not inspired by base fondness for commercialism and economic man. Such factors played a role in the development of liberal attitudes toward the public/private distinction; but they were neither alone nor primary. Indeed, Constant's arguments suggest that he valued the public/ private boundary because it was inherently creative and could serve the interests of the community as well as of the individual.

THE ANTONYMS OF SELF-INTEREST

What accounted for Constant's sympathy with certain dimensions of the private, with the realm of modern liberty? Some reasons, the obverse of those motivating his skepticism toward the public, need no rehearsal. But other considerations should be mentioned here. For example, Maistre was not the first Christian to assert the nullity of human individuality from God's point of view.[37] Self-interest was a dimension of self-affirmation. It was directly opposed to the passivity of grace. There were, moreover, two specifically political reasons for Constant's qualified bias toward the private.

The liberal glorification of self-interest has often been misunderstood as the ignoble repudiation of a virtuous concern for the public good. But no one ever considered self-interest an attractive human motive simply because it releases men from public-spiritedness. On the contrary, liberals affirmed self-interest because they saw it as the best means for domesticating motives that were much more violently antisocial than self-interest itself. Interests were opposed to two sources of social friction: hereditary privilege and bloodthirsty passions.[38] Unlike privileges, interests are distributed without regard to birth: they are just as independent of the social status of your family as they are of your religious beliefs. To act upon interest is to claim the status of an equal—of a masterless man. Liberals turned a friendly eye toward self-interest to discredit the degrading ranks of prestige and chains of dependency characterizing the old regime. Even today, antiliberal attacks on self-interest often express nostalgia for systems of deference, authority, and condescension.[39]

Second, self-interest was opposed to passions and to passions of two sorts: religious zealotry and the revenge-mindedness of barons and clans. Those who believe that eternal salvation hinges upon a willingness to murder the heterodox pose the same threat to social cooperation as those who purchase immortal honor by retaliating personally for every perceived wrong. By focusing on interests, and by attributing paramount importance to self-preservation, Hobbes strove to put an end to the English civil wars. His aim was not to promote the interests of the merchant class, though that may have been a side-effect of what he did. By discrediting the ideals of glory and salvation, he hoped to encourage peace. At the end of the eighteenth century and during another civil war, a similar strategy suggested itself to Constant. Antiliberals typically accuse liberalism of having defiled mankind by rejecting the ethical code of a military aristocracy. They belittle self-interest by contrasting it with manliness and courage.[40] Willingness to die for a cause, however, is better understood as willingness to kill for a cause. Murder is manly indeed, and is precisely the sort of transcendent experience which, through self-interest, liberals hoped to discourage.

Paternalism was another antonym of self-interest. For the public record, Constant said that individuals could estimate their own interests better than functionaries: "monopolies and privileges . . . are ostensibly introduced in the public interest." They are "justified by the presumed blindness of self-interest." But self-interest is "always more enlightened, a thousand times more enlightened, than our government."[41] It may happen, of course, that other individuals know what is good for us better than we know ourselves; but this empirical truth cannot safely be made into an axiom of government. Liberalism is a theory of politics, not a theory of man. To deny that others can define our profoundest interests is not to enunciate a psychological generalization or to affirm the ultimate privacy of self-knowledge. It is to remove a certain kind of justification from the arsenal of public officials.

There is probably no better illustration of the liberal attitude toward commercialism than the following passage from Voltaire's *Lettres philosophiques*: "Enter the Exchange of London, that place more respectable than many a court; you will see there agents from all nations assembled for the utility of mankind. There the Jew, the Mohammedan, and the Christian deal with one another as if they were of the same religion, and give the name of infidel only to those who go bankrupt."[42] Voltaire's sociological insight here was absolutely central for Constant: social cooperation presupposes mutual indifference. Reciprocal disengagements promote civilized involvements. In a modern society, concreteness presupposes abstraction. Humanly meaningful relations with some can only be achieved by deeroticizing relations with others. With the privatization of religion, I become indifferent to the question of your eternal salvation. But this indifference, this barrier or boundary, cannot reasonably be interpreted as antisocial. Indeed, it creates conditions for social cooperation and mutual learning that never existed before. Montesquieu urged the same theme: "Commerce cures destructive prejudices."[43] Commerce allows for cooperation without common aims. It teaches people that agreement on rules is compatible with disagreement about the meaning of life. Economic activity deemphasizes sectarian passions, providing individuals with a chance to develop mutualities of a noneconomic sort. Most social relations (in religion, the family, science, and politics) cannot be patterned after economic exchange. But an element of market indifference will loosen the conditions for social compatibility and thus create conditions for more broadly based political cooperation. Markets cordialize inherited hatreds. They help turn factions into parties, sects into interest groups. In this way, commerce makes self-government possible. Like his Enlightenment predecessors, Constant viewed commerce as a tool of citizen control. Private independence was an indispensable resource in the service of public participation. What we call "the private" or economic sphere was valued because of its publicly beneficial consequences. Compartmentalization, including the public/private frontier, played an important role in strengthening social, and even political, integration.

THE SIMULTANEOUS EXPANSION OF PUBLIC
AND PRIVATE REALMS

Sovereignty and freedom are often conceived as opposites. Similarly, there is a tendency to view the private and the public as mutually exclusive alternatives and to assume that the more we have of one the less we have of the other. Usually unspoken, this assumption underlies many interpretations of Constant's theory of modern liberty. For example, C. J. Friedrich

claimed that "the larger the sphere of . . . private freedom, the more restricted will public freedom be and vice versa."[44] It is easy to understand
the source of this idea. Think of time: the more time we spend with our
family or at work, the less time we spend voting and thinking about politics
or acting politically.[45] Time is a scarce resource, and if we spend it one way
we will not spend it another. But the zero-sum model obscures the meaning
of the public/private boundary in liberal thought. When tempted to view
public and private simply as opposites, we should recall that the two are a
pair. Neither had an important place in medieval society. Like individual
rights and political sovereignty, they arose together in the early modern era.
Indeed, the public/private scheme was introduced as a joint alternative to
the politics of caste, kinship, blood feuds, and religious sectarianism. Sieyès
argued explicitly that the public/private dichotomy should replace the absurd and injurious distinction between the three "orders."[46] The contrast
between public and private should supplant the much more invidious contrasts among social strata. Constant followed this same line of reasoning.
Private independence and civic involvement can be creatively combined.
Together they can eradicate the painful social boundaries afflicting the old
regime. Considered separately, both ancient and modern liberty are flawed.
Once allied, however, their defects become mutually correcting and furnish
the conditions for a complex form of liberal freedom.

After the Revolution, the increasing importance of the person/office
distinction meant that sycophants gradually found less opportunity to win
preferments through personal toadying. But it was only in the nineteenth
century, with the beginnings of impersonal bureaucracy and the public
scrutiny of budgets, that marriage for love became socially routine. In other
words, the public and the private (in this case, the impersonal and the
personal) expanded simultaneously.[47] The creative dualism of Constant's
own career corroborates this claim: "[my] own life has been divided until
now between public office, where I have served to the best of my ability
and according to my own judgment, and the scholarly research which separates me from the world."[48] Constant's private life was not devoted exclusively to research. What matters, however, is that his society allowed
him to lead both public and private lives. His biography corroborates his
theory: the public can become more public as the private becomes more
private. The exclusion of personal salvation and damnation from the political agenda made businesslike government by discussion possible. Conversely, as political power and political allegiances became less dependent
on kinship ties, the family itself became more intimate and personalized.

SOCIAL DISJUNCTIONS AND LIBERAL EQUALITY

The person/office distinction goes back to antiquity.[49] It was crucial for the medieval church, which used it not only internally but also to help justify its claim of a right to depose kings. Augustine believed that sacraments were valid even if performed by sinners. But while the distinction is old, its radical and egalitarian implications were fully drawn out only in the modern age. "In modern times, everything is developed and implemented through offices."[50] As an essential feature of the modern state, the person/office distinction is obviously closely linked to the public/private boundary. The earliest political parties arose when party membership no longer depended on kinship. Brother could fight brother and father, son.[51] The widening gulf between the private and the public made such realignments possible. Politics became uprooted from personality and family. The court politics of the European monarchies was still quite personal. Most peace treaties between kingdoms involved marriage pacts. But the struggle for rationalization— and that meant depersonalization—began in the sixteenth and seventeenth centuries. In his *Political Testament,* Richelieu warned the king against listening to women because they evoked the king's personal and passionate side, a side that must be kept quiescent for the sake of rationalizing the state.[52]

According to ancient theorists, the endurance of regimes depended as much upon psychological qualities as upon institutional arrangements. Liberals broke this ancient alliance between personal and political stability. Constant saw the privatizing of personal qualities as a step toward increasing the rational content of public life. Impersonality is one of the great advantages of the liberal state: "The loose morals of Louis XV and the irresoluteness of Louis XVI would have had very little importance in England, because the king's personal character means nothing in a constitutional regime."[53] The constitutionalization of politics meant liberation from the tyranny of personality.

Legally defined roles encourage personal forbearance, the exiling of emotional expressivism into the private domain. In this sense, the confused and pathetic author of love letters to Juliette Récamier and the lucidly clear, ironic, and strong-willed author of the *Principes de politique* were different men. Liberal justice, we might add, assumes that statesmen, with all their prejudices and passions, are alienated from their offices. At the very least, justice thrives on selectively applied indifference. Institutional filters screen out the irrelevant allegiances of citizens and the irrelevant passions of political officials.

BOUNDARIES OF THE POLITICAL

The liberal achievements usually associated with the public/private distinction are religious toleration, freedom of inquiry, and the decentralization of the economy. Constant's writings demonstrate that the democratic trend toward self-rule and a responsible citizenry should also be included here. Government by discussion requires that certain motives be privatized and certain topics be ruled out of bounds.

Popular sovereignty also requires the secret ballot. In order to manipulate the elections, the ultras managed to make secret voting difficult: "private virtues and affections were thereby put into conflict with public virtue."[54] Constant advocated the secret ballot in order to make personal loyalties compatible with civic responsibility. The secret ballot falls inside the political sphere but outside the public. It is an enclave of privacy within the public world. Court trials provide another example of how publicity and secrecy, opened and closed doors, can be mutually supportive. The publicity of procedures is reinforced by the secrecy of jury deliberation. This special combination of concealment and disclosure allows the court to learn, to respond appropriately to new arguments and new facts. Publicity stimulates learning by ensuring criticism and allowing for an influx of new information and unsettling views. On the other hand, secrecy can also stimulate learning, because uninterrupted exposure to public scrutiny may paralyze the imagination and foster playing to the gallery.

Social boundaries also have a democratic function in the system of representation. Constant praised representative government as the only modern system that allows citizens to change their rulers without killing them. For this, rulers should be grateful, and so should citizens. The individual is one thing, the office another. Power is invested in the office, not in the person. The person wields power only so long as he holds office, and he holds office only so long as he abides by certain rules. Most importantly, politicians know that if they are ousted they will not be murdered, which probably makes them somewhat more amenable to engaging in the public debate we call democracy.

Government by discussion requires that limits be imposed on political officials and political themes. Striking testimony to democracy's need for liberal boundaries was provided by the Jacobin attempt to revive the ancient citizen in modern France. In ancient Greece there was no clear state/society distinction. Indeed, there was no "state." Citizens, at least as their modern admirers imagined them, were total participants. In Jacobin France, men were persecuted for *incivisme,* for political absenteeism and indifference.

This conflation of the social and the political, the absorption of the private into the public, did not serve the cause of democracy but only of dictatorship. We could have predicted this from a study of Rousseau. Rousseau brought the image of the ancient *polis* into the center of modern consciousness. He cursed the public/private distinction and, in his political writings, glorified a Sparta where the private vanished before the public. But at the same time he had the courage to admit that this was not democracy: there were neither discussions nor debates in his Sparta. There were no creative encounters of diverse points of view because there were no diverse points of view. To praise Sparta was to praise the great Legislator, who molded citizens from birth, made them of one mind by religious ceremonies, and prepared them to dissolve their personal contrariness into a common enterprise. To glorify the ancient *polis* in modern Europe meant repudiating the private/public boundary. Robespierre and other second-rate Rousseauists did not have Rousseau's lucidity or courage. They wrongly believed that they could erase the "line" between the public and the private and still have democratic government. An attentive reader of Rousseau, Constant knew better.

THE LIMITS OF CONSTANT'S LIBERALISM

Constant's liberalism was openly cosmopolitan and therefore unlike the nationalistic liberalisms that emerged at mid-century with Mazzini and the anti-Prussian forty-eighters. In the 1820s, with the Greek revolt against the Turks, Constant did take up the cause of national independence—the emancipation of a culturally homogeneous group from foreign rule. But this revolt pitted a Christian nation against the Turks, making the "nationalist" element unclear even here.[55] In his polemics against the ultras, he sometimes associated freedom with national autonomy. With hindsight, however, we can see that he was largely unaware of the volcanic power of European nationalism. His cosmopolitanism was complacent, never conceived as a defense against ultranationalism. That was a choice and a dilemma that lay in the future.

A glance at Tocqueville and Mill reveals another discrepancy between Constant and the weightiest of his successors. For both Tocqueville and Mill, the threat to the individual posed by conformism and collective mediocrity was almost as great as the threat posed by an overcentralized state. Their works were pervaded by a fear that refined culture was in decay, standards of excellence were being eroded, and eccentric geniuses were a vanishing species. In Constant's writings, and the contrast could not be more stark, there was no sign of *Kulturkritik*. Although he had few illusions

about modern society and many worries about its vulnerability to Bonapartist dictatorship, he did not conceive of social leveling as a threat to
philosophy, culture, science, art, or individuality. His hatred of the old
regime and his distrust of military heroes were too deeply ingrained to allow
him any obsession with "mediocrity."

Constant's egalitarianism, his lack of nostalgia for feudal hierarchy
and the age of heroes, as well as his relative clarity about the anomie of
modern society, all conspire to make his position more attractive to current
readers than, say, Tocqueville's fond regret for servant-master relations
under the old regime. But there are other features of Constant's liberalism
that, from our point of view, appear time-bound and irrelevant to present
concerns.

One illustration is his repeated insistence that the first virtue of any
legal system is "la lenteur."[56] Courts are now so overburdened, procedures
so cumbrous and arthritically slow, that mechanisms for inhibiting hasty
decisions often seem counterproductive, obstacles to legal justice. This is
just one example of a general problem: liberalism arose partly as a defensive
reaction against arbitrary government. Few liberals wrote as if their *sole*
aim was to limit state authority and obstruct its interventionist acts. For
example, Locke's famous chapter on "the prerogative" shows that even he
believed limited government to be insufficient: a government also had to
work positively for the public good.[57] But mainstream liberalism left its
followers ill-equipped to deal with the problem of governmental paralysis
and incoherence. How should liberals respond to the inability of a government to make consistent policies and act upon them in a decisive manner?[58]
Constant often said that "Of all offices, that of deputy is the noblest and
most independent."[59] He was very comfortable criticizing governments.
Would he have been able to govern? During his lifetime, liberalism remained
on the defensive; so he never had to face this problem.[60] But it seems easier
for liberals to adopt a critical than a constructive stance. Constant's position
has not, therefore, become superannuated. But liberalism may now be a
partial truth in a way largely unforseen by Constant.

A similar conclusion follows from a different objection, one based on
concern not for political paralysis but for the erosion of individual rights.
Constant's liberalism was typical in this respect: it located the principal
threat to social pluralism and the integrity of individual lives in the agents,
especially the subaltern agents, of the state. By the eighteenth century, the
centralized state had effectively eliminated most rivals to its monopoly on
power. As a result, supporters of security and independence naturally focused their attacks on the government and its officials, while looking with

favor on free enterprise in an exchange economy. In the course of the
nineteenth century, however, unprecedented accumulations of power were
built up in economic sectors of society. Unregulated freedom of contract,
having disintegrated the illiberal corporations of the old regime, began to
engender illiberal patterns of its own. Novel forms of personal dependency
emerged, no longer based on patronage and possession of land, but nevertheless recognizable *as* dependency and as violations of the Enlightenment
ideals of autonomy and freedom.[61] How could the liberal state be "neutral"
between parties with such grossly unequal bargaining power? An otiose
fixation on the state as the sole menace to social pluralism made liberals
such as Spencer insensitive to the new ubiquity of threats posed by wielders
of nonpolitical power. The emergence first of compulsory education and
finally of the welfare state signaled a sharpened awareness that freedom of
contract could not be the sole organizing principle of a liberal society. Here
again, the liberal worry about political tyranny did not become obsolete.
Soviet-style command economies have demonstrated conclusively that
workers can be harmed by the excessive power of the state. But the old
liberal fixation must now be balanced by a more comprehensive concern
for multiple threats to social pluralism or the freedom to cooperate socially
outside of politics.

Virulent nationalism, political paralysis, accumulations of economic
power, and the necessity for the state to assume some redistributive welfare
functions are four of the many problems for which Constant's writings
provide little or no instruction. But, despite historical remoteness, Constant's
political theory cannot be considered utterly passé. To some extent, his
problems are still our problems. The fundamental theoretical alternatives
that preoccupy social philosophers today, from libertarian individualism to
communitarian socialism, were originally formulated during his lifetime. As
France was recovering from the Revolution, Constant staked out another
position. Articulating his fundamental ideas in response to dramatic historical events, he explicitly aimed at providing a theoretical alternative to
both communitarian and antipolitical ideals. There are thus good prima
facie reasons for taking Constant's position seriously even today.

To denigrate Adam Smith by reading him through the eyes of Aristotle
has been a common theoretical ploy at least since Hegel's *Philosophy of
Law*. Constant's fundamental contribution to the contemporary debate lies
here: he presented a tightly argued and cogent case for the limited relevance,
and even the danger, of the ancient ideal of total citizenship in modern
contexts. But he urged his position with subtlety and nuance, stressing that
privatized citizens have something important to learn from ancient republics.

Constant speaks to late twentieth-century readers in other ways as well. The lure of ideology has not abated and the need for a deflating form of skepticism is still strong. Faced with uncompromisingly hostile ideological groups, Constant tried to promote governmental neutrality toward conflicting ideals as a formula for ensuring social stability, coexistence, and mutual learning. This ideal had precapitalist roots in the sixteenth-century *politique* advocacy of religious toleration. The *politiques* did not see the centralized state as the source of all social problems. Because they were primarily worried about competing sects and rival magnates, they actually sought to strengthen sovereign power. Curiously enough, Constant's debt to these sixteenth-century theorists may help to explain why his political theory seems illuminating even today—that is to say, why it has not been discredited by unforeseen nineteenth-century developments. Since his liberalism had precapitalist roots, it has also had the resilience to survive telling arguments against the identification of freedom with economic laissez-faire.

Notes

INTRODUCTION

1 Denis Leduc-Fayette, *Jean Jacques-Rousseau et le mythe de l'antiquité* (Paris: Vrin, 1974).
2 Twelve years after Constant's death, Marx wrote: "Freedom, that feeling of man's dignity ... disappeared from the world with the Greeks." Letter of May 1843. *Writings of the Young Marx on Philosophy and Society*, ed. Loyd Easton and Kurt Guddat (New York: Doubleday, 1967), p. 206.
3 Influential examples of neo-Aristotelian political theory are Hannah Arendt, *The Human Condition* (Chicago: University of Chicago Press, 1958); and Alasdair MacIntyre, *After Virtue* (Notre Dame, Ind.: University of Notre Dame Press, 1981).
4 Guy Dodge, *Benjamin Constant's Philosophy of Liberalism. A Study in Politics and Religion* (Chapel Hill: University of North Carolina Press, 1980); Etienne Hofmann, *Les "Principes de politique" de Benjamin Constant. La Genèse d'une oeuvre et l'évolution de la pensée de leur auteur (1789–1806)* (Geneva: Droz, 1980); Marcel Gauchet, "L'illusion lucide du libéralisme," preface to *De la liberté chez les modernes* (Paris: Pluriel, 1980), pp. 11–91. For an exhaustive bibliography of writings on Constant, readers may now consult the *Bibliographie analytique des écrits sur Benjamin Constant (1796–1980)*, ed. Etienne Hofmann (Oxford: The Voltaire Foundation, 1980).
5 Acquiescence in the 18th Brumaire came from "un peuple fatigué d'une ré-publique nominale." "Souvenirs historiques, I," *Revue de Paris* 9 (1830): 118.
6 This is the crux of Franz Neumann's criticism in *The Democratic and Authoritarian State* (New York: Free Press, 1957), pp. 138–43, 160ff.
7 Other distinctive criticisms of liberalism can be found in Sheldon Wolin, *Politics and Vision* (Boston: Little Brown, 1960), pp. 286–351; and Roberto Unger, *Knowledge and Politics* (New York: Free Press, 1975).

8   See pp. 258–60 above.

9   Isaiah Berlin refers to Constant, together with Mill, as "the fathers of liberalism." *Four Essays on Liberty* (Oxford: Oxford University Press, 1969), p. 161.

10 ". . . il arrive sans cesse que les hommes oublient une moitié de leurs opinions, quand ils veulent faire prévaloir l'autre moitié." *Commentaire sur Filangieri,* 2:55.

11 Pierre Deguise, *Benjamin Constant méconnu* (Geneva: Droz, 1966).

12 Etienne Hofmann, whose excellent study of the early Constant is cited in note 4 above, attends closely to developmental factors, with (in my view) slender theoretical results.

13 Even a subtle interpreter of Constant's position can be misled by an exclusive focus on the unrepresentative writings of 1814–15. See George Kelly, "Liberalism and Aristocracy in the French Restoration" *Journal of the History of Ideas* 26 (October–December 1965): 509–30.

14 He maintained personal relations with the de Broglies, but his political allies stood further to the left.

15 As did his marriage (1808–30) to a foreigner, Charlotte von Hardenberg, a cousin of the Prussian minister.

16 "Robespierre et les Jacobins dans la correspondance de Benjamin Constant (1793–1794)," ed. Gustave Rudler, *Annales révolutionnaires* 3, no. 1 (January–March 1910): 100. All translations are mine except where noted.

17 The best study of Constant's early "nihilism" is still Gustave Rudler's *La Jeunesse de Benjamin Constant (1767–1794)* (Paris: Armand Colin, 1908), pp. 135ff.

18 For example, Hofmann, Les *"Principes de politique,"* pp. 194, 200.

19 Despite the basic thrust of his argument (quite similar to Constant's), Ronald Dworkin asserts that "Liberalism cannot be based on skepticism." "Liberalism," in *Public and Private Morality,* ed. Stuart Hampshire (Cambridge: Cambridge University Press, 1978), p. 142.

20 Alfred Cobban, *A History of Modern France,* 1:256.

21 Jean Bodin, *The Six Bookes of a Commonweale* (Cambridge, Mass.: Harvard University Press, 1962), p. 537; Julian Franklin, *Jean Bodin and the Rise of Absolutist Theory* (Cambridge: Cambridge University Press, 1973), p. 41ff; Quentin Skinner, *The Foundations of Modern Political Thought* (Cambridge: Cambridge University Press, 1978), 2:249–50.

22 Les *"Principes de politique" de Benjamin Constant,* p. 424.

23 For my understanding of Voltaire's premise that sovereignty can serve freedom, I am indebted to Peter Gay's *Voltaire's Politics* (Princeton: Princeton University Press, 1959).

24 M. J. Sydenham, *The French Revolution* (New York: Capricorn Books, 1966), pp. 13–34.

25 Jacques Necker, *De la Révolution française* (Paris, 1796); Mme. de Staël, *Considérations sur les principaux événements de la Révolution française,* 3 vols. (Paris: Delaunay, 1818).

26 Mme. de Staël, *Considérations,* 3:8–9.

27 The claim that Tocqueville radically broke with the self-understanding of all

members of the revolutionary generation is thus untenable. See François Furet's *Penser la Révolution française* (Paris: Gallimard, 1978), p. 30.

28 Cited in Guy Dodge, *Benjamin Constant's Philosophy of Liberalism*, p. 96, from a manuscript of a lecture on the English constitution delivered (as was "Ancient and Modern Liberty") at the Paris Atheneum in 1819.

29 "Des réactions politiques" and a speech of 16 September 1797, *Ecrits et discours politiques*, 1:87, 119.

30 According to Constant "madame de Staël assigne fréquemment aux distinctions héréditaires, et surtout aux souvenirs historiques dans les organisations modernes, une place qu'il me paraît impossible de leur accorder aujourd'hui." Article of 15 June 1818, *Recueil d'articles: Le Mercure, la Minerve, la Renommée*, p. 456.

31 "Souvenirs historiques, I" and "Souvenirs historiques, II," *Revue de Paris* 9 (1830): 120; 16 (1830): 103; *Mémoires sur les Cent-Jours*, p. 186. See also the memoirs dictated to Coulmann in 1829: "Sieyès est un des hommes qui ont fait le plus de bien à la France en 89. . . . Il a rendu d'immenses services lorsqu'il a fallu démasquer et anéantir les classes privilégiées." Jean-Jacques Coulmann, *Réminiscences* (Geneva: Slatkine Reprints, 1973), 3:52. Here, and in the "Souvenirs," devoted largely to Sieyès, Constant goes on to level some harsh criticisms at Sieyès's character.

32 I thus disagree with Roland Mortier's otherwise convincing article, "Constant et les lumières," *Europe*, no. 467 (March 1968), p. 9. Far from being a consistent disciple of Montesquieu, Constant repeatedly echoed the fierce attack on *De l'esprit des lois* contained in the famous letters formerly attributed to Helvétius. The "intermediate orders" which Montesquieu praised were actually "tyrants of the people," whose main function was to prevent the grievances of the people from being heard by the king. (These letters are translated as an appendix to Destutt de Tracy's *Commentary and Review of Montesquieu's Spirit of the Laws* [Philadephia: William Duane, 1811], pp. 286 and 288.) For Constant's echo of this attitude, see *Commentaire sur Filangieri*, 1:4. Needless to say, Constant still greatly admired numerous other aspects of Montesquieu's thought: his skepticism, anticlericalism, demand for toleration and penal reform, and his belief that personal traits were only marginally relevant to the endurance and moderation of constitutional regimes.

33 As he wrote: "nous sentons enclins à pardonner les forfaits de Louis XI et les cruautés de Richelieu en faveur de leur résultat, la destruction de la féodalité" (*Fragmens d'un ouvrage abandonné*, Nouvelles acquisitions françaises (hereafter cited as Naf.) 14363, fol. 13b. Writers who wrongly claim that Constant was an unflinching antagonist of sovereign power include: Michael Oakeshott, *On Human Conduct* (Oxford: Oxford University Press, 1975), pp. 245–46; Bertrand de Jouvenel, *On Power* (Boston: Beacon Press, 1962), p. 294; and Paul Bastid, *Benjamin Constant et sa doctrine* (Paris: Armand Colin, 1966), 2:867–68. Recall that the dismal failure of absolutism resulted from its spectacular success. By the end of the eighteenth century, religious civil wars and baronial feuds had been so thoroughly quelled that the original raison d'être of a strong state had been largely forgotten. The civil war in France at the end of the eighteenth century helped to renew liberal sympathy

for sovereign power, to be based this time on constitutionally organized popular consent, not on divine right. Constant thus expressly defended the sovereignty of public discussion, founded on an inviolable right of opposition and dissent. Unlike the *politique* state, however, public debate was not merely an instrument in the service of freedom; it was also a channel for the exercise of freedom.

34   John Dunn claims that, among liberals, the Revolution weakened the eighteenth-century commitment to freedom, equality, reason and tolerance ("Liberalism," in *Western Political Theory in the Face of the Future* [Cambridge: Cambridge University Press, 1979], p. 30). The reverse is true in the case of Constant. Indeed, it would have been extraordinary if the Terror had *not* reinforced the liberal belief in the value of procedural justice and a protected sphere of private rights.

35   "Réflexions sur la tragédie" (1829), *Oeuvres*, p. 902.

36   Hereafter cited as *Force du gouvernement actuel de la France.*

37   Reprinted in *Cours de politique*, vol. 2.

38   *Ecrits et discours politiques*, 1:49.

39   See *Suites de la contre-révolution en Angleterre*, p. 45; and also G. de Bertier de Sauvigny, "Liberalism, Nationalism and Socialism: The Birth of Three Words," *Review of Politics* 32 (1970): 152.

40   George Kelly, "Constant Commotion: Avatars of a Pure Liberal," in the *Journal of Modern History* 54, no. 3 (September 1982): 512.

41   In a famous letter of 22 October 1797 to Bonaparte, Talleyrand said of Constant: "son caractère est ferme et modéré; républicain inébranlable et libéral." This letter is reprinted in *Recueil d'articles: Le Mercure, la Minerve, La Renommée*, p. 1244.

42   *Suites de la contre-révolution en Angleterre*, p. 28.

43   *Commentaire sur Filangieri*, 2:289. Similarly: "l'anarchie n'est autre chose que l'arbitraire exercé tour à tour par beaucoup d'hommes qui se le disputent et se l'arrachent." *Du polythéisme romain*, 1:209.

44   The partial elections of April 1797, in which the former Conventionnels were severely defeated, had given counterrevolutionaries hope of taking power by peaceful means. In response, the Fructidor putschists preemptively brought the army into the center of political life. Arbitrarily exiling and executing a few hundred opponents of the regime, they also banned opposition journals and nullified the legal election of almost two hundred royalist sympathizers. The Fructidorians thus "saved" the Republic by abolishing all the basic principles of representative government. Constant's speech in defense of the coup is reprinted in *Ecrits et discours*, 1:115–28.

45   For Constant's strong reservations about Bonaparte's coup, see his letter to Sieyès, probably written on the 19th Brumaire. "Les lettres de Benjamin Constant à Sieyès," *Annales Benjamin Constant* 3 (1983): 96–97; also reprinted in Etienne Hofmann, *Les "Principes de politique" de Benjamin Constant,* (Geneva: Droz, 1980), 1:189.

46   Compare Franz Neumann: "The rise of liberal theories (such as Locke's) is understandable and has meaning only if the monopoly of the state's coercive powers is no longer challenged so that restraints upon sovereignty will no

longer lead to its disintegration." *The Democratic and the Authoritarian State*, p. 182.

47 Letter of 24 November 1803. "Lettres de Benjamin Constant à Fauriel (1802–1823)," In Victor Glachant, *Benjamin Constant sous l'oeil du guet* (Paris: Plon, 1906), p. 94.

48 Composed sometime between 1800 and 1803. Naf. 14363 and 14364. Bibliothèque Nationale, Paris. Cited hereafter as *Fragmens d'un ouvrage abandonné*.

49 Composed between 1802 and 1806, and published as the second volume of Etienne Hofmann's book cited in note 4; herein cited as *Les "Principes de politique" de Benjamin Constant*.

50 *Fragmens d'un ouvrage abandonné*, Naf. 14363, fol. 40b.

51 Published in *Oeuvres*, pp. 187–789.

52 Some of Constant's correspondence has yet to be published. Among the more important printed collections are these: Jean H. Menos, ed., *Lettres de Benjamin Constant à sa famille, 1795–1830* (Paris, 1888), hereafter cited as Menos; D. Mélégari, ed., *Journal intime de Benjamin Constant et lettres à sa famille et à ses amis* (Paris, 1895), cited as Mélégari; Ephraim Harpaz, ed., *Benjamin Constant et Goyet de la Sarthe correspondance, 1818–1822* (Geneva: Droz, 1973); George Dierolf, ed., "Lettres de Benjamin Constant à Prosper de Barante, 1805–1830. *Revue des deux mondes* 34 (1906): 241–72, 528–67; Ephraim Harpaz, ed., *Lettres à Madame de Récamier (1807–1830)* (Paris: Klincksieck, 1977).

53 All printed in *Oeuvres*.

54 Volume 1 was first published in 1824; vol. 2, in 1825; vol. 3, in 1827; and vols. 4 and 5, posthumously in 1831.

55 First published in 1833.

56 "On a négligé jusqu'à présent de séparer avec assez de soin les religions dominées par les prêtres, des religions qui demeurent indépendantes de la direction sacerdotale" (*De la religion*, 1:136). Constant also described this difference as a distinction between "la religion imposée" and "la religion libre" (*De la religion*, 5:173). An idealization of apostolic Christianity, spontaneous and uncorrupted by a worldly priesthood, was a commonplace in early Protestant thought. In Constant's own writings, the distinction between sacerdotal and nonsacerdotal religions dates back at least to 1813, when he completed the "Cahier bleu," one of the early manuscripts of *De la religion*.

57 *De la religion*, 5:194.

58 *Commentaire sur Filangieri*, 2:269, similarly, in Rome, the priesthood "fut toujours subordonné à l'état." *Du polythéisme romain*, 1:40.

59 *De la religion*, 2:467–69.

60 "De la guerre de trente ans," *Mélanges*, 2:14–15.

61 "Je veux trouver un pays où l'on dorme tranquille, et je le trouverai en Allemagne" ("Journaux intimes," 28 October 1804, *Oeuvres*, p. 363); cf. *De la religion*, 1:ix–x.

62 Reprinted in *Cours de politique*, vol. 2.

63 *Cours de politique*, 2:275.

64 Ibid., pp. 189–90.

65 Indeed, almost immediately afterward, Constant wrote that *la légitimité* was utterly worthless without the guarantees of the Charter. Article of 21 April 1814, *Recueil d'articles: 1795–1817*, pp. 142–43.

66 The new constitution of 1814, regally "granted" to the nation by Louis XVIII, retained the Civil Code and recognized legal equality, religious toleration, and the right of purchasers of "national lands" to keep their property. To understand the liberal–ultra battles of the Restoration, it is important to note that the Charter was a blatantly ambiguous document which, for instance, did not make clear how power was to be apportioned between the king and the Chambers. Guillaume de Bertier de Sauvigny, *The Bourbon Restoration* (Philadelphia: University of Pennsylvania Press, 1966), pp. 65–72.

67 Reprinted in *Cours de politique*, vol. 1.

68 *Mémoires sur les Cent-Jours*, p. 122.

69 Article of 19 March 1815, *Recueil d'articles: 1795–1817*, p. 149ff.

70 Mme. de Staël asked this question: *Considérations sur les principaux événements de la Révolution française*, 3:135–43.

71 He was also fascinated by what he perceived as Napoleon's eerie stoic detachment from his own fate.

72 Reprinted in *Cours de politique*, vol. 1, and to be clearly distinguished from the manuscript "Principes de politique," written between 1802 and 1806.

73 *Cours de politique*, 1:83.

74 Ibid., p. 35.

75 See the notes added in 1818 to the reissued "Réflexions sur les constitutions" *Cours de politique*, 1:251, 308–18. Consider also: "depuis la renaissance des lumières, les défenseurs de la liberté n'ont jamais cru que son établissement fût possible sans l'abolition des castes prédominantes. . . . On ne trouve pas un écrivain ami de la liberté, dans les temps modernes, qui ne veuille enlever la puissance aux nobles." Article of 15 June 1818, *Recueil d'articles: Le Mercure, la Minerve, la Renommée*, p. 453.

76 Richard Cobb, "The White Terror," *A Second Identity: Essays on France and French History* (London: Oxford University Press, 1969), p. 199. No liberal, aware of "the apparently anarchical violence of the murder gangs of the south" (ibid., p. 198), could define "liberty" as the antonym of "sovereignty."

77 Reprinted in *Cours de politique*, vol. 2.

78 The Doctrinaires, intellectual heirs of Necker and Mme. de Staël, were a handful of deputies at the center or center-left of the parliamentary spectrum, with intellectual prestige but without the kind of national constituency possessed by either ultras or "Independents." They were less committed to the Revolution, fonder of the "mixed" English constitution, and readier to compromise with the ultras (i.e., more deferential toward *la légitimité*) than Constant's party.

79 Paul Bastid, *Benjamin Constant et sa doctrine* (Paris: Armand Colin, 1966), 1:333; William W. Holdheim, *Benjamin Constant* (London: Bowes & Bowes, 1961), p. 80; Alfred Cobban, *A History of Modern France* (Harmondsworth: Penguin, 1965), 2:77.

80 *Cours de politique*, 2:558.

81 "Des élections prochaines" (1817), *Cours de politique*, 2:311.

82 Hereafter cited as *Discours*.

83 Collected in *Recueil d'articles: Le Mercure, la Minerve, la Renommée* and *Recueil d'articles, 1820–1824*.

84 Herein cited as *Commentaire sur Filangieri*.

85 *Commentaire sur Filangieri*, 2:272.

86 Ibid., p. 56.

87 Helvétius, "De l'homme, de ses facultés intellectuelles, et de son éducation," *Oeuvres* (Paris: Briand, 1793), 4:186. In Constant's view, the most dangerous aspect of the myth of antiquity was not the suggestion of citizen participation but, rather, an exaggerated notion of the power of legislators over morals. Diderot's *Encyclopédie* confirms the appropriateness of this concern: "L'éducation des enfans sera pour *le législateur* un moyen efficace pour attacher les peuples à la patrie, pour leur inspirer l'esprit de communauté, l'humanité, la bienveillance, les vertus publiques, les vertus privées, l'amour de l'honnête, les passions utiles à l'état, enfin pour leur donner, leur conserver la sorte de caractère, de génie qui convient à la nation." Continuing in a vein that reminds postrevolutionary readers of Robespierre, the author added: "Les jeux publics, les spectacles, les assemblées seront un des moyens dont les *législateur* se servira pour unir entr'eux les citoyens; les jeux des Grecs . . . nos fêtes, nos spectacles, répandent l'esprit de société qui contribue à l'esprit de patriotisme." *Encyclopédie, ou Dictionnaire raisonné des sciences, des arts et des métiers* (Neuchâtel: Faulche, 1765), 9:360 and 361.

88 On the tension, in the eighteenth century, between individual self-determination and moral education at the hands of a philosophic elite, see Peter Gay, *The Enlightenment: An Interpretation*, vol. 2 of *The Science of Freedom* (New York: Norton, 1969), p. 497ff.

89 *Commentaire sur Filangieri*, 1:7; throughout this study I have taken the *Commentaire* as a yardstick by which to gauge Constant's mature views.

90 "Contre la traite des noirs" (5 April 1822), "Sur la traite des noirs" (31 July 1822), and "Sur le projet de loi relatif à la traite des noirs" (31 March 1827), *Discours*, 2:137–44, 179–81, 569–73. A speech of 17 July 1824 against "le plus abominable trafic qui ait jamais déshonoré l'espèce humaine" is reprinted in *Ecrits et discours*, 2:65–74; citation from p. 66. Constant's reformism, which also included his battles to secure legal protection for the inhabitants of French colonies and to end discrimination against Protestants and Jews, helps modify Sheldon Wolin's claim that "In France . . . liberalism emerged as a post-revolutionary reaction. Voltaire's boast, '*Je suis grand démolisseur,*' was as alien to the temperament of the nineteenth-century French liberals as Rousseau's theory of popular sovereignty." *Politics and Vision*, p. 294.

91 Benjamin et Rosalie Constant, *Correspondance 1786–1830*, (Paris: Gallimard, 1955), p. 300. Constant identified totally and enthusiastically with the Revolution of 1830. See speech of 11 September 1830, *Archives parlementaires*, deuxième série, 63:452.

92 Edgar Leon Newmann, "The Blouse and the Frock Coat: The Alliance of the Common People of Paris with the Liberal Leadership and the Middle Class during the Last Years of the Bourbon Restoration," *Journal of Modern History* 46 (1974): 26–59. This alliance, which was viewed as self-evident at the time,

only becomes surprising when examined with a distorting Marxist lens.

93   *Commentaire sur Filangieri,* 2:150.

94   "En général, il faut éviter de proclamer les changements, si la nécessité n'est pas urgente. C'est leur susciter des résistances." *De la religion,* 5:203.

95   Speech 11 September 1830, *Archives parlementaires,* 63:452.

96   "Conquête et usurpation." *Cours de politique,* 2:217.

97   *Fragmens d'un ouvrage abandonné,* Naf. 14363, fol. 71b.

98   Jacques Godechot, *France and the Atlantic Revolution of the Eighteenth Century, 1770–1799* (New York: Free Press, 1965), p. 246.

99   John Plamenatz, "Liberalism," *Dictionary of the History of Ideas* (New York: Scribner's, 1973), 3:45. According to Guy Dodge, "Constant's liberalism was aristocratic because the Terror and Bonapartism resulted in an antidemocratic liberalism that was antagonistic to the egalitarian ideas of Rousseau" *(Benjamin Constant's Philosophy of Liberalism,* p. 144.) J. L. Talmon, too, enlists Constant in the Great Struggle of "liberalism versus democracy." *Political Messianism: The Romantic Phase* (New York: Praeger, 1960), pp. 317–22.

100 Speech of 6 April 1829, *Ecrits et discours,* 2:140. Unconcerned about majority tyranny in the nation, Constant was nevertheless always worried about a tyranny of the ultra majority in the Chamber.

101 *Les "Principes de politique" de Benjamin Constant,* p. 523. Constant affirmed popular sovereignty with this caveat: "la souveraineté du peuple ne va pas jusqu'à donner à des fractions du peuple le droit de se présenter soit en armes, soit d'une manière menaçante, pour imposer leur voeu comme le voeu général" (speech of 6 November 1830, *Archives parlementaires,* 64:272).

CHAPTER 1

Epigraph: "Souvenirs historiques, II," *Revue de Paris* 16 (1830): 103.

1   "De la liberté des anciens comparée à celle des modernes," delivered at the Paris Athenuem in 1819 and reprinted in *Cours de politique,* 2:539–60, cited hereafter as "Anciens et modernes." Besides this lecture, the basic texts in which Constant discussed the distinction between ancient and modern liberty are chapters 6 through 8 of *De l'usurpation* of 1814, reprinted in *Cours de politique,* 2:204–17, and, most important of all, Book 16 of the recently published manuscript, originally composed between 1802 and 1806, *Les "Principes de politique" de Benjamin Constant,* ed. Etienne Hofmann (Geneva: Droz, 1980), pp. 419–55. This early sketch of Constant's argument is itself a rewritten and expanded version of chapter 3 of Mme. de Staël's *Des Circonstances actuelles qui peuvent terminer la Révolution* (Geneva: Droz, 1979), pp. 106–12, a work composed around 1798 but left unpublished until the twentieth century. According to an authoritative work on Mme. de Staël, "Le manuscrit des *Circonstances actuelles pour terminer la Révolution* porte de nombreuses traces de l'écriture de Constant. . . . Lui-même a corrigé le ms." (Simone Balayé, *Madame de Staël. Lumières et liberté* [Paris: Kincksieck, 1979], p. 60.) Constant must also have been involved with the initial con-

ception of the chapter in question and may possibly be considered its spiritual coauthor. The actual degree of Constant's collaboration, however, is bound to remain a matter of dispute. Because he later took whole sentences from the book and simply transplanted them unrevised into his own published works, we can assume he felt a proprietary attitude toward the manuscript of 1798. The relevant chapter also has a kind of Constantian ring that is discordant with de Staël's ordinary tone. But there is room for légitimate disagreement on this question. The answer to it is also of limited importance.

2   J. B. Bury, *The Idea of Progress* (New York: Macmillan, 1932), pp. 78–97; Antoine Adam, *Grandeur and Illusion: French Literature and Society 1600–1715* (New York: Basic Books, 1972), pp. 142–64.

3   The basic tension marking Constant's attitude toward ancient liberty also appeared in Voltaire's article of 1765. "Les Anciens et les modernes ou la toilette de Madame de Pompadour," in *Mélanges,* ed. Jacques van den Heuval (Paris: Pléiade, 1961), pp. 731–38. As proof of the superiority of the moderns over the ancients, Voltaire recited a standard list: the compass, gunpowder, the telescope; and he also compared Racine and Molière favorably with Euripides and Terence. Today, he wrote, "les jeunes gens, en sortant des écoles, en savent plus que tous [les] philosophes de l'antiquité." On the other hand, the ancients had political greatness (for, unlike Frenchmen, they *had* politics); and more striking still: "nous respectons Cicéron et tous les anciens qui nous ont appris à penser" (pp. 736 and 738).

4   See Thomas Hobbes's dismissal of ancient liberty, *Leviathan* (Oxford: Oxford University Press, 1965), pt. 2, chap. 21, p. 165.

5   David Hume, "Of the Populousness of Ancient Nations," *Essays: Moral, Political and Literary* (Oxford: Oxford University Press, 1963), pp. 381–451.

6   Hume, "Ancient Nations," p. 418. Cf. Alexander Hamilton: "The industrious habits of the people of the present day, absorbed in the pursuits of gain and devoted to the improvements of agriculture and commerce, are incompatible with the condition of a nation of soldiers, which was the true condition of the people of those [ancient] republics." *The Federalist Papers* (New York: New American Library, 1961), p. 69.

7   Compare Books II–VIII of *De l'esprit des lois,* with Books XI and XII.

8   Montesquieu, *De l'esprit des lois,* in *Oeuvres complètes* (Paris: Pléiade, 1951), 2:431 (XII, 2).

9   Montesquieu, *De l'esprit des lois,* p. 396 (XI, 5) and p. 354 (VIII, 6). Anglophiles also commonly contrasted English liberty to the fund-raising techniques of the French and Spanish monarchies. See J. H. Hexter, "The Birth of Modern Freedom," *Times Literary Supplement,* 21 January 1983, pp. 51–54.

10   Montesquieu, *De l'esprit des lois,* p. 397 (XI, 6).

11   Montesquieu, *Causes de la Grandeur des Romains,* in *Oeuvres complètes,* p. 119.

12   Montesquieu, *De l'esprit des lois,* pp. 363 (VIII, 16); 272 (IV, 8); 269 (IV, 6); 273 (IV, 8).

13   Ibid., p. 252 (III, 3): "Les politiques grecs, qui vivoient dans le gouvernement populaire, ne reconnoissoient d'autre force qui pût les soutenir que celle de la vertu."

14 Montesquieu, *De l'esprit des lois,* p. 303 (V, 19).

15 Max Weber, *Wirtschaft und Gesellschaft* (Tübingen: J. C. B. Mohr, 1972), p. 809.

16 Montesquieu, *De l'esprit des lois,* pp. 274 (V, 2); 362 (VIII, 16); 252 (III, 3).

17 Montesquieu's definition of freedom as personal security (with no reference to self-government, character development, or the satisfactions afforded participants in a common endeavor) was echoed in Jaucourt's article on political liberty in the *Encyclopédie:* "La *liberté politique* du citoyen est cette tranquillité d'esprit qui procède de l'opinion que chacun a de sa sûreté, & pour qu'on ait cette sûreté, il faut que le gouvernement soit tel, qu'un citoyen ne puisse pas craindre un citoyen." *Encyclopédie, ou Dictionnaire raisonné des sciences, des arts et des métiers* (Neuchâtel: Faulche, 1765), 9:472.

18 Jean-Louis de Lolme, *The Constitution of England* (London: Wilkie and Robinson, 1807), p. 246.

19 Joseph Priestly, *An Essay on the First Principles of Government and of the Nature of Political, Civil and Religious Liberty* (London, 1768), pp. 12–13, 54; Adam Ferguson, *An Essay on the History of Civil Society* (London, 1767), p. 92; Jean-Charles-Leonard Sismondi, *Histoire des républiques italiennes du moyen-âge* (Paris: H. Nicolle, 1809), 4:369–70. These texts are all cited in Guy Dodge, *Benjamin Constant's Philosophy of Liberalism,* pp. 43–44.

20 "Anciens et modernes," *Cours de politique,* 2:539.

21 Ibid., p. 547.

22 Les *"Principes de politique" de Benjamin Constant,* p. 432.

23 Isaiah Berlin, "Two Concepts of Liberty," in *Four Essays on Liberty* (Oxford: Oxford University Press, 1969), pp. 118–72; Berlin suggests that Constant's idea of liberty derives from ancient stoicism; but Constant explicitly criticized the human inadequacy of the "liberté intérieure" sought by the ancient stoics. *Du polythéisme romain,* 1:88.

24 Some radically ascetic nos may not entail any yeses; but this is not the case with modern liberty.

25 Les *"Principes de politique" de Benjamin Constant,* pp. 421–24.

26 "Anciens et modernes," *Cours de politique,* 2:556–57.

27 "Presque tous les hommes d'Etat et les philosophes de l'antiquité voulaient concentrer le pouvoir entre les mains des classes supérieures, et plaçaient la naissance, c'est-à-dire la noblesse, au nombre des titres valables sur lesquels devait se fonder la suprématie de ces classes. Aristote exige cette condition, même dans une démocratie bien constituée." *Mémoires sur les Cent-Jours,* p. 185.

28 Describing Filangieri's position, but in full agreement with it, Constant wrote: "toute liberté civile, toute garantie individuelle, est impossible avec l'absence de l'égalité." *Fragmens d'un ouvrage abandonné,* Naf. 14363, fols. 10a–10b.

29 Larry Siedentop develops this point in "Two Liberal Traditions" (in *The Idea of Freedom,* ed. Alan Ryan [Oxford: Oxford University Press, 1979], pp. 153–74); his contrast between French and British liberalism is ultimately unconvincing, however, as it requires the expulsion of Adam Smith from the British tradition.

30 "Conquête et usurpation," *Cours de politique,* 2:213–17.

31 Constantin François de Volney, "Leçons d'histoire," in *Oeuvres complètes* (Paris: Didot Frères, 1846), p. 592.

32 Robert L. Herbert, *David, Brutus, Voltaire and the French Revolution* (New York: Viking, 1972).

33 "Conquête et usurpation," *Cours de politique*, 2:217.

34 Constant's analysis of the masks worn by "modern imitators of ancient republics" was echoed thirty-five years later in Karl Marx's discussion of the role played by Roman costumes and phrases in the great French Revolution. (Karl Marx, "Der achtzehnte Brumaire de Louis Bonaparte," *Marx-Engels Werke* [Berlin: Dietz, 1978], 8:116). Curiously enough, in the very same passage where Marx tacitly echoed Constant, he explicitly *said* that Constant was another bourgeois propagandist unaware that "ghosts from the days of Rome" had watched over the demolition of feudalism in France. Marx's principal point, in any case, was that history had instructed the French revolutionaries to create bourgeois society. They had to drug themselves to the banality of their task; and thus they mouthed public-spirited slogans and struck patriotic poses borrowed from ancient citizens. Marx went on to predict that the proletarian revolution would be quite different. It would be truly heroic, neither requiring nor admitting any form of self-deception. Unlike Marx, Constant did not believe the emergence of revolutionary cults of antiquity could be traced to the cunning of reason. He thought that the Jacobin fixation on classical virtue was a contingent fact: it was caused by the classical education of middle-class French elites and especially by the paucity of alternative languages available for attacking royalism and religious orthodoxy.

35 "Anciens et modernes," *Cours de politique*, 2:548–49.

36 *Les "Principes de politique" de Benjamin Constant*, p. 420.

37 Cf. Judith Shklar, *Men and Citizens: A Study of Rousseau's Social Theory* (Cambridge: Cambridge University Press, 1969).

38 "Anciens et modernes," *Cours de politique*, 2:555.

39 Ibid., pp. 559–60.

40 Cf. George Sabine, "Two Democratic Traditions," *Philosophical Review* 61 (October 1952): 451–74.

41 Mme. de Staël, *Circonstances actuelles*, p. 106.

42 Here is a somewhat more comical image of the political participation worth withdrawing from: "Je suis profondément fatigué de Paris. J'y ai fait assez de connaissances . . . mais ces connaissances . . . sont tellement difficiles à ménager entre elles, il y a tant de tracasseries personnelles, auxquelles on ne peut pas rester étranger, il est si difficile de ne pas déplaire aux uns pour plaire aux autres, enfin on a si fréquemment l'occasion de se faire un ennemi ardent pour se conserver un ami tiède que je suis harassé de toutes les considérations de détails qui m'ont occupé depuis huit jours; je partirai dans peu de jours pour ma campagne et j'irai oublier loin de Paris les hommes et les factions." Letter of 8 May 1796, Mélégari, p. 255.

43 Mme. de Staël, *Circonstances actuelles*, p. 106.

44 Ibid, pp. 106–07.

45 Ibid., pp. 108–11.

46 Ibid., p. 111.

47   Ibid.

48   John Plamenatz, *The Revolutionary Movement in France 1815-71* (London: Longmans, Green, 1952), pp. 21-22; Georges Weill, "L'Idée républicaine en France pendant la Restauration," *Revue d'histoire* 2, no. 11 (September-October 1927): 334-35.

49   Speech of 8 June 1824, *Discours*, 2:259.

50   "Anciens et modernes," *Cours de politique*, 2:540.

51   Ibid.

52   Ibid.

53   Bonald was bold enough to embrace this sort of comparison: "On nous parle de la liberté des Grecs et des Romains, et ils n'avaient ni jugements par jurés ni liberté de la presse." Louis de Bonald, "Observations sur Mme. de Staël," *Oeuvres complètes*, 2:643.

54   Ibid., pp. 554; 542.

55   Ibid., p. 542.

56   Ibid., p. 553.

57   Reprinted in *Cours de politique*, 2:53-69.

58   *Cours de politique*, 1:17, 180, 310; *Archives parlementaires*, 63:63.

59   "D'une assertion de M. Bailleul dans sa brochure contre M. de Chateaubriand" (1818), *Recueil d'articles: Le Mercure, la Minerve, la Renommée*, 1:349.

60   "Anciens et modernes," *Cours de politique*, 2:556.

61   Ibid., pp. 547; 556 (see also 557); 560.

62   Ibid., pp. 545-46.

63   Ibid., p. 559.

64   Rousseau, *Oeuvres complètes*, ed. Bernard Gagnebin et Marcel Raymond (Paris: Pléiade, 1964), 3:430.

65   "Anciens et modernes," *Cours de politique*, 2:542.

66   Ibid., p. 553.

67   *Commentaire sur l'ouvrage de Filangieri*, 2:182-83.

68   Albert Hirschman, *The Passions and the Interests: Political Arguments for Capitalism before its Triumph* (Princeton: Princeton University Press, 1977), pp. 123-24.

69   Article of 23 May 1819, *Recueil d'articles: Le Mercure, la Minerve, la Renommée*, 2:829.

70   Louis Bergeron, *France under Napoleon* (Princeton: Princeton University Press, 1981), p. 87.

71   "Anciens et modernes," *Cours de politique*, 2:552.

73   The freedom from politics which Constant enjoyed in Germany had its limits: "Je veux trouver dans l'étude et dans la poursuite de mon grand ouvrage [on religion] de quoi oublier tout ce qu'on entend et tout ce qu'on voit. Mais, il faut un terrain solide pour construire même un hermitage, et je ne vois pas un désert où la terre ne tremble comme partout." Letter of 15 September 1810, "Lettres de Benjamin Constant à Fauriel (1803-1823)," in Victor Glachant, *Benjamin Constant sous l'oeil du guet* (Paris: Plon, 1906), p. 127.

74   "Anciens et modernes," *Cours de politique*, 2:559.

75   Ibid., p. 558.

76   Ibid.

77 Ibid.
78 Ibid., p. 547.
79 Ibid., p. 559.
80 Ibid.
81 Ibid., p. 560.
82 In the manuscripts of 1802–06, written under the shadow of Napoleon, we find: "lorsqu'il n'y a dans un pays libre ni liberté de la presse, ni droits politiques, le peuple se détache entièrement des affaires publiques. Toute communication est rompue entre les gouvernants et les gouvernés. L'autorité, pendant quelque temps, et les partisans de l'autorité peuvent regarder cela comme un avantage. Le gouvernement ne rencontre point des obstacles. Rien ne le contrarie. Il agit librement mais c'est que lui seul est vivant et que la nation est morte" (Les "Principes de politique" de Benjamin Constant, p. 137). The liberal constitutionalism Constant advocated was obviously not intended to detach citizens entirely from public affairs.
83 Jean-Louis de Lolme, The Constitution of England (London: Wilkie and Robinson, 1807), p. 245. Referring specifically to the French revolutionaries and their followers, Edmund Burke drew a similar distinction: "the right of the people is almost always confounded with their power." Reflections on the Revolution in France (London: Penguin, 1969), p. 153.
84 Albert Hirschman, Exit, Voice and Loyalty (Cambridge, Mass.: Harvard University Press, 1970), pp. 30–43. Constant, however, was thinking of "interdependence" rather than a mere "mixture."
85 Commentaire sur Filangieri, 1:73.
86 Ibid., p. 72.
87 According to Isaiah Berlin, Constant defended democratic self-government "only for the reason . . . that without it negative liberty may be too easily crushed." Four Essays on Liberty, p. xlvii. Consider also: "que tout l'effort des libéraux, après la Révolution, ait été de rendre à la liberté politique le caractère de moyen de défense de la liberté du particulier." Bertrand de Jouvenel, Les Débuts de l'état moderne (Paris: Fayard, 1976), p. 116.
88 Letter to Mme. de Nassau, 20 January 1800, Mélégari, pp. 298–99; translated from the corrected text in Hofmann, Les "Principles de politique," p. 194.
89 Hippolyte Taine, L'Ancien Régime (Paris: Hachette, 1877).
90 Fragmens d'un ouvrage abandonné, Naf. 14363, fol. 92b.
91 Ibid., fol. 15b.
92 "Fragmens sur la France," Mélanges de littérature et de politique, 1:68.
93 As Gay and others have stressed, the appeal to antiquity was only one aspect of the Enlightenment tradition; and it was counterbalanced by a belief that, in many domains, the moderns had outstripped the ancients.
94 In his essay "Of Refinement in the Arts," Hume wrote: "To declaim against present times, and magnify the virtue of remote ancestors, is a propensity almost inherent in the human mind." Essays, p. 285.
95 Under the Directoire, republicans still tended to sacralize freedom: "Cette fraction du parti patriote aimait la liberté comme une divinité occulte, mystérieuse, bonne à servir par tous les moyens." "Souvenirs historiques, II," Revue de Paris 16 (1830): 103.

96   Les *"Principes de politique" de Benjamin Constant,* p. 438.

97   "During a conversation in which [Robespierre] attacked the representative system, it is reported that, asked what he would put in its place, he replied, 'Celui de Lycurge.' " Alfred Cobban, "The Political Ideas of Robespierre during the Convention," *Aspects of the French Revolution* (New York: Braziller, 1968), p. 186; consider also R. R. Palmer, *The Age of the Democratic Revolution* (Princeton: Princeton University Press, 1964), 2:124.

98   *Oeuvres de Maximilien Robespierre,* ed. Laponneraye (New York: Burt Franklin, 1970), 3:518.

99   Ibid., p. 608; but also see 3:194, where Robespierre notes of Sparta that "il n'y a rien de commun entre cette famille de républicains austères et une nation de 25 millions d'hommes." Robespierre was flexible enough that, in order to attack the *sectionnaires* and the Commune, he often reversed himself and denounced urban self-government on the ancient model (ibid., 3:544).

100 This thesis has been recently explored by Michel Villey, "Sur l'inexistence des droits de l'homme dans l'Antiquité," *Le Droit et les droits de l'homme* (Paris: Presses Universitaires de France, 1983), pp. 81–104; see also *Leçons d'histoire de la philosophie du droit* (Paris: Dalloz, 1962), pp. 221–50.

101 According to Moses Finley, "Classical Greeks and Republican Romans possessed a considerable measure of freedom, in speech, in political debate, in their business activities, even in religion. However, they lacked, and would have been appalled by, inalienable rights. There were no theoretical limits to the power of the state, no activity, no sphere of human behavior in which the state could not legitimately intervene provided the decision was properly taken for any reason that was held to be valid by a legitimate authority." *The Ancient Economy* (London: Chatto and Windus, 1973), pp. 154–55.

102 "Fragmens sur la France," *Mélanges de littérature et de politique,* 1:68.

103 Norman Hampson, *The Social History of the French Revolution* (Toronto: University of Toronto Press, 1965), p. 223.

104 *Fragmens d'un ouvrage abandonné,* Naf. 14363, fol. 97a.

105 "Suspicion was directed not only towards probable authors of acts already committed, on grounds of definite circumstances susceptible of discussion and of proof, but also towards the possible perpetrators of eventual crimes, who were believed capable of them because of their opinions or even their real or simulated indifference." Georges Lefebvre, *The French Revolution* (London: Routledge and Kegan Paul, 1968), 2:118.

106 François Furet and Denis Richet, *La Révolution française* (Paris: Marabout, 1979), p. 210.

107 Robespierre, *Oeuvres,* 3:514.

108 Ibid., 3:698 and 612; Norman Hampson, *The Life and Opinions of Maximilien Robespierre* (London: Duckworth, 1974), pp. 139 and 173.

109 Robespierre, *Oeuvres,* 3:551.

110 On the execution of Louis XVI as an attempt to furnish a republican reeducation for the miseducated French nation, see Michael Walzer, *Regicide and Revolution* (Cambridge: Cambridge University Press, 1974), pp. 1–89.

111 According to Plutarch, Lycurgus "bred up his citizens in such a way that they neither would nor could live by themselves; they were to make themselves

one with the public good, and, clustering like bees around their commander, be by their zeal and public spirit carried all but out of themselves, and devoted wholly to their country." *The Lives of the Noble Grecians and Romans* (New York: Modern Library, n.d.), p. 69.

112 Robespierre, *Oeuvres,* 1:156; 3:541.

113 Ibid., 3:541.

114 "Conquête et usurpation," *Cours de politique,* 2:213.

115 For Montesquieu's idea of the "general spirit" of a country or age, see *De l'esprit des lois,* Book XIX, chaps. 4 and 5.

116 *Suites de la contre-révolution en Angleterre,* pp. 56–57.

117 Consider the two uses of the word *revolution* at the beginning of Turgot's "A Philosophical Review of the Successive Advances of the Human Mind," in *On Progress, Sociology and Economics,* ed. R. L. Meek (Cambridge: Cambridge University Press, 1973), pp. 41–42. See also Felix Gilbert, "Revolution," in *Dictionary of the History of Ideas* (New York: Scribner's, 1973), 4:152–63.

118 Robespierre, *Oeuvres,* 3:736; Hampson, *Life and Opinions of Maximilien Robespierre,* pp. 133–34.

119 Les *"Principes de politique" de Benjamin Constant,* p. 432.

120 "Adolphe," in *Oeuvres,* p. 32.

121 Les *"Principes de politique" de Benjamin Constant,* p. 434.

122 Ibid., pp. 620, 86, 438.

123 In most constitutional and organizational questions, "L'expérience de la Grèce n'est point applicable aux grands états modernes. Ce qui leur est applicable dans cette expérience, ce sont les bienfaits de la liberté. La Grèce nous apprend jusqu'à quel point de bonheur et de gloire la liberté porte les nations. La Grèce nous présente une cité de vingt mille citoyens . . . éclairant le monde entier" (*Fragmens d'un ouvrage abandonné,* Naf. 14363, fol. 85a). Viewed properly, the Greek city can teach modern Europeans the wisdom of supplementing their private independence with citizen involvement.

124 This caveat distinguishes Constant's position from the views advanced by Karl Popper, *The Open Society and Its Enemies,* 2 vols. (Princeton: Princeton University Press, 1966).

125 M. J. Sydenham, *The French Revolution* (New York: Capricorn, 1966), p. 178; Hampson, *Life and Opinions of Maximilien Robespierre,* p. 198.

CHAPTER 2

Epigraph: Marquis de Condorcet, "Premier mémoire sur l'éducation," in *Oeuvres,* 12 vols. (Paris: F. Didot frères 1847–49), 8:417.

1 Max Weber, *Gesammelte Aufsätze zur Wissenschaftslehre* (Tübingen: J. C. B. Mohr, 1922), p. 206.

2 According to Robert Nozick, the ultimate point of reference for liberal theory is a set of ahistorically defined "characteristics of persons" (*Anarchy, State*

and Utopia [New York: Basic Books, 1974], p. 48). Among Constant's contemporaries, the Idéologues made an even more radical leap from traits to rights, i.e., from physical characteristics to political claims. See Emmet Kennedy, *A Philosophe in the Age of Revolution. Destutt de Tracy and the Origins of "Ideology"* (Philadelphia: American Philosophical Society, 1978), pp. 151–52.

3 *Fragmens d'un ouvrage abandonné,* Naf. 14363, fol. 60ᵇ.

4 See, for example, Jacques Droz, *Histoire des doctrines politiques en France* (Paris: Presses Universitaires de France, 1956), where it is said of Constant, "Chez aucun écrivain les préoccupations de la bourgeoisie ne sont plus évidentes," and where his works are rather unsubtly dismissed as providing "la justification de la domination de la bourgeoisie" (pp. 70 and 73); cf. Godechot, Dyslop, Dowd, *The Napoleonic Era in Europe* (New York: Holt, Rinehart and Winston, 1971), p. 259.

5 Constantin François de Volney, "Leçons d'histoire," in *Oeuvres complètes* (Paris: Didot Frères, 1846), p. 593. Volney summarizes his violent denunciation of the ancient city in the following manner: "Guerres éternelles, égorgements de prisonniers, massacres de femmes et d'enfants, perfides factions intérieures, tyrannie domestique, oppression étrangère; voilà le tableau de la Grèce et l'Italie pendant 500 ans, tel que nous le tracent Thucydide, Polybe et Tite-Live" (p. 593).

6 *Les "Principes de politique" de Benjamin Constant,* pp. 482; 428; *Fragmens d'un ouvrage abandonné,* Naf. 14363, fol. 19b.

7 Cf. Hegel's claim that "the Greeks knew nothing of conscience." *Grundlinien der Philosophie des Rechts* (Hamburg: Felix Meiner, 1955), p. 417.

8 *Les "Principes de politique" de Benjamin Constant,* pp. 420, 421.

9 "Anciens et modernes," *Cours de politique,* 2:547.

10 Ibid., p. 541; my emphasis.

11 Ibid., p. 557.

12 Unlike Isaiah Berlin (*Four Essays on Liberty,* pp. 163–64), Constant distinguished sharply between two senses of independence, between apolitical withdrawal into philosophy and apolitical engagement in commerce and other sectors of social life. *Les "Principes de politique" de Benjamin Constant,* pp. 432–33.

13 Consider this: "The Athenians also took part in the Assembly, which had 40 ordinary meetings a year, and public slaves rounded them up from the agora onto the Pnyx for these meetings with the aid of a ruddled rope: anyone found afterwards with red on his clothes was fined." T. B. L. Webster, *Everyday Life in Classical Athens* (New York: Putnam, 1969), p. 69.

14 *Les "Principes de politique" de Benjamin Constant,* p. 419.

15 "Anciens et modernes," *Cours de politique,* 2:542; this is confirmed rather than denied by Pericles' statement: "we are not angry with a neighbor for doing what he likes, nor do we cast sour looks at him" (Thucydides, *Peloponnesian War,* bk. 2, chap. 37). Pericles was bragging about Athenian exceptionalism, the implication being that all other Greeks *would* have been angry with signs of nonconformity on the part of a neighbor. Elsewhere, Pericles gives quite Rousseauist advice to his fellow citizens: "you must daily

fix your gaze upon the power of Athens and become lovers of her" (bk. 2, chap. 43).

16 "Anciens et modernes," *Cours de politique*, 2:542.
17 "Conquête et usurpation," ibid., p. 254.
18 Ibid., p. 543.
19 Les *"Principes de politique"* de Benjamin Constant, p. 426; cf. *Circonstances actuelles*, p. 109.
20 In many premodern societies, "L'individu ne trouvait de récompense que dans l'éclat qu'il procurait à l'ordre dont il était membre." *De la religion*, 2:123.
21 Hobbes, *Leviathan* (Oxford: Oxford University Press, 1965), pt. 1, chap. 5, p. 35.
22 "Montesquieu's characterization of republican virtue as an unreasoning passion is something new in political thought. . . . Aristotle calls virtue a habit, but he would have been shocked at the suggestion that it is a passion." Bernard Yack, "The Longing for Total Revolution: A New Form of Social Discontent and Its Philosophic Sources, 1750–1900" (Ph.D. diss., Harvard University, 1981), p. 37.
23 Les *"Principes de politique"* de Benjamin Constant, p. 419; in contrast to Hannah Arendt, *The Human Condition* (Chicago: University of Chicago Press, 1958).
24 "Anciens et modernes," *Cours de politique*, 2:548.
25 Ibid., p. 541.
26 Les *"Principes de politique"* de Benjamin Constant, p. 420.
27 "Anciens et modernes," *Cours de politique*, 2:542, 547.
28 Ibid., p. 543.
29 Ibid., p. 545; compare Montesquieu: "On étoit fort embarrassé dans les républiques grecques. On ne vouloit pas que les citoyens travaillassent au commerce, à l'agriculture, ni aux arts; on ne vouloit pas non plus qu'ils fussent oisifs. Ils trouvoient une occupation dans les exercices qui dépendoient de la gymnastique, et dans ceux qui avoient du rapport à la guerre." *De l'esprit des lois* in *Oeuvres complètes*, ed. Roger Caillois (Paris: Pléiade, 1951), 2:272 (IV, 8).
30 "Anciens et modernes," *Cours de politique*, 2:546. Compare Thucydides' statement that Athenians "regard untroubled peace as a far greater calamity than laborious activity." *The Peloponnesian War*, bk. 1, chap. 70.
31 Aristotle *Politics* 1337a. 27.
32 David Hume, *A Treatise of Human Nature* (Oxford: Oxford University Press, 1967), p. 477ff.
33 *Fragmens d'un ouvrage abandonné*, Naf. 14363, fol. 164b.
34 "Réflexions sur les constitutions," *Cours de politique*, 1:246–47.
35 "Anciens et modernes," *Cours de politique*, 2:545.
36 Mme. de Staël, *Des circonstances actuelles qui peuvent terminer la Révolution* (Geneva: Droz, 1979), p. 110.
37 Les *"Principes de politique"* de Benjamin Constant, p. 424.
38 Aristotle *Politics* 1252a. 7. No pacifist, Aristotle was nevertheless opposed to war among Greek cities (*Politics* 1324b. 1–1325a. 10). His teleological theory of the *polis*, however, may still have mirrored the single-minded focus on war

that marked the Greek cities during their most glorious years.

39 Constant's derivation of the ancients' intense attachment to the common good from the stringent needs of war recalls his analysis of political zealotry (see above pp. 114–15). To the extent that ancient life was dominated by the public good, citizens were *incapable of being distracted,* of straying off in pursuit of partial considerations. This bias against contrariness and distraction was Constant's essential complaint about the ancient city. It was precisely what Rousseau had admired most.

40 *Politics* 1225b. 35–38.

41 "Anciens et modernes," *Cours de politique,* 2:558.

42 Ibid., p. 543; this is a paraphrase of Condorcet.

43 Ibid., p. 548.

44 Indeed, the astonishing energy of the ancients was due to their *lack* of awareness of human freedom: "Presque toutes les nations livrées à des passions énergiques penchent vers le fatalisme. . . . Ces nations se sentent en quelque sorte entraînées par une impulsion irrésistible, elles se pénètrent de la croyance d'une destinée qui les protége, et cette croyance fortifie la passion dominante qui en a suggéré l'idée." *Du polythéisme romain,* 1:18.

45 *The Federalist Papers* (New York: Mentor, 1961), p. 81.

46 In ancient republics, "deux classes, les riches et les pauvres se disputaient et s'arrachaient la totalité de la puissance sociale." *Fragmens d'un ouvrage abandonné,* Naf. 14363, fol. 84b.

47 Thomas Hobbes, *Leviathan* (Oxford: Clarendon Press, 1965), p. 166.

48 "Anciens et modernes," *Cours de politique,* 2:551.

49 For a further analysis of Constant's philosophy of history, see chapter 7.

50 Aristotle *Politics* 1326b. 25 and 15–16.

51 "Anciens et modernes," *Cours de politique,* 2:545.

52 *Les "Principes de politique" de Benjamin Constant,* p. 420.

53 Ibid., p. 421.

54 Mme. de Staël, *Des circonstances actuelles qui peuvent terminer la Révolution,* p. 109.

55 On the controversial concept of "liberal neutrality," see chapter 5.

56 For a recent exploration of these metaphors and of their central importance for a theory of liberal equality, see Michael Walzer, *Spheres of Justice* (New York: Basic Books, 1983).

57 Augustine defined man as a "social" rather than a "political" being; and Thomas Aquinas translated Aristotle's *zōon politikon* as *animal social* (*The City of God,* bk. 19, chap. 5; *Summa Theologica,* pt. 1, qu. 96, art. 4). In contrast to Aristotle, both assigned politics a meager function in the economy of individual salvation.

58 Ferdinand Braudel writes that "the peasant who uprooted himself from his land and arrived in town was immediately another man. . . . If the town had adopted him, he could snap his fingers when his lord called for him." *Capitalism and Material Life 1400–1800* (New York: Harper & Row, 1967), pp. 402–03.

59 "Anciens et modernes," *Cours de politique,* 2:554.

60 Ibid., p. 545.

61 "LIBERTY, or FREEDOME, signifieth (properly) the absence of Opposition; (by
    Opposition I mean externall impediments of motion;)." Hobbes, *Leviathan*
    (Oxford: Oxford University Press, 1965), pt. 2, chap. 21, p. 161. The shocking
    radicalness of this redefinition of freedom can best be appreciated against the
    background of the traditional English "liberties," a bundle of owned privileges
    or powers allocated according to birthrank.

62 It is a fundamental principle of liberalism that such mutual learning can be
    nonpolitical as well as political.

63 Isaiah Berlin sometimes identifies positive freedom with self-determination
    and negative freedom with the absence of inward or outward obstacles (*Four
    Essays on Liberty*, p. 131). This way of reformulating Constant's distinction
    misses the essential point that in modern Europe, where polity and society
    are no longer identical, self-determination will necessarily have both political
    and extrapolitical dimensions. Freedom from authority, and even from time-
    consuming participation, will enhance one's chances for controlling one's own
    life.

64 "Anciens et modernes," *Cours de politique*, 2:541.

65 Ibid., p. 545.

66 Alexis de Tocqueville, *De la démocratie en Amérique* (Paris: Gallimard, 1961),
    2:313–14.

67 "Anciens et modernes," *Cours de politique*, 2:546.

68 Article of 20 August 1818, *Recueil d'articles: Le Mercure, la Minerve, la
    Renommée*, 1:496. So much for "the little platoon we belong to in society"
    lauded by Burke, *Reflections on the Revolution in France* (Harmondsworth:
    Penguin, 1969), p. 135.

69 By monopolizing the legitimate use of force, the modern state also centralized
    most threats to individual security. This concentration of danger made it easier
    for individuals to conceive of workable strategies for self-defense (e.g., rights).

70 In his challenge to Constant's understanding of ancient liberty, Gomme asserts
    that "individual ownership of land is as potent an aid to personal freedom
    as trading." Arnold W. Gomme, "Concepts of Freedom," *More Essays in
    Greek History and Literature* (Oxford: Blackwell's, 1962), p. 141. But he
    presents no evidence for this view.

71 *Les "Principes de politique" de Benjamin Constant*, p. 426; on the entire issue
    of moveable property as a restraint on the state, see Albert Hirschman, *Essays
    in Trespassing: Economics to Politics and Beyond* (Cambridge: Cambridge
    University Press, 1981), pp. 253–58.

72 *Les 'Principes de politique' de Benjamin Constant*, p. 426 (cf. *Commentaire
    sur Filangieri*, 2:557); ibid., p. 427. This linkage between the rise of credit
    and the emergence of political freedom was also a theme in Mme. de Staël's
    work. *Considérations sur les principaux événements de la Révolution fran-
    çaise*, 2:322.

73 *Les "Principes de politique" de Benjamin Constant*, pp. 426; 427.

74 "Anciens et modernes," *Cours de politique*, 2:546–47.

75 This is the theme of Harold Laski, *The Rise of Liberalism* (New York: Harper
    and Brothers, 1936).

76 *Mémoires sur les Cent-Jours*, p. 191.

77 Speech of 25 January 1801, *Ecrits et discours*, 1:166–67, 185.

78 Speech of 23 February 1825, ibid., 2:98.

79 Article of 7 June 1823, *Recueil d'articles 1820–1824*, p. 317.

80 Marx sometimes embraced this absurd position, as when he denounced the bourgeois Rights of Man for destroying community by preventing individuals from harming one another. "Zur Judenfrage," in Karl Marx and Friedrich Engels, *Werke* (Berlin: Dietz, 1972), p. 366.

81 Albert Hirschman reviews the history of the idea that commercial calculation might serve to harness destructive emotionalism in *The Passions and the Interests*.

82 "Principes de politique" (1815), *Cours de politique*, 1:112–13.

83 Ibid., p. 113.

84 *Fragmens d'un ouvrage abandonné*, Naf. 14363, fols. 18a–18b; and *Recueil d'articles: 1820–1824*, pp. 268–69.

85 "Principes de politiques" (1815), *Cours de politique*, 1:114.

86 Excellent on this point is Paul Bénichou, *Le Temps des prophètes: Doctrines de l'âge romantique* (Paris Gallimard, 1977), pp. 16–17.

87 Arguing that liberal constitutionalism gives only minimal content to the concept of citizenship, Alexander Bickel emphasized the all-importance of the right of expatriation. *The Morality of Consent* (New Haven: Yale University Press, 1975), pp. 33–54.

88 Timing was crucial: "Dans les troubles civils, notamment en France, l'important est de se soustraire au premier moment. On est sûr que le parti où est la force la perdra bientôt, en se donnant des torts. On avait disparu coupable, on reparaît victime." "Souvenirs historiques, II," *Revue de Paris 16 (1830): 110.*

89 *Commentaire sur Filangieri*, 2:61.

90 *Les "Principes de politique" de Benjamin Constant*, p. 445.

91 "La division même de l'Europe en plusieurs Etats, est, grâce au progrès des lumières, plutôt apparente que réelle. Tandis que chaque peuple, autrefois, formait une famille isolée, ennemie-née des autres familles, une masse d'hommes existe maintenant sous différents noms, et sous divers modes d'organisation sociale, mais homogène de sa nature. . . . Les chefs peuvent être ennemis; les peuples sont compatriotes" ("Anciens et modernes," *Cours de politique*, 2:543 and 557). This passage is a monument to Constant's lack of prescience. He remained unaware that a particular European *patrie* might still be the object of intense emotional attachment: "L'amour de la patrie ne sauroit exister chez nous comme il existoit chez les anciens." *Commentaire sur Filangieri*, 2:60–61.

92 *Fragmens d'un ouvrage abandonné*, Naf. 14363, fol. 88a.

93 Ibid., Naf. 14363, fols. 88a–88b. Moreover, despite the experiences of his own generation, he believed that commercial linkage could provide an effective deterrent to nationalistic wars. For our present purposes, however, this passage has a different significance. It helps reiterate one of Constant's most fundamental beliefs: unintended social change has a decisive impact on the plausibility of political ideals.

94 "Anciens et modernes," *Cours de politique*, 2:558.

95 Ibid., p. 556.
96 Menos, p. 486.
97 "Anciens et modernes," *Cours de politique*, 2:541. This passage provides an occasion to comment on claims that Constant's liberalism is essentially antidemocratic. Under the influence of Isaiah Berlin's one-sided portrait of Constant, a recent English editor of the *Cours de politique* has summarized Constant's catalogue of modern rights thus: "The list Constant gives is one which covers most, but not all, of those objectives which remained the staples of liberal programmes in the nineteenth century—personal liberty, trial by jury, freedom of religion, careers open to talents, the inviolability of property and (above all) freedom of expression including freedom of speech and of the press. There is one notable omission from the list, for *there is no mention of political rights*. Here Constant drives a deep wedge between liberal and democratic ambitions." Jack Lively, introduction to the Arno Press reprint of *Cours de politique* (New York, 1979), 1:4; my emphasis.
98 Isaiah Berlin, *Four Essays on Liberty*, p. xlvi; similarly, "Benjamin Constant constate que dans les temps modernes, la vie privée est la part la plus précieuse de l'existence." André Jardin and André-Jean Tudesq, *La France des notables, 1815–1848* (Paris: Seuil, 1973), 1:99.
99 "Anciens et modernes," *Cours de politique*, 2:555; "Réflexions sur les constitutions," *Cours de politique*, 1:176; *Fragmens d'un ouvrage abandonné*, Naf. 14363, fol. 129a. Cf. "la liberté civile, c'est-à-dire les jouissances, ne sont assurées que par la liberté politique." *Mémoires sur les Cent-Jours*, p. 14.
100 Cf. Hannah Arendt, "What Is Freedom?" in *Between Past and Future* (New York: Viking, 1961), p. 155.
101 *Les "Principes de politique" de Benjamin Constant*, p. 463. Describing Napoleon, Mme. de Staël wrote: "Je l'ai vu un jour s'approcher d'une Françoise très-connue par sa beauté, son esprit et la vivacité de ses opinions; il se plaça tout droit devant elle comme le plus roide des généraux allemands, et lui dit: 'Madame, je n'aime pas que les femmes se mêlent de politique.' 'Vous avez raison, général,' lui répondit-elle, 'mais dans un pays où on leur coupe la tête, il est naturel qu'elles aient envie de savoir pourquoi.' " (*Considérations sur les principaux événements de la Révolution française*, 2:201–02). Even if people desired nothing more than private security, they would be driven to active involvement in public affairs.
102 "Anciens et modernes," *Cours de politique*, 2:540. This was a common view at the time. Adam Smith wrote: "the idea of representation was unknown in ancient times" (*An Inquiry into the Nature and Causes of the Wealth of Nations* [New York: Modern Library, 1965], p. 588). Also referring to the representative system, Kant concurred: "None of the ancient so-called republics knew such a system" ("Zum ewigen Frieden," *Kleinere Schriften zur Geschichtsphilosophie: Ethik und Politik*, ed. Karl Vorländer (Hamburg: Felix Meiner, 1964), p. 130. For a counterargument, see Madison: " the position concerning the ignorance of the ancient governments on the subject of representation is by no means precisely true in the latitude commonly given to it." *The Federalist Papers*, no. 63 (New York: Signet, 1961), p. 386.

103 "Anciens et modernes," *Cours de politique*, 2:540.
104 Paine, too, believed that "Representation was a thing unknown in the ancient democracies. In those the mass of the people met and enacted laws (grammatically speaking) in the first person." But he justified modern representative institutions not by reference to the scarcity of time, but on the grounds that contemporary societies have become "too populous, and too extensive for the simple democratical form" (*Rights of Man* [Harmondsworth: Penguin, 1969], p. 199); cf. Albert Hirschman, *Shifting Involvements, Private Interest and Public Action* (Princeton: Princeton University Press, 1982), pp. 96–99.
105 "Anciens et modernes," *Cours de politique*, 2:557–58.
106 Aristotle *Politics* 1318b. 12–13.
107 *Commentaire sur Filangieri*, 2:182.
108 Ibid., 1:4
109 "Anciens et modernes," *Cours de politique*, 2:558.
110 Karl Marx, "Der achtzehnte Brumaire de Louis Bonaparte," in Karl Marx and Friedrich Engels, *Werke*, 8:116.
111 "Anciens et modernes," *Cours de politique*, 2:553–54.
112 "Conquête et usurpation," *Cours de politique*, 2:175.
113 "Anciens et modernes," *Cours de politique*, 2:555.
114 "Principes de politique" (1815), *Cours de politique*, 1:114, cf. "Anciens et modernes," ibid., 2:555.
115 Carl Friedrich writes, less ambitiously, that the "task of maximizing freedom involves a balancing of the two dimensions of freedom." *Man and his Government* (New York: McGraw-Hill, 1963), p. 360.

CHAPTER 3

Epigraph: *Mémoires sur les Cent-Jours*, p. 201.

1 Alasdair MacIntyre, *Against the Self-Images of the Age* (Notre Dame, Ind.: University of Notre Dame Press, 1978) p. 284.
2 "Additions et notes" (1818), *Cours de politique*, 1:285; Les *"Principes de politique"* de Benjamin Constant, p. 30.
3 For example, the word *prétexte* occurs repeatedly in Helvétius. See, for example, "De l'homme," *Oeuvres* (Paris: Briand, 1793), 5:115; also see Constant, "Préface" (1818), *Cours de politique*, 1:liv. The notion that modern liberals are aware of external but not internal obstacles to freedom (e.g., Charles Taylor, "What's Wrong with Negative Liberty," in *The Idea of Freedom*, ed. Alan Ryan [Oxford: Oxford University Press, 1979], pp. 176 and 186) is, to put it mildly, difficult to reconcile with the Enlightenment battle against prejudice and superstition. This complaint might be more appropriately leveled against Aristotle, who defined a free man simply as one who exists for his own sake and not for the sake of another (*Metaphysics* 982b. 20–983a. 5).
4 Les *"Principes de politique"* de Benjamin Constant, p. 101. The Jacobins were not the first guilty party to appear on the European scene. Already in the

seventeenth century, John Locke had noted that religious sectaries would often "color their spirit of persecution and un-Christian cruelty with a pretense of care for the public weal." (*A Letter Concerning Toleration* [Indianapolis: Bobbs-Merrill, 1975], p. 16). Like Constant, Locke denounced the "pretense of public good" (ibid., p. 40) precisely because he believed that "the public good is the rule and measure of all lawmaking" (ibid., p. 36).

5   "Conquête et usurpation," *Cours de politique,* 2:157.

6   François de la Rochefoucauld, *Maximes* (Paris: Garnier, 1967), p. 48; *Commentaire sur Filangieri,* 2:271, and *De la religion,* 1:81 and 278; "Réflexions sur la tragédie" (1829), *Oeuvres,* p. 919; *Du polythéisme romain,* 1:136; "Additions et notes," *Cours de politique,* 1:301.

7   *Commentaire sur Filangieri,* 2:160.

8   Ibid., 1:11.

9   "Adolphe," *Oeuvres,* p. 41.

10 Les *"Principes de politique" de Benjamin Constant,* p. 111; *Fragmens d'un ouvrage abandonné,* Naf. 14363, fol. 123a; *Commentaire sur Filangieri,* 1:65; cf. Les *"Principes de politique" de Benjamin Constant,* p. 94; "De M. Dunoyer," *Mélanges,* 1:127–28; letter of 3 September 1799, Menos, p. 161; speech of 7 March 1820, *Discours,* 1:195; speech of 11 September 1830, *Archives parlementaires,* 63:452; Les *"Principes de politique" de Benjamin Constant,* p. 181; *Fragmens d'un ouvrage abandonné,* Naf. 14363, fol. 177[a]; "Souvenirs historiques, III," *Revue de Paris* 16 (1830): 223.

11 "Conquête et usurpation," *Cours de politique,* 2:217, my italics; cf. article of 16 August 1817, *Recueil d'articles: Le Mercure, la Minerve, la Renommée,* 1:291; Constant expressed a similar view about the Long Parliament: "what we detest with good reason in those who dominated the English republic" is "all the scaffolding of despotism in the name of the people" (*Suites de la contre-révolution en Angleterre,* p. 101). Referring to Robespierre, Mme. de Staël wrote: "on savoit qu'il ne connoissoit d'autre manière d'écarter ses concurrens, que de les faire périr par le tribunal révolutionnaire, qui donnait au meurtre un air de légalité" (*Considérations sur les principaux événements de la Révolution française,* 2:143).

12 *Fragmens d'un ouvrage abandonné,* Naf. 14363, fol. 20[a].

13 Crane Brinton, *A Decade of Revolution, 1789–1799* (New York: Harper & Row, 1963), p. 155. In general, Constant agreed that self-interest is a relatively feeble human motivation. Not interests but ideas rule the world ("Perfectibilité," *Mélanges,* 2:129–30; cf. "Or, dans tous, les opinions ou la vanité sont plus fortes que les intérêts" [*Du polythéisme romain,* 2:63]). The exorbitant claims to selflessness advanced by the Terrorists, however, led him to renew the unmasking technique of the philosophes.

14 *Suites de la contre-révolution en Angleterre,* p. v; David Hume spoke of Cromwell's attempt to establish "the face of a commonwealth" (*The History of England* [New York: Harper and Brothers, 1850], 5:440). He also registered his concern with pretexts when discussing political factions: "there are enow of zealots on both sides who kindle up the passions of their partisans, and under pretense of public good pursue the interests and ends of their particular faction" ("That Politics May Be Reduced to a Science," *Essays: Moral, Po-*

litical and Literary, [Oxford: Oxford University Press, 1963], pp. 23–24). Finally, he discussed "The sanctified hypocrites, who called their oppressions the spoiling of the Egyptians, and their rigid severities the domination of the elect, interlarded all their iniquities with long and fervent prayers, saved themselves from blushing by their pious grimaces, and exercised in the name of the Lord, all their cruelty on men. An undisguised violence could be forgiven: but such a mockery of the understanding, such an abuse of religion, were, with men of penetration, objects of peculiar resentment" (ibid., pp. 339–40).

15 *De la religion,* 1:267; *Les "Principes de politique" de Benjamin Constant,* pp. 77, 460–61; *De la religion,* 1:xxxv; "Principes de politique" (1815), *Cours de politique,* 1:75; *Commentaire sur Filangieri,* 1:63.

16 Like most other claims about historical novelty, this one can be challenged. Augustus preceded Napoleon in calling himself "Emperor of the Republic." For Constant's own discussion of Augustus as "un usurpateur hypocrite," see article of 13 September 1817, *Recueil d'articles: Le Mercure, la Minerve, la Renommée,* 1:302; cf. *Fragmens d'un ouvrage abandonné,* Naf. 14363, fol. 64a.

17 "Conquête et usurpation," *Cours de politique,* 2:195.

18 *Les "Principes de politique" de Benjamin Constant,* p. 535; "Additions et notes," *Cours de politique,* 1:285; *Les "Principes de politique" de Benjamin Constant,* p. 30. Cf. "Le prétexte de l'intérêt public a servi de tout temps à toutes les tyrannies" (speech of 25 July 1828), *Archives parlementaires,* 55:417.

19 *Commentaire sur Filangieri,* 2:123; *Les "Principes de politique" de Benjamin Constant,* p. 444.

20 Johann Wolfgang Goethe, *Gedenkausgabe der Werke, Briefe und Gespräche,* ed. Ernest Beutler (Zürich: Artemis, 1949), 12:630.

21 *Fragmens d'un ouvrage abandonné,* Naf. 14363, fol. 147a.

22 *Les "Principes de politique" de Benjamin Constant,* p. 30.

23 Ibid., p. 108; "le prestige du mot de sûreté publique aveugle les meilleurs esprits." *Commentaire sur Filangieri,* 2:191.

24 For example, Alfred Cobban, *A History of Modern France* (Harmondsworth: Penguin, 1965), 1:250.

25 François Furet and Denis Richet, *La Révolution française* (Paris: Marabout, 1979), pp. 211–12.

26 The psychological roots of intolerance, according to Constant, lie in man's natural "sociability"—that is, in his insecurity and profound need for company in matters of belief: "l'intolérance qui l'on attribue à l'orgueil de l'homme a plutôt pour principe la défiance de lui-même et une espèce d'humilité." *Du polythéisme romain,* 2:130.

27 John Plamenatz, "Liberalism," *Dictionary of the History of Ideas* (New York: Scribner's, 1973), 3:45; Guido de Ruggiero, *The History of European Liberalism* (Boston: Beacon, 1959), p. 370.

28 *Commentaire sur Filangieri,* 1:82. This is no evidence at all, of course, because Constant plausibly argued that the protection of minority rights, including the right of political opposition, were intrinsic to government by discussion.

29 For a counterargument, see chapter 5.

30 *Commentaire sur Filangieri,* 1:101.

31 He wrote unequivocally of "tous les citoyens, sans exception." "Anciens et modernes," *Cours de politique*, 2:559; cf. *Mélanges*, pp. iv–v.

32 Alfred Cobban, *In Search of Humanity: The Role of Enlightenment in Modern History* (New York: George Braziller, 1960), pp. 190–93.

33 Les *"Principes de politique" de Benjamin Constant*, p. 164; *Commentaire sur Filangieri*, 2:175; "Principes de politique" (1815), *Cours de politique*, 1:10; "Réflexions sur les constitutions," ibid., p. 278; and Les *"Principes de politique" de Benjamin Constant*, p. 45.

34 "De la souveraineté," in *Le Temps*, 1830. Cited in Guy Dodge, *Benjamin Constant's Philosophy of Liberalism*, p. 57.

35 Speech of 10 March 1820, *Discours*, 1:211; cf. "Additions et notes," *Cours de politique*, 1:285.

36 "Additions et notes," *Cours de politique*, 1:280; Les *"Principes de politique" de Benjamin Constant*, pp. 37–38.

37 We would probably have to look to the polemics of Talmon to find a denunciation of Rousseau's political thought more vitriolic and one-sided than this. See J. L. Talmon, *The Origins of Totalitarian Democracy* (New York: Praeger, 1960).

38 As a debater in the Chamber of Deputies, Constant liked to acknowledge the merits of his opponents. But his praise of Rousseau went far beyond ritual politeness. On Constant's affinity to Rousseau, see also William Holdheim, *Benjamin Constant* (London: Bowes and Bowes, 1961), pp. 67–72, 82–83, 88.

39 "De la doctrine politique qui peut réunir les partis en France" (1816), *Cours de politique*, 2:303; and "Anciens et modernes," ibid., p. 547; cf. Les *"Principes de politique" de Benjamin Constant*, p. 163.

40 "Additions et notes," *Cours de politique*, 1:278; Les *"Principes de politique" de Benjamin Constant*, p. 44.

41 Rousseau, "Du contrat social," bk. 2, chap. 6, *Oeuvres complètes*, (Paris: Pléiade, 1964), 3:379.

42 "Principes de politique" (1815), *Cours de politique*, 1:7; Les *"Principes de politique" de Benjamin Constant*, p. 44; "Additions et notes," *Cours de politique*, 1:278 and "Anciens et modernes," ibid., 2:549.

43 "Anciens et modernes," *Cours de politique*, 2:549.

44 Constant unhesitatingly defends the social convention of private property in these non-Rousseauist terms: "L'abolition de la propriété serait destructive de la division du travail, base du perfectionnement de tous les arts et de toutes les sciences." *Cours de politique*, 1:114.

45 Rousseau, "Du contrat social," bk. 3, chap. 5, *Oeuvres complètes*, 3:431.

46 Cf. Rousseau, *Politics and the Arts, Letter to M. d'Alembert on the Theatre* (Ithaca: Cornell University Press, 1968), pp. 34–47.

47 "Adolphe," *Oeuvres*, p. 83.

48 Rousseau, "Considérations sur le gouvernement de Pologne," *Oeuvres complètes*, 3:957.

49 Adam Ferguson, *An Essay on the History of Civil Society*, ed. Duncan Forbes (Edinburgh: Edinburgh University Press, 1966); cf. Alexander Hamilton: "Sparta was little more than a well-regulated camp." *The Federalist Papers*

(New York: New American Library, 1961), p. 57; *Commentaire sur Filangieri,* 2:34.

50 "Anciens et modernes," *Cours de politique,* 2:540; 557. Rousseau, "Gouvernement de Pologne," *Oeuvres complètes,* 3:956–57; *Commentaire sur Filangieri,* 2:60–61; "Anciens et modernes," *Cours de politique,* 2:543 and 557.

51 *Du polythéisme romain,* 1:189–90; Rousseau, "Lettres écrites de la montagne," *Oeuvres complètes,* 3:881.

52 "Fragmens sur la France," *Mélanges,* 1:65; *Commentaire sur Filangieri,* 2:31–32.

53 Judith Shklar, *Men and Citizens: A Study of Rousseau's Social Theory* (Cambridge: Cambridge University Press, 1969); Rousseau, "Du contrat social," bk. 1, chap. 7, *Oeuvres complètes,* 3:364. Though, as mentioned, independence of a personal master was purchased at the cost of total dependence on a social group.

54 "Additions et notes," *Cours de politique,* 1:309; *Commentaire sur Filangieri,* 2:80–81; 1:16–17; "Réflexions sur la tragédie" (1829), *Oeuvres,* p. 925.

55 *Commentaire sur Filangieri,* 1:2; cf. Franklin Ford, *Robe and Sword: The Regrouping of the French Aristocracy after Louis XIV* (New York: Harper & Row, 1965), pp. 238–43.

56 See, for example, *Commentaire sur Filangieri,* 1:27.

57 In the *Fragmens,* he explicitly rejects the notion, advanced by Montesquieu and Mme. de Staël (and later by Tocqueville), that "liberty is ancient" in France: "il n'y nul rapport entre l'esclavage de la glèbe, réuni à des privilèges tellement atroces que je me refuse à les retracer, et tellement absurdes qu'on ne peut y croire, et une constitution qui garantit les droits de tous et qui rend aux yeux de la loi le paysan le plus obscur égal au premier pair du Royaume." *Fragmens d'un ouvrage abandonné,* Naf. 14363, fols. 13ᵃ–13ᵇ.

58 "Principes de politique" (1815), *Cours de politique,* 1:7, 9.

59 Rousseau, "Lettres écrites de la montagne," *Oeuvres complètes,* 3:826.

60 Les *"Principes de politique" de Benjamin Constant,* p. 39; cf. "Additions et notes," *Cours de politique,* 1:277.

61 Les *"Principes de politique" de Benjamin Constant,* p. 43; cf. "Rousseau . . . détruit avec emportement ce qu'il relève avec enthousiasme" (*Commentaire sur Filangieri,* 2:247).

62 Les *"Principes de politique" de Benjamin Constant,* pp. 44, 43.

63 Letter of 25 June 1811, "La Correspondance de Benjamin Constant et de Sismondi (1801–1830)," *Revue européenne des sciences sociales* 18, no. 30 (1980): 126.

64 Rousseau, "Emile," *Oeuvres complètes,* 4:250.

65 Entry of 19 January 1805, "Journaux intimes," *Oeuvres,* p. 415; *De la religion,* 1:82–83.

66 Rousseau, "Du contrat social," bk. 1, chap. 6, *Oeuvres complètes,* 3:360–62.

67 Ibid., bk. 2, chap. 7, pp. 381–84.

68 Maurice Cranston, "Liberalism," in *The Encyclopedia of Philosophy* (New York: Free Press, 1967), 3:459; cf. George Sabine, "The Two Democratic

Traditions," *Philosophical Review,* October 1952, pp. 451–74.

69 In "Emile," Rousseau wrote that social deformations set man "en contradiction avec soi" (*Oeuvres complètes,* 4:491). In the "Contrat social" (bk. 4, chap. 8), he added: "Toutes les institutions qui mettent l'homme en contradiction avec lui-même ne valent rien." Ibid., 3:464.

70 The revolutionaries appreciated the speechlessness of the total citizen: "L'enfant, le citoyen appartiennent à la patrie. . . . On élève les enfants dans l'amour du silence et le mépris des rhéteurs. Ils sont formés au laconisme du langage." Saint-Just, *Oeuvres choisies* (Paris: Gallimard, 1968), p. 341.

71 Rousseau, "Du contrat social," bk. 2, chap. 3, and bk. 4, chap. 2, *Oeuvres complètes,* 3:371, 439.

72 Thus, although Constant agreed with Rousseau that all legitimate government is based on the "general will," he used the term in a non-Rousseauist manner. For Rousseau, the general will was what all men would agree upon if they obeyed their consciences; while for Constant, the general will was the decision of the majority made within a procedural framework that guaranteed freedom of dissent and minority rights: while a defeated minority must abide by majority rule, it can legitimately continue its attempt to persuade members of the majority to reverse their decision. Rousseau, by contrast, believed that a defeated minority will realize, upon losing the vote, that the decision of the majority represents its own "true" will.

73 *Fragmens d'un ouvrage abandonné,* Naf. 14363, fol. 77ᵃ; *Les "Principes de politique" de Benjamin Constant,* p. 426: "Réflexions sur les constitutions," *Cours de politique,* 1:208.

74 *Commentaire sur Filangieri,* 1:4; Guizot, who identified "democracy" with social chaos and believed that it would destroy the ascendancy of the middle class, promoted the maxim: "tout pour le peuple, rien par le peuple" (cited in Dominique Bagge, *Les Idées politiques en France sous la Restauration* [Paris: Presses Universitaires de France, 1952], p. 165). But Constant's political quarrels with Guizot went back at least to 1814. Cf. the "Journal intime" of August 12, 1814: "Dispute avec Guizot. Le plus petit pouvoir est un grand corrupteur" (*Oeuvres,* p. 703). According to Douglas Johnson, the dispute mentioned here concerned Guizot's decision to favor censorship of the periodical press. *Guizot: Aspects of French History* (London: Routledge & Kegan Paul, 1963), p. 30. After the July Revolution, Guizot supported the government's decision to force newspapers to pay caution-money. The press, he argued, must be kept in enlightened hands. To this argument, Constant responded: "Messieurs, je ne connais point en France de classe plus élevée que la totalité des Français" (speech of 9 November 1830, *Archives parlementaires,* 64:311).

75 *Cours de politique,* 1:276.

76 *Fragmens d'un ouvrage abandonné,* Naf. 14363, fol. 172ᵇ; the same passage occurs earlier in an expanded version: "Rien n'est plus terrible que les assemblées législatives, lorsqu'elles [sont] de purs instrumens de l'autorité exécutive. Les citoyens, livrés sans défense à cette coalition monstrueuse, ne retirent de l'existence de ceux qui s'intitulent encore leurs représentans que le triste avantage d'être opprimés au nom de la loi. Ce genre d'oppression est de tous le

plus avilissant, le plus atroce. Rien n'est plus affreux que le despotisme d'un seul ou de quelques hommes, régnant avec l'autorité et au nom de tous. Ce mode de tyrannie dispense de toute pudeur les gouvernans. Ils oppriment bien plus hardiment le peuple, lorsqu'ils s'autorisent de la volonté exprimée par ses mandataires, que lorsqu'ils sont obligés de convenir qu'ils l'oppriment malgre lui." *Fragmens d'un ouvrage abandonné*, Naf. 14363, fol. 121ᵃ.

77   "Additions et notes," *Cours de politique*, 1:279, 277.

78   Ibid., p. 279.

79   Ibid., p. 280; "Réflexions sur les constitutions," ibid., p. 187.

80   "Additions et notes," *Cours de politique*, 1:279.

81   Article of 13 March 1818, *Recueil d'articles: Le Mercure, la Minerve, la Renommée*, 1:358. During the Restoration, Constant took a very radical stand on "responsibility," arguing that subordinates should never be able to excuse their infractions of law with the claim that they were simply following orders: "Si vous ne punissiez que le chef qui donne l'ordre et non les agens qui l'exécutent, vous placeriez la réparation si haut que le citoyen lésé ne pourrait l'atteindre" (article of 19 March 1823, *Recueil d'articles 1820–1824*, p. 314).

82   As part of his argument against political censorship, Constant also attacked the bogus anonymity which a quirk of language bestows upon personal choices: "Impersonal verbs seem to have deceived political writers. They thought they were saying something when they said: one must repress the opinions of men; one must not abandon men to the vagaries of their spirits; it is necessary to preserve the thoughts of men from the deviations into which sophism may drag them. But do not these words, 'one must,' 'one must not,' 'it is necessary,' refer to men? Is a different species being discussed? All these phrases amount to saying: men must repress the opinions of men; men must prevent men from yielding to the vagaries of their own spirits; men must preserve men from dangerous deviations of thought. Impersonal verbs seem to have persuaded us that the instruments of authority are not human" ("Réflexions sur les constitutions," *Cours de politique*, 1:258–59; *Commentaire sur Filangieri*, 1:40). This passage illustrates how Rousseauism can function as a political pretext. By defining "le corps politique" as "un être moral qui a une volonté," demagogues can disguise the fact that far-reaching decisions are made by individuals. Well-meaning opponents of individualism may thus be unwitting accessories to political obfuscation and hypocrisy.

83   "Additions et notes," *Cours de politique*, 1:279–80; *Commentaire sur Filangieri*, 1:52.

84   Cheryl Welch makes a similar argument in her study of the Idéologues: hostility to democratic rhetoric provides no evidence for hostility to democratic politics. *Liberty and Utility: The French Idéologues and the Transformation of Liberalism* (New York: Columbia University Press, 1984).

85   "Additions et notes," *Cours de politique*, 1:275.

86   Ibid., p. 284.

87   Rousseau, "Du contrat social," bk. 3, chap. 4, *Oeuvres complètes*, 3:404–05.

88   Diderot, "Autorité politique," in *Oeuvres politiques*, ed. Paul Vernière (Paris: Garnier Frères, 1963), pp. 9–20.

89 Les *"Principes de politique" de Benjamin Constant,* pp. 135, 504, 113. A well-armed executive "peut, quand les troupes sont rassemblées, arracher au pouvoir législatif l'apparence du consentement." *Fragmens d'un ouvrage abandonné,* Naf. 14363, fol. 162ᵇ; *Les "Principes de politique" de Benjamin Constant,* p. 114; "Additions et notes," *Cours de politique,* 1:280.

90 Les *"Principes de politique" de Benjamin Constant,* p. 36.

91 Ibid., p. 37; "Additions et notes," *Cours de politique,* 1:279.

92 "Qui ne sent pas que plus un gouvernement est despotique, plus les citoyens épouvantés s'empressent de porter à ses pieds leur adhésion tremblante ou leur enthousiasme commandé?" *Fragmens d'un ouvrage abandonné,* Naf. 14364, fol. 5ᵃ.

93 *Fragmens d'un ouvrage abandonné,* Naf. 14363, fol. 91ᵃ; *Les "Principes de politique" de Benjamin Constant,* p. 113; "La sanction du peuple, les adresses d'adhésion sont les inventions de la violence hypocrite" (*Fragmens d'un ouvrage abandonné,* Naf. 14634, fol. 5ᵃ).

94 "L'opinion publique est la vie des Etats." *Les "Principes de politique" de Benjamin Constant,* p. 137. And see chapter 5.

95 Ibid., p. 421.

96 Robespierre, *Oeuvres* (Paris, 1840), 3:191; *Commentaire sur Filangieri,* 1:37.

97 Les *"Principes de politique" de Benjamin Constant,* p. 44.

98 Ibid., pp. 618–19.

99 "Additions et notes," *Cours de politique,* 1:278.

100 Rousseau, "Les Confessions," *Oeuvres complètes,* 1:112.

101 Rousseau, preface to "Narcisse," *Oeuvres complètes,* 2:972.

102 Rousseau, "Du contrat social," bk. 4, chap. 1, *Oeuvres complètes,* 3:438; Rousseau also said that unanimity may be a sign of tyranny as well as of freedom (ibid., bk. 4, chap. 2, 3:439); and that a sure sign of tyranny is the decision to legislate morality in a time of social turmoil (ibid., bk. 2, chap. 10, 3:390).

103 Constant repeats this argument: "Les richesses . . . donnent aux individus de nouveaux besoins, et des habitudes corruptrices, et de la sorte, loin de les rendre indépendans, elles les plongent pour le reste de leur vie, dans la plus funeste des dépendances." *Fragmens d'un ouvrage abandonné,* Naf. 14363, fol. 117ᵇ.

104 *Du polythéisme romain,* 2:7.

105 Referring to the psychological trauma experienced by suddenly emancipated serfs, Constant recognized explicitly that an individual's capacity for choice can be disabled for "internal" reasons: "pour donner la liberté à des hommes, il ne faut pas les avoir dégradés par l'esclavage, au dessous de la condition humaine; alors sans doute la liberté n'est qu'un présent illusoire et funeste, comme le jour devient inutile et douloureux pour celui dont la vue est affaiblie par les ténèbres d'un cachot: mais c'est un crime de plus de la tyrannie." *Fragmens d'un ouvrage abandonné,* Naf. 14363, fol. 13ᵇ.

106 Berlin states the liberal view of freedom with admirable succinctness: "it is the actual doors that are open that determine the extent of someone's freedom, and not his own preferences." " 'From Hope and Fear Set Free,' " in *Concepts and Categories* (Harmondsworth: Penguin, 1978), p. 193; for a recent criti-

cism of this radical attempt to define freedom without regard to happiness, self-realization, or achieving what one wants, see Jon Elster, *Sour Grapes: Studies in the Subversion of Rationality* (Cambridge: Cambridge University Press, 1983), p. 127ff.

107 "Tout homme peut graver des tables de pierre, ou acheter un oracle, ou feindre un secret commerce avec quelque divinité, ou trouver un oiseau pour lui parler à l'oreille, ou trouver d'autres moyens grossiers d'en imposer au peuple" ("Du contrat social," bk. 2, chap. 7, *Oeuvres complètes*, 3:384).

CHAPTER 4

Epigraph: letter of 8 May 1796, Mélégari, p. 255.

1   Mme. de Staël called this "la véritable époque de l'anarchie en France." *Considérations sur les principaux événements de la Révolution française*, 2:146.

2   "Des élections prochaines" (1817), *Cours de politique*, 2:335.; *Commentaire sur Filangieri*, 1:19. Compare: "La délation, jugée infamante sous l'Ancien Régime, devient une vertu et un devoir parce qu'on est en république" (François Furet and Denis Richet, *La Révolution française*, p. 211). What Constant called "l'exécrable loi des otages" (July 1799), whereby men were held responsible for the purported crimes of their brothers, was a terrible commentary on the revolutionary ideal of "fraternité" (see speech of 5 January 1800, *Ecrits et discours*, 1:146).

3   Harold Nicolson, *Benjamin Constant* (Garden City, N.Y.: Doubleday, 1949), p. 149.

4   Montesquieu, *De l'esprit des lois*, XII, 23–24, in *Oeuvres complètes*, 2:452–53; *Suites de la contre-révolution en Angleterre*, p. 94; On informing as a profession rather than a mere duty, see "Lettre à M. Odillon-Barrot sur l'affaire de Wilfrid Regnault" (1818), *Cours de politique*, 2:409–10; and Richard Cobb, *The Police and the People* (Oxford: Oxford University Press, 1970), pp. 5–13.

5   *Suites de la contre-révolution en Angleterre*, pp. 91, 93, 92 ("chacun se tait, chacun s'isole"), p. 90.

6   Ibid., pp. 93, 94.

7   Speeches of 7 March 1820 and 22, and 27 July 1822, *Discours*, 1:199; 2:158–59, 169–78; also see the chapter "De la dénonciation" in *Commentaire sur Filangieri*, 2:175–80. Denunciations were not always strictly anonymous. Referring to authors of an ultra journal, who were known by name, Constant wrote: "que la dénonciation soit un mensonge, c'est ce qui leur importe peu" (article of 12 July 1823, *Recueil d'articles 1820–1824*, p. 320).

8   "Lettre à M. Odillon-Barrot sur l'affaire de Wilfrid Regnault," *Cours de politique*, 2:411.

9   Letter of 15 June 1802, "Lettres de Benjamin Constant à Fauriel (1802–1823)," *Benjamin Constant sous l'oeil du guet* (Paris: Plon, 1906), p. 47.

10 Referring to Stendahl, Franz Neumann remarks that "in certain periods of

history, it is the liar who becomes the hero. The lie (in its many forms) becomes the protection of the individual against a universalized system of propaganda" (*The Democratic and the Authoritarian State*, p. 18).

11 Voltaire, *Correspondance*, ed. T. Bestermann, 5:280; cited in Peter Gay, *Voltaire's Politics*, p. 89. See also Norman L. Torrey, "Duplicity and Protective Lying," in *Voltaire*, ed. William F. Bottiglia (Englewood Cliffs, N.J.: Prentice-Hall, 1968), pp. 18–30.

12 Crane Brinton, *A Decade of Revolution, 1789–1799*, p. 134; Jacques Godechot, *The Counter-Revolution: Doctrine and Action* (London: Routledge and Kegan Paul, 1972), p. 206.

13 According to Richard Cobb, the all-invasiveness of the Jacobin state produced, as an allergic reaction, "the private man . . . anxious to escape attention." *Reactions to the French Revolution* (Oxford: Oxford University Press, 1972), p. 129.

14 See Basil Munteanu, "Episodes kantiens en Suisse et en France sous le Directoire," *Revue de littérature comparée* 15 (1935): 387–454.

15 Cf. "Niemand kann mich zwingen, auf seine Art (wie er sich das Wohlsein anderer Menschen denkt) glücklich zu sein" (Immanuel Kant, "Über den Gemeinspruch: Das mag in der Theorie richtig sein, taugt aber nicht für die Praxis," *Kleinere Schriften zur Geschichtsphilosophie: Ethik und Politik*, ed. Karl Vorländer [Hamburg: Felix Meiner, 1964], p. 87).

16 Kant, "Zum ewigen Frieden," ibid., p. 151; the same unconditional prohibition against lying occurs in Kant's *Metaphysik der Sitten*, ed. Karl Vorländer (Hamburg: Felix Meiner, 1966), pp. 277–81.

17 *Fragmens d'un ouvrage abandonné*, Naf. 14363, fol. 105[a].

18 "Principes de politique" (1815), *Cours de politique*, 1:29; *Commentaire sur Filangieri*, 2:178–79.

19 *Suites de la contre-révolution en Angleterre*, pp. 44, 74.

20 "Réflexions sur les constitutions," *Cours de politique*, 1:248.

21 "Des réactions politiques," *Ecrits et discours*, 1:68.

22 Ibid., p. 69.

23 Immanuel Kant, "Über ein vermeintes Recht, aus Menschenliebe zu lügen," *Kleinere Schriften zur Geschichtsphilosophie: Ethik und Politik*, pp. 201–06. For a context-free discussion of the Kant/Constant controversy, see Charles Fried, *Right and Wrong* (Cambridge, Mass.: Harvard University Press, 1978), pp. 69–72.

24 Kant, "Zum ewigen Frieden," in *Kleinere Schriften*, p. 151.

25 Kant did not recommend unconditional veracity as a *means* for achieving the moral purity of the agent. Moral purity was the unintended, though foreseeable, side-effect of the strict observance of duty regardless of consequences. But Kant apparently did not believe that there was anything abhorrent about the causal association of one's own purity with the undeserved and preventable suffering of others.

26 "Des réactions politiques," *Ecrits et discours*, 1:69–70.

27 As he wrote: "eine Kollision von Pflichten und Verbindlichkeiten [ist] gar nicht denkbar." *Metaphysik der Sitten*, p. 27.

28 "Souvenirs historiques, II," *Revue de Paris* 16 (1830):105; he also wrote of

"l'ineptie, tantôt pusillanime et tantôt persécutrice, du gouvernement directorial" (*Mémoires sur les Cent-Jours*, p. 6).

29 M. J. Sydenham, *The First French Republic 1972–1804* (Berkeley: University of California Press, 1973), pp. 153–54; François Furet and Denis Richet, *La Révolution française*, p. 501.

30 Postrevolutionary individualism was a philosophical correlate not of entrepreneurial capitalism but of the mutual suspicions engendered by civil war. Social atomization had immediate political advantages. It could separate the combatants, disaggregate the community of hate. Lies, strategically employed, could help maintain small islands of trust in a sea of turbulent suspicion. Withdrawal, mutual dissociation, and deceit, however, were not stable solutions. Under conditions of political stability, individualism might promote dynamic and creative forms of social cooperation. (For example, the clashing of different perspectives might conceivably shed light on public issues and improve the quality of public decisions.) But France was a sovereignless nation, a country in upheaval. National consensus could not be fashioned by an accumulation of protective lies. While justifiable as a reaction to civil war, turning one's back on one's neighbor was inadequate as a political response.

31 Les "*Principes de politique*" *de Benjamin Constant*, p. 632; also see p. 499.

32 Hume, "That Politics May Be Reduced to a Science," *Essays: Moral, Political and Literary*, pp. 22–23. See also Duncan Forbes, *Hume's Philosophical Politics* (Cambridge: Cambridge University Press, 1975), pp. 224–30. On Montesquieu's belief that the English enjoyed moderate government without the benefit of personal moderation, see Judith Shklar, "Virtue in a Bad Climate: Good Men and Good Citizens in Montesquieu's *L'Esprit des lois*." in *Enlightenment Studies in Honor of Lester G. Crocker*, ed. Alfred J. Bingham and Virgil W. Topazio (Oxford: Voltaire Foundation, 1979), pp. 315–28.

33 Kant, "Zum ewigen Frieden," in *Kleinere Schriften*, p. 146.

34 Reprinted in *Recueil d'articles 1795–1817*, pp. 15–24. Aware that anonymity would safeguard his freedom of maneuver, Constant refrained from signing these letters.

35 "L'Universalité des citoyens français est le souverain." *Les Constitutions de la France depuis 1789*, ed. Jacques Godechot (Paris: Garnier-Flammarion, 1970), p. 103.

36 "Lettres à un député," *Recueil d'articles 1795–1817*, p. 22. After the fall of Robespierre, as Constant recalled in 1829, "Les membres de la Convention ... s'étaient mis à se dénoncer les uns les autres et à se faire expulser ou arrêter réciproquement" ("Mémoires inédits de B. Constant," in Jean-Jacques Coulmann, *Réminiscences* [Geneva: Slatkine, 1973], 3:45).

37 "Lettres à un député," *Recueil d'articles 1795–1817*, p. 20.

38 Compare: "dans les dissensions civiles les hommes finissent toujours par prendre les opinions dont on les accuse." Mme. de Staël, *Considérations sur les principaux événements de la Révolution française*, 2:178.

39 *Recueil d'articles 1795–1817*, pp. 20, 16.

40 *Force du gouvernement actuel de la France*, p. 61; *Fragmens d'un ouvrage abandonné*, Naf. 14363, fol. 205ª.

41 Les "*Principes de politique*" *de Benjamin Constant*, pp. 138–39; *Commentaire*

sur Filangieri, 1:71–81; *Suites de la contre-révolution en Angleterre,* p. 80.

42   *Commentaire sur Filangieri,* 1:188. Cf.: "les partis modérés conservent ce qui existe, mais ne peuvent rien établir; leur modération laisse trop de place à tous les calculs, à toutes les prétentions individuelles." *Du polythéisme romain,* 2:230.

43   Les *"Principes de politique"* de Benjamin Constant, p. 496.

44   "La Convention était en 95, comme le Sénat de Bonaparte en 1814, une digue de sang et de boue contre les partisans de l'ancien régime. C'était une vilaine digue, mais il ne fallait pas la renverser." "Mémoires inédits de B. Constant," in Coulmann, *Réminiscences,* 3:54.

45   *Force du gouvernement actuel de la France,* pp. 46, 43, 19–20, 3.

46   Etienne Hofmann, Les *"Principes de politique"* de Benjamin Constant. La *Genèse d'une oeuvre et l'évolution de la pensée de leur auteur (1786–1806),* pp. 103 and 112.

47   *Force du gouvernement actuel de la France,* p. 38.

48   Ibid., p. 11.

49   Ibid., p. 8.

50   "Des réactions politiques," *Ecrits et discours,* pp. 42, 43.

51   "Réflexions sur les constitutions," *Cours de politique,* 1:203 (cf. *Fragmens d'un ouvrage abandonné,* Naf. 14363, fol. 122[b]); "Des réactions politiques," *Ecrits et discours,* 1:79.

52   Niccolò Machiavelli, "Il Principe," chap. 7 in *Tutte le opere,* ed. Mario Martelli (Florence: Sansoni, 1971), p. 266.

53   Mathiez and others have described the *Force du gouvernement actuel* as an unabashed piece of political flattery penned by Constant in order to ingratiate himself with the Directorial regime. See Albert Mathiez, "Saint-Simon, Lauraguais, Barras, Benjamin Constant, etc., et la réforme de la Constitution de l'an III," *Annales historiques de la Révolution* 6 (1929): 5–23. The pamphlet does contain a subtle *theory* of political flattery and its moderating influence. But did it actually sooth the egos of the men in power? Without flinging quotable insults, Constant suggested that these men were vulgar, violent, infantile, stupid, and insecure. This was not especially flattering.

54   *Force du gouvernement actuel de la France,* pp. 8–9.

55   Ibid., pp. 102–03.

56   Les *"Principes de politique"* de Benjamin Constant, p. 150; "Des réactions politiques," *Ecrits et discours,* p. 50.

57   *Force du gouvernement actuel de la France,* p. 9.

58   Ibid., p. 8.

59   Joseph de Maistre, "Considérations sur la France," *Oeuvres complètes* (Lyon: Vitte, 1891), 1:41–54.

60   *Force du gouvernement actuel de la France,* pp. 11, 70.

61   Ibid., p. 9.

62   "Souvenirs historiques, I," *Revue de Paris* 9 (1830): 118; "Souvenirs historiques, II," ibid. 16 (1830): 107.

63   Alfred Cobban, *A History of Modern France,* 1:256; and Norman Hampson, *A Social History of the French Revolution* (Toronto: University of Toronto Press, 1965), p. 248; Patrice Higonnet, *Class, Ideology, and the Rights of*

Nobles during the French Revolution (Oxford: Oxford University Press, 1981), pp. 219–56.

64 The Directorial pamphlets have frequently been interpreted as political flattery aimed at securing citizenship for Constant and a passport for Mme. de Staël. See note 53.

65 *Force du gouvernement actuel de la France,* p. 85.

66 Pascal, *Oeuvres complètes,* ed. Jacques Chevalier (Paris: Pléiade, 1954), pp. 1216–17. See also Nannerl Keohane, *Philosophy and the State in France: The Renaissance to the Enlightenment* (Princeton: Princeton University Press, 1980), p. 273; "Adolphe," *Oeuvres,* p. 48; *Commentaire sur Filangieri,* 2:43–44.

67 David Hume, "Of Commerce," *Essays: Moral, Political and Literary,* p. 261; Montesquieu, *Oeuvres complètes,* 2:230.

68 "De la doctrine qui peut réunir les partis en France" (1816), *Cours de politique,* 2:286.

69 *Force du gouvernement actuel de la France,* p. 65.

70 Aristotle *Nichomachean Ethics* 1103.

71 "Cécile," *Oeuvres,* pp. 150–51; *Force du gouvernement actuel de la France,* p. 15.

72 Rousseau, "La Nouvelle Héloïse," *Oeuvres complètes,* 2:236.

73 Leo Gershoy, *The French Revolution and Napoleon* (New York: Appleton-Century-Crofts, 1933), p. 293.

74 "Mémoires inédits de B. Constant," in Coulmann, *Réminiscences,* 3:44.

75 *Fragmens d'un ouvrage abandonné,* Naf. 14363, fol. 126ᵃ (cf. "Réflexions sur les constitutions," *Cours de politique,* 1:212); *Fragmens d'un ouvrage abandonné,* Naf. 14363, fol. 126ᵃ; *Du polythéisme romain,* 2:41; article of April 1818, *Recueil d'articles 1817–1820,* 1:369.

76 *Recueil d'articles 1817–1820,* 1:291. Cf. "L'hypocrisie fut dans tous les temps plus persécutrice que la croyance" (speech of 14 April 1825, *Ecrits et discours* 2:81).

77 *Force du gouvernement actuel de la France,* pp. 83–84, 85.

78 Outside the *Principes de politique* of 1802–06, Constant's main discussion of Bentham can be found in "De l'obéissance à la loi," an article of 8 November 1817, *Recueil d'articles: Le Mercure, La Minerve et La Renommée,* 1: 317–28; reprinted as "Note V" to the "Réflexions sur les constitutions," *Cours de politique,* 1:347–56. A shortened version of this same text appears in "De M. Dunoyer, et de quelques-uns de ses ouvrages," in *Mélanges,* 1: esp. 122–27. Like Kant, Bentham drew a distinction between morality and legality ("Principles of Legislation," in *The Theory of Legislation,* ed. Upendra Baxi [Bombay: Tripathi, 1979], p 36). He, too, denied that the state had a right to "improve" citizens or enforce virtue. Constant also appreciated Bentham's persistent defense of toleration, freedom of the press, and the equal worth of all citizens. The principle of utility was essentially liberal because it decentralized the authority to define happiness, dispersing it into the hands of individuals (cf. Shirley Letwin, *The Pursuit of Certainty* [Cambridge: Cambridge University Press, 1965], pp. 127–88). The state must promote the greatest happiness of the greatest number, and happiness should be defined by unsupervised individuals in a variety of eccentric ways. Political officials

cannot prescribe obligatory goals or override diverse ideas of happiness on the grounds that wise statesmen must be their brothers' keepers. From a *political* point of view (and the restriction is essential), pushpin is as good as poetry. Governors must satisfy the wishes of the governed, not "lift" them above themselves. If political authorities can legitimately define happiness, resistance to governmental policy will be extremely difficult to justify. Constant found all this quite congenial.

79 Bentham, "Principles of the Civil Code," *Theory of Legislation*, p. 87; Letwin, *Pursuit of Certainty*, p. 153. Bentham's writings also substantiated the thesis that distrust of democratic rhetoric does not imply distrust of democratic government. With his mind on Robespierre, Constant repeatedly stressed Bentham's adage: "the name of the people is a signature counterfeited in order to justify their rulers" (*Les "Principes de politique" de Benjamin Constant*, pp. 114 and 519). His understanding of revolutionary language was heavily indebted to Bentham's discussion of "certain pompous maxims which are a mixture of truth and falsehood, and which give to a question, however simple, an air of depth and political mystery" ("Principles of the Civil Code," *Theory of Legislation,* p. 87). Bentham's individualism seemed a perfect antidote to inflated Jacobin rhetoric about "community" and the General Will. Here is a passage which Constant found especially relevant to revolutionary hyperbole in France: "The interest of individuals, it is said, ought to yield to the public interest. But what does that mean? . . . This public interest, which you introduce as a person, is only an abstract term; it represents nothing but the mass of individual interests" (Bentham, "Principles of the Civil Code," *Theory of Legislation,* p. 87).

80 "Principles of the Penal Code," ibid., pp. 259, 279, 256–57, 258.

81 James Madison also affirmed the "unavoidable inaccuracy" of political language. *The Federalist Papers*, No. 37 (New York: Mentor, 1961), p. 229.

82 Bentham, "Principles of Legislation," *Theory of Legislation*, pp. 49–52; "Anarchical Fallacies, being an Examination of the Declarations of Rights Issued during the French Revolution," in *The Works of Jeremy Bentham*, ed. J. Bowring (Edinburgh, 1843), 2:506.

83 *Commentaire sur l'ouvrage de Filangieri*, 1:65; cf. *Les "Principes de politique" de Benjamin Constant*, p. 94; *Commentaire sur l'ouvrage de Filangieri*, 1:65.

84 For a parallel argument, see John Rawls, *A Theory of Justice* (Cambridge, Mass.: Harvard University Press, 1971), p. 181; and Jon Elster, *Sour Grapes: Studies in the Subversion of Rationality*, pp. 91–100.

85 Bentham, "Principles of the Penal Code," *The Theory of Legislation*, pp. 266–71.

86 *Les "Principes de politique" de Benjamin Constant*, p. 60.

87 For a similar defense of rights against Bentham, see H. L. A. Hart, *Essays on Bentham: Jurisprudence and Political Theory* (Oxford: Oxford University Press, 1982), pp. 85–86.

88 *Suites de la contre-révolution en Angleterre* (1799) concludes with an appeal to recast the defective Constitution of the Year III (pp. 81–86).

CHAPTER 5

Epigraph: "De la liberté des brochures, des pamphlets et des journaux" (1814/1818), *Cours de politique,* 1:461.

1 For the negative view that "the object of constitutionalism" is exclusively "the limitation of all governmental power," see Friedrich Hayek, *The Constitution of Liberty* (Chicago: Gateway, 1972), p. 182.

2 Cf. "The separation of the judicial from the executive power seems originally to have arisen from the increasing business of society, in consequence of its increasing improvement." Adam Smith, *Wealth of Nations* (New York: Modern Library, 1937), p. 680.

3 Cf. "Montesquieu établit très bien ce qui devrait être, mais il ne donne aucun moyen pour que cela soit." *Fragmens d'un ouvrage abandonné* Naf. 14363, fol. 159ᵇ.

4 Ibid., fol. 61ᵇ.

5 He was able to do so because the framers of the Charte, in an effort to reconcile the old and the new France, left many important issues shrouded in ambiguity, including the relative importance of the king and the Chamber of Deputies.

6 Montesquieu, *Oeuvres complètes,* 2:304.

7 Aristotle *Politics* 1252a.7. For Aristotle, the best social order represented the fulfillment of man's "highest" inborn potentials.

8 Georg Jellinek, *Allgemeine Staatslehre* (1913) (Kronberg: Athenäum, 1976), pp. 246–50.

9 John Locke, *The Second Treatise of Government,* ed. Thomas Peardon (New York: Bobbs-Merrill, 1952), p. 71 (chap. ix, sec. 124). Locke defined *property,* in turn, in an extraordinarily broad manner. It included both life and liberty; but both of these were understood as means for the effective pursuit of further ends.

10 Like Montesquieu, Constant did not ultimately justify his adherence to the constitutional state by pointing to a set of natural "rights" that such a state must protect. Rights were crucial but not foundational. The state drew its legitimacy from a general public consciousness of a *summum malum*—for example, blood vengeance or religious civil war—that political officials succeed in avoiding or suppressing. Legitimate authority had no foundation on which it might be built, but only a problem it could solve.

11 David Hume, *A Treatise of Human Nature* (Oxford: Clarendon Press, 1967), p. 477ff. All students of European liberalism are indebted to John Mackie for his reconstruction of Hume's antiteleological theory of justice. J. L. Mackie, *Hume's Moral Theory* (London: Routledge and Kegan Paul, 1980), pp. 76–119.

12 Jürgen Habermas, *Theory and Practice* (Boston: Beacon Press, 1973), p. 42; Leo Strauss, *Natural Right and History* (Chicago: University of Chicago Press, 1953), p. 169 and passim.

13   Henry. G. Liddell and Robert Scott, eds., *A Greek-English Lexicon* (Oxford: Oxford University Press, 1940), p. 1434.

14   Aristotle *Politics* 1295ª.40-ᵇ1; Isocrates *Aereopag.* 14. Also see Victor Ehrenberg, *The Greek State* (New York: Norton, 1964), p. 39.

15   For a related distinction, see C. H. McIlwain, *Constitutionalism Ancient and Modern* (Ithaca, N.Y.: Cornell University Press, 1966), pp. 36–38.

16   For reasons to be examined, however, Constant found it very useful to stress the educative side-effects of citizen involvement.

17   "Eloge de Sir Samuel Romilly," delivered at the Paris Atheneum, 26 December 1818. Cited in Guy Dodge, *Benjamin Constant's Philosophy of Liberalism,* p. 110.

18   *Les "Principes de politique" de Benjamin Constant,* p. 620.

19   *Commentaire sur Filangieri,* 1:37 and 62. Paraphrasing Rousseau, the young Constant wrote: "Le genre humain est né sot et mené par des fripons, c'est la règle." Letter to Mme. de Charrière, 10 December 1790, reproduced in Gustave Rudler, *La Jeunesse de Benjamin Constant 1767–1794* (Paris: Armand Colin, 1908), p. 475.

20   The authors of *The Federalist Papers,* although they knew civil war only at second hand, concurred with Constant on most constitutional questions. Madison argued that the latent causes of disagreement and faction were sown in the nature of man (Alexander Hamilton, James Madison, John Jay, *The Federalist Papers* [New York: Mentor, 1961], p. 79). Similarly, Constant wrote: "On ne peut se flatter d'exclure les factions d'une République. Il faut donc travailler à les rendre les moins malfaisantes possibles, et comme elles doivent quelquefois être victorieuse, il faut d'avance prévenir ou adoucir les inconvéniens de leur victoire" (*Fragmens d'un ouvrage abandonné,* Naf. 14363, fol. 119ᵇ). While it is impossible to give men harmonious outlooks through civic education (the Rousseauist dream of producing social unanimity through an imposed morality is especially preposterous in modern times), it may still be possible to compensate for a permanent deficit in moral consensus by a shrewd outfitting of institutions. Even though public officials will not resemble angels, "inventions of prudence" (*The Federalist Papers,* p. 322) can take into account the most obvious human infirmities and actually put man's conflict-prone nature to good use.

21   *Fragmens d'un ouvrage abandonné,* Naf. 14363, fols. 34ª, 33ᵇ; "Réflexions sur les constitutions," *Cours de politique,* 1:187.

22   *Fragmens d'un ouvrage abandonné,* Naf. 14363, fols. 180a, 108b.

23   Ibid., fols. 7a, 32a, 31b.

24   Ibid., fol. 112ª; "Réflexions sur les constitutions," *Cours de politique,* 1:227; *Fragmens d'un ouvrage abandonné* Naf. 14363, fols. 31ᵇ–32ª.

25   "Toute société dans laquelle la garantie des droits n'est pas assurée, ni la séparation des pouvoirs déterminée, n'a point de constitution" (Article 15). Similarly, the Constitution of the Year III (1795): "La garantie sociale ne peut exister si la division des pouvoirs n'est pas établie" (Article 22). *Les Constitutions de la France depuis 1789,* ed. Jacques Godechot (Paris: Garnier-Flammarion, 1970), pp. 35 and 102. Cf. Montesquieu, *Oeuvres complètes,* 2:397.

26   *Fragmens d'un ouvrage abandonné,* Naf. 14363, fols. 33ª, 32ª.

27   Speech of 25 January 1801, reprinted in *Ecrits et discours,* 1:156–89.

28   Ibid., pp. 164–65, 159, 161; cf. speech of 5 January 1800, ibid., p. 148.

29   "Principes de politique" (1815), *Cours de politique,* 1:16; *Fragmens d'un ouvrage abandonné* Naf. 14363, fol. 32ᵃ.

30   "Réflexions sur les constitutions," *Cours de politique,* 1:271. Consider also: "il faut donner à toutes les autorités l'intérêt d'observer la constitution et de rester dans leurs limites." *Fragments d'un ouvrage abandonné,* Naf. 14363, fol. 187ᵃ.

31   *Fragmens d'un ouvrage abandonné,* Naf. 14363, fols. 55ᵃ, 180ᵃ, 87ᵇ; "Réflexions sur les constitutions," *Cours de politique,* 1:206.

32   *Fragmens d'un ouvrage abandonné,* Naf. 14363, fol. 94ᵇ.

33   "Réflexions sur les constitutions," *Cours de politique,* 1:201; *Fragmens d'un ouvrage abandonné,* Naf. 14363, fol. 169ᵃ.

34   "Additions et notes tirées en partie des Principes de politique et autres ouvrages antérieurs" (1818), *Cours de politique,* 1:308–18. Compare *Commentaire sur Filangieri,* 1:97.

35   *Mémoires sur les Cent-Jours,* pp. 155–60.

36   *Fragmens d'un ouvrage abandonné,* Naf. 14363, fol. 84ᵇ. "Montesquieu démontre parfaitement que l'idée de la division des pouvoirs politiques est restée toujours entièrement étrangère à l'Antiquité" (ibid.).

37   Cf. Crane Brinton, *A Decade of Revolution* (New York: Harper & Row, 1963), p. 127; Albert Goodwin, *The French Revolution* (New York: Harper & Row, 1966), pp. 148 and 158.

38   *Fragmens d'un ouvrage abandonné,* Naf. 14363, fols. 147ᵃ–148ᵃ.

39   Ibid., fol. 120ᵃ.

40   Ministers "ne peuvent être accusés que pour fait de trahison ou de concussion." *Constitutions de la France depuis 1789,* ed. Godechot, p. 223.

41   "Principes de politique" (1815), *Cours de politique,* 1:18.

42   Article of 5 January 1830, *Le Courrier français,* cited in Guy Dodge, *Benjamin Constant's Philosophy of Liberalism,* p. 91.

43   Here again Constant was much more progressive than Royer-Collard or Guizot. See M. J. C. Vile, *Constitutionalism and the Separation of Powers* (Oxford: Oxford University Press, 1967), pp. 202–06.

44   Constant's lack of sympathy for the Chambre introuvable and his recognition that a strict construction of the Charte was the liberals' best weapon against the ultras cannot be cited as evidence for his hostility to public opinion and legislative supremacy. Cf. Mary S. Hartman, "Benjamin Constant and the Question of Ministerial Responsibility in France, 1814–1815," *Journal of European Studies* 6 (1976): 248–61.

45   Cf. "The Liberals pretended to accept the Charter so as to embarrass the Ultras but really accepted neither the return of the Bourbons nor the Restoration." René Rémond, *The Right Wing in France from 1815 to De Gaulle* (Philadelphia: University of Pennsylvannia Press, 1966), p. 41.

46   Cf. "Les ministères ne sont remplacés alors, que lorsqu'ils ont perdu l'appui de l'opinion, et par suite, celui des Chambres" (speech of 13 March 1822, *Discours,* 2:112).

47   *Fragmens d'un ouvrage abandonné* Naf. 14363, fols. 161ᵇ, 91ᵇ.

48 "La faiblesse d'une partie quelconque du gouvernement est un mal." Ibid., fol. 33b; cf. "Réflexions sur les constitutions," *Cours de politique*, 1:173. Reflecting back on the Constitution of the Year III, Constant told Coulmann, "Les deux grands vices de cette Constitution étaient l'absence de la faculté, par le Directoire, de dissoudre l'un ou l'autre des Conseils et la réélection par tiers, le plus mauvais de tous les systèmes d'élection possibles. Le Directoire ne pouvant pas en appeler à la nation pour la consulter sur ses ennemis, fut obligé de mutiler les Conseils et d'en déporter les membres jusqu'au moment où les haines qu'il avait ainsi accumulées le renversèrent" ("Mémoires inédits de B. Constant," in Coulmann, *Réminiscences*, 3:53).

49 "Réflexions sur les constitutions," *Cours de politique*, 1:174; *Fragmens d'un ouvrage abandonné*, Naf. 14363, fol. 111a; "Réflexions sur les constitutions," *Cours de politique*, 1:268.

50 After 18 Fructidor, "Les dépositaires inquiets d'une autorité devenue illégale, étaient profondément avertis que cette autorité périrait, dès qu'elle cesserait d'être tyrannique." The Directorate knew it had committed "un grand délit politique." Thus, "il se croyait toujours en péril." *Fragmens d'un ouvrage abandonné*, Naf. 14364, fol. 7a, and Naf. 14363, fol. 91a.

51 Ibid., Naf. 14363, fol. 91a, Naf. 14364, fol. 7a.

52 "Réflexions sur les constitutions," *Cours de politique*, 1:214; *Fragmens d'un ouvrage abandonné*, Naf. 14363, fols. 141b–142a.

53 "Réflexions sur les constitutions," *Cours de politique*, 1:215.

54 Ibid., 1:214; *Fragmens d'un ouvrage abandonné*, Naf. 14363, fol. 142a; cf. *De la démocratie en Amérique*, ed. J. P. Mayer (Paris: Gallimard, 1961), 2:206–18 and passim, where Tocqueville argued—against his ultracist family and friends—that the internalization of repression can effectively replace old-style repression by hangmen and priests.

55 *Fragmens d'un ouvrage abandonné*, Naf. 14363, fol. 37a. He also spoke of creating interior counterweights against personal ambition: "Il faut établir contr'elle dans l'individu même le contrepoids d'un intérêt pressant" (ibid., Naf. 14364, fol. 8a).

56 "Réflexions sur les constitutions," *Cours de politique*, 1:221.

57 *Fragmens d'un ouvrage abandonné*, Naf. 14363, fol. 112a.

58 Ibid., fol. 113b; "Réflexions sur les constitutions," *Cours de politique*, 1:228. Hamilton used exactly the same argument to support the indefinite reeligibility of the American president. *The Federalist Papers*, pp. 437–38.

59 *Commentaire sur Filangieri*, 2:193.

60 Les *"Principes de politique" de Benjamin Constant*," p. 209.

61 "Réflexions sur les constitutions," *Cours de politique*, 1:190.

62 *Fragmens d'un ouvrage abandonné*, Naf. 14363, fol. 114a; Les *"Principes de politique" de Benjamin Constant*, p. 232; "Réflexions sur les constitutions," *Cours de politique*, 1:228.

63 Speech of 8 June 1824, *Discours*, 2:250.

64 "Réflexions sur les constitutions," *Cours de politique*, 1:225, 224.

65 *Commentaire sur Filangieri*, 2:58.

66 'Réflexions sur les constitutions," *Cours de politique*, 1:186. Cf. "Quand vos espions ne trouvent pas de coupables, ils en créent, quand ils ne peuvent pas

en créer, ils en inventent" (article of 12 July 1822, *Recueil d'articles 1820–1824*, p. 172).

67 Les "*Principes de politique*" de Benjamin Constant, p. 638; *Commentaire sur Filangieri*, 2:98.

68 In the *Fragmens*, Constant assigned the veto to the legislatively elected executive, while in the *Réflexions*, he gave this prerogative to the "neutral" monarch.

69 Les "*Principes de politique*" de Benjamin Constant, p. 186; cf. *Commentaire sur Filangieri*, 2: 204; Robespierre dismissed liberal concern for formal procedures as reflecting a lack of moral commitment: "Nous invoquons des formes, parce que nous n'avons pas de principes." *Oeuvres*, ed. Laponneraye (New York: Burt Franklin, 1970), 3:10.

70 Comparing the Polignac ministry with the Second Directory, Constant wrote: "Même dédain pour la liberté des élections . . . même nécessité prétendue de préserver les électeurs de leur propres excès, même monopole de sagesse et de lumières en faveur du pouvoir, mêmes appels à un principe alors dit républicain, occulte, indéfinissable, comme le principe dit aujourd'hui monarchique" ("Souvenirs historiques, II," *Revue de Paris* 16 (1830): 105).

71 "Principes de politique" (1815), *Cours de politique*, 1:33.

72 "Procès de MM. Benjamin Constant et Paul-Louis Courier" at the Tribunal de Police correctionnelle (14 November 1822), *Rec. 1820–1824*, p. 219. Constant admired British government despite its many faults, because "En Angleterre, la liberté de la discussion dans les assemblées représentatives est portée plus loin qu'elle ne l'a jamais été dans aucun autre pays." *Fragmens d'un ouvrage abandonné*, Naf. 14363, fol. 114ᵇ.

73 *Fragmens d'un ouvrage abandonné*, Naf. 14363, fol. 104ᵇ.

74 Speech of January 1800, *Ecrits et discours*, 1:139–41.

75 Speech of 1 February 1800, *Archives parlementaires*, 1:132–35.

76 Speech of 5 January 1800, *Ecrits et discours*, 1:140, 146.

77 Cf. George Sabine, "The Historical Position of Liberalism," *American Scholar* 10 (1940–41): 49–58.

78 "La liberté de rendre compte de vos séances tient à l'essence du gouvernement représentatif" (speech of 30 January 1822, *Discours*, 2:27–28; on the need to combine universal with particularistic perspectives, see Montesquieu, *Oeuvres complètes*, 2:399–400.

79 "Réflexions sur les constitutions," *Cours de politique*, 1:211.

80 This argument was part of a polemic against Cabanis and other Idéologues for whom lack of expertise was a sufficient reason for disenfranchising most citizens. For Constant's criticism of Cabanis's undemocratic reliance on political experts, see *Fragmens d'un ouvrage abandonné*, Naf. 14363, fols. 113ᵃ–114ᵇ.

81 Ibid., fol. 134ᵇ; "Réflexions sur les constitutions," *Cours de politique*, 1:210.

82 *Fragmens d'un ouvrage abandonné*, Naf. 14363, fol. 135ᵇ; Les "*Principes de politique*" de Benjamin Constant, p. 392; "Réflexions sur les constitutions," *Cours de politique*, 1:211.

83 "Une assemblée n'est pas juge de ses membres" because self-selection would violate popular sovereignty and *also* discourage government by discussion:

"tous les efforts des partis se dirigeront vers l'expulsion de leurs adversaires; leur répondre paraîtra moins sûr et moins facile que les chasser." *Fragmens d'un ouvrage abandonné*, Naf. 14363, fols. 98ᵇ and 100ᵃ.

84 Ibid., fols. 101ᵇ, 205ᵇ. In his republican constitution, Constant's main argument for a plural executive was that such a system encouraged government by discussion: "Un pouvoir exécutif complexe, nécessitant la discussion, conserve du raisonnement au moins les formes et l'habitude" (ibid., fol. 82ᵃ).

85 "Réflexions sur les constitutions," *Cours de politique*, 1:229; *Fragmens d'un ouvrage abandonné*, Naf. 14363, fols. 97ᵃ, 123ᵃ.

86 "Réflexions sur les constitutions," *Cours de politique*, 1:230.

87 Les "*Principes de politique*" de Benjamin Constant, pp. 138, 137, 141.

88 "De la liberté des brochures, des pamphlets et des journaux" (1814/1818), *Cours de politique*, 1:459–60; Les "*Principes de politique*" de Benjamin Constant, p. 137.

89 Hannah Arendt and Jürgen Habermas are wrong to suggest that, for liberalism, public debate is "only a means to protect society" or a "mere limit on violence" (Arendt, *The Human Condition* [Chicago: University of Chicago Press, 1958], p. 31; Habermas, *Strukturwandel der Offentlichkeit* [Berlin and Neuwied, 1971], p. 166). For classical liberals, such as Constant and Mill, public discussion had a creative, not merely a defensive, function. Here, Constant parted company with his *politique* ancestors. He saw popular sovereignty, not merely as a technique for arresting civil war, but also as a means of organizing the nation. National disagreements could be domesticated and rendered creative through public debate. Constant was no ultranationalist. By later standards, he remained bloodlessly cosmopolitan. But he believed in sustaining a limited national venture through the sovereign power of public discussion.

90 Voltaire, "Lettres philosophiques," *Mélanges*, ed. Jacques van den Heuvel (Paris: Pléiade, 1961), p. 21.

91 In the "Principes" of 1815, he performed the same service for a briefly restored Napoleon.

92 "Réflexions sur les constitutions," *Cours de politique*, 1:181; cf., *Fragmens d'un ouvrage abandonné*, Naf. 14363, fol. 188ᵃ; *Commentaire sur Filangieri*, 1:91.

93 *Fragmens d'un ouvrage abandonné*, Naf. 14363, fol. 131ᵃ; "Réflexions sur les constitutions," *Cours de politique*, 1:207–08.

94 It was this more comprehensive conception of neutrality that associated Constant's idea of a *pouvoir neutre* with James Madison's claim, published in 1787, that "sovereignty" should be rendered "neutral between different interests and factions." *The Mind of the Founder*, ed. Marvin Meyers (Indianapolis: Bobbs-Merrill, 1973), p. 91.

95 "Du discours de M. de Marchangy" (1818), *Cours de politique*, 2:15.

96 *Commentaire sur Filangieri*, 2:107.

97 Referring to the Jacobin attempt to legislate morality, Constant wrote: "C'est en confondant ainsi le but de la législation et celui de la morale, qu'on a donné à la législation l'extension qui est devenue si funeste" (Les "*Principes de politique*" de Benjamin Constant, p. 524). To secure social peace, some questions must be placed beyond politics, beyond the competence of political

officials. Constitutionalism must thus draw the difficult-to-draw boundaries of the political; it must (to some extent) depoliticize morals and de-moralize politics.

98 *De la religion,* 1:108.

99 For glory-seekers, convulsionaries, and even "possessive individualists" of a precapitalist sort, the peacekeeping state was not neutral. But for most others it was neutral enough. It provided a framework compatible with the lives of those individuals whose goals presupposed common survival. See Thomas Hobbes, *Leviathan* (Oxford: Oxford University Press, 1965), p. 116.

100 For an argument against the possibility of "the state's total neutrality," see Brian Barry, *Political Argument* (London: Routledge and Kegan Paul, 1965), p. 75ff.; William Galston also asserts that "neutrality . . . is never possible" in "Defending Liberalism," *The American Political Science Review* 76, no. 3 (September 1982): 627.

101 Speech of 5 May 1819, *Discours,* 1:87.

102 In his own eyes, Constant's gravest political error had been his decision to support the coup of Fructidor without afterward seeking a revision of the constitution. The speech he delivered at the Constitutional Circle (16 September 1797), twelve days after the coup, was a plea against arbitrary government and for a strict observation of formal procedures. Nevertheless, he justified the illegal annulment of the recent elections on the grounds that the newly elected deputies were royalists intent on using the constitution to overthrow the constitution. The idea of a temporary dictator, able to act outside the law in order to save the Republic, had a long tradition (cf. Machiavelli, "Discorsi," bk. 1, chap. 33, *Tutte le opere,* pp. 114–16; Rousseau, "Du contract social," bk. 4, chap. 6, *Oeuvres complètes,* 3:455–58). Constant picked up on this idea, justifying the coup by focusing on the limits of governmental neutrality: "Let us not confuse impartiality with justice. Justice is a duty for governors; impartiality is but madness and crime. To make liberty function, we must be partisans of liberty. When we see liberty on one side and its enemies on the other, we must not make the imbecile boast of knowing how to remain in the middle" (*Ecrits et discours,* 1:119). A constitutional government cannot be neutral toward anticonstitutional forces trying to destroy it. But Constant soon became convinced that extraconstitutional measures could never preserve a constitutional regime. The myth of "republican dictatorship" was another false legacy of antiquity (cf. "Si la Charte renfermait la possibilité de la dictature, la Charte serait un non-sens, une illusion," speech of 16 February 1822, *Discours,* 2:92). When a liberal government finds itself faced with the choice of being defeated by anticonstitutional forces or making use of extraconstitutional measures, it is already lost. The secret of liberal government is to avoid getting maneuvered into this hopeless situation.

103 "De l'état constitutionnel de la France," article of 15 June 1819, *Recueil d'articles: Le Mercure, la Minerve et la Renommée,* 2:1232.

104 "C'est par des faits que j'aime à répondre aux assertions dogmatiques" (*Commentaire sur Filangieri,* 2:292; compare Voltaire's adage: "*Au fait!* est ma devise." Letter of 1 August 1739, cited in Peter Gay, *Voltaire's Politics,* p. 3; speeches of 13 March 1822 and 1 February 1800; *Discours,* 2: 111; *Archives*

parlementaires, 1:132. "Sur la loi d'exception contre la liberté de la Presse" (1820), *Discours*, 1:247; *Commentaire sur Filangieri*, 2:12ff., 88. As these passages suggest, social science was born out of the needs of representative government, not from the spirit of reaction (cf. Robert Nisbet, "Conservatism," *A History of Sociological Analysis*, ed. Tom Bottomore and Robert Nisbet [New York: Basic Books, 1978], pp. 88–118).

105 Theorists who wished to invest unlimited powers of moral education in the government were not morally culpable but unrealistic: "On suppose d'abord que le gouvernement sera tel qu'on le désire. On voit toujours en lui un allié, sans réfléchir qu'il peut devenir un ennemi. L'on ne sent pas que les sacrifices qu'on impose aux individus peuvent ne pas tourner au profit de l'institution que l'on croit parfaite, mais au profit d'une institution quelconque" (*Commentaire sur Filangieri* 2:237). Each party in France should imagine what constitution it would desire on the assumption that its enemies might come to power. This thought-experiment was profoundly realistic, Constant believed, and it would increase support for a limited government, one that strove for neutrality in questions of moral dispute.

106 "De la liberté des brochures, des pamphlets et des journaux," *Cours de politique*, 1:448.

107 "Du discours de M. de Marchangy" (1818), *Cours de politique* 2:15.

108 "Fragmens sur la France, du 14 juillet 1789 au 31 mars 1814," *Mélanges*, 1:67.

109 *Mélanges*, 1:iv–v.

110 *Commentaire sur Filangieri*, 1:106ff.

111 Norman Gash, *Aristocracy and People* (London: Edward Arnold, 1979), p. 152.

112 Seeking a third alternative between popular sovereignty and royal sovereignty, the Doctrinaires affirmed a nebulous "sovereignty of reason" or "sovereignty of the constitution." Gabriel Rémond, *Royer-Collard. Son essai d'un système politique* (Paris: Sirey, 1933), pp. 35–42; Douglas Johnson, *Guizot: Aspects of French History 1787–1874* (London: Routledge & Kegan Paul, 1963), pp. 37–42. In general, it is safe to say that the Doctrinaires favored a representative and constitutional monarchy with guarantees against democratic developments, while Constant advocated a parliamentary system open to democratic reform. In 1814, when the Bourbons were first restored and royalists were again brandishing the archaic doctrine of divine right, Constant wrote that discussions of "the origin of sovereignty" were "dangerous" and "useless" ("Réflexions sur les constitutions," *Cours de politique*, 1:174). During the Hundred Days, he publicly affirmed the sovereignty of the people ("Principes de politique" [1815], *Cours de politique*, 1:7–8). He reprinted a somewhat milder but still explicit version of this affirmation in the additions to the "Réflexions" published in 1818 ("Additions et notes" [1818], *Cours de politique*, 1:275–87).

113 ". . . Dans les principes de la liberté, c'est-à-dire, dans toute constitution qui reconnoit pour origine la volonté nationale. . . ." *Fragmens d'un ouvrage abandonné*, Naf. 14363, fol. 34ᵃ.

114 *Les "Principes de politique" de Benjamin Constant*, p. 397.

115 "Nul . . . n'est le représentant de ses concitoyens, que lorsque ses concitoyens lui ont donné mission de les représenter" and "Ni le gouvernement, ni le corps représentatif même ne peuvent s'arroger la faculté de juger la capacité ou la moralité des elus." *Fragmens d'un ouvrage abandonné*, Naf. 14363, fols. 122ᵃ and 99ᵃ; cf. 128ᵃ.

116 Réflexions sur les constitutions, *Cours de politique*, 1:187–90.

117 *Fragmens d'un ouvrage abandonné*, Naf. 14363, fol. 120ᵇ.

118 For example, "le paiement de 300 francs de contributions directes, suppose incontestablement un revenu trop élevé" (article of 18 January 1817, *Recueil d'articles: Le Mercure, la Minerve, et la Renommée*, 1:40); "l'abaissement du cens est indispensable" (speech of 7 August 1830, *Archives parlementaires*, 63:74); cf. speech of 6 April 1829, *Ecrits et discours*, 2:130, 134.

119 "Réflexions sur les constitutions," *Cours de politique*, 1:251.

120 Ibid., p. 255.

121 In England, Montesquieu had written, *all* inhabitants of a district should have a right to vote at the election of a representative, "excepté ceux qui sont dans un tel état de bassesse, qu'ils sont reputés n'avoir point de volonté propre." Montesquieu, *Oeuvres complètes*, 2:400.

122 "Réflexions sur les constitutions," *Cours de politique*, 1:216.

123 Les *"Principes de politique" de Benjamin Constant*, p. 221.

124 Speech of 6 April 1829, *Ecrits et discours*, 2:136.

125 *Fragmens d'un ouvrage abandonné*, Naf. 14363, fols. 17ᵃ, 51ᵃ.

126 "Réflexions sur les constitutions," *Cours de politique*, 1:235 and 238.

127 Quoted in ibid, 2:236.

128 In the 1818 reissue of "Réflexions sur les constitutions," Constant publicly acknowledged that he had been mistaken to restrict the vote to owners of land. Industrial property was even more important in the modern age than landed property. Unfortunately, this liberal-minded reversal introduced an additional difficulty into his argument for a restricted definition of the *pays légal*. On his own account, modern industrial property left its owners with little free time: not leisure but agitation characterized their lives. Thus, the inevitable shift from landed to industrial property drastically weakened Constant's rationale for restricting the vote to the propertied.

129 *Fragmens d'un ouvrage abandonné*, Naf. 14364, fol. 26ᵇ.

130 Ibid., Naf. 14363, fol. 123ᵃ; cf. fols. 89ᵃ and 124ᵃ.

131 Ibid., 87ᵃ.

132 Ibid., 162ᵃ.

133 "Réflexions sur les constitutions," *Cours de politique*, 1:254.

134 Cf. "La crainte de perdre ce qu'on a rend tout aussi pusillanime ou aussi furieux que l'espoir d'acquérir ce qu'on n'a pas." Les *"Principes de politique" de Benjamin Constant*, p. 207.

135 When he actually attempted a theoretical reply to the proponents of universal manhood suffrage, Constant showed signs of tripping over his own feet: "It will be objected perhaps that in according . . . political rights to proprietors alone, I diminish the advantage of the representative system. But, (1) I grant these rights to possessors of such modest holdings that they will always be, despite their properties, in at least a relative if not an absolute dependence

on the opulent classes; (2) there does not exist between the small proprietors and the nonproprietors a line of demarcation such that the rich can reconcile the first while oppressing the second. The nonproprietors, the artisans in the market towns and the villages and the day laborers in the hamlets, are all relatives of proprietors. They will make common cause against the oppressor. It is therefore necessary to treat them all with care and concern in order to obtain the vote of those who have the franchise. In this way property will be respected and the concern owed to the indigent will acquire a guarantee." (See "Réflexions sur les constitutions," *Cours de politique*, 1:212: this passage first appears in *Fragmens d'un ouvrage abandonné*, Naf. 14363, fols. 126ᵃ–126ᵇ; *Les "Principes de politique" de Benjamin Constant*, p. 394.) If Constant's modest property-owners were still dependent on the rich, their autonomy was compromised; and Constant's argument from independence is undermined.

136 Alan B. Spitzer, "Restoration Political Theory and the Debate over the Law of the Double Vote," *Journal of Modern History* 55 (March 1983): 55.

137 Speech of 18 September 1830, *Archives parlementaires*, 63: 485.

138 *Du polythéisme romain*, 2:15; *Mémoires sur les Cent-Jours*, p. 4; speech of 9 February 1822, *Discours*, 2:72; 2:560.

139 "Anciens et modernes," *Cours de politique*, 2:560.

140 Constant's argument at the end of "Ancient and Modern Liberty" was echoed in Mill's *Considerations on Representative Government* (1861). Mill's thesis was that liberal democracy is the government best able to fulfill three functions: protecting the interests of citizens; improving their intellect and moral sentiments; and enlisting the intelligence and imagination of all members of the community to solve common problems. (On the second function of liberal government, see Dennis Thompson, *John Stuart Mill and Representative Government* [Princeton: Princeton University Press, 1976], pp. 36–53; on the third function, see Samuel H. Beer, "The Strengths of Liberal Democracy," in *A Prospect for Liberal Democracy*, ed. William Livingston [Austin: University of Texas Press, 1979], pp. 215–29.) Like Constant, Mill argued explicitly against the disenfranchisement of citizens on grounds of purported incompetence.

141 *Fragmens d'un ouvrage abandonné*, Naf. 14363, fols. 100ᵃ, 59ᵃ, 149ᵇ.

142 "Anciens et modernes," *Cours de politique*, 2:545.

CHAPTER 6

Epigraph: Friedrich Schiller, *Über die ästhetische Erziehung des Menschen* (Stuttgart: Philipp Reclam, 1973), p. 18.

1 "Lettres de Benjamin Constant à Prosper de Barante, 1805–1830," *Revue des deux mondes* 34 (1906): 549.

2 Carl Schmitt, *Ex Captivitate Salus* (Cologne: Greven, 1950), p. 76; *Verfassungslehre* (Berlin: Duncker und Humblot, 1928), p. 201; *Politische Romantik* (Berlin: Duncker und Humblot, 1925), p. 209.

3   Cited in Lothar Gall, *Benjamin Constant* (Wiesbaden: Steiner, 1963), p. 87.

4   "Il existe un traditionalisme, un socialisme, un nationalisme romantiques. Mais le libéralisme français apparaît longtemps—et peut-être encore aujourd'hui—comme imperméable au romantisme." Jean Touchard, *Histoire des idées politiques* (Paris: Presses Universitaires de France, 1965), 2:515.

5   "Adolphe," in *Oeuvres*, p. 9; "Conquête et usurpation," *Cours de politique*, 2:278. Cf. Mme. de Staël, *Considérations sur les principaux événements de la Révolution française*, 2:198.

6   *De la religion*, 1:27, 3; 3:29; "De Madame de Staël, et de ses ouvrages," *Mélanges*, 1:151.

7   *Commentaire sur Filangieri*, 1:72; "Conquête et usurpation," *Cours de politique*, 2:147; "Anciens et modernes," ibid., p. 559.

8   Novalis, *Werke*, ed. G. Schulz (Munich: Beck, 1969), p. 400; Friedrich Schleiermacher, *Monologen* (Hamburg: Felix Meiner, 1978), p. 59; Johann Gottlieb Fichte, *Die Grundzüge des gegenwärtigen Zeitalters* (Hamburg: Felix Meiner, 1956), p. 149; Adam Müller, *Die Elemente der Staatskunst* (Berlin: Sander, 1809), 1:51; Friedrich Schiller, *Über die ästhetische Erziehung des Menschen*, pp. 11–15. For political romanticism in general, see Friedrich Meinecke, *Cosmopolitanism and the National State* (Princeton: Princeton University Press, 1970).

9   Novalis, "Christendom or Europe," *The Political Thought of the German Romantics 1793–1815*, ed. Hans Reiss (Oxford: Blackwell, 1955), pp. 128 and 129.

10   Ibid., p. 127.

11   J. L. Talmon, *Romanticism and Revolt: Europe 1814–1848* (New York: Norton, 1967), p. 148.

12   "De la tragédie de Wallstein, par Schiller," *Mélanges*, 2:23; Novalis, "Christendom or Europe," p. 141.

13   Schiller, *Ästhetische Erziehung*, pp. 8, 125, 37, 18–19, 68.

14   Ibid., pp. 56, 127–28; it is tempting to respond that the Greeks themselves conceived of freedom quite unromantically as a condition awarded or withheld at birth, not as an ideal toward which men must ceaselessly strive.

15   Ibid., pp. 9, 91, 24–25, 63, 81.

16   Ibid., pp. 20–21.

17   Ibid., pp. 23, 84, 126, 27, 128, 32–33.

18   Novalis, *Werke*, p. 358.

19   "Journaux intimes," 27 May and 5 November 1804, in *Oeuvres*, pp. 277, 370.

20   Les *"Principes de politique" de Benjamin Constant*, p. 554. And consider once again a passage cited above: "Il faut que les institutions achèvent l'éducation morale des citoyens" ("Anciens et modernes," *Cours de politique*, 2:560).

21   *Force du gouvernement actuel de la France*, pp. 80–81.

22   Ibid., p. 81; Les *"Principes de politique" de Benjamin Constant*, p. 398; "Réflexions sur les constitutions," *Cours de politique*, 1:204.

23   Cf. Kurt Kloocke, "Benjamin Constant et les débuts de la pensée nihiliste en Europe," *Benjamin Constant, Madame de Staël et le groupe de Coppet*, ed.

Etienne Hofmann (Oxford: The Voltaire Foundation, 1982), pp. 182–220.

24 Letter of 4 June 1790, cited in Gustave Rudler, *La Jeunesse de Benjamin Constant (1767–1794* (Paris: Armand Colin, 1908), p. 376. Much later, he wrote the following about a novel under review: "On y rencontre des aperçus très-ingénieux sur la vie humaine. Ces aperçus sont tristes, cela doit être, puisqu'ils sont vrais" (article of 30 July 1821, *Recueil d'articles 1820–1824,* p. 64); similarly, "Fait-on autre chose dans la vie que de remplacer la douleur par la douleur?" (letter of 29 April 1802, "Lettres de Benjamin Constant à Fauriel," in Victor Glachant, *Benjamin Constant sous l'oeil du guet,* p. 39).

25 Number 13 signified "incertitude sur tout." *Oeuvres,* pp. 486–87.

26 Letter of 4 June 1790, in Rudler, *La Jeunesse de Benjamin Constant,* p. 377.

27 "Nous ne nous arrêterons pas aussi à examiner les fins que Dieu s'est proposées en créant le monde, et nous rejetterons entièrement de notre philosophie la recherche des causes finales" (Descartes, "Les Principes de la philosophie," *Oeuvres et lettres,* ed. André Bridoux [Paris: Pléiade, 1953], pp. 583–84).

28 Novalis, "Christendom or Europe," pp. 137, 138, 133.

29 *De la religion,* 2:466–67.

30 Article of 18 January 1817, *Recueil d'articles: Le Mercure, la Minerve, la Renommée,* 1:33, 31–32.

31 "Conquête et usurpation," *Cours de politique,* 2:163; "De la doctrine politique qui peut réunir les partis en France," ibid., p. 278.

32 "Conquête et usurpation," ibid., p. 146.

33 Charles Taylor, "What's Wrong with Negative Liberty," in *The Idea of Freedom,* ed. Alan Ryan (Oxford: Oxford University Press, 1979), p. 187.

34 "Adolphe," *Oeuvres,* pp. 13, 48; Cf. Mme. de Staël, *De l'Allemagne* (Paris: Garnier-Flammarion, 1968), 2:301–16.

35 Rousseau, "La Nouvelle Héloïse," *Oeuvres complètes,* 2:232–36; "Discours sur les sciences et les arts," ibid., 3:8; "Emile," ibid., 4:515; "Lettre à Christophe de Beaumont," ibid., 4:966. "Journaux intimes," 1 December 1804, *Oeuvres,* p. 385.

36 "Journaux intimes," 1 December 1804, *Oeuvres,* p. 385. Emerson offered a more romantic view: "Every man alone is always sincere. At the entrance of a second person, hypocrisy begins." *Emerson's Essays,* ed. Irwin Edman (New York: Harper, 1951), pp. 145–46.

37 "Journaux intimes," 18 December 1804, *Oeuvres,* p. 394.

38 "Journaux intimes," 12 June 1804, *Oeuvres,* p. 285; cf. "Les autres sont les autres, on ne fera jamais qu'ils soient soi. . . . Il y a entre nous et ce qui n'est pas nous une barrière insurmontable" (ibid., 18 December 1804, *Oeuvres,* p. 394).

39 Les *"Principes de politique"* de Benjamin Constant, p. 110; "Journaux intimes," 6 June 1804, *Oeuvres,* p. 282; ibid., 5 November 1804, *Oeuvres,* p. 370.

40 Cf. Blandine Barret-Kriegel, *L'Etat et les esclaves* (Paris: Calmann-Levy, 1979), pp. 193–206.

41 The same argument might be made about Constant's "refus d'unifier politique et amour" (Tzvetan Todorov, "Benjamin Constant, politique et amour," *Poétique* 56 [November 1983], p. 510).

42 *Du polythéisme romain,* 1:80–81.

43 Victor Hugo, originally a romantic conservative, eventually came to define Romanticism quite simply as "liberalism in literature." *Oeuvres complètes* (Paris, 1880), 22:1–4.

44 *De la religion,* 1:xix, xx; *Du polythéisme romain,* 2:81, 91–92.

45 Ibid., pp. xxiv, xxix, xxx, xxxii, xl.

46 Ibid., p. 235; speech of 8 June 1824, *Discours,* 2:250; François de la Rochefoucauld, *Maximes* (Paris: Garnier, 1967), p. 15; cf. *Commentaire sur Filangieri,* 1:298; *du polythéisme romain* 1:71.

47 *Mélanges,* 1:iii. Constant retitiled *Wallenstein* as *Wallstein.*

48 "Du théâtre français et du théâtre étranger," article of 13 December 1817, *Recueil d'articles: Le Mercure, la Minerve, la Renommée,* 1:335.

49 "De la tragédie de Wallstein, par Schiller," *Mélanges,* 2:21.

50 According to Victor Klemperer, French Romantics always retained a sobering sense of limits and never followed their German counterparts in "die völlige und dauernde Entgrenzung." See "Romantik und französische Romantik," *Begriffsbestimmung der Romantik,* ed. Helmut Prang (Darmstadt: Wissenschaftlichebuchgesellschaft, 1972), p. 69.

51 "De la tragédie de Wallstein, par Schiller," *Mélanges,* 2:41–42, 44–45.

52 Ibid., p. 40; "Réflexions sur la tragédie," *Oeuvres,* p. 905.

53 "Réflexions sur la tragédie," *Oeuvres,* pp. 905–06.

54 Ibid., pp. 906–08.

55 "La liberté de la presse, je l'ai défendue sous tous les gouvernemens; car il ne faut pas se tromper sur les mots de république, d'empire et de monarchie; tous les gouvernemens sont ennemis de cette liberté, tous s'attachent à la détruire" (speech of 13 February 1827, *Discours,* 2:539; see also *Force du gouvernement actuel de la France,* p. 98; and the "Avant-propos" of 1819 to "Des réactions politiques," in *Cours de politique,* 2:70).

56 *Force du gouvernement actuel de la France,* p. 101.

57 "De la tragédie de Wallstein, par Schiller," *Mélanges,* 2:27 (Robert Nisbet claims oddly that the basic tenet of liberalism is "the innate stability of the individual." *The Sociological Tradition* [New York: Basic Books, 1966], p. 9); *Force du gouvernement actuel de la France,* p. 28.

58 The image of ancient citizens "recognizing themselves" in their city was useful as a foil against which to denounce the inequality of ranks and the servile dependency characteristic of the religiously based, old-regime monarchy. It became "romantic" only when it was conceived (as it was by Rousseau) as a communitarian reproach to the secular, bourgeois order and to the cold constitutional state, administered bureaucratically and based on equality before the law.

59 Article of 3 November 1818, *Recueil d'articles: Le Mercure, la Minerve, la Renommée,* 1:578; letter of 8 November 1815, *Lettres à Madame Récamier (1807–1830),* p. 277; cf. *Ecrits et discours,* 1:188; Menos, p. 512; more painfully: "Je ne parle avec personne que du bout des lèvres" ("Journaux intimes," 1 June 1804, *Oeuvres,* p. 279).

60 "Du Discours de M. de Marchangy" (1818), *Cours de politique,* 2:17–18.

61 Charles Taylor, *Hegel* (Cambridge: Cambridge University Press, 1975), pp. 544, 541.

62 Fichte, *Die Grundzüge des gegenwärtigen Zeitalters,* pp. 24, 29. The only virtue modern citizens know, according to Fichte, is the pursuit of personal advantage; the only vice they acknowledge is failure in this pursuit. The organic bonds of traditional society have snapped. Modern society is but a loose assemblage: "a whole pieced together out of parts." History should be judged in black and white categories, as a struggle between "the noble" and the "ignoble," of sinister egoism against healthy community. Fichte defined his moral mission as the preparation of men for a new age in which organic togetherness would be restored. Displaying contempt for his puny contemporaries, he formulated his own ethical code: "there is only one virtue, to forget oneself as a person, and only one vice, to think about oneself." Politically, this implied a complete erasure of the boundary between public and private—that is to say, a repudiation of the liberal ideal of simultaneously occupying public and private roles. No individual can set himself a goal that is not identical with the *Gesamtzweck,* the goal of the community. In the "perfect state" all legitimate individual purposes will be included in the purposes of the state and the community will provide for their realization (ibid., pp. 34, 29, 39, 38, 157, 153–54). It was a short step from this conviction to the nationalism of the *Addresses to the German Nation.*

63 "Journaux intimes," 27 May 1804, *Oeuvres,* p. 277.

64 Excellent on the differences between Schiller and Humboldt is Robert Leroux, "Schiller, Théoricien de l'Etat," *Revue germanique* 28 (January-March 1937): 1–28.

65 Wilhelm von Humboldt, *The Limits of State Action* (Cambridge: Cambridge University Press, 1969), p. 26.

66 *Commentaire sur Filangieri,* 2:43; 1:73, 74; 2:117.

67 "De la tragédie de Wallstein, par Schiller," *Mélanges,* 2:22.

68 Humboldt, *Limits of State Action,* p. 17; *Force du gouvernement actuel de la France,* p. 61; *Mélanges,* 1:ii; "Lettres à Prosper de Barante," *Revue des deux mondes* 34 (1906): 262–63; *De la religion,* 3:28; "Adolphe," *Oeuvres,* p. 14; cf. "Je ne m'intéresse guère plus à moi qu'aux autres" ("Journaux intimes," 28 October 1804, ibid., p. 361); similarly: "écrire des mémoires me répugne. . . . Je ne m'intéresse pas assez à moi pour en occuper si longuement les autres" ("Souvenirs historiques, I," *Revue de Paris* 9 (1830): 116).

69 Humboldt, *Limits of State Action,* p. 16; "Lettres à Prosper de Barante," p. 534; "Journaux intimes," 11 April 1804, *Oeuvres,* pp. 256–57.

70 Schiller, *Über die ästhetische Erziehung des Menschen,*" p. 27.

71 "Cécile," *Oeuvres,* p. 179; "Journaux intimes," 16 September 1812, *Oeuvres,* p. 662.

72 "Adolphe," in *Oeuvres,* p. 23; article of 15 October 1818, *Recueil d'articles: Le Mercure, la Minerve, la Renommée,* 1:557; letter of 1 February 1796 (dated by editor), Mélégari, p. 250.

73 One could say that Constant rejected both sides of the romantic advice: "strive to be a whole, and if you fail, join a whole." Cited in Sheldon Wolin, *Politics and Vision* (Boston: Little Brown, 1960), p. 401.

74 Isaiah Berlin, *Four Essays on Liberty* (Oxford: Oxford University Press, 1969), p. xlv. The belief that liberalism is hostile to democracy has been exacerbated

by a confusing usage of the term *positive liberty*. In his classic reformulation of Constant's distinction, Isaiah Berlin employs "positive liberty" indiscriminately to refer to democratic self-government and the realization of the real self. This confusion of two quite distinct concepts has enabled antiliberals to cite the liberal distrust of the idea of a "real self" as evidence for liberalism's purportedly antidemocratic tendencies. But popular government and romantic authenticity are unrelated logically, psychologically, and historically.

75 "Réflexions sur la tragédie," *Oeuvres*, pp. 921–22.

76 Letter of 29 January 1814, Menos, p. 512; *Les "Principes de politique" de Benjamin Constant*, p. 432.

77 *Les "Principes de politique" de Benjamin Constant*, p. 482. For example, a liberally organized legal system will not compel children and wives to testify against their parents and husbands.

78 "Journaux intimes," 18 August 1804, *Oeuvres*, p. 321.

79 *Les "Principes de politique" de Benjamin Constant*, p. 428, 443, 430.

80 Arthur Lovejoy, *The Great Chain of Being* (New York: Harper, 1965), p. 250. Alasdair MacIntyre unconvincingly assumes that he can reject Aristotle's doctrine of the "unity of the virtues" and still remain an Aristotelian. *After Virtue* (Notre Dame, Ind.: University of Notre Dame Press, 1981), p. 168.

81 Lovejoy, *The Great Chain of Being*, pp. 304–08.

82 Friedrich Schiller, "The Legislation of Lycurgus and Solon," *An Anthology for Our Time* (New York: Ungar, 1959), pp. 156, 158, 157.

83 Introducing an infinite variety of choiceworthy goals would enrich man; it would not, as some neo-Aristotelians suggest, debase him to the status of a pleasure-pain machine.

84 Schiller, *Über die ästhetische Erziehung des Menschen*, p. 22.

85 Robespierre, *Oeuvres*, 3:190.

86 *Commentaire sur Filangieri*, 1:56–59.

87 *Les "Principes de politique" de Benjamin Constant*, pp. 521, 482.

88 "Principes de politique" (1815), *Cours de politique*, 1:144; "Conquête et usurpation," ibid., 2:269; "Anciens et modernes," ibid., p. 555; speech of 13 May 1821, *Discours*, 1:517; article of 11 October 1817, *Recueil d'articles: Le Mercure, la Minerve, la Renommée*, 1:316.

89 *De la religion*, 1:xl; Benjamin et Rosalie de Constant, *Correspondance 1786–1830*, p. 216.

90 "Journaux intimes," 15 April 1804, *Oeuvres*, p. 259; "Conquête et usurpation," *Cours de politique*, 2:207.

CHAPTER 7

Epigraph: Letter of 17 July 1816, Menos, p. 543.

1 Karl Löwith, *Meaning in History* (Chicago: University of Chicago Press, 1949); Carl Becker, *The Heavenly City of the Eighteenth-Century Philosophers* (New Haven: Yale University Press, 1932); John Passmore, *The Perfectibility of*

Man (New York: Scribner's, 1970); Karl Popper, *The Poverty of Historicism* (London: Routledge and Kegan Paul, 1961).

2 J. L. Talmon, *The Origins of Totalitarian Democracy* (New York: Norton, 1970), pp. 132–35.

3 Peter Gay, *The Enlightenment* (New York: Norton, 1962), 2:92–125; Gay also emphasizes the realistic and reformist dimensions of the Enlightenment concept of progress.

4 Condorcet, *Esquisse d'un tableau historique des progrès de l'esprit humain* (Paris: Vrin, 1970), p. 238.

5 Cf., on the difference between Voltaire and Condorcet, Friedrich Meinecke, *Historism* (London: Routledge and Kegan Paul, 1972), pp. 144–45.

6 "The term perfectible . . . not only does not imply the capacity of being brought to perfection, but stands in express opposition to it" (William Godwin, *Enquiry concerning Political Justice*, ed. Isaac Kramnick [Harmondsworth: Penguin, 1976], p. 145).

7 For a more broadly conceived attempt to defend the concept of progress against its antiliberal critics, see Hans Blumenberg, *The Legitimacy of the Modern Age* (Cambridge: MIT Press, 1983), pp. 3–120.

8 *Du polythéisme romain*, 1:84; 2:168.

9 Cf. "Die Franzosen . . . der Revolution bemächtigten sich des römischen Altertums in einer Weise, zu der wir nicht den Mut mehr hätten—dank unserem höhern historischen Sinne" (Friedrich Nietzsche, "Die fröliche Wissenschaft," *Werke*, ed. Karl Schlechta [Munich: Carl Hanser, 1966], p. 91).

10 *Commentaire sur Filangieri*, 1:106.

11 *Du polythéisme romain*, 1:2; *Commentaire sur Filangieri*, 2:22; article of 8 May 1819, *Recueil d'articles: Le Mercure, la Minerve, la Renommée*, 2:825.

12 Cf. Hugh Trevor-Roper, "The Scottish Enlightenment," *Studies on Voltaire and the Eighteenth Century* 58 (1967): 1640.

13 Leo Strauss, *Natural Right and History* (Chicago: University of Chicago Press, 1953), p. 318. Even without a transhistorical fulcrum, however, moral agents are not thrown back on whim. They can still judge between available alternatives on the basis of accompanying costs, disposable resources, and other pressing problems that will be affected. Choices will in part be guided by culturally shared moral norms. Indeed, historical relativism excludes whim more effectively than natural law—which has never been known to interpret itself.

14 Cited in *Adolphe*, ed. Jacques-Henry Bornecque (Paris: Garnier, 1966), pp. 304–05.

15 Cf. Henry Vyverberg, *Historical Pessimism in the French Enlightenment* (Cambridge, Mass.: Harvard University Press, 1958).

16 *De la religion*, 1:3; *Les "Principes de politique" de Benjamin Constant*, pp. 430–31; cited in Pierre Deguise, *Benjamin Constant méconnu* (Geneva: Droz, 1966), p. 150; "Lettres de Benjamin Constant à Prosper de Barante, 1805–1830," *Revue des deux mondes* 34 (1906): 547.

17 Benjamin et Rosalie de Constant, *Correspondance, 1786–1830*, pp. 215–16; *Les "Principes de politique" de Benjamin Constant*, p. 430.

18 Letter of 30 May 1809, Menos, p. 302; article of 21 October 1818, *Recueil*

314 NOTES TO PAGES 185–95

d'articles: Le Mercure, la Minerve, la Renommée, p. 560; *De la religion,* 1:7.

19 Les *"Principes de politique" de Benjamin Constant,* p. 431.

20 Ibid., p. 430; "Conquête et usurpation," *Cours de politique,* 2:207.

21 For example, Turgot, *On Progress, Sociology and Economics,* ed. Ronald Meek (Cambridge: Cambridge University Press, 1973), p. 47.

22 *De la religion,* 1:316.

23 "Des élections prochaines," *Cours de politique,* 2:314.

24 "Conquête et usurpation," *Cours de politique,* 2:135–36.

25 Les *"Principes de politique" de Benjamin Constant,* p. 430. On the background for this thesis, see René Wellek, "The Price of Progress in Eighteenth-Century Reflections on Literature," *Studies of Voltaire and the Eighteenth Century* 155 (1976): 2268–84.

26 Bertrand de Jouvenel, "Rousseau, évolutionniste pessimiste," *Rousseau et la philosophie politique* (Paris: Presses Universitaires de France, 1965), pp. 1–19.

27 *Du polythéisme romain,* 1:188.

28 "Perfectibilité" *Mélanges,* 2:126.

29 *Commentaire sur Filangieri,* 2:82.

30 "Du développement progressif des idées religieuses," *Mélanges,* 1:80.

31 "Conquête et usurpation," *Cours de politique,* 2:273.

32 *Commentaire sur Filangieri,* 1:46.

33 Ibid., 1:60; speech of 8 June 1824, *Discours,* 2:247; cf. Frederick Artz, *France under the Bourbon Restoration,* (Cambridge, Mass.: Harvard University Press, 1931), p. 55.

34 *Commentaire sur Filangieri,* 1:9, 10.

35 Speech of 22 May, 1824, *Discours,* 2:242.

36 *Fragmens d'un ouvrage abandonné,* Naf. 14363, fol. 205ᵃ.

37 Montesquieu, *Causes de la Grandeur des Romains,* in *Oeuvres complètes* (Paris: Pléiade, 1951), 2:203. See also *De l'esprit des lois* (XIX, 4–6), pp. 558–59.

38 *Commentaire sur Filangieri,* 2:279.

39 Ibid., p. 42.

40 Raymond Aron, *Démocratie et totalitarisme* (Paris: Gallimard, 1965), pp. 25–35.

41 *Commentaire sur Filangieri,* 1:72.

42 See Henri Gougelot, *L'Idée de la liberté dans la pensée de Benjamin Constant* (Melun: Legrand et fils, 1942), p. 186.

43 *Fragmens d'un ouvrage abandonné,* Naf. 14363, fol. 8ᵃ.

44 "Réflexions sur les constitutions," *Cours de politique,* 1:271.

45 Letter of 6 December 1816, Benjamin and Rosalie de Constant, *Correspondance, 1786–1830,* p. 219.

46 *De la religion,* 2:338–39.

47 "Perfectibilité," *Mélanges,* 2:125.

48 Speech of 9 February 1822, *Discours,* 2:70; cf. Robert Nisbet, *History of the Idea of Progress* (New York: Basic Books, 1980), pp. 179–86.

49 "De la tragédie de Wallstein, par Schiller," *Mélanges,* 2:51; speech of 13 February 1827, *Discours,* 2:541; "Perfectibilité," *Mélanges,* 2:140; see also

article of 11 January 1817, *Recueil d'articles: Le Mercure, la Minerve, la Renommée,* 1:18.

50 "Journaux intimes," 4 May 1804, *Oeuvres,* pp. 268–69.

51 "Réflexions sur la tragédie," *Oeuvres,* p. 927; *Du polythéisme romain,* 2:290; similarly: "Le cours des choses est bien plus fort que les volontés des hommes" (letter of 20 June 1800, Menos, p. 162).

52 Promulgating the Charter in a kingly manner, Louis XVIII nevertheless acquiesced in the idea of progress: "Nous avons dû, à l'exemple des rois nos prédécesseurs, apprécier les effets des progrès toujours croissants des lumières, les rapports nouveaux que ces progrès ont introduits dans la société, la direction imprimée aux esprits depuis un demi-siècle, et les graves altérations qui en sont résultées." *Les Constitutions de la France depuis 1789,* ed. Godechot, p. 217.

53 *De la religion,* 1:36–37, 490; 2:175, 178, 180, 190, 201.

54 Tocqueville, *De la démocratie en Amérique,* 1:4–5; 2:339.

55 *De la religion,* 4:477.

56 Speech of 13 September 1830, *Archives parlementaires,* 63:485.

57 Turgot, *On Progress, Sociology and Economics,* p. 41.

58 "Conquête et usurpation," *Cours de politique,* 2:273.

59 *Commentaire sur Filangieri,* 1:30.

60 "Pensées détachées," *Mélanges,* 2:169.

61 "Des élections prochaines," *Cours de politique,* 2:329.

62 "Perfectibilité," *Mélanges,* 2:145.

63 *Fragmens d'un ouvrage abandonné,* Naf. 14363, fol. 12[b].

64 Ibid., fol. 11[b].

65 Article of 23 January 1820, *Recueil d'articles: Le Mercure, la Minerve, la Renommée,* 2:1135.

66 *Commentaire sur Filangieri,* 1:83

67 "Additions et notes," *Cours de politique,* 1:294.

68 Judith N. Shklar, "Jean d'Alembert and the Rehabilitation of History," *Journal of the History of Ideas,* 1982, p. 654.

69 "Pensées détachées," *Mélanges,* 2:170–71.

70 "Réflexions sur les constitutions," *Cours de politique,* 1:231.

71 *Force du gouvernement actuel de la France,* pp. 95–96; compare Tocqueville's famous sentence: "Le livre entier qu'on va lire a été écrit sous l'impression d'une sorte de terreur religieuse produite dans l'âme de l'auteur par la vue de cette révolution irrésistible [he means the weakening of landed aristocracy] qui marche depuis tant de siècles à travers tous les obstacles, et qu'on voit encore aujourd'hui s'avancer au milieu des ruines qu'elles a faites" (*De la démocratie en Amérique,* 1:12).

72 "Perfectibilité," *Mélanges,* 2:142.

73 Ibid., p. 136.

74 *Les "Principes de politique" de Benjamin Constant,* p. 226.

75 *Mélanges,* 2:146.

76 Ibid., p. 147.

77 "Il arrivera donc, ce moment où le soleil n'éclairera plus sur la terre que des hommes libres, ne reconnaissant d'autre maître que leur raison" (Condorcet,

Esquisse d'un tableau historique des progrès de l'esprit humain [Paris: Vrin, 1970], p. 210).

78   "Perfectibilité," *Mélanges,* 2:147.

79   According to Mill, "Politics as conceived by the ancients consisted wholly in this [i.e., "an unceasing struggle against causes of deterioration"]. The natural tendency of men and their works was to degenerate, which tendency, however, by good institutions virtuously administered, it might be possible for an indefinite length of time to counteract" (*Considerations on Representative Government* [New York: Bobbs-Merrill, 1958], p. 22); cf. Hannah Arendt: "bodies politic have always been designed for permanence and their laws always understood as limitations imposed upon movement" (*The Human Condition* [Chicago: University of Chicago Press, 1958], p. 47).

80   *Fragmens d'un ouvrage abandonné,* Naf. 14363, fol. 204ᵃ.

81   John Stuart Mill, *On Liberty* (New York: Norton, 1975), p. 22.

82   *Commentaire sur Filangieri,* 2:65ff.

83   "Conquête et usurpation" *Cours de politique,* 2:207.

84   *Les "Principes de politique" de Benjamin Constant,* p. 431.

85   "Perfectibilité," *Mélanges,* 2:142.

86   John Plamenatz convincingly argues that "the connections between knowledge, illusion and happiness are less simple than Condorcet supposed" (*Man and Society* [London: Longmans, 1963], 2:444).

87   "Anciens et modernes," *Cours de politique,* 2:548; *Commentaire sur Filangieri,* 2:115.

88   John Passmore, "The Malleability of Man in Eighteenth-Century Thought," in *Aspects of the Eighteenth Century,* ed. Earl Wassermann (Baltimore: Johns Hopkins University Press, 1965), pp. 21–46.

89   "Journaux intimes," 15 April 1804, *Oeuvres,* p. 259.

90   John Locke, *An Essay concerning Human Understanding,* bk. 2, chap. 21 (London: Everyman's, 1969), 1:193–238.

91   Romantics and neo-Aristotelians refuse to identify freedom with "getting what one [immediately] wants" because they believe men may be cognitively mistaken about their God-given or "authentic" wants (Charles Taylor, "What's Wrong with Negative Liberty," *The Idea of Freedom,* ed. Alan Ryan, pp. 179–93). Liberals such as Constant and Berlin also refuse to identify freedom with getting what one wants, but only because they believe that freedom includes the liberty to *revise* one's goals and wishes.

92   *Commentaire sur Filangieri,* 1:24.

93   *Mélanges,* 1:iii.

CHAPTER 8

Epigraph: Las Cases, *Le Mémorial de Sainte-Hélène* (Paris: Pléiade, 1935), 1:762 (10 June 1816).

1   The authoritarian regimes discussed in the recent literature are post-traditional, military autocracies, sharing little in common with the royal absolutism

to which Constant contrasted pseudodemocratic dictatorship. Cf. Juan Linz, "Totalitarian and Authoritarian Regimes," *Handbook of Political Science*, ed. Greenstein and Polsby (Reading, Mass.: Addison-Wesley, 1975), 3:175–411. The most important intermediary between Constant and contemporary writers was probably Guglielmo Ferrero, *Pouvoir: Les génies invisibles de la cité* (New York: Brentano's, 1942).

2 For an earlier attempt to solve the mystery of *Conquête et usurpation*, see my "Liberal Uses of Bourbon Legitimism," *The Journal of the History of Ideas* 43, no. 2 (April-June 1982): 229–48.

3 "De l'usurpation," in "Conquête et usurpation," *Cours de politique*, 2:183–97.

4 "De l'esprit de conquête," in ibid., pp. 170–75.

5 Duc Achille de Broglie, *Souvenirs 1785–1870* (Paris: Calmann Lévy, 1886), 1:282.

6 "Conquête et usurpation," *Cours de politique*, 2:172 and 186.

7 Ibid., pp. 264–73.

8 Ibid., pp. 274–82.

9 November 1813 through March 1814, *Oeuvres*, pp. 689–92; also see Bengt Hasselrot, *Nouveaux documents sur Benjamin Constant et Mme. de Staël* (Copenhagen: Ejnar Munksgaard, 1952); see also the same writer's introduction to Benjamin Constant, *Lettres à Bernadotte* (Geneva: Droz, 1952); and Norman King, "La Candidature de Bernadotte," in *Europe* 467 (March 1968): 85–92.

10 The second edition was published at London in March.

11 Reprinted in *Oeuvres*, pp. 1587–89. In her correspondence with Constant, Mme. de Staël explicitly referred to Bernadotte as "le Guillaume III de la France." *Lettres de Madame de Staël à Benjamin Constant*, ed. P. Leon (Paris: Simon Kra, 1928), p. 61.

12 At Paris in April 1814.

13 Charles-Maurice de Talleyrand, *Mémoires* (Paris: Bonnot, 1967), 2:155.

14 *Du polythéisme romain*, 1:105; "Conquête et usurpation," in *Cours de politique*, 2:281, 262, 247.

15 *Cours de politique*, 2:157–58.

16 Ibid., pp. 189–90; cf. "L'on a beaucoup déclamé contre les rois fainéants. Dieu nous rende leur fainéantise, plutôt que l'activité d'un usurpateur" (ibid., p. 188).

17 Ibid., pp. 189 and 190.

18 Ibid., p. 189.

19 Montesquieu, *Oeuvres complètes*, 2:356.

20 "Conquête et usurpation," *Cours de politique*, 2:244; speech of 13 September 1830, *Archives parlementaires*, 63:484.

21 "Conquête et usurpation," *Cours de politique*, 2:186.

22 Ibid., pp. 188–93.

23 Cited in Gustave Rudler, *La Jeunnesse de Benjamin Constant*, p. 474; "Conquête et usurpation," *Cours de politique*, 2:172.

24 Edmund Burke, *Reflections on the Revolution in France* (Harmondsworth: Penguin, 1969), pp. 91, 130.

25 "Journaux intimes," 19 March 1804, *Oeuvres,* p, 246; cf. "Des réactions politiques," *Ecrits et discours,* 1:73–81.

26 Speech of 6 April 1829, *Ecrits et discours,* 2:134; a seeming exception to this rule can be found in a speech of 22 May 1824, where the conservative themes of *Conquête et usurpation* are repeated. For example: "tout pouvoir nouveau se voit condamné, fût-ce malgré lui, à être tyrannique" (*Discours,* 2:241). At this moment, however, Constant had just been returned to the chamber as one of 17 liberal deputies facing an ultra majority of 413. In a fruitless attempt to gain the ear of such a hostile assembly, he interlarded his first speeches with misleadingly "aristocratic" doctrines.

27 Article of 20 August 1818, *Receuil d'articles: Le Mercure, la Minerve, la Renommée,* 1:496.

28 *Fragmens d'un ouvrage abandonné,* Naf. 14363, fols. 73b, 57a, 51a–52b, Naf. 14364, fol. 18ª.

29 Gilbert Highet, *The Classical Tradition* (New York: Oxford University Press, 1949), p. 356.

30 "De la tragédie de Wallstein, par Schiller," *Mélanges,* 2:47; article of 9 September 1819, *Receuil d'articles: Le Mercure, la Minerve, la Renommée,* 2:951; cf. "Bonaparte, enivré de flatteries et importuné des formes républicaines, eut proclamé l'Empire, et modelé sa Cour d'après celle des rois ses vassaux" (*Mémoires sur les Cent-Jours,* p. 187).

31 Similarly, the Directory had engaged in unjust and disastrous wars, not because it was controlled by "new men," but "parce qu'il n'y avoit plus de représentation nationale qui pût l'arrêter." *Fragmens d'un ouvrage abandonné,* Naf. 14363, fol. 91ª.

32 "Conquête et usurpation" *Cours de politique,* 2:189–90; Metternich dwelt on this point in his *Memoirs:* "One thing which [Napoleon] always regretted extremely was that he could not invoke the principle of Legitimacy as the basis of his power. Few men have been so profoundly conscious as he was that authority deprived of this foundation is precarious and fragile, and open to attack." And when the Allies advised Napoleon to make peace and withdraw behind less extensive frontiers: " 'Well now, what do they want me to do?' said Napoleon, 'do they want me to degrade myself? Never! I shall know how to die, but I shall not yield one handsbreadth of soil. Your sovereigns, born to the throne, may be beaten twenty times, and still go back to their palaces; that cannot I—the child of fortune; my reign will not outlast the day when I cease to be strong, and therefore to be feared' " (Prince Metternich, *Memoirs* [New York: Scribner's], 1:185ff., 275). Napoleon, or so Metternich wants us to believe, did not have the flexibility that was second nature to Legitimate kings. Napoleon dethroned himself. He did it by stubbornly refusing to make peace when he had the chance. This refusal, in turn, reflected a fatal inability to compromise which accompanied Napoleon's sense of the illegitimacy of his rule.

33 *Fragmens d'un ouvrage abandonné,* Naf. 14364, fol. 8ᵇ.

34 Edmund Burke, *Reflections on the Revolution in France,* p. 315; "Conquête et usurpation" *Cours de politique,* 2:173, 170.

35 *Les "Principes de politique" de Benjamin Constant,* pp. 385–403.

36 Alfred Cobban, *A History of Modern France*, 2:23–24.

37 *Les "Principes de politique" de Benjamin Constant*, p. 397; "Conquête et usurpation" *Cours de politique*, 2:170.

38 *Les "Principes de politique" de Benjamin Constant*, p. 388; the same passage appeared earlier in *Fragmens d'un ouvrage abandonné*, Naf. 14363, fols. 199ᵇ–200ᵃ, and later in "Additions et notes," *Cours de politique*, 1:288.

39 Article of 20 August 1818, *Recueil d'articles: Le Mercure, la Minerve, la Renommée*, 1:496.

40 If slavery is not abolished simultaneously throughout a country, resistance to comparative disadvantage will prevent its being abolished anywhere. *Les "Principes de politique" de Benjamin Constant*, p. 386.

41 "Lecture" on the English Constitution, delivered at the Atheneum in 1819. Cited in Guy Dodge, *Benjamin Constant's Philosophy of Liberalism*, p. 98.

42 Cf. "The substance of the ideas of 1789 is not the limitation of sovereign power, but the abrogation of intermediary powers." Lord Acton, *Essays in the Liberal Interpretation of History* (Chicago: University of Chicago Press, 1967), p. 141.

43 Franklin Scott, "Propaganda Activities of Bernadotte, 1813–1814," in *Essays in the History of Modern Europe*, ed. D. McKay (New York: Harper, 1936), pp. 16–30; "Bernadotte and the Throne of France, 1814," *The Journal of Modern History* (1933), pp. 465–78; "Benjamin Constant's 'Projet' for France in 1814," *The Journal of Modern History* (1935), pp. 41–44.

44 Several years later, in a discussion of *Conquête et usurpation*, Constant wrote: "alors, comme à présent, j'accusais moins l'homme que le siècle" (*Mémoires sur les Cent-Jours*, p. 203); the essential modernity of Napoleon is also stressed by Emerson, in "Napoleon; or the Man of the World," *Representative Men* (Boston: Houghton, Mifflin, 1884), pp. 215–45.

45 Montesquieu, *Oeuvres complètes*, 2:584; Kant, "Zum ewigen Frieden," *Kleinere Schriften zur Geschichtsphilosophie: Ethik und Politik*, p. 148.

46 "Conquête et usurpation" *Cours de politique*, 2:140. In the fourth edition, Constant reported the following criticism of his argument: "On m'a reproché d'avoir affirmé que les conquêtes étaient impossibles au moment où l'Europe entière était la proie d'une vaste conquête" (ibid., p. 282).

47 "Have there not been as many wars founded on commercial motives since that has become the prevailing system of nations, as were before occasioned by the cupidity of territory or dominion?" *The Federalist Papers*, No. 6 (New York: Mentor, 1961), p. 57.

48 "Conquête et usurpation," *Cours de politique*, 2:139; cf. Joseph Schumpeter, *Imperialism and Social Classes* (New York: Meridian, 1955), pp. 4–98.

49 "Conquête et usurpation" *Cours de politique*, 2:141.

50 Cf. Albert Hirschman, *The Passions and the Interests*, p. 124.

51 "Conquête et usurpation" *Cours de politique*, 2:140, 278, 139–42.

52 Ibid., pp. 180, 181.

53 Ibid., p. 173; "Lettres de Benjamin Constant à Prosper de Barante 1805–1830," *Revue des deux mondes* 34 (1906): 547.

54 "Journaux intimes," 2 October 1813, *Oeuvres*, pp. 682–83.

55 "Conquête et usurpation" *Cours de politique*, 2:149–50. Here again, Constant

echoed Burke: the revolutionaries converted France "into a nation of gamesters who live on chances." *Reflections on the Revolution in France*, p. 310.

56   "Souvenirs historiques, I," *Revue de Paris* 9 (1830): 117; *Mémoires sur les Cent-Jours*, p. 203.

57   Les *"Principes de politique" de Benjamin Constant*, p. 143.

58   "Du parlement sous Cromwel, et du Tribunat, dans la constitution de l'an VIII, jusq'à son épuration," *Mélanges*, 1:41.

59   Speech of 9 February 1822, *Discours*, 2:60.

60   Les *"Principes de politique" de Benjamin Constant*, p. 286. In the Tribunat, Constant had artfully tailored his style of criticism to fit Bonaparte's democratic hypocrisy. He embarrassingly invoked the Constitution of the Year VIII against the regime's legislative proposals, attempting—not very successfully— to box in the dictatorship with its own pretexts. Bonaparte expressed his exasperation with Constant and other opposition Tribunes by calling them "metaphysicians." In fact, they were much more annoying than this: they spoke common sense, intelligible to all.

61   "Conquête et usurpation," *Cours de politique*, 2:195.

62   Ibid., p. 196.

63   Ibid. Consider also: "cette hypocrisie serait d'autant plus corruptrice que personne n'y croirait" (ibid., p. 158).

64   "Conquête et usurpation," *Cours de politique*, 2:197.

65   Cf. "il y a dans les hommes une grande propension à croire aux bonnes intentions de la puissance, et . . . quand la conviction n'existe pas, la lâcheté en prend la forme pour paraître moins vile" ("Du parlement sous Cromwel, et du Tribunat," *Mélanges*, 1:42).

66   "Adolphe," *Oeuvres*, p. 48.

67   Cf. Jean Bodin, *Six Bookes of a Commonweale* (Cambridge, Mass.: Harvard University Press, 1962), pp. 210–18.

68   Article of 14 July 1824, *Receuil d'articles 1820–1824*, p. 322.

69   *Commentaire sur Filangieri*, 1:8.

CHAPTER 9

Epigraph: Louis de Bonald, "Observations sur l'ouvrage ayant pour titre: *Considérations sur les principaux événements de la Révolution française*, par Mme. la baronne de Staël," *Oeuvres complètes* (Paris: Migne, 1859), 2:647.

1   Speech of 9 February 1822, *Discours*, 2:71.

2   The Law of Sacrileges of 1825, though never actually invoked, prescribed the death penalty to anyone profaning the consecrated host. See Louis de Bonald, "Discours sur le projet de loi relatif au sacrilège" (Chamber of Peers, 15 February 1825), *Oeuvres complètes*, 1:1297–302; Constant's speech of 14 April 1825 against the proposed law is reprinted in *Ecrits et discours*, 2:80–95.

3   "Ce qui distingue la révolution française, et ce qui en fait un événement unique

dans l'histoire, c'est qu'elle est mauvaise radicalment." Joseph de Maistre, "Considérations sur la France," *Oeuvres complètes* (Lyon: Vitte, 1891), 1:50.

4   Misled by Constant's theory of the "pouvoir neutre," advanced in 1814–15, Roman Schnur was perplexed to discover that, faced with the ultras, Constant was an engaged "Parteimann" rather than an impartial "Staatsmann" ("Wiedergutmachung: Benjamin Constant und die Emigranten," *Der Staat* 19, Heft 2 [1980]: 161–80).

5   *Mémoires sur les Cent-Jours*, pp. 6, 128, and 202; article of 9 march 1820, *Recueil d'articles: Le Mercure, la Minerve, la Renommée*, 2:1200; speeches of 9 February, 7 August, and 25 July 1822; *Discours*, 2:59, 169, 202; speech of 6 April 1829, *Ecrits et discours*, 2:143; *De la religion*, 5:185; letters of 30 March and 15 June 1822, Constant and Goyet, *Correspondance 1818–1822*, pp. 661 and 690.

6   Speech of 9 February 1822, *Discours*, 2:63.

7   Letter of 28 December 1820, Constant and Goyet, *Correspondance 1818–1822*, p. 465.

8   Speech of 5 August 1822, *Discours*, 2:192.

9   Article of 27 January 1823, *Recueil d'articles 1820–1824*, pp. 281–82.

10 Bonald, "Théorie du pouvoir politique et religieux dans la société civile," *Oeuvres complètes*, 1:123.

11 Sometimes antiliberals attack individualism as a false description, inadequate to the reality of "social bonds." At other times, they claim that it is a fully accurate description of modern society, but that modern society itself is detestably atomized and must be replaced by a warm and cohesive community. This double strategy allows antiliberals to pose simultaneously as dry-eyed realists, undeceived by liberal abstractions, and as moral prophets, nursing hopes of human redemption through social change.

12 According to Kenneth Minogue, "liberalism is a purely political doctrine, whereas most other political 'isms' are more portentous doctrines, part political and part religious, purporting to be guides to life as well as to politics." "Liberalism," *Encyclopedia Americana* (Danbury, Conn.: Grolier, 1983), 17:296.

13 *De la religion*, 1:20.

14 "Chacun professe sa religion avec une égale liberté, et obtient pour son culte la même protection." *Les constitutions de la France depuis 1789*, ed. Godechot, p. 219.

15 *Mémoires sur les Cent-Jours*, p. 15.

16 Bonald, "Législation primitive," *Oeuvres complètes*, 1:1373–74.

17 *Commentaire sur Filangieri*, 2:123–24.

18 This thesis is nevertheless intelligently defended by William Sewell, *Work and Revolution in France* (Cambridge: Cambridge University Press, 1980), pp. 279–81.

19 Guillaume de Bertier de Sauvigny, *The Bourbon Restoration* (Philadelphia: University of Pennsylvania Press, 1966), pp. 164ff.; see also "Sur une pétition accusant M. de Cazes de l'assassinat du duc de Berry" (28 April 1820), *Discours*, 1:310–18.

20 *Commentaire sur Filangieri*, 2:58.

21 "Réflexions sur les constitutions" (1814), *Cours de politique,* 1:215; this was also Montesquieu's argument against cruel punishment and for judicial leniency (*Oeuvres complètes,* 1:253).

22 *Commentaire sur Filangieri,* 1:1; 2:48, 50, 65ff. Cf. "Les peuples tendent au bon ordre, ils l'aiment, ils en ont besoin; quand ils en sortent, c'est que des vexations les y contraignent" (speech of 2 March 1822, *Discours,* 2:100).

23 *De la religion,* 4:487; see also *Commentaire sur Filangieri,* 2:144.

24 *Commentaire sur Filangieri,* 2:17; cf. David Hume, *A Treatise of Human Nature* (Oxford: Oxford University Press, 1967), p. 535.

25 "Réflexions sur les constitutions," *Cours de politique,* 1:257.

26 "Enseigner, c'est gouverner, et si chacun peut enseigner, chacun gouverne; et il ne faut plus de gouvernement public." Bonald, "Sur la liberté de la presse" (1816), *Oeuvres complètes,* 2:509.

27 Henri Mouliné, *De Bonald* (Paris: Felix Alcan, 1916), pp. 107–21.

28 "Réflexions sur les constitutions," *Cours de politique,* 1:261; the same argument surfaced in the "Letters to a Deputy" of 1795.

29 "Réflexions sur les constitutions," *Cours de politique,* 1:260.

30 ". . . l'esclavage de la presse irrite, et . . . la liberté légale apaise les esprits" (speech of 13 February 1827, *Discours,* 2:544).

31 ". . . il n'y a point de souveraineté limitée; toutes sont absolues et infaillibles, puisque nulle part il n'est permis de dire qu'elles se sont trompées" (Maistre, "Du Pape," *Oeuvres complètes,* 2:178; also see, pp. 1–12). Similarly: "il faut toujours quelque chose d'absolu dans un Etat, sous peine de ne pouvoir gouverner." Bonald, "Observations sur Mme. de Staël," *Oeuvres complètes,* 2:627.

32 *Commentaire sur Filangieri,* 1:105.

33 ". . . les gouvernements ont un penchant remarquable à supprimer tout ce qui leur semble entraîner un inconvénient quelconque" (speech of 30 May 1828, *Archives parlementaires,* 54:408).

34 ". . . il n'est pas bon que le pouvoir ne connaisse pas l'état des choses; il ne peut le connaître que par la publicité libre, indépendante" (ibid.).

35 "Réflexions sur les constitutions," *Cours de politique,* 1:269; cf., "Il est donc indispensable, à mesure que les vices ou les superfluités d'une constitution se découvrent, qu'elle puisse être corrigée, modifiée successivement et partiellement" (*Fragmens d'un ouvrage abandonné,* Naf. 14634, fol. 2[b]).

36 *Commentaire sur Filangieri,* 2:4, 5, 6.

37 "Je conçois que quand il est question, soit des citoyens français accusés, soit des nègres voués au fouet ou à la roue, on doit entendre des éclats de rire dans une portion de cette Chambre" (speech of 31 July 1822, *Discours,* 2:179).

38 Speech of 12 Feb. 1825, cited in Mouliné, *De Bonald,* p. 129.

39 Bonald, "Législation primitive," *Oeuvres complètes,* 1:1260.

40 Bonald, "Observations sur Mme. de Staël," *Oeuvres complètes,* 2:638–40.

41 Maistre, "Du Pape," *Oeuvres complètes,* 2:4.

42 Bonald, "Sur les élections" (30 December 1816), *Oeuvres complètes,* 2:1319.

43 Maistre, "Du Pape," *Oeuvres complètes,* 2:342; Bonald, "Observations sur Mme. de Staël," *Oeuvres complètes,* p. 602.

44 Edmund Burke, *Reflections on the Revolution in France* (Harmondsworth: Penguin, 1969), p. 187.

45 *De la religion,* 5:170.

46 Ibid., p. 207; cf. Voltaire, "Lettres philosophiques," *Mélanges* (Paris: Pléiade, 1961), pp. 17–18.

47 Speech of 14 April 1825, *Ecrits et discours,* 2:92.

48 *De la religion,* 5:174. This was the classic liberal argument for toleration; see, for example, John Locke, *A Letter concerning Toleration* (Indianapolis: Bobbs-Merrill, 1975), p. 18.

49 Speech of 25 January 1822, *Discours,* 2:16.

50 Antiliberals typically see disorder and "crisis" in modern societies because these societies have developed unprecedented patterns of stability and integration.

51 For example, Frederick Gentz blamed the Terror on "the deadly passion for making political experiments with abstract theories, and untried systems." *The French and American Revolutions Compared* (1800), trans. John Quincy Adams (Chicago: Regnery, 1955), p. 62.

52 Bonald, "Observations sur Mme. de Staël," *Oeuvres complètes,* 2:657.

53 "Des effets du régime qu'on a nommé révolutionnaire," *Mélanges,* 2:95.

54 *Fragmens d'un ouvrage abandonné,* naf. 14363, fols. 125ᵃ–125ᵇ.

55 *Du polythéisme romain,* 1:202.

56 Article of 22 August 1821, *Recueil d'articles 1820–1824,* p. 71.

57 "Messieurs, il y avait en France, en 1788, une monarchie absolue avec ses lits de justice, ses lettres de cachet, sa police, sa censure! Ces choses amenèrent la révolution" (speech of 31 January 1822, *Discours,* 2:36).

58 Cf. "Ainsi nous crions aux ministres: La route que suivait l'ancien régime a conduit la France dans un abîme; et il réplique, pour nous rassurer: Soyez tranquilles, nous suivons la même route" (speech of 9 May 1827, *Discours,* 2:620).

59 "La raison humaine est manifestement convaincue d'impuissance pour conduire les hommes; car peu sont en état de bien raisonner, et nul ne l'est de bien raisonner sur tout; en sorte qu'en général il est bon, quoi qu'on dise, de commencer par l'autorité." *Les Soirées de Saint-Pétersbourg* (1820) (Paris: Editions de la Maisnie, 1980), p. 108. Aware of the limited capacity of reason to lend meaning to life, Constant sometime appealed to religious sentiment, but he never appealed to authority. See Article of 24 June 1824, *Recueil d'articles,* p. 344.

60 Article of 15 March 1823, *Recueil d'articles 1820–1824,* p. 311.

61 "Réflexions sur les constitutions," *Cours de politique,* 1:271.

62 Bonald, "Observations sur Mme. de Staël," *Oeuvres complètes,* 2:625 and 599.

63 Maistre, "Du Pape," *Oeuvres complètes,* 2:168.

64 Bonald, "Essai analytique sur les lois naturelles de l'ordre social," *Oeuvres complètes,* 1:992, 995.

65 *De la religion,* 5:197.

66 Ibid., 2:61; speech of 8 July 1824, *Discours,* 2:285. It was paradoxical, of course, for denigrators of human reason to celebrate authority, for if man is incapable of governing himself, how can he govern others? Cf. "Sometimes it is said that man cannot be trusted with the government of himself. Can he,

then, be trusted with the government of others?" Thomas Jefferson, "First Inaugural Address" (1801), *The Portable Jefferson*, ed. Merrill Peterson (Harmondsworth: Penguin, 1977), p. 292.

67 Speech of 9 February 1822, *Discours*, 2:68–69.

68 ". . . l'aristocratie n'est d'aucun pays, elle n'a de compatriotes que dans les autres aristocraties d'Europe; elle est une caste; hors de cette caste, elle n'a point de patrie." Speech of 25 July 1822, *Discours*, 2:167.

69 Constant briefly revived this argument in 1824, at a time when the ultras had an overwhelming majority in the Chamber of Deputies. Constant was one of 17 liberals faced with 413 ultra representatives. Judging from the (in part) positive reaction he received, this thesis struck a resonant cord with the majority in the Chamber even though Constant was arguing against a proposal of the ultra ministry. Speech of 8 June 1824, *Discours*, 2:243–73; see especially pp. 261–64.

70 Speech of 13 September 1830, *Archives parlementaires*, 63:484.

71 Under the July Monarchy, Constant argued vigorously against the government's proposal to ban "popular societies." Speech of 25 September 1830, *Archives parlementaires*, 63:672–73.

72 Karl Mannheim drew an analogous distinction between traditionalism and conservativism in "Conservative Thought," *From Karl Mannheim*, ed. Kurt Wolff (Oxford: Oxford University Press, 1971), pp. 152ff.

73 Bonald, "Théorie du pouvoir," *Oeuvres complètes*, 1:358.

74 Ibid., pp. 145–51.

75 Robert Spaemann, *Der Ursprung der Soziologie aus dem Geist der Restauration. Studien über L. G. A. de Bonald* (Munich: Kösel, 1959); Robert Nisbet, "Bonald and the Concept of the Social Group," *The Journal of the History of Ideas* (January 1944); *The Sociological Tradition* (New York: Basic Books, 1966), pp. 11–13.

76 Maistre, "Essai sur le principe générateur des constitutions politiques," *Oeuvres complètes*, 1:265.

77 "Nulle langue n'a pu être inventée, ni par un homme, qui n'aurait pu se faire obéir, ni par plusieurs qui n'auraient pu s'entendre." *Les Soirées de Saint-Pétersbourg* (1820), p. 87; language was also one of Bonald's major preoccupations (cf. *Oeuvres complètes*, 1:1063; 3:64 and 172).

78 Maistre, "Essai sur le principe générateur des constitutions politiques," *Oeuvres complètes*, 1:286–87.

79 Ibid., p. 158. As this statement reveals, Maistre's thought was considerably more complex than that of the average ultraroyalist.

80 Guillaume de Bertier de Sauvigny, *The Bourbon Restoration* (Philadelphia: University of Pennsylvania Press, 1966), pp. 377–79. According to Marc Bloch: "Rien ne fait mieux sentir le déclin définitif de l'ancien religion monarchique que cette dernière tentative, si timide et si médiocrement accueillie, pour rendre à la royauté le lustre du miracle." *Les Rois thaumaturges* (Paris: Gallimard, 1983), pp. 403–04.

81 Ernest Gellner, *The Legitimation of Belief* (Cambridge: Cambridge University Press, 1974), p. 24.

82 Referring to theocracy, Harold Laski wrote that "The claims of its represen-

tatives have grown as their acceptance has become more impossible. . . . the garment has been the more royally displayed that the shrunken body may be the better concealed." *Authority in the Modern State* (New Haven: Yale University Press, 1919), p. 123.

83 *Fragmens d'un ouvrage abandonné*, Naf. 14363, fols. 71b–74b.

84 Ibid., fols. 64a–64b.

85 *Commentaire sur Filangieri*, 1:27.

86 "Réflexions sur les constitutions," *Cours de politique*, 1:265.

87 Article of 8 May 1819, *Recueil d'articles: Le Mercure, la Minerve et la Renommée*, 2:824–25.

88 Réflexions sur les constitutions," *Cours de politique*, 1:265–66.

89 *Recueil d'articles 1820–1824*, p. 62.

90 "Des réactions politiques," *Ecrits et discours*, 1:70.

91 *Mémoires sur les Cent-Jours*, p. 12.

92 Stephen Holmes, "Two Concepts of Legitimacy: France after the Revolution," *Political Theory* 10, no. 2 (May 1982): 165–83.

93 As Constant wrote: "l'Europe est fatiguée" (letter of 24 May 1814, Menos, p. 521). Revulsion from Napoleon's *impôt du sang*, not piety, was the principal source of popular loyalty toward the old dynasty.

94 *Mémoires sur les Cent-Jours*, p. 81.

95 Bonald, "Observations sur Mme. de Staël," *Oeuvres complètes*, 2:637.

96 "Réflexions sur les constitutions," *Cours de politique*, 1:271, 269, 270.

97 According to René Rémond, "the Ultra party represented by its nature an extremism which could not accommodate itself to the necessities of power nor resign itself to the servitudes of reality." *The Right in France* (Philadelphia: University of Pennsylvania Press, 1968), p. 38.

98 Speech of 7 August 1830, *Archives parlementaires*, 63:63.

99 Moreover, when Legitimacy ceased to be a guarantee of international peace, it naturally alienated its liberal adherents. In 1819, Constant sharply denounced "the principles of social order," by which he meant the Legitimist ideology advanced by Metternich and the other members of the Holy Alliance. The intransigence of these autocrats, imitated by the ultras inside France, was a sign that "the sovereigns of Europe are restless about their own security." They are, Constant suggests, more paranoid than Napoleon: "they believe that they are surrounded by shadowy conspirators and frenzied revolutionaries" (article of August 1819, *Recueil d'articles: Le Mercure, la Minerve, la Renommée*, 2:931–32). Their commitment to "social order" may be nothing but a *pretext* for invading France. As an excuse for war, Legitimacy could certainly not retain the loyalty of those who longed for peace.

100 Speeches of 7 August and 6 September 1830, *Archives parlementaires*, 63:63 and 401.

EPILOGUE

1 Liberals are said to believe that the state and citizen are mutually hostile or opposed, that sovereign power is a force fundamentally alien to man, that the

social whole is a mere tool in the service of its parts. (See Franz Neumann, *The Democratic and Authoritarian State*, pp. 142, 160.) Before "the second half of the nineteenth century," according to John Dewey, liberalism affirmed "a natural antagonism between ruler and ruled, interpreted as a natural opposition between the individual and society" (*Liberalism and Social Action* [New York: Perigee, 1980], p. 5). Classical liberals interpreted "political action" as "an invasion of individual liberty" (pp. 8–9). Embarrassingly, this is also the fascist critique of liberalism and "bourgeois rights" developed in Giovanni Gentile, *Genesi e struttura della società* (Florence: Sansoni, 1946), pp. 61–66.

2 Harold Laski, *The Rise of Liberalism* (New York: Harper, 1936), p. 110.

3 "Les intérêts matériels que nous défendons ne sont pas non plus le seul motif qui nous anime" (speech of 14 April 1825, *Ecrits et discours*, 2:98).

4 "Des élections prochaines" (1817), *Cours de politique*, 2:311; speech of 2 February 1827, *Discours*, 2:534; speech of 19 August 1830, *Archives parlementaires*, 63:182.

5 Letter of 13 September 1807, "La Correspondance de Benjamin Constant et Sismondi (1801–1830)," *Revue européenne des sciences sociales* 18, no. 50 (1980): 107; speeches of 2 March and 3 August 1822, *Discours*, 2:98, 189; speech of 30 May 1828, *Archives parlementaires*, 54:404; speech of 18 March 1827, *Discours*, 2:582.

6 *Commentaire sur Filangieri*, 1:34. My emphasis.

7 Speech of 30 June 1828, *Archives parlementaires*, 55:439.

8 Jacques Necker, *De la Révolution française* (Paris: Drisonnier, 1797), p. 77.

9 *Fragmens d'un ouvrage abandonné*, Naf. 14363, fol. 70ᵃ; speech of 30 January 1822, *Discours*, 2:28.

10 *Fragmens d'un ouvrage abandonné*, Naf. 14363, fol. 66b.

11 Montesquieu, *De l'esprit des lois*, in *Oeuvres complètes*, 2:452–53; *Commentaire sur l'ouvrage de Filangieri*, 2:175–80.

12 "Dans les Monarchies modérées par l'opinion, la célébrité qui est un danger est en même temps une défense. Les individus obscurs paraissent moins exposés; mais la multiplicité des agens subalternes rend le peril égal pour eux, et la défense est nulle: car lorsqu'ils sont frappés, victimes ignobles et ignorées, il ne leur reste aucun recours." *Fragmens d'un ouvrage abandonné*, Naf. 14363, fol. 67ᵃ.

13 See "Lettre à M. Odillon-Barrot sur l'affaire de Wilfrid Regnault," in *Cours de politique*, 2:395–434.

14 *Fragmens d'un ouvrage abandonné*, Naf. 16343, fols. 158ᵃ and 196ᵃ.

15 Statement in court, 29 November 1822, *Recueil d'articles 1820–1824*, p. 253.

16 Cf. Sheldon Wolin, *Politics and Vision* (Boston: Little, Brown, 1960), p. 291; Hannah Arendt, *The Human Condition* (Chicago: University of Chicago Press, 1958), p. 31; Robert Paul Wolff, *The Poverty of Liberalism* (Boston: Beacon, 1968), p. 172; Alasdair MacIntyre, *After Virtue*, p. 24.

17 Article of 19 September 1822, *Recueil d'articles 1820–1824*, p. 186; see also *Fragmens d'un ouvrage abandonné*, Naf. 14363, fol. 205a.

18 Libertarians writing in the *Rechtsstaat* tradition seldom go beyond this point.

For example, Friedrich Hayek conceives democracy as essentially illiberal, not as government by discussion but rather as a triumph of the will (which now takes the form of a short-sighted scramble for benefits). See "The Principles of a Liberal Social Order," *Studies in Philosophy, Politics and Economics* (Chicago: University of Chicago Press, 1980), p. 166.

19 Speech of 8 June 1824, *Discours*, 2:247.

20 During the Restoration, moreover, he sympathized with the goals of many secret organizations, but he consistently refused to join any such group: "je n'ai jamais été et je ne serai jamais d'une association secrète" (article of 15 November 1822, *Recueil d'articles 1820–1824*, p. 237).

21 "De la tragédie de Wallstein, par Schiller," *Mélanges*, 2:16.

22 Les *"Principes de politique"* de Benjamin Constant, p. 628.

23 Letter of 13 September 1807, "La Correspondance de Benjamin Constant et Sismondi," p. 106.

24 "Des effets de la terreur," *Cours de politique*, 2:59.

25 John Locke, *A Letter concerning Toleration* (Indianapolis: Bobbs-Merrill, 1976), p. 50.

26 Les *"Principes de politique"* de Benjamin Constant, p. 540; *Commentaire sur l'ouvrage de Filangieri*, vol. 1 (1822), p. 54 and vol. 2 (1824), p. 162; Les *"Principes de politique"* de Benjamin Constant, p. 73; article of 23 January 1800, *Recueil d'articles: Le Mercure, la Minerve, la Renommée*, 2:1137. See also Benjamin Barber, *The Death of Communal Liberty* (Princeton: Princeton University Press, 1974), p. 135.

27 *Commentaire sur Filangieri*, 1:56.

28 *Fragmens d'un ouvrage abandonné*, Naf. 14363, fol. 134[b].

29 Cf. "Je ne connais que deux partis, celui des bons et celui des mauvais citoyens." Robespierre, *Oeuvres* (New York: Burt Franklin, 1970), 3:698.

30 "Souvenirs, I," *Revue de Paris* 9 (1830): 121.

31 Speeches of 30 May 1828 and 4 October 1830, *Archives parlementaires*, 54:409 and 64:39; speech of 13 February 1827, *Discours*, 2:538.

32 Letter of August 1813, Menos, p. 495.

33 *Commentaire sur Filangieri*, 1:67–69.

34 Les *"Principes de politique"* de Benjamin Constant, p. 73.

35 Speech of 25 January 1801, *Ecrits et discours*, 1:161.

36 *Fragmens d'un ouvrage abandonné*, Naf. 14363, fol. 96a; Naf. 14364, fol. 21a.

37 Maistre, *Les Soirées de Saint-Pétersbourg*, 1:26–27.

38 My remarks here are based partly on Albert Hirschman, *The Passions and the Interests*. Hirschman, however, deals principally with the second of these motives, though both were equally important for the liberal tradition.

39 Alasdair MacIntyre condemns liberal modernity as "a culture to which the notion of authority is alien and repugnant" (*After Virtue*, p. 41). This statement may shed light on "the lost morality of the past" (p. 21), which he would like to see revived.

40 Cf. letter of 2 July 1802, "Lettres de Benjamin Constant à Fauriel," in Victor Glachant, *Benjamin Constant sous l'oeil du guet*, p. 51.

41 Speech of 20 November 1830, *Archives parlementaires*, 64:515.

42 Voltaire, "Lettres philosophiques" in *Mélanges* (Paris: Pléiade, 1961), pp. 17–18.

43 Montesquieu, *Oeuvres complètes,* 2:585.

44 C. J. Friedrich, *Man and His Government* (New York: MacGraw-Hill, 1963), p. 356; cf. Albert Hirschman, *Shifting Involvements: Public and Private Action,* p. 125.

45 Robert Dahl, *After the Revolution* (New Haven: Yale University Press, 1970), pp. 40–55.

46 Unlike nobility, priesthood was a public office: "Si le clergé n'était qu'un *ordre,* il ne serait rien de réel. Il n'y a dans une société politique que des professions privées et des professions publiques. Hors de là, ce ne sont que billevesées ou dangereuses chimères." Emmanuel Sieyès, *Qu'est-ce que le Tiers Etat?* (Paris: Presses Universitaires de France, 1982), p. 30.

47 Cf. Georg Simmel, *The Sociology of Georg Simmel,* ed. Kurt Wolff (New York: Free Press, 1964), p. 336.

48 Court proceedings, 14 February 1823, *Recueil d'articles 1820–1824,* p. 303.

49 The classical definition of a tyrant as a ruler who treats the public domain as a piece of private property (cf. Thucydides, *Peloponnesian War,* bk. 1, chap. 37) shows that the private/public boundary also has a lengthy genealogy.

50 *Commentaire sur Filangieri,* 2:161.

51 Michael Walzer, *The Revolution of the Saints* (New York: Atheneum, 1976), p. 14.

52 Richelieu, *Political Testament* (Madison: University of Wisconsin Press, 1961), p. 116.

53 *Commentaire sur Filangieri,* 1:86.

54 Article of 31 December 1823, *Recueil d'articles 1820–1824,* p. 333.

55 Cf. Constant's "Appel aux nations chrétiennes en faveur des Grecs" (1825); and speech of 14 April 1828, *Archives parlementaires,* 54:57.

56 For example, *Archives parlementaires,* 1:33.

57 John Locke, *The Second Treatise of Government,* chap. 14 (Indianapolis: Bobbs-Merrill, 1952), pp. 91–96.

58 Constant had confronted but not resolved the problem of governmental paralysis under the Directory.

59 Speech of 27 August 1830, *Archives parlementaires,* 63:284.

60 Rudolf von Albertini, *Freiheit und Demokratie in Frankreich: Die Diskussion von der Restauration bis zur Résistance* (Freiburg: Karl Alber, 1957), p. 10.

61 Catholic critics of modernization complained that commercial relations were too voluntary; liberals claimed that these relations were not voluntary enough.

Chronology of Constant's Writings Discussed in This Book

1819   "De la liberté des anciens comparée à celle des modernes"

1822–24   *Commentaire sur l'ouvrage de Filangieri*

1824–31   *De la religion considérée dans sa source, ses formes et ses développements*

1833   *Du polythéisme romain considéré dans ses rapports avec la philosophie grecque et la religion chrétienne*

(These last two works represent a lifelong project, begun in the 1780s and only fully published after Constant's death.)

Editions Cited

Commentaire sur l'ouvrage de Filangieri. 2 vols. Paris: Dufart, 1822–24.

Mémoires sur les Cent-Jours. Edited by O. Pozzo di Borgo. Paris: Pauvert, 1961.

Cours de politique constitutionnelle ou collection des ouvrages publiés sur le gouvernement représentatif. 2 vols. Edited by Edouard Laboulaye. Paris: Guillaumin, 1872.

Discours de Benjamin Constant à la Chambre des Députés. 2 vols. Paris: Ambroise Dupont, 1827.

Ecrits et discours politiques. 2 vols. Edited by O. Pozzo di Borgo. Paris: Pauvert, 1964.

De la force du gouvernement actuel de la France et de la nécessité de s'y rallier. Lausanne, 1796.

Benjamin and Rosalie Constant. *Correspondance, 1786–1830.* Paris: Gallimard, 1955.

Lettres à Madame Récamier (1807–1830). Edited by Ephraim Harpaz. Paris: Klincksieck, 1977.

Mélanges de littérature et de politique. 2 vols. Brussels: Libraire Romantique, 1829.

Lettres de Benjamin Constant à sa famille, 1775–1830, Edited by J. H. Menos. Paris: Savine, 1888.

Oeuvres. Edited by Alfred Roulin. Paris, Pléiade, 1964.

Les "Principes de politique" de Benjamin Constant. Edited by Etienne Hofmann. [This is the second and companion volume to Hofmann's thesis, *Les "Principes de politique" de Benjamin Constant: La Genèse d'une oeuvre et l'évolution de la pensée de leur auteur (1789–1806)*.] Geneva: Droz, 1980.

Du polythéisme romain considéré dans ses rapports avec la philosophie grecque et la religion chrétienne. 2 vols. Paris: Bechet, 1833.

De la religion considérée dans sa source, ses formes et ses développements. 5 vols. Paris: Béchet Ainé, 1825–31.

Recueil d'articles, 1795–1817. Edited by Ephraim Harpaz. Geneva: Droz, 1978.

Recueil d'articles: Le Mercure, la Minerve et la Renommée. 2 vols. Edited by Ephraim Harpaz. Geneva: Droz, 1972.

Recueil d'articles (1820–1824). Edited by Ephraim Harpaz. Geneva: Droz, 1981.

Des suites de la contre-révolution de 1660 en Angleterre. Paris: Buisson, 1799.

Manuscript

Fragments d'un ouvrage abandonné sur la possibilité d'une constitution républicaine dans un grand pays. Paris, Bibliothèque Nationale, Nouvelles acquisitions françaises, 14363 and 14364.

Index

333

1994